Military Chaplains as Agents of Peace

Military Chaplains as Agents of Peace

*Religious Leader Engagement in
Conflict and Post-conflict Environments*

S. K. Moore

LEXINGTON BOOKS
Lanham • Boulder • New York • Toronto • Plymouth, UK

Published by Lexington Books
A wholly owned subsidiary of The Rowman & Littlefield Publishing Group, Inc.
4501 Forbes Boulevard, Suite 200, Lanham, Maryland 20706
www.rowman.com

10 Thornbury Road, Plymouth PL6 7PP, United Kingdom

British Library Cataloguing in Publication Information Available

Library of Congress Cataloging-in-Publication Data

Moore, S. K., 1952-
Military chaplains as agents of peace : religious leader engagement in conflict and post-conflict environments / S. K. Moore.
p. cm.
Includes bibliographical references and index.
ISBN 978-0-7391-4910-2 (cloth : alk. paper) -- ISBN 978-0-7391-8016-7 (electronic)
1. Military chaplains. 2. Postwar reconstruction--Social aspects. 3. Peace-building--Religious aspects 4. Reconciliation--Religious aspects. 5. Military chaplains--History--Case studies. 6. Christianity and other religions--Islam--Case studies. 7. Islam--Relations--Christianity--Case studies. I. Title.
UH20.M55 2013
355.3'47--dc23
2012037187

Printed in the United States of America

Dedicated to Deborah Anne Moore,
my life's partner and best friend,
who, in her selfless giving
and continual support,
has made this book
possible.

Contents

Acknowledgments

Vern Neufeld Redekop
Jim Pambrun
John Van den Hengel

LCol Leslie Dawson

Concepts Cell
(Canadian Army Land Warfare Centre)

Preface

Military Chaplains as Agents of Peace: Religious Leader Engagement in Conflict and Post-Conflict Environments

Andrea Bartoli

Who is in charge of peace? Whose job is it to find, secure, and maintain peace? Is it a military task? A civilian one? Is it something that can be done by one person alone? Or is it a collective enterprise? How do diverse, even contradictory elements come together in a sustainable "whole"? These are some of the questions that come to mind after reading Steve Moore's book. Granted that chaplains as religious figures traditionally played important roles in the armed forces of different countries, could it be that the ever changing nature of war opens new spaces for individual and collective responsibility that alter the understanding of the role of chaplains, civilians, and local actors on the ground and in relation to the military apparatus in general? What is the contribution of these multiple actors identified by the author as Religious Leader Engagement (RLE) to Whole of Government formulations?

Religious peacemaking is not new. Religiously motivated leaders like Gandhi have led countries such as India to independence using profoundly spiritual terms. Military actors, such as Ashoka, stunned the world with their religious conversion and the subsequent compassionate polices that stem out of that transformation. In the United States there is a rediscovery of the remarkable contributions of the Emir Abd el Kader, the Algerian leader who resisted the French, spared the lives of prisoners and saved more than five thousands Christians while in exile in Damascus. The calling of Pope John Paul II of the International Prayer for Peace in Assisi in 1986 preceded the fall of communist Soviet Union and led to an unprecedented encounter of Christians of all denominations, Muslims, Jews, Hindu, Buddhists, and many other traditions.Yet, in the middle of a conflict, when parties are actively seeking the enemy to kill, when patrolling is a dangerous task and the outcome of a power struggle is far from being settled, it is not easy to imagine pathways of engagement through which peace can be imagined, experimented with, and sustained.

Through these pages, Dr. Moore offers an overview of the current understanding of the role of religion in conflict and the emergence—through that understanding and beyond—of the new roles and responsibilities for chaplains. This book is neatly organized, and both the theory section and the case studies offer significant insights into this emerging and encouraging trend. The thread I observed throughout the book is it is possible to see more; it is possible to try more; it is possible to do more for peace while in the midst of conflict. What is presented in the book is not a hodgepodge list of cases and practices, but a careful evaluation of experiences that actually occurred and must be taken very seriously. Military officers all over the world are preparing, today, for the next engagement. They are planning. They are creating doctrines. They are creating, today, the conditions under which their military forces will serve in a new crisis tomorrow. There is a responsibility of doing, but there is also a responsibility of learning and of paying attention to what already occurred to make sure the next deployment is more successful, effective, and fruitful than the previous one. For this reason alone Dr. Moore's volume is essential.

Let's pay attention, for a moment, to the cases presented in the text and to the Whole of Government formulations—like the Provincial Reconstruction Teams—where Religious Leader Engagement (RLE) could possibly find even greater expression. The Canadian (Afghanistan) and American (Iraq) Case Studies bring this out in particular. We have stories of Canada involvement in Bosnia and Afghanistan; the study of the Ulema Shura; the account of Breaking Bread Together and Building Trust through Apology in Kosovo; a presentation of the Baghdad Accords; examples of reconstruction roles in Afghanistan and in Bosnia-Herzegovina where we encounter a model of reconciliation in process. These cases are preliminary. They tell us religious leaders, in many theaters of war, are engaging communities that seek new spaces for engagement. Are these all the cases in existence? My hunch is they are not and the book will be received as an invitation to speak up, to share more stories of constructive engagement, and to explore new opportunities in current and future deployments.

However, it is not sufficient to collect stories, anecdotes, and examples of what was done. It is necessary—as in this case—to include these episodes in a deeper understanding of the emerging trend. This volume, indeed, contributes in its own way to the practice-to-theory movement that aims to seek insights from actual cases, while opening the pathway to shared understandings.

Canada has been at the forefront of the peacekeeping revolution, the movement that led military forces away from active war of aggression into stabilization and reconstruction priorities. It seems quite appropriate that this book comes out of that milieu and it is presented as part of an international conversation that will hopefully include an always-greater array of diverse actors. It will be extremely important to see how these insights will contribute to the interagency environment of operations. Plans are not made in a vacuum and the possibility of relevant contributions coming from religious actors is going to be part of the emerging trends. Let's welcome this volume as a groundbreaker, a resource for years to come as government leadership (both civilian and military) debate this emerging role of religious peacebuilders working alongside their interagency partners.

Andrea Bartoli is S-CAR's Drucie French Cumbie Chair and its Dean. He has been at the School for Conflict Analysis and Resolution (S-CAR) at George Mason University since 2007. He works primarily on peacemaking and genocide prevention. An anthropologist from Rome, Dr. Bartoli completed his Italian *dottorato di ricerca* (PhD equivalent) at the University of Milan and his *laurea* (BA–MA equivalent) at the University of Rome. His most recent book *Peacemaking: From Practice to Theory* was published in 2011. He has been involved in religious peacemaking especially through the Community of Sant'Egidio of which he is the Representative to the United Nations and the United States of America.

Part I

Theoretical Considerations of the Role of Religion in the Conflict Environment

Chapter One

Introduction

The events of 9-11 resonate as an iconic moment for the entire world—people everywhere will remember for the remainder of their lives where they were and what they were doing when airliners began crashing into buildings in New York, Washington and a field in rural Pennsylvania. Terrorist bombings on buses in London,[1] trains in Madrid,[2] and resort areas in Bali,[3] among a myriad of other homicidal acts around the globe, punctuate for us the seismic shift in how conflict now manifests globally. These complexities continually summon from the international community a response of ever-increasing sophistication and ongoing adaptation. This has resulted in a re-assessment by government and military leadership the world over with respect to: how conflict has altered the international landscape; how such aggression may effectively be confronted; what approaches hold the greatest promise in mitigating its impact while ameliorating structural development; and how best to employ such strategies. In certain quarters this continues to be an exacting exercise as traditional methods and long-held positions to resolving conflict have had to bend to more innovative processes. The Comprehensive Approach to operations has emerged from this examination, representing a more integrative process leading to greater cooperation and collaboration among a confluence of organizations (military, government and civilian—an entity now commonly referred to as the Whole of Government) in stabilizing countries experiencing turbulent conflict and reconstructing societies in its wake, formerly known as nation building. It is imperative to the thinking brought forward in this book that the reader appreciate the expansive and integrative nature of the endeavors presently brought to bear on the taxing conditions posed by today's conflict and post-conflict environments.

It is in such operational venues that an irenic *impulse* among military chaplains is leading to a peacebuilding role among religious leaders and their respective communities within indigenous populations. In no way meant to undermine the principal function of sacramental and pastoral support of the troops (internal operational ministry), chaplains are increasingly afforded opportunity to engage the religious *other* in operational environments (external operational ministry). It is under Commander's authority and in his explicit intent that chaplains are advancing peaceful relations among fractured communities providing opportunity for *encounter* to occur—creating a safe and transformative space for dialogue where conflict, or its residual effects, have left intercommunal relations either strained or non-existent. In some instances, exchanges with those of *tolerant voice* have precipitated shared ritual events and collaborative activities resulting in engendered trust and renewed cooperation across ruptured ethnic divides. It is this reframing of relation that provides the impetus for beginning the journey of reconciliation—actual religious diplomacy in certain cases. Known as Religious Leader Engagement (RLE), this *facilitative* role of chaplains will be explored for its pertinence to fulfilling mission mandates. *Ad hoc* examples in the form of documented case studies from Bosnia, Kosovo, Iraq and Afghanistan will be consulted for their veracity, weighing its potential and considering its limitations. Indicative of the relevancy of such engagement to strategic planning is the recent endorsement and continued advancement of RLE (June 2011) by the Canadian Forces Army as a new capability under development, e.g., the institutionalization of RLE as an operational construct.

Salient to this discussion as well is the increased number of government and civilian organizations (Whole of Government) participating in reconstruction and stabilization efforts in conflict and post-conflict environments. Contrary to Western society, in many cultures around the world religious observance is revered, permeating all levels of society in both government and civilian sectors. In such regions, religious leaders are held in high esteem by the people and carry considerable credibility with government officials, frequently holding public office. In light of the integrative strategy of the Comprehensive Approach, this begs the larger question of what contribution could RLE make to processes of reconciliation in collaboration with government departments and agencies in their dealings with local, regional, and in some instances, national level religious leaders? Perplexing for some. Inspiring for others. RLE stands as an emerging, yet, sometimes controversial, capability in a world where, paradoxically, extreme expressions of religion factor into conflict, while its peaceful themes await implementation. These principal themes, and other related topics, will be considered for their strategic merit and operational effectiveness within collaborative approaches to conflict transformation.

The approach taken here will be that of participatory-action research. As a military chaplain, having served on the outskirts of Sarajevo during the Bosnian war (1993) and conducted research in Kandahar, Afghanistan (2006), the personal experience of engaging religious leaders and their communities engulfed in the greater conflict of their respective ethno-religious becomes transformative and instructive. One moves beyond the *primal self,* which speaks of one engaged in the experience of war, yet remaining at that level of comprehension, to that of the *distal self,* which steps back from the experiential, observes, and contemplates its significance for individuals, groups, and the future. Critical reflection and theoretical concepts will be brought to these events and those that others have entrusted to this process. These stories carry within them the hopes and tragedies of imperiled people trapped in conflicts not of their making. That said, one should not lose sight of the sanctity of these stories, for in a very real sense we are guests invited to observe these accounts in the hopes that all may benefit in the mitigation of conflict, the healing of relation and the strengthening of mutuality—seeding reconciliation.

It is believed that a candid examination of the strengths and weaknesses of RLE will advance the discussion with respect to its credibility and applicability to conflict and post-conflict environments. In religious and secular circles alike, the religious peacebuilding of chaplains or others working in similar fashion is provoking debate as to its place within the domain of multi-track diplomacy.[4] However, to truly value what is to follow, an appreciation for today's context of operations for both military and civilian actors is critical. Aside from providing an overview of the book, this INTRODUCTION will situate the context for what is to follow. By no means exhaustive, yet informative, the following constitutes a brief overview of contemporary conflict and the response of the international community known as the Comprehensive Approach.

THE CONTEMPORARY CONTEXT

Jack S. Levy states that, "The typical wars of the past pitted state armies against each other. Particularly for great-power conflicts, but also for many other European *interstate* conflicts, wars were "symmetric" in the sense that the two sides were of roughly equal strength and fought with the same kinds of weapons."[5] The open warfare that, until recent years, has preoccupied the more 'elite' countries in North America and Europe, as well as centers of power among third world countries, in many instances, has been eclipsed by non-state organizations, extremely elusive in terms of their structure and activities. Such groups are unable to seriously challenge major state power. Notwithstanding, the potential for them to inflict material damage and loss of life is impossible to disclaim. Worrisome is their ability to strike at civil society in ways that are hard to foresee and still more difficult to combat,[6] evoking fear and creating instability. The movement from the more traditional *interstate* warfare to what may be described as *intrastate*[7] conflict has ushered in hostilities that tend to be more asymmetric in nature.

Leslie, Gizewski, and Rostek offer one of the more sweeping descriptions of today's security environment. By way of comparison, the authors delineate the numerous levers applied as tactics, most of which are unaccustomed to the terrain of traditional warfare.

> That environment is ever more dynamic, uncertain, and challenging. Often, it involves irregular and asymmetric conflict conducted by a range of foes, including highly adaptive 'media-savvy' terrorist organizations, intent less upon defeating armed forces than in eroding their will to fight, warlords seeking to retain power and influence over local populations at any price, and transnational criminal organizations ready, willing, and able to buy, sell, and trade everything from drugs to armaments for personal gain. Frequently, it involves failed and failing states whose tenuous existence and inability to meet popular demands offer ready breeding ground for rebellion and civil war, as well as a secure base from which adversaries can function. And, it involves complex human and physical terrain—with large, densely populated cities and highly diverse populations (i.e., ethnically, religiously, economically, and culturally) often serving as the backdrop for military operations.[8]

The authors illuminate for the reader the breadth and depth of the complexity facing governments in confronting today's *intrastate* conflict. Mary Kaldor defines conflicts of this nature as *new wars*. She lists Identity Politics[9] as its first trait contrasting it with the geopolitical or ideological goals known to the more traditional wars of the past. The claim to power on the basis of a particular identity is among the principal drivers of today's conflicts: national, clan, religious or linguistic. Such claims often hearken to the past, which leans towards identity politics becoming more exclusive and fragmented— sure footing for conflict. Terrell Northrup concurs that threatened identity is at the heart of today's intractable conflict.[10] Such inter-group violence is most often associated with the challenging of one's core constructs. These go to the very roots of one's being, organizing how a person approaches life and the roles that one plays. The seeds of intractable conflict are sown in a threatened core sense of self, which strikes at identity.[11] Tied closely to the shaping of one's inner self is the significance of social or group identity. Suffice it to say that where conflict is concerned, the sense of loss becomes unit forming when a common fate or shared threat is present. Such loss contributes markedly to the dynamics between identity and conflict found in both interpersonal and intergroup conflict. Intractable conflict is a trademark of the contemporary context where fighting among local populations is commonplace to insurgents. In *fighting among the people*, as Sir Rupert Smith coins it, rather than capturing territory by military means, insurgents control territory through political control of the people, mostly by extremist politics aimed at inducing fear and, insidiously, cultivating hatred.[12] *New wars* entail Western forces and insurgents fighting amongst the people over the *will of the people*. The strategic objective is to win the trial of strength by capturing the *will of the people*. For insurgents, attacking civilian populations is a proven method of assailing that *will*.[13]

Continuing with Kaldor's reasoning, economies are decentralized in *new wars*, characterized by low levels of participation in the war while unemployment remains extremely high. Insurgent groups are partially dependent on external sources of funding, leaving fighting units little choice but to finance themselves through plunder, hostage taking or the black market. As indicated in the above quote by Leslie et al., legal trade in arms, drugs or valuable commodities such as diamonds, oil or human trafficking are but a few examples.[14] Expert in foreign security policy and noted peace-builder, Sean McFate elucidates that on the African conflict in particular, most armed threats are *intrastate* in nature. As such, they rely upon the support of local populations to hide, survive, and thrive within the borders of a country most often accomplished by exploiting public grievances, real or perceived, emanating from the failures of development.[15]

Stein and Lang further articulate the political dimension of contemporary conflict and its strategic reliance on popular support among the people is characteristic of insurgencies.

> Insurgency is deeply political warfare, where military and political strategies reinforce each other. Insurgents depend on a mass base of support, which they win or lose through politics. They use military strategies to build political strength and alienate people from their governments, to create the political preconditions for success. In insurgences, there is no neatly defined "front," and once the front is gone, the "safe space" behind the lines disappears for civilians as well as soldiers.[16]

No one understood this strategy more completely than Mao Zedong, who is often cited by historians as the most successful insurgent of the twentieth century. His oft-repeated metaphor poignantly articulates where his success lay: "The people are the sea in which the insurgent fish swims and draws strength."[17] As such, easily identifiable lines of conflict are pretty much a thing of the past. The concept of the Comprehensive Approach was born out of the realization that force alone would not resolve the kinds of conflicts impacting global trouble spots. As such, it is a novel construct, an integrated and holistic strategy to resolving conflict, re-establishing governments and normalcy for populations.

THE COMPREHENSIVE APPROACH

The complexity of contemporary conflict has elicited a more decisive response from the international community. Emerging in appreciable degrees is a more integrative strategy of grappling with intrastate conflict and/or its oft-ensuing insurgencies. Referred to here as the comprehensive approach, western governments and multinational organizations are increasingly adopting such interdependence. The call is to break out of their silos and look to one another for creative and collaborative solutions to the political, security, economic and social realms.[18] Contributing to such complexity is the complicity of certain governments in providing refuge for extremist groups bent on training and exporting violence to Western nations, urgently summoning a need for a coordinated multinational response. Subsequently, eradicating terrorist elements embedded in "failed" or "failing" states that either lack the capacity or will to root out such groups, has become of vital interest to western governments. Out of this necessity, the Comprehensive Approach (CA) has emerged as a measured peace enforcement policy melded to extensive reconstruction and stabilization efforts. The international community views the CA as the most realistic means of grappling with the sweeping challenges impacting imploding societies. That said, it is not an exact science, rather an evolving domain with varying approaches all working toward the same goal. An ever-expanding range of actors contributes to resolving the complex issues facing Western initiatives. The objective is to effect change by achieving a synergy of effort among other government departments (OGD), other government agencies (OGA) and civilian organizations, supported by military forces. These now range from "important allied governments, subject matter experts, functional specialists, non-government actors and others as the situation dictates."[19]

The military offers support by providing the necessary security to carry out such endeavors more commonly known as Stability Operations. Poignant to this discussion is the recognition by military leadership of the need for a CA to achieve mission success. *Stability Operations*, a Field Manual of the US Army, offers the following overview of such an integrated approach,

> Through a comprehensive approach to stability operations, military forces establish conditions that enable the efforts of the other instruments of national and international power. By providing the requisite security and control to stabilize an operational area, those efforts build a foundation for transitioning to civilian control and, eventually, to the host nation. Stability operations are usually conducted to support a host-nation government or a transitional civil or

military authority when no legitimate, functioning host-nation government exists. Generally, military forces establish or restore basic civil functions and protect them until a civil authority or the host nation is capable of providing these services for the local populace. They perform specific functions as part of a broader response effort, supporting the complementary activities of other agencies, organizations, and the private sector.[20]

As early as 2006, British thinking included an evolving CA to Operations,

[A] cohesive plan of action used to aid objectives in a variety of complex situations—these objectives are to delay, contain or resolve crises that arise, which can include humanitarian and natural disasters. Comprehensive approach work has also been undertaken in the post-conflict reconstruction environment—Iraq and Afghanistan are two of the most recent examples. Groups or organizations involved can include: civilian, para-military, military groups and individuals, and international and non-governmental organizations.[21]

In articulating the characteristics of the comprehensive approach, the framers of the *Guiding Principles for Stabilization and Reconstruction* at the United States Institute of Peace cite *interdependence* as paramount. Such connectivity among actors is seen to create the requisite synergy essential to providing the conditions enabling fledgling governments to gain their footing.

Security requires the rule of law, essential services require governance, the rule of law is dependent on security, sustainable economies are dependent on the rule of law, ownership requires capacity, and meeting basic human needs requires all of the above. It is a spider web of interdependence that requires as much integration as possible.[22]

On a broader scale, some of the more prominent multinational organizations now employ versions of the comprehensive approach.[23] This is an evolving domain with varying approaches all working toward the same goal. For the United Nations (UN) it is the Integrated Mission (IM);[24] the European Union (EU) has developed a concept known as Emergency and Crisis Coordination Arrangements (CCA);[25] the North Atlantic Treaty Organization (NATO) approaches gravitate more toward Effects-Based Approach to Operations (EBAO);[26] and the Organization for Security and Cooperation in Europe (OSCE) has created a consensus-based strategy addressing three dimensions of security: the politico-military, the economic-environmental, and the human dimension.[27] The test before governments is how best to integrate these efforts so as to minimize duplication of effort and maximize results.

European and North American delegates came together for a conference in Helsinki, Finland, in 2008 to deliberate on the comprehensive approach—Comprehensive Approach: Trends, Challenges and Possibilities for Cooperation in Crisis Prevention and Management. The consensus was that today's complex conflicts and crises necessitate bringing together a wide range of internal and external actors from within governments, civil society, the private sector and international agencies to work collaboratively.[28] It was determined that a multilateral and networked approach effectively combining all available civil and military instruments was essential to resolving such convoluted crises. Integral to resolving conflict were the following: an analysis of the situation; determining its root causes, identifying presenting issues in the field; and an awareness of other actors' networks. In terms of collaborative efforts, sharing perspectives were viewed as an important step towards de-conflicting actions and complementing the efforts of others. The social sphere was seen to be interdependent with the political, security and economic: failure in one, risked failure in all others.[29] Today's reality dictates that all must adapt to the pre-existing networked environments that await them in Operations, be that at the micro or macro level. Such networking depends on trust with its "commitment to cultivating the will and developing the means to establish such relationships."[30]

The United States makes sweeping reference to more integrative approaches as integral to the *National Security Strategy*, citing the capacity of diplomacy and development to ". . . prevent conflict, spur economic growth, strengthen weak and failing states, lift people out of poverty, combat climate change and epidemic disease, and strengthen institutions of democratic governance."[31] Underscored below, the policy stipulates the necessity for multilateral strategies to combat insecurity, networking with critical constituencies as a means of tapping into essential capabilities and resources, all of which harness collective action—all attributes of the CA.

> Our mutual interests must be underpinned by bilateral, multilateral, and global strategies that address underlying sources of insecurity and build new spheres of cooperation. To that end, strengthening bilateral and multilateral cooperation cannot be accomplished simply by working inside formal institutions and frameworks. It requires sustained outreach to foreign governments, political leaderships, and other critical constituencies that must commit the necessary capabilities and resources to enable effective, collective action. And it means building upon our traditional alliances, while also cultivating partnerships with new centers of influence. Taken together, these approaches will allow us to foster more effective global cooperation to confront challenges that know no borders and affect every nation.[32]

Implementing such an integrative strategy filters through numerous governmental departments and agencies, not the least of which is the U.S. Department of State. Fostering international reconstruction and stabilization goes to the heart of their recent report, *2009 Year in Review: Smart Power in Action*, prepared by the Coordinator for Reconstruction and Stabilization, Ambassador John E. Herbst. Networking through international channels and partnering with scores of civilian agencies world wide, the Dept. of State engenders greater collaboration.

> As a cornerstone of President Obama's foreign affairs and national security policy, U.S. stabilization efforts abroad necessitate bilateral and multilateral engagements with international partners possessing civilian reconstruction and stabilization (R&S) capabilities who are able to help achieve effective outcomes in countries emerging from conflict and civil strife.[33]

There is increasing agreement among world governments that mitigating the effects of asymmetric warfare and its accompanying insurgencies will require much more than the brute military force of the cold war era. One indication of this recognition is the Dept. of State's recent (Oct. 2009) development of the International Stabilization and Peacebuilding Initiative (ISPI). Another tool for the WoG toolbox, their *2009 Year in Review* outlines its purpose,

> This network [ISPI] of governments and multilateral and international organizations will establish a Stabilization and Peacebuilding Community of Practice to deepen cooperation among the emerging international community of implementing partners engaged in stabilization and peacebuilding issues, and will share information via the German Center for International Peace Operations' CivCap Web-Portal.[34]

Although not the focus of this book, it should be mentioned that the Comprehensive Approach, with its emphasis on integration is now embraced as the *modus operandi* for many governments and organizations tackling such domains as collective security among and within nations, e.g., the American *National Security Strategy*[35] as well as the recent collaboration of the governments of the United Kingdom and the Netherlands on mutual security concerns.[36] Both documents cite the array of today's security challenges and the need for multinational resourcing of the necessary capabilities. Again, in the realm of economic recovery, the Organization for Economic Cooperation and Development (OECD) makes the compelling case "that successful long-term development in impoverished nations is impossible when incapacitated states cannot deliver the collective goods of basic security and effective governance."[37] As stated in their *Principles for Good International Engagement in Fragile States*, "the political, security, economic and social spheres are interdependent: failure in one risks failure in all others."[38] As a means of creating sound economic management in recovering states, they call for greater coherence of effort within the international community in terms of policies and among the bodies that implement them.

The preceding discussion is offered as a means of situating the main theme of this book: Religious Leader Engagement (RLE). By no means on the scale of other approaches to resolving conflict, nonetheless, RLE is deemed a timely and considerable contribution to situations where conflict exhibits a religious dimension—a small piece of a much larger puzzle. As an operational capability, RLE lends itself to bridging to religious communities of indigenous populations where intractable conflict has left significant ruptures between ethno-religious groups. The forthcoming case studies from a number of nations will demonstrate in varying degrees the adaptability of RLE to more integrated approaches. Offered for consideration here is its relevance to stabilization and peacebuilding endeavors within the CA.

THE BOOK

The offering of this book is an attempt to capture the essence of Religious Leader Engagement (RLE) as an evolving domain of ministry among operational chaplains internationally. Increasingly, chaplains gravitate toward peacebuilding initiatives of various descriptions within indigenous religious communities in conflict and post-conflict environments. Be that expeditionary, humanitarian or domestic, the value and relevance of RLE to operational environments will continue to make its presence felt. The intent here is not only to inform the present but also to chart probable applications for the future. In this sense, it is hoped that what is to follow will serve as a reference source for the military chaplaincy, the Whole of Government community— an aspect of the CA—and academia.

The opening section of this introductory chapter to *Military Chaplains as Agents of Peace* appropriately provides the backdrop to this entire book. It is presented as an overview of the contemporary context of intra-state conflict—its complexities and compulsions—coupled with a description of the CA as a collaborative response by the international community to confronting such aggression and rebuilding societies caught in its throes.

Chapter 2 will serve as a primer to grasping more fully the dynamics of deep-rooted conflict and, therefore, is more theoretical in nature. Possessing something of a knowledge base will aid the reader in appreciating Religious Leader Engagement as a viable approach, among others, to mitigating conflict and promoting reconciliation. An element of praxis will follow forging a place for practical application, as engaging the *tolerant religious voice* is probed for its relevance to reconciling differences across ethnic divides. It will be for the reader to decide to either work through this chapter or to continue on to chapter 3. The upcoming case studies will showcase the theory and praxis offered here, citing where the supporting material may be found. As such, chapter 2 becomes a resource for reference purposes. A number of theoretical constructs will be explored.

In terms of theoretical underpinnings, Terrell A. Northrup is a noted scholar and authority in the domain of *intractable conflict*. Striking at core identity, her four stages of threat, distortion, rigidification and collusion poignantly describe the titanic struggles facing contemporary conflict. These will serve as a descriptive backdrop of this overview. Amplifying the effects of conflict further will be the *mimetic theory* of French anthropologist René Girard as framed by scholar/practitioner and Mennonite pacifist Vern Neufeld Redekop. He elucidates how the 'mirroring' effect of violence feeds conflict: a victim of aggression is "avenged" by offering violence to the perpetrator, who, in so doing becomes the new perpetrator. The desire for revenge becomes such that reciprocal violence is perpetuated in the spiraling effect of the human urge to "strike back twice as hard," hence the oft-quoted idiom, "Violence begets violence . . . with interest." Mimetic violence will be examined for its relevance to conflict and post-conflict environments. *Human identity needs* may be best interpreted as a theoretical construct linking one's profound beliefs, desires and emotions with one's actions and motivations. When identity needs are threatened a strong emotional reaction occurs. Groups caught in the nexus of deep-rooted conflict rarely comprehend the effect that the satisfaction or dissatisfaction of these needs have on conflict outcomes. Some exposure to *wounded memory* is deemed necessary, as the seeds of conflict that germinate in the present are often sown in earlier times, where actual or perceived wrongs have lived in the collective memory of individuals and/or groups over extended periods of time. *Relational Systems* will reveal how within certain contexts groups become locked in rigid and opposing positions, known as *closed relational systems*. Balancing this are *open relational systems*, to be discussed in the case studies. Here a third party becomes a catalytic force in bringing leaders and communities out of their alienating entrenched positions.

For the purposes of this book, praxis is understood to be the practical application of theory. In this regard, *Cultural Competency* becomes more than assimilated knowledge. How one moves and communicates within a given culture is critical to achieving mission outcomes. More than a crafted technique, the *Place of Hospitality* in building relation with the *other* looks to engendering trust, kindness and a sense of safety, without which it is impossible to lay the foundation for further dialogue and cooperation. *Ritual* events are non-referential symbolic acts that, although a dimension of the concrete, communicate subliminally through symbols, myths and metaphors. Such events offer to individuals and groups a means to receive new truths that, due to an on-going conflict or its residual effects, may be too taxing to consider or beyond their capacity to grasp at that moment. The power of *Ritual and Symbol* is its facility to communicate tacitly, activities that may be cultural, religious or a synthesis of both. These may not be unique to the chaplain's role, however a spiritual component does exist, rendering certain of these events as common ground for clerics.

Preceding the full treatment of Religious Leader Engagement (RLE), chapter 3 prepares the ground more thoroughly by presenting an overview of the paradoxical nature of religion: a component of conflict, yet, a purveyor of peace. Broached is the gnawing question of the hollowing out of the faith experience as contributing to the polarizing of "us" and "them" in the negation of the *other* often detected at the heart of conflict. The balance of the discussion focuses on the emerging domain of religious *peacebuilding* and its value to reconciling efforts the world over. Examples of such efforts are given citing principal traits of *peacebuilding* practitioners from Christianity, Judaism, Islam and Buddhism, a persuasive precursor to the full treatment of RLE.

The operational role of chaplains engaging in RLE activities will be the thrust of chapter 4. This emerging capability will be presented as a conceptual model well suited to contemporary operational structures, a construct possessing principles easily generalized from one context to another. The building blocks of RLE will be assembled, offering explanation of how these components interrelate. An aspect of RLE, Religious Area Analysis (RAA) will exhibit the skill chaplains now bring to Command in offering an analysis of the religious terrain of an Area of Operations (AO), inclusive of the potential impact of the nuances of local religious belief and practice. The dénouement of RLE reveals how the chaplain's capacity to build relation with indigenous religious leaders and their communities serves as a prelude to bringing together in *encounter* those who remain estranged due to conflict or its residual effects. Engendered trust and its subsequent cooperation facilitate the initiation of collaborative activities designed to more closely integrate communities at the tactical, operational and strategic levels. The relevancy of RLE to the Whole of Government community will also be explored, in particular, chaplains *partnering* with other government department and agency personnel in promoting dialogue and collaboration with indigenous religious communities.

Chapters 5 through 8 will bring RLE to life, showcasing the operational experience of a number of chaplains from various countries. Case studies from Canada, France, the United States, New Zealand and Norway will: (1) effectively illustrate the theory and praxis of chapter 2; and (2) concretize RLE as a conceptual model presented in chapter 4, complete with references to earlier presented theory and praxis. Each operational anecdote features a unique theoretical lens while presenting a distinctive application of RLE: from ritual and cultural events in Bosnia and Afghanistan, to religious diplomacy in Kosovo and Iraq, culminating in partnering in the Whole of Government environment of Provincial Reconstruction Teams in Afghanistan. The objective is to demonstrate the scope of RLE as an operational construct, establishing its capacity to be contextualized, regardless of venue: expeditionary, humanitarian or domestic operations. Informative as well is the unprecedented contribution of a Muslim chaplain to what is predominantly a Christian domain of ministry. Before leaving the actual case studies, the reader will benefit from the hope-filled journey of the Religious Directors of the Bosnia and Herzegovina Defense Forces: Bosniak Muslim, Croatian Roman Catholic and Serbian Orthodox. From war to reconciliation, the collaboration of these men of faith stands today as an inspiration to all of how conflict may be transcended in the writing of new narratives as the healing of memory begins for their people.

To fully appreciate the value of a new concept, one must be willing to wrestle with the difficult issues as well as extolling its benefits. Chapter 9—*Religious Leader Engagement in Implementation*—will deliberate a number of the more challenging questions related to institutionalizing RLE as well as delineate some of the practical approaches to its utilization. Principal among these "Caveats for Consideration" will be such themes as RLE as an Influence Activity, Information Gathering as an Intelligence Activity and what impact, if any, would either of these have on the protected (non-combatant) status of chaplains according to International Humanitarian Law—the Geneva Conventions and Protocols. Elucidated also will be how four days of deliberation in the forum of a Seminar War Game with all of the principal stakeholders contributed to greater comprehension of the above themes. This section will close with a candid appraisal of the insidious nature of Instrumentalism. Balancing this discussion, "Areas for Advancement" will address a number of topics pertaining to application. Suggestions as to how one identifies the *religious tolerant voice* noting key organizations that may be of assistance will be considered as well as the collaborative potential chaplains offer a role to Whole of Government configurations, e.g., Provincial Reconstruction Teams. Raised, too, will be the efficacy of integrating indigenous religious peacebuilders into local initiatives as a means of sustaining gains made with religious communities. Lastly, questions relating to the interface between Christian chaplains and Islamic religious leaders will be briefly introduced as a theme requiring further reflection. This point follows on the thinking of a number of leading Islamic scholars who, although, encouraged with the efforts of Christian peacebuilders among Islamic religious leaders, yet, believe greater success would result from more familiarity with Islamic approaches to resolving conflict.

An examination of ministry so closely related to *peacebuilding* and reconciliation would not be complete without consulting theology. As the closing chapter—*A Practical Theology of Reconciliation in Theaters of War*—imparts a hermeneutic of peace, demonstrating a new self-understanding of the *agency* of chaplains. The invitation is for all to draw on the beliefs, imagination and requisite values of their collective faith traditions to further the development of the practical theology commenced here. Miroslav Volf's theology of exclusion and embrace factor centrally in this work. Relation of the *self* with the *other* will be probed for its significance theologically. Exclusion diminishes relation leading to the de-humanizing of the *other* with its egregious violence often witnessed in conflict zones as "ethnic cleansing." Factoring into exclusion also are the themes of willful independence and the logic of purity, both contributing to the negation of the *other*. It is the opening of the *self* in the *will to embrace* that creates the space for re-humanizing the *other*. In facilitating encounter, chaplains seed reconciliation, creating bridges out of barriers, repelling the evil that stalks the vulnerable of conflict zones.

As a capability, nascent within operational environments, RLE is predicated on the notion that, as effective as it has been with the support of military leadership, its genesis and value will only be fully realized in collaboration with its Interagency partners—Whole of Government. As such, RLE is offered to the reader as a viable operational ministry of chaplains among the religious communities of indigenous populations in theatres of operation—one approach among others in lessening conflict and promoting peace.

NOTES

1. See "London Attacks," BBC News, http://news.bbc.co.uk/2/shared/spl/hi/uk/05/london_blasts/html/, accessed 6 Jan. 2012.

2. See "2004: Many die as bombs destroy Madrid trains," BBC News, http://news.bbc.co.uk/onthisday/hi/dates/stories/march/11/newsid_4273000/4273817.stm, accessed 6 Jan. 2012.

3. See "Bali terrorist blast kill at least 26, http://edition.cnn.com/2005/WORLD/asiapcf/10/01/bali.blasts/index.html, accessed 6 Jan. 2012.

4. Multi-track diplomacy is a term coined by Louise Diamond referring to an approach to peacebuilding "involving as many different tracks as possible when implementing projects [designed to promote conflict transformation]. This way, even when doing social peacebuilding work, [people are involved] from government, media, or other social institutions, which provide a link between the structural peacebuilding and political peacebuilding processes. Just as conflict transformation and peacebuilding are understood in terms of systems change, multi-track diplomacy takes a systems approach to understanding the nature of international peacebuilding." Together, Diamond and Ambassador John Macdonald expanded on what Joseph Montville termed Track II diplomacy to include the following domains: conflict resolution professionals, business, private citizens, the media, religion, activism; research, training, and education; and philanthropy, or the funding community. See The Institute for Multi-Track Diplomacy, http://www.imtd.org/publications/occasional-papers/building-peace-and-transforming-conflict-multi-track-diplomacy-in-practice/, accessed 16 Mar. 2012. See also Louise Diamond and John MacDonald, *Multi-track Diplomacy: A Systems Approach to Peacebuilding* (West Hartford, Connecticut: Kumarian Press, 1996).

5. Jack S. Levy, "International Sources of Interstate and Intrastate War" in *Leashing the Dogs of War: Conflict Management in a Divided World*, eds. Chester A. Crocker, Fen Osler Hampson and Pamela Aall, (Washington, D.C.: United States Institute of Peace, 2007), 19. Italics mine.

6. Martin Ewans, *Conflict in Afghanistan: Studies in Asymmetric Warfare* (Oxon and New York: Routledge, 2005), 2, 173.

7. *Interstate* warfare refers to what historically has been the more traditional conflict of state against state, whereas *intrastate* conflict identifies conflict among groups within the borders of a sovereign nation inclusive of insurgencies.

8. Lieutenant-General Andrew Leslie, Mr. Peter Gizewski, and Lieutenant-Colonel Michael Rostek, "Developing a Comprehensive Approach to Canadian Forces Operations" in *The Canadian Military Journal*, Vol. 9. No. 1, 2008, 12.

9. Mary Kaldor, "Introduction" in *New & Old Wars: Organized Violence in a Global Era, 2nd Edition* (Stanford, California: Stanford University Press, 2006), 7-8.

10. Northrup's research into intractable conflict will be examined more thoroughly in Chapter Two.

11. Terrell A. Northrup, "The Dynamic of Identity in Personal and Social Conflict" in *Intractable Conflicts and Their Transformation*, eds. Louis Kriesberg, Terrell A. Northrup and Stuart Thorson (Syracuse, New York: Syracuse University Press, 1989), 65.

12. Kaldor, 2006, 8–9.

13. Smith, 2006, 277.

14. Kaldor, 2006, 10.

15. Sean McFate, "U.S. Africa Command: A New Strategic Paradigm?" *Military Review* 17 (January-February 2008), 20.

16. Janice Gross Stein and Eugene Lang, *The Unexpected War* (Toronto: Viking Canada, 2007), 211-212.

17. Timothy K. Deady, "Lessons from a Successful Counterinsurgency: The Philippines, 1899-1902" in *Parameters*, Spring 2005, 58.

18. *Guiding Principles for Stabilization and Reconstruction*, the United States Institute of Peace, see http://www.usip.org/publications/guiding-principles-stabilization-and-reconstruction, 5-30, accessed 17 Jan. 2012.

19. *The Comprehensive Approach: Road Map 21 April 2010*, Version 4.0, Chief of Force Development, Canadian Forces, 4.

20. *Stability Operations*, Field Manual, Dept. of the Army, Washington, D.C., "Introduction," p. vii, http://downloads.army.mil/docs/fm_3-07.pdf accessed 29 March 2009.

21. Joint Doctrine and Concepts Centre. Joint Discussion Note 4/05, *The Comprehensive Approach.* 2006. www.google.ca/search?client=safari&rls=en&q=Joint+Doctrine+and+Concept+Centre,+The+comprehensive+Approach&ie=UTF-8&oe=UTF-8&redir_esc=&ei=ukPQS_C1KIT68Abvh62oDw, accessed 22 April 2010.

22. *Guiding Principles for Stabilization and Reconstruction*, the United States Institute of Peace, see www.usip.org/publications/guiding-principles-stabilization-and-reconstruction, 5-30, accessed 17 Jan. 2012.

23. Joint Doctrine and Concepts Centre. Joint Discussion Note 4/05, *The Comprehensive Approach.* 2006. www.google.ca/search?client=safari&rls=en&q=Joint+Doctrine+and+Concept+Centre,+The+comprehensive+Approach&ie=UTF-8&oe=UTF-8&redir_esc=&ei=ukPQS_C1KIT68Abvh62oDw, accessed 22 April 2010.

24. "An '*Integrated Mission*' is an instrument with which the UN seeks to help countries in the transition from war to lasting peace, or to address a similarly complex situation that requires a system-wide UN response, through subsuming actors and approaches within an overall political-strategic crisis management framework." Executive Summary, *Report on Integrated Missions: Practical Perspectives and Recommendations,* www.google.ca/search?q=Report+on+Integrated+Missions&ie=utf-8&oe=utf-8&aq=t&rls=org.mozilla:en-US:official&client=firefox-a; see also Planning a Peacekeeping Operation, 5.1 The Integrated Approach, 5.2 The Integrated Mission Planning Process in *United Nations Peacekeeping Operations: Principles and Guidelines*, http://www.un.org/en/peacekeeping/operations/newoperation.shtml, 53–57.

25. The *EU Emergency and Crisis Coordination Arrangements* was born out of a concern of terrorist attacks but is not specific to such events. Poignant to the argument here is the trend toward a *comprehensive approach to cooperation.* "While the London bombings . . . provided momentum for this work, the emergency and crisis co-ordination arrangements proposed in this paper is not specific to counter-terrorism. Rather, they would provide a generic arrangement

applicable to and which may be triggered by all types of crises, such as natural disasters, industrial accidents, or flu pandemic, as well as terrorist attacks. They are also designed to provide co-ordination capability across all areas of EU activity to be used in response to emergencies both inside and outside the Union. . . ." www.google.ca/search?hl=en&client= firefox-a&hs=wWX&rls=org.mozilla:en-US:official&sa=X&ei=XpAPT-znCILl0QHM58ipAw&ved=0CBoQvwUoAQ&q=Emergency+and+Crisis+Coordination+ Arrangements&spell=1&biw=1232&bih=651, accessed 12 Jan. 2012.

26. "In simple terms, an effects-based approach ensures that the military activities are integrated with those of other agencies and that military activities are directly linked to operational objectives—the results or effects of the activities directly contribute to operational objectives." *Land Force: Counter-Insurgency Operations* B-GL-323-004/FP-003 (Kingston, ON: Army Publishing Office, 2008), p. 5–8. Also, "NATO's new Strategic Concept, adopted at the Lisbon Summit in November 2010, underlines that lessons learned from NATO operations show that effective crisis management calls for a *comprehensive approach* involving political, civilian and military instruments. Military means, although essential, are not enough on their own to meet the many complex challenges to Euro-Atlantic and international security. Allied leaders agreed at Lisbon to enhance NATO's contribution to a comprehensive approach to crisis management as part of the international community's effort and to improve NATO's ability to contribute to stabilization and reconstruction." See *A Comprehensive Approach to Crisis Management*, http://www.nato.int/cps/en/natolive/topics_51633.htm, accessed 12 Jan. 1012.

27. For an overview of CA approaches specific to the UN, EU, NATO and the OSCE, see the Conference Report, Chapter 3, pp. 13–17. www.defmin.fi/files/1316/Comprehensive_ Approach__Trends_Challenges_and_Possibilities_for_Cooperation_in_Crisis_Prevention_ and_Management.pdf; see also *OSCE Uses Comprehensive Approach in Fighting Terrorism, Secretary General Tells UN Committee*, http://www.osce.org/sg/75766, accessed 12 Jan. 2012; (4) regarding the EU, "EU efforts at implementing a *comprehensive approach* – and what it has termed Civil-Military Coordination (CMCO) – must be understood in the context of both the growth of the EU as a security provider by means of civilian and military crisis operations under the European Security and Defense Policy (ESDP), and of a changing security environment in which state failure and international terrorism increasingly require both civilian and military solutions. Operational experience in the Balkans, sub-Saharan Africa and more recently Afghanistan has further demonstrated the need to combine civilian and military crisis management in order to address security challenges that include the fight against organized crime, the need to reform the police and justice sector, or the provision of military forces on a short-term basis in support of larger peace-keeping missions." See EU and the Comprehensive Approach in *The Civil-Military Agenda*, Danish Institute for International Studies, http:// www.diis.dk/sw69236.asp, accessed 12 Jan. 2012.

28. *Comprehensive Approach: Trends, Challenges and Possibilities for Cooperation in Crisis Prevention and Management* Based on Comprehensive Approach Seminar 17 June 2008 Helsinki, Articles from International Actors and from National Delegations, Work of the CAS Research Team and Expertise of the Crisis Management Initiative (Ministry of Defence: Helsinki, Finland, 2008), 11.

29. Helsinki, 2008, 11.

30. Helsinki, 2008, 24.

31. *National Security Strategy*, http://www.whitehouse.gov/sites/default/files/rss_viewer/ national--_security-_strategy, accessed 6 July 2010, 11.

32. Helsinki, 2008, 41.

33. *2009 Year in Review: Smart Power in Action*, United States Department of State, Coordinator for Reconstruction and Stabilization, http://www.state.gov/r/pa/ei/subject/index.htm accessed 7 July 2010.

34. Ibid., p. 13.

35. National Security Strategy, 11.

36. Sharon L. Caudle and Stephan de Spiegeleire, "A New Generation of National Security Strategies: Early Findings from the Netherlands and the United Kingdom" in *Journal of Homeland Security and Emergency Management*, Vol. 7, Issue 1, 2010, Article 35.

37. *Whole of Government Approaches to Fragile States: Governance, Peace and Security*, DAC Guidelines and Reference Series, Organization for Economic Cooperation and Development (OECD), 2006, p. 10. http://www.oecd.org/dataoecd/15/24/37826256.pdf, accessed 6 July 2010.

38. See OECD's *Principles for Good International Engagement in Fragile States*, http://www.oecd.org/document/40/0,3343,en_21571361_42277499_42283112_1_1_1_1,00.html, accessed 7 July 2010.

Chapter Two

Theory and Praxis

Where conflict exists or its residual effects continue to linger, stoking any embers of division often becomes an effective means of polarizing ethno-religious communities for political gain. Volatility and violence can be expected outcomes if people are outraged by their victimization at the hands of the *other*, rendering their deep emotional currents and prejudices easily exploited.[1] Such vulnerability is often leveraged to become hostile words and violent acts in what is perceived as warranted retribution against the *other*, hence the escalating effect of deep-rooted conflict begins. As someone once said, "Perception is very real in its consequences."

The purpose of this chapter is to offer a brief primer outlining the theory of conflict and the praxis of peacebuilding utilized in the upcoming chapters and case studies. Albeit, this book speaks primarily of the role of chaplains, the nature of the following is of sufficient scope to be useful to a range of actors engaging indigenous communities in nation building endeavors. By no means exhaustive, the theory and praxis examined here will sufficiently acquaint the reader with the dynamics at play in such engagement, providing additional background knowledge for further reflection. A study in and of itself, it is for the reader to decide to continue with the present analysis or to return to these pages for additional expansion on theoretical points while working through the case studies. For ease of reference, theory introduced deeper into this text will cite the more in-depth explanations offered here.

INTRACTABLE CONFLICT

Terrell A. Northrup contends that threatened identity is at the heart of inter-group hostilities. Related to identity are one's "core constructs," which "are of particular importance for organizing a person's approach to life and to the roles he or she plays [which] cannot be changed significantly without disturbing the very roots of our being."[2] It is when one's core sense of self—identity—is threatened that conflict looms large. Also woven into Northrup's notion of the shaping of the inner self is the significance of social or group identity. Here, the crucial element is the sense of loss that becomes unit forming when such variables as common fate or shared threat are present. Her assertion is that the notion of loss is pivotal to the dynamics relating to identity and conflict, found in both interpersonal and intergroup conflict. Reinforcing Northrup's thesis that identity goes to the core of conflict is the work of Harvard's Herbert C. Kelman, known for his leadership of the Oslo Accord. He maintains that the deep-seated negation of the *other* is a main driver of conflict, which in turn shapes collective identity[3] as boundaries are drawn to secure one's safety and identity from the alien *other*. In such situations, this is achieved largely by exclusion, placing beyond the boundary of the *self* those who are not "us," rather, who are "them". . . these are the ones made *other*.[4] A paraphrase of Northrup's four stages of intractable conflict is offered here as a descriptive backdrop to the larger discussion of deep-rooted conflict: Threat, Distortion, Rigidification and Collusion.

Stage One: Threat

Attempts to invalidate another's core sense of identity elicit feelings of being threatened. Most commonly, threats to one's core constructs undermine meaning and an individual's ability to predict. In conflict among groups one of the more pronounced dynamics is the threat of the loss of land. For many, identity and meaning are tied to the land; to lose it is to lose a sense of *self* or, as Northrup defines it, psychic annihilation. Reinforcing Northrup, R. Scott Appleby articulates the religious overtones of such "sacredness of land." He states,

> All religions have their "sacred spaces," and woe to those who transgress their borders and violate their sanctity. Sacred spaces function in part as territorial markers, heavily fortified reminders that the religious community, while geographically diffuse and otherworldly in its spiritual orientation, is not indifferent to the questions of peoplehood and land.[5]

The Israeli-Palestinian conflict is a case in point: national identity is so invested in the land that to see the national aspirations of one party fulfilled is for the other to experience identity somehow denied; zero sum outcomes.

Stage Two: Distortion

Distortion is a psychological response to information that poses a threat. In order to deal with an incoming threat, individuals or groups may force a different meaning onto the construct as a way of invalidating it, thus preserving their own sense of identity. This may take the form of denying incoming information or redefining it altogether. Either way, the information is invalidated as a means of affirming one's own identity, e.g., keeping one's own sense of identity intact by misconstruing actual events. This is how propaganda is spawned. In Afghanistan, for example, the intended message of the efforts by the international community to improve governance and to rehabilitate infrastructure is *distorted* by the insurgents as being nothing more than a ploy by "today's Crusaders" intent rather on occupying the land and changing the way of life of the people. In so doing, linkages of the perceived Western agenda to the historical memory of East/West—Islam/Christianity enmity are rekindled all the while leaving their core sense of *self* "intact" as true followers of Islam.

Stage Three: Rigidification

Northrup explicates further that over time the intractability of conflict moves from invalidating information (distortion), as a means of protecting one's core sense of identity, to developing increasingly impermeable constructs. At this stage interpretations of the world become more rigid, making change far more difficult. Minor characteristics of the other party once deemed more acceptable due to a resemblance to their own now become threatening. Rigidification introduces the process of crystallizing or hardening of the "us" and "them" dynamic. Where once a degree of contact between the parties was evident, distance now becomes a more defining trait—communication shuts down or focuses totally on invalidating the *other* as boundaries of the *self* are secured. Over time, stories of the *other* develop portraying them as bad, evil or lazy while projecting a self-image of being noble and courageous. Dehumanization is manifest at this stage, making violence more tolerable. Simply put, it is far easier to harm someone who is believed to be sub-human. Objectification becomes the result—reducing the *other* to an "it," removing any reticence to inflicting pain or, worse still, eradicating them and their memory.

Stage Four: Collusion

Finally, alienation becomes so entrenched at this stage that conflict takes on a life of its own. Both parties *collude* in maintaining the dispute as the hostilities begin to shape identity. Criticisms and rejections, precipitating violent acts toward the *other*, increasingly become the behavioral norm, validating *distortions* that have contributed to the conflict.

Albeit guarded, Northrup does offer hope for situations where intractable conflict persists. She explains that where changes in the dynamics of relation occur, there is reason for cautious optimism. For many, the temptation is to think of intractable conflict as insurgencies transpiring far from our shores. Notwithstanding, conflict of this nature manifests itself in various places and in sundry ways, some of which are close to home.

President Obama's foray into the abortion debate in the early months of his presidency provides a window through which to view some of what Northrup's theory entails. Speaking at the Convocation of Notre Dame University in May of 2009, as *Guardian* columnist Andrew Clark notes, Obama reluctantly was drawn into the debate due to its fierce polarization between the pro-choice and pro-life camps. He acknowledged the conflict's seeming *intractability*, evidenced in its *rigidification*; the development of increasingly impermeable constructs and the hardening of the 'us' versus 'them' mentality. He asserted, "No matter how much we may want to fudge it—indeed, while we know that the views of most Americans on the subject are complex and even contradictory—the fact is that, at some level, the views of the two camps are irreconcilable."[6] Intoning further his concern of the escalating volatility, he urged those on either side of the debate not to "demonize" the *other*. Here *distortion* had already led to *rigidification.* "Each side will continue to make its case to the public with passion and conviction. But surely we can do so without reducing those with differing views to caricature."[7] In the United States, some pro-life proponents have become so vociferous in their opposition to pro-choice advocates that they have resorted to violence, and, in some instances, murder.

The killing of abortionist Dr. George Tiller of Wichita, Kansas, by a professed pro-life supporter just days after President Obama's address at Notre Dame is a poignant example of the manifested violence of, what has become for some, intractable conflict.[8] *Collusion* is evidenced as increasingly identity is shaped by the conflict itself. Aggression against pro-choice physicians and staff are often carried out with resigned resolve, as acts of violence, in some instances, are "religiously compelled." As is the case, those suffering at the hands of the *other* have been reduced to the status of sub-human—butchers in the eyes of some—becoming instead recipients of deserving judgment and punishment.

Integral to grasping something of the inner workings of deep-rooted conflict is the insidious nature of *mimesis*. Alluded to in Northrup, intractable conflict's dynamics of threat, distortion, rigidification and collusion testify of spiraling and violent reciprocity. The contribution of *mimetic* theory from anthropological research offers insight into the phenomenon of the oft-witnessed escalating effects of violence among groups caught in its throes. The following overview of the stages of *mimesis* will highlight its ubiquitous nature as an aspect of the human condition and its role in intensifying conflict.

MIMESIS: THE RECIPROCAL NATURE OF ESCALATING VIOLENCE

In its original Greek, *mimesis* carries with it the sense of *desire*. The words "mime" and "imitate" are derivative of this Greek root. René Girard, originator of the concept, contends that our understanding of language and culture are realized through the *mimetic* process.[9] From an early age children learn from their surroundings by watching what others do and, in some fashion, imitating their behavior. Another may possess, do or even become something that is seen as highly desirable, to the point that steps are taken to acquire whatever that something may be. "Girard's key insight is that what we desire, what motivates to extend our reach to do, become, or acquire something is arrived at mimetically."[10] Known as *mimetic* desire, it is a driving factor of the human condition and, as will be seen, results in positive or negative outcomes.

Mimetic Desire

Mimetic desire in its classic form involves a Self, a Model and an Object. As *mimesis* unfolds in the everyday lives of individuals or groups, the Self observes the Model as exhibiting for what may be a physical object, a relationship, prestige, honor, a skill, recognition, status, life conditions or sex.[11] As intimated in this list of potential desires, it is not uncommon for someone to *mimetically* desire the interiority of another, e.g., "I want to be like him or her." Depending on the Model, that may be beneficial or detrimental to the Self. In military training it often occurs that a new recruit will want to emulate a member of the Directing Staff; a Sergeant or Warrant Officer whose demeanor earns the respect of all, epitomizing the ethical behavior, self-discipline, and honor that a young recruit would "*mimetically* desire," envisioning what they may one day become. Conversely, this same phenomenon is found where the criminal element shapes their underlings, be that on the street or in prison. A young delinquent will recognize the aura of a seasoned villain and its cowering effect on others as something desirable. Such emulation is *mimetic*. In other circumstances, desire within Self may intensify if others assign value to what the Model possesses. Believing the object the Model possesses or desires to be of such significance, the Self cannot feel complete until the object is acquired.[12] Tension is exacerbated if the Model stands between the Self and that which is deemed essential to the

Self's identity fulfillment. At this point the Model becomes an obstacle to be dealt with in whatever manner the Self deems effective.

Mimetic Desire

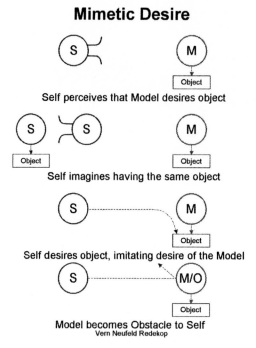

Self perceives that Model desires object

Self imagines having the same object

Self desires object, imitating desire of the Model

Model becomes Obstacle to Self

Vern Neufeld Redekop

Figure 2.1.   Mimetic Desire. Used by Permission of Vern Neufeld Redekop.

Mimetic Rivalry

In conflict situations *mimetic* desire often reveals itself in the dynamics between opposing groups frequently in competition over such things as scarce resources or the support of influential or powerful outside parties to the conflict. Here desire becomes actual rivalry, where one group becomes preoccupied with what the other may possess. Mimetic rivalry emerges as preoccupation becomes reciprocal; as one advances the other reacts believing they are somehow being treated unfavorably or placed at disadvantage. Objects of desire become coveted possessions, provoking resentment and eventual reaction. Where conflict renders certain geographical areas inaccessible, food and water become highly desirable staples, as groups position themselves to 'acquire' aid intended for a rival group. *Mimetic* rivalry may also be seen as one group becomes desirous of the 'seeming' curried favor that their opponent may have with certain International Organizations (IOs) or NGOs, an interim administration or outside governments and agencies. Groups will go to great lengths to discredit the *other* in an attempt to supplant what they deem as an enviable position of favoritism.

Mimetic Violence

The *mimetic* nature of violence is an insidious dynamic of conflict. Its spiraling effect of reciprocity takes on a life of its own, precipitating its oft-intractable nature. Anthony Storr rightly depicts the incendiary nature of violence and its capacity to spread seemingly unchecked—a *mimetic* reality. He states, "It is far more difficult to quell an impulse toward violence than it is to rouse it."[13] Many an interventionist—military or civilian—has watched powerlessly as hostilities of one group toward another were repaid with exacting vengeance, escalating uncontrollably with incalculable cost. Girard metaphorically describes the seeming unappeasable nature of *mimetic* violence, as a consuming fire.

> The mimetic attributes of violence are extraordinary—sometimes direct and positive, at other times indirect and negative. The more [people] strive to curb their violent impulse; the more these impulses seem to prosper. The very weapons used to combat violence are turned against their users. Violence is like a raging fire that feeds on the very object intended to smother its flames . . . the mimetic character of violence is so intense that once violence is installed in a community, it cannot burn itself out.[14]

Violence is epitomized in deep-rooted conflict by its "escalating" effect, as "one gives back as good as one gets, and then some." Cooler heads seldom prevail once the bloodletting begins; escalation develops into an inferno rapidly. A poignant example of such escalating *mimesis* can be detected in the incendiary statement made by Muslim leaders to their community after suffering severe violence at the hands of the Hindu mobs in Bombay, India, during the winter of 1992–1993.[15] Understandably shaken by the severity of recent events, they wittingly stoked the embers of revenge by intoning, "For every bottle they throw, this time we will throw two."[16]

Also, within the domain of deep-rooted conflict, *mimetic* violence is often depicted metaphorically as a 'contagion' due to its contribution to the escalation of violence. The concept of contagion originates in Girard. He states, "being eminently contagious, desire follows the most unexpected paths in order to spread from one person to another." It is in the crescendo of *mimetic* intensity, *self* (subject) rivaling the *other* (model) for the much-sought object, that one "catches" a nearby desire just as one would catch the plague or cholera, simply by contact with an infected person."[17]

Redekop and Paré's research suggests that *mimetic* contagion is seen in gathering crowds as word of mouth spreads the news that something is happening. As people assemble momentum mounts; the logic becomes that there must be legitimacy to the accusations because so many are rallying to the cause. It may be that a particular action become the *mimetic* contagion, usually an act of violence. Their contention is that people "choose to imitate those who are within the closest relational system to us—those who we admire most. It is the size of the commonality that determines the extent of the contagion."[18]

In situations where the international community deems intervention necessary, those deploying frequently come face to face with the death and destruction of such *quid pro quo*. Such *mimetic* violence contributes to the taking of entrenched positions of "us" and "them": the *rigidification* of intractable conflict. *Mimetic* structures of violence manifest in conflict taking on a life of its own: the *collusion* of intractable conflict.

Mimetic Structures of Violence

Mimetic structures of violence emerge when the dominating attitude and orientation of those embroiled in conflict becomes such that attempts to control, hurt, diminish or otherwise do violence to the *other* becomes the main driver of the conflict.

Structure as a construct is introduced; as it identifies how a number of interrelated parts are dominated by the whole. Redekop explains further,

> In this case, the parts include human identity need satisfiers; feelings of "envy, greed and impotent hatred" inspired by mimetic desire; and memories of victimization and bystander encouragement—all are dominated by the whole, which is violence. When people in mimetic structures of violence interact with one another they are worse off for the encounter.[19]

Paraphrasing Redekop, it is *mimetic* because groups are imitating one another in hurting each other; it is a structure because it is an ongoing pattern that creates and sustains harm. *Mimetic* structures of violence constrict the movement of people, limit life's options, and are directed toward death. In this context, violence may be understood to mean that which takes away from the well-being of the *other*. Groups develop competing interpretive frameworks and public relation strategies to disclaim any culpability of their own all the while maximizing the responsibility for the violence on the other side—the "perpetrator." It is not just that groups strike back in retaliation, reversing the roles of victim and perpetrator, but a relationship builds up in such a way that the parties in the relationship continually say and do things to harm one another. In that sense it becomes a structure that can be prolonged over extended periods of time, even decades or longer.[20] Structures of this nature take on a life of their own in conflict situations, inciting people to do or say things to the *other* that would normally go against their nature. It holds within it an intention to do harm or get at the *other*.

Violence is manifested and perpetuated in the following ways:

Violence as *control*, keeps people form achieving their ends, holds them back, and puts obstacles in their way.

Violence, as *force*, inflicts goals, actions, or behaviors on people. It makes people subservient, doing what they do not wish to do. It is the work of extortion and brutality. It forces people to choose between two unacceptable options, as when women are forced to choose between unwanted sexual activity or seeing their children hurt.

Violence *extracts*, from people what they cherish. It may be the theft of possessions or it may mean extracting information through torture, trickery, or treachery.

Violence *diminishes* people. It makes them lose face, humiliates them, and removes all dignity and self-respect.

Violence *hurts* people. It maims them, burns them, makes them bleed, and kills them. With the physical hurt comes the inner hurt of being deceived or betrayed.

Violence can take place at another level—that of *curse*. Curses involve a desire to see the other harmed. It imagines and desires ill for the *other*. Curses have a verbal dimension of demanding that harmful things happen to the object of the curse. They may also have a spiritual dimension where forces are involved to perpetrate evil against the *other*.

Violence can also take the form of *withholding help* from someone who is suffering.[21]

The Israeli-Palestinian conflict is a poignant example of a *mimetic* structure of violence in action. For many in this conflict there exists mutual distrust; for some, perhaps, even mutual hate. The Israeli stance has always been to strike back when attacked. This is public knowledge. True to *mimesis*, the response is often more forceful that the original attack. This conflict has continued now for a number of years with sustained reciprocal retaliation. The cycles of violence have on more than one occasion erupted into serious conflict, the more recent conflicts in both southern Lebanon (2006) and the Gaza (2009) being cases in point. The *mimetic* nature of this ongoing conflict can be seen in its continual reciprocity. As a structure it perpetuates a pattern of creating and sustaining harm; movement is constricted for many, limiting life's options; security is persistently threatened; violence toward the *other* results in death within both communities.

Mimetic Structures
of *Violence*

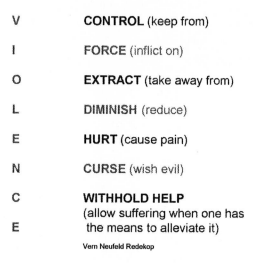

V	**CONTROL** (keep from)
I	**FORCE** (inflict on)
O	**EXTRACT** (take away from)
L	**DIMINISH** (reduce)
E	**HURT** (cause pain)
N	**CURSE** (wish evil)
C	**WITHHOLD HELP**
E	(allow suffering when one has the means to alleviate it)

Vern Neufeld Redekop

Figure 2.2.   Mimetic Structures of Violence Used by Permission of Vern Neufeld Redekop.

Mimetic Structures of Blessing

Redekop uses the term "blessing" as a descriptor of reconciliation, an English word translated from the Hebrew and Arabic words *berikah* and *barakat* respectively. Together these words connote an orientation, attitude and actions intended to enhance mutual well-being.[22] When infused with the reciprocal nature of *mimesis*, blessing becomes "the mutual concern for, and actions that reciprocally enhance the well-being of those within a relationship."[23] *Mimetic* structures of blessing look to a broad ethical vision that transcends antagonistic polarities. Redekop insists that such inclusivity does not relegate past injustice to the margins. From a relational perspective, one benefits from the good found in relations without becoming locked into old and unproductive patterns of relatedness. As such, *mimetic* structures of blessing do not necessarily preclude conflict but provide a framework in which conflict is transformed into something creative with options expanding to include new people, new paradigms and new ways of doing things—a reciprocity manifest in the openness of the *self* that aids in creating space for the development of new things for the *other*.[24] Such mutual respect and even care for the *other* are key to reconciliation without prescribing how they might be expressed.[25] The spirit of generosity infuses relation with reciprocal giving, cultivating a structure of abundance as mutual generosity produces more. Together, such openness and receptivity of generosity together elicits a continual strengthening of trust and love for the *other*.[26]

Mimetic Modeling: Creating Openness to the Other

In conflict and post-conflict environments, *mimesis* may also be experienced in a positive light, as will be seen in the case studies. Stated earlier, *mimetic* desire encompasses not only imitating one's behavior but may include the 'interiority' of the *other* as well. Where an intervener models trust, acceptance, tolerance and hospitality, the desire for such subjectivity—internalizing similar sentiments—may find expression within a local leader. Openness to broader engagement may ensue, something that previously neither leader could have entertained. During such encounters, *re-humanizing* of the *other* has a chance to take root, something that Miroslav Volf refers to as the *will to embrace*—that hesitant yet hopeful opening of the *self* to the *other* in the arduous task of bridging the chasm of alienation and separation.[27] Where the desire exists within the *other* for a reconciling of differences and a return to coexistence/relation, movement toward such renewed interdependence may emerge. In such instances, a transformative narrative may begin, a positive first step on the long road to reconciliation and the healing of memory.

Human identity needs complement *mimetic* systems as a means of grasping something of the dynamics of conflict. As individuals or groups, satisfaction of the need for meaning, connectedness, security, action and recognition is an additional lens through which to identify what can become the layered effect of deep-rooted conflict.

HUMAN IDENTITY NEEDS

John Burton was the first theorist/practitioner to bring forward the notion of human identity needs and their satisfiers/dissatisfiers as applicable to conflict resolution. He contends that essential to understanding the nature of conflict is the realization that one must move beyond the consideration of interests to that of the human needs of the real person. Processes can be introduced that will move individuals/groups from an aggressive mode to that of problem solving.[28] Resolving conflicts consists of discovering appropriate need satisfiers, determining their association within the analyses of the problems of relations, and costing out the long-term consequences of the decided need satisfiers, with the likely responses of the *others*.[29]

Since Burton's work in the 1980's, other scholars have expanded on his theories; further describing the various need categories and how they function in relation to human experience. After extensive research in this domain, Vern Neufeld Redekop[30] defines over twenty such need categories developed within the literature, synthesizing them into the following six broader categories: *connectedness*, *meaning*, *security*, *action*, and *recognition*, all of which function together to create the need for *being*, or an integrated sense of the *self*. Need categories may be understood to be universal satisfiers based on a complex amalgam of culture and personal experience. The theory referred to here, while drawing on additional scholars, principally reflects Redekop's adaptation of the construct.

Relevant as well are the emotions attached to each, which under certain circumstances may lead to trauma. Essential to this examination is the emphasis placed on relation: the *self* with the *other*. Relation is the lens through which the various dynamics that take place among individuals and groups are viewed; for it is in relation with the *other* that identity is negotiated. No one is an island. Each person is a unique individual, yet identity is created by integrating something of the *other* within the *self* through encounter, an aspect of mutuality. Whether alienation or acceptance, the common denominator may be traced to the relation of the *self* with the *other*.

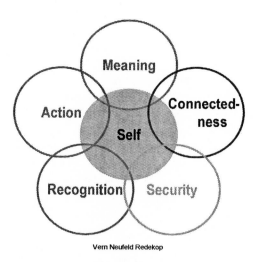

Identity Needs Implicated In Deep-Rooted Conflict

Vern Neufeld Redekop

Figure 2.3.   Human Identity Needs. Used by Permission of Vern Neufeld Redekop.

Meaning

The inner worlds we develop are rooted in the understanding of meaning, which provide an overall perspective for surveying the worlds of *others* around us. Our viewpoints of purpose and why we want to live are grounded in this identity need. Integral to our world of meaning is what we deem as a sense of justice: the understanding of healthy relation, what is fair, and what is a reasonable expectation for the behavior of *others* in response to our well-intentioned actions. Conflict emerges when our perception of the way of meeting the identity need of meaning is endangered, as aggression against us strikes at the core of who we are. Relation becomes adversarial, as the *self* is pitted against the *other*, laying sole claim to existing need satisfiers as rightfully deserved, thus sparking reciprocity. "The need for meaning is so profound, our identity is so wrapped up in that meaning, that we defend our deepest beliefs and assumptions with enormous emotional force—sometimes with ferocity!"[31]

Although in slightly different language, Robert Schreiter speaks of violence as "an attack on our sense of safety and selfhood," the later being another way of saying "meaning." Violence at the hands of the *other* is a reminder of our vulnerability (*security*). Often culminating in violence, such *relational* collapse is typical of conflict situations that engender entrenched positions of the *self* against the *other*. Schreiter states that egregious violence illegitimately empowers perpetrators to terrorize victims. Undermining our need for *meaning* is the attack on our sense of "selfhood," where our narratives of life and culture are being brutalized by the *other*. He illumines,

> [Our narratives are] the stories that we tell about ourselves, both to ourselves and to others. These stories become foundational not only for describing ourselves to *other(s)*, but also for our very understanding of our-*selves*. They constitute our truths. They tell us what we need to know about ourselves, how we remember what has happened to us, how we may have changed, and how we have stayed the same—in other words, how we manage to be who we are.[32]

The violence of the *self* (perpetrator) against the need for *meaning* of the *other* (victim) is manifested in causing us to doubt the cohesion of the narratives that sustain our identity, while attempting to supplant it with a surrogate narrative. The *self's* violent targeting the human need for *meaning* of the *other* leaves a residual anger, which, under traumatic conditions, leads to questioning, or, as Schreiter states, doubting. [33]

In *Shattered Assumptions*, Ronnie Janoff-Bulman explains how for victims of heinous crimes, the world can become malevolent suddenly, not solely because something bad comes into their lives but because the world changes for them, it becomes tainted. The capacity to trust others is seriously eroded. She speaks of how extreme negative events violate the core schemas, the repositories of those positive pre-existing assumptions that give life meaning and order.[34]

> [C]ultural truisms—beliefs that are so widely accepted we are unpractised in defending them—are highly vulnerable to influence and persuasion . . . Traumatic life events challenge these core schema; we have no "counterarguments," and they come tumbling down.[35]

On a more helpful note, Janoff-Bulman also states that even though positive core assumptions may undergo a period of psychological upheaval, our core schema are associated with long-term recovery.[36]

In conflict situations, the tendency for individuals and/or groups to find meaning in violence is very real; the "fight or flight" reaction is all too familiar. In the intensity of violence—real or perceived—individuals may be influenced to frame their hostilities as revenge or glory,[37] giving credence to what—under normal circumstances—they might not condone. Where the negative satisfiers of the human identity need of security are in effect, uncertainty compounds insecurity, undermining our sense of meaning: aggressive posturing soon leads to overt violence.

Connectedness

Delineated earlier, as individuals we are not islands; we need community. It is in connecting with those around us that we find inner fulfillment. The *other(s)* becomes a reference point enhancing our capacity to describe ourselves. We cannot be a *self* on our own; we need a degree of bonding with the *other* as an aspect of the human condition. Charles Taylor cites the need of connectedness and its relation to community in his "webs of interlocution, [which lead to] a reference point of some fashion to a defining community."[38] Paul Ricoeur echoes our need for connectivity with the *other* in his statement, "selfhood of oneself implies the otherness to such an intimate degree that one cannot be thought of without the other."[39] Social identity and the desire to belong are among the most prominent requirements known to the human species, with a rupture of such "bonding produc[ing] separation, alienation, ostracism, and humiliation."[40] In terms of identity, connectedness is tied to our need for collective continuity whereby we see ourselves as members belonging to a group. As can be expected, the need for survival comes into play when our group or lineage is threatened with extinction.[41] Research among tribal peoples further reveals that violence is more likely tied to threats and hurt feelings, disloyalty and unkindness, which can be attributed to relational conflicts and the absence of social stability.[42] People belong to many communities. When fundamental needs are threatened individuals turn to the groups most likely to preserve them. Which particular identity group is most important at any point in time could be a function of the needs that are best met by that group or the satisfaction of which needs are most threatened.

In intense conflict where violence is either real or perceived, external threats to human identity needs may reach such emotional intensity so as to cause trauma. People dominated by violence usually experience trauma and, as such, express a need for identity need satisfiers linked to violence, such as the impulse for revenge, a dynamic that feeds into the spiraling effect of deep-rooted conflict. It is the crisis of an outside threat that often reinforces the need for *connectedness* to a group as a means of maintaining meaning and preserving a sense of identity.

Security

As a human identity need, security is linked to self-identity and the need for a long-term future. The need for emotional security manifests itself in the desire to be among our own people where language, experience and feelings are held in common. Threats, harassment and the dashing of our built-up expectations threaten emotional security. Compounding this is the need for economic security, which telegraphs to the satisfaction of other needs, i.e., welfare needs.

The linkage between positively satisfying the identity need of security and our fulfillment of the bonds of connectedness has already been established. It is in such positive connectedness that relation is sustained, and, in so doing, a strengthened self-confidence re-emerges, bringing with it a bolstered sense of security as a human identity need. Where security erodes, freedom from threats, violence and injury, coupled with the endangering of the welfare needs of food, shelter and clothing creates palpable *fear*. Trauma may result as the need for security is threatened, thus inhibiting the *self's* ability to connect with the *other* in relation. With violence, real or perceived, the need for security intensifies to such a degree that relation is reframed adversarially in an "us and them" mentality.

> When a group feels a sustained threat . . . identity need satisfiers are defined in terms of security and are expressed in black and white terms. Meaning systems become rigid, people are either friends or enemies; action becomes very focused on security accompanied by a passionate need for validation of one's hurt and vulnerability. Striking first or striking back becomes the rule of the day as violence begins to escalate. It doesn't have to make sense.[43]

The above quote underscores the breadth of effect of alienation. It is the loss of security that leads to the undermining of one's ability to act, possibly the worst form of violence.

Action

If we are to be actor or agent it must translate into our ability to take meaningful and significant action. The human identity need of action represents choice, i.e., exhibiting some control over our immediate social and physical environment. One of the worst forms of violence is for the capacity to act to be withheld from us, resulting in having "no choice" but to be acted upon. The inability to take action is concomitant with a diminution of self-esteem. Some of the most egregious cases of violence are found in concentration camps where incomprehensible atrocities are inflicted upon those who have no recourse but to endure unspeakable cruelty and torment; those who survive live to face another day of further torture. In fleshing out our understanding of being "acted on" and its impact on the individual, there is value in drawing on the thinking of a few authors who have written in this domain.

Reading through Elie Wiesel's *Night* pulls back the curtain on the horrific suffering of the Jewish people at the hands of the Nazi SS run concentration camps in World War Two. A heart-wrenching read, it depicts a people totally deprived of their capacity to "act," subjected to the continued deprivation and violence of being 'acted on' by their sadistic masters. Wiesel's recounting of the hopelessness and depth of anguish of some of those he knew in the camp leaves you with a seldom-experienced solemnness as you encounter evil on such a large scale. Yet, in the midst of such inconceivable darkness, totally shredded of their ability to resist, many continued with their practice of faith. There are not many more descriptive accounts of people being "acted on" by the *other* than the Jewish people in the Holocaust.

Paul Ricoeur offers insight here. In *Oneself as Another* he relates that for every action there is an actor, one who acts and one who suffers—one who is acted on. However, Ricoeur recognizes the moral problem associated with an incremental hostility resulting in the "essential dissymmetry between the one who acts and the one who undergoes, culminating in the violence [action] of the powerful agent."[44] It is in such situations that the "sufferer" is left with no recourse but to remain the "acted on." In Robert Schreiter's language, being "acted on" may be understood as the *self's* attack on the *other's* sense of "selfhood," the brutalizing of the narratives of one's life and culture. Emmanuel Levinas adroitly discerns the potential treachery of the *self's* will forcefully imposed on the *other*. Levinas states,

> Violence does not consist so much in injuring and annihilating persons as in interrupting their continuity, making them play roles in which they no longer recognize themselves, making them betray not only commitments but their own substance, making them carry out actions that will destroy every possibility of action.[45]

In conflict situations, the loss of security and its oft accompanying absence of the ability to act leaves in its wake fear and depression for many who are forced to endure hardship that is beyond most to comprehend. Being "acted upon" with little or no recourse leads to the human identity need category of recognition where being appreciated as someone of value and importance becomes a crucial aspect of self-fulfillment.

Recognition

Tied to the human identity needs of connectedness, meaning, security and action is the need to feel that you are appreciated for who you are; that your identity is acknowledged as important along with its meaning system, actions and connections. It is the exceptional person who is confident enough in themselves for the need for recognition to be met internally. Most of us need that recognition from others; that "congruence between what one has determined within oneself as being a ground for recognition and what is acknowledged from the *other*."[46]

Conflict situations exacerbate the effects of exclusion, often traumatizing its victims. In withholding appropriate recognition, the *self* deprives the *other* of dignity, resulting in indignation and anger. The intensely charged conditions of conflict lead to the traumatically induced state of shame as exclusion negates the *self*-worth of the *other* and, by extension, recognition. The scars of unmet human identity needs contribute to the perpetuation of skewed narratives by groups with a history of conflict, narratives that engender myth. Recalling their story of woundedness impacts the present and shapes the future.

Being: An Integrated Sense of Self

It is in the satisfying of human identity needs of connectedness, meaning, security, action and recognition that we grasp something of self-actualization—a sense of fulfillment for our inner being. Human Identity Needs testify to how the externality of conflict impacts individual and groups internally. The palpable threat to one's physical security is often accompanied by intense inner desire for integration tied to human identity needs—something that significantly deteriorates in overt or perceived conflict. Deep-rooted conflict begins at the level of interiority—the conflicting processes and dynamics that originate deep within us.

When people are severely threatened (extreme cases) they can become traumatized. As outlined above, when *human identity needs* are intensely threatened, questions relating to meaning and purpose are dominant; depression in its various manifestations is often evident; and, a person's state of well-being is undermined. Trauma ensues. Feelings of belonging erode, fray-

Trauma and
Human Identity Needs

Despair = Depression + Fear
Frustration = Anger + Depression
Vern Neufeld Redekop

Figure 2.4.   Trauma and Human Identity Needs. Used by permission of Vern Neufeld Redekop.

ing at one's notion of *connectedness*, only to be compounded by a sustained sense of a loss of *security* at various levels—physical, emotional, and economic. Depending on the dynamics at play, chaplains may come in contact with those experiencing trauma directly related to Identity Needs. For many of the people, the need for security takes over the core of their being and they become dissociated, unable to empathize or connect with others. In some situations physiological processes related to identity needs are so overdone within the body that the result is Post-Traumatic Stress Disorder.

When a group feels a sustained on-going threat, mimetic structures of entrenchment take over. Identity need satisfiers are defined in terms of security and become expressed in black and white terms. Meaning systems become rigid; people are either friends or enemies; action becomes very focused on security; and there is a passionate need for validation of one's hurt and vulnerability. Striking first or striking back becomes the rule of the day as violence begins to escalate. It doesn't have to make sense.

Time becomes a critical factor in limiting the effects of entrenchment. International intervention is a must as the need for security becomes paramount. People are unable to consider a new beginning if their present situation is still fraught with daily reminders of the violations they have suffered. Securing the peace by deploying troops into conflict areas gives the reconcil-

Mimetic Structures
of Entrenchment

- All needs developed around security
- Self criticism impossible
- Everything is black and white
- Fundamentalist approach to meaning
- Terminal identity – all that matters is "Are you on our side?"

Figure 2.5. Mimetic Structures of Enlightenment. Used by permission of Vern Neufeld Redekop.

iation process a chance to take root. Mimetic structures of entrenchment, which often lead to a spiralling effect with respect to rivalry and violence, are, at least to a degree, forced into a state of suspension.

WOUNDED MEMORY

Historical enmity between groups may remain dormant for extended periods of time, containing any visceral demonstration of resented victimization of one group toward another. It is true, younger generations are schooled by their elders of past injustices visited upon them by an historical foe. Latent themes, unresolved inner conflicts, unasked questions, demoralizations, victimizations and aspirations of a former epoch may be catapulted forward by the political involvements of a future generation. In deep-rooted conflict, this anachronistic phenomenon is known as intergenerational transmission,[47] a potential powder keg under the right circumstances. Middle-eastern scholar and practitioner Raymond Cohen concurs that "past humiliations are not consigned to the archives but continue to nourish present concerns."[48] Speaking of the 'Troubles' of Northern Ireland, John Agnew notes that conflict is exacerbated among groups through the usage of mutually exclusive rituals, "which recover in the present symbolic events and places from the past."[49]

Prior to the Good Friday Accord, during the famed "marching season," Protestants used these large parades to continually revive the memories of the former victories of the late seventeenth century: the Battle of the Boyne (July 12, 1690)[50] and the Siege of Londonderry (August 10, 1689).[51] Referring to the "marching season," Kenny states, "The ritual form and symbolic content insure every year that the message is the traditional one. The continuing antagonism and cultural incompatibility between Protestants and Catholics is the implicit but ambiguous meaning of the annual Protestant statement."[52]

Vamik Volkan's contribution to understanding the links between historical memory and deep-rooted conflict is illuminating. He states that parallels exist between individual and group mourning; individuals find it difficult to accept change without mourning what has been lost. Individuals also mourn the loss of hated persons or things. Like love, hate connects people deeply to one another. Volkan contends that when a tragedy occurs to a given people, they may not be able to resolve their feelings of humiliation. He likens this traumatized self-image to psychological DNA implanted in the personality of the younger generation through its relationship with the previous one. Unable to initiate or resolve the mourning of their losses or reverse their feelings of humiliation, these traumatized self-images are passed down to later generations in the hopes that others may be able to mourn and resolve what prior generations have not. This becomes a part of the ethnic group identity and mythology, something he identifies as *chosen trauma*.[53] Reinforcing Volkan's conception, Rabbi Marc Gopin explicates how deep-rooted conflict myths "can allow communication to proceed by means of its own expansion and development, or extension, into modern constructs that often elude rationalistic methods of negotiation and diplomacy, especially those intended for masses of people."[54] Gopin uses the terminology of 'perpetuated mourning' to describe "the state in which human beings find one way or another to keep old wounds open, to keep attachment to the loss by perpetuating some state of affairs in which that loss is kept at the surface level of experience, in addition to the perpetuation of moral justifications for that position."[55]

Ambitious leaders frequently exploit the intensity and volatility of an emotionally charged "collective memory of a calamity that once befell a group's ancestors."[56] As can be imagined, emerging from such 'ravaged' memories are an 'enhanced' ethnic pride, a reinforced sense of victimization and an oft-witnessed revitalization to avenge one's ancestor's hurts.[57] The deft employment of the historical memory by unscrupulous and radical leaders is of grave concern. Too often, vulnerable and uninformed populations have been duped into believing the propaganda of their leaders, be that a complete misconstruction of the past or total distortion of the present. Miroslav Volf articulates this concern well, "Some of the most brutal acts of exclusion depend on hatred, and if the common history of persons and communities does not contain enough reasons to hate, masters of exclusion will rewrite the histories and fabricate injuries in order to manufacture hatreds."[58] When conflict is reduced to its lowest common denominator—the *self/other* relation becomes the primary unit. It is the lens of 'relation' in particular that will come into view as relational systems are introduced as an aspect of conflict.

RELATIONAL SYSTEMS

Implicit in Redekop theory is the notion that deep-rooted conflict transpires within the context of *relation* between oneself and another. His coining of the term relational systems holds particular bearing on deep-rooted conflict due to its "relational" orientation, "an adjective emphasiz[ing] the interrelating of people."[59] Drawing from the Greek, he defines "system" as "literally, standing together."[60] Redekop contends that relational systems are contextual,[61] "bring[ing] individuals or groups into significant contact with one another . . . frequently [in] geographical proximity."[62] The dynamics of open and closed relational systems provide further definition and understanding for the inherent complexities of intercommunal relation of the *self/other* encounter in conflict settings.

Open and Closed Relational Systems

In figure 2.6, the larger horizontal circle depicts a *closed relational system* in which the *self* and the *other* are maintaining rigid exclusivity in relation. In

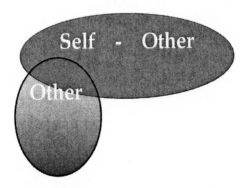

Open and Closed Relational Systems

Figure 2.6.   Relational Systems. Used by permission of Vern Neufeld Redekop.

such systems, groups are consumed with the spiraling effect of their conflict, often spilling over into overt violence. Amplifying closed relational systems, Shibutani and Kwan speak of the peculiar interrelationship that develops over the course of the conflict: "What each side does is a response to the actual or anticipated moves of its opponents; thus the course of events is built up by social interaction."[63] With such dysfunctional interaction, the focus of energies becomes one of monitoring—a *mimetic* exercise of calculating how to retaliate to the latest affront or violent act of the *other*. Closed relational systems may be "as small as a family or two people or may be larger—going from clans to ethnocultural identity groups to states to international groupings or multinational corporations."[64]

The vertical circle containing the *Other* intersecting the closed relational system depicts an open relational system, implying an openness to relation beyond the rigid focus that becomes all consuming within closed relational systems. Miroslav Volf speaks of the *self-other* relation as "differentiation": negotiating identity in interaction one with another.[65] The human *self* is not formed through a rejection of the *other* but, rather, through a complex process of "taking in" and "keeping out," something that occurs in relation. Explicating further he offers, "We are who we are not because we are separate from the others who are next to us, but because we are both separate and connected, both distinct and related; the boundaries that mark our identities are both barriers and bridges."[66] Open relational systems engender such interdependence envisioned here by the *self* bridging to the *other*. Individuals and/or groups in pluralistic societies enjoy multiple relationships concurrently. Such receptivity denotes that various ethnic and cultural distinctions are respected and valued. As depicted here, interjecting a third party into a closed relational system potentially disrupts rigid patterns that have either left groups estranged or locked in conflict.

Expanding further, figure 2.7 illustrates the range of factors that contribute to closed relational systems developing in conflict and post-conflict environments. The case studies to come will draw on this overview.

Closed Relational Systems

The uneven line (violet) portrays the unpredictability and uncertainty of life's circumstances intensified by a conflict environment. The *self* (purple S) and the *other* (red O) are representative of either individuals or groups ensnared in a closed relational system exclusive of other groups, characterized by entrenched positions and frequently punctuated with overt violence. As indicated, *mimetic* desire manifests in the *other* becoming an obstacle to what the *self* believes to be in their best interests. *Mimetic* rivalry exacerbates the intensity of the mounting conflict, resulting in spiraling violence that witnesses the reciprocal dynamic of victim and perpetrator continually exchang-

Theatre of Operations

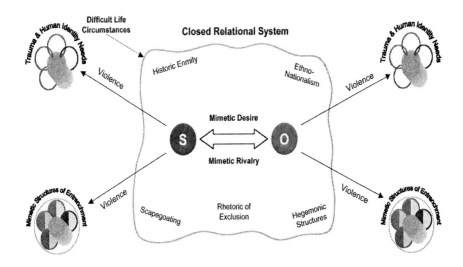

Figure 2.7. Closed Relational System in an Operational Environment (Conflict & Post-Conflict). Used by permission of Vern Neufeld Redekop.

ing roles in escalation. Noted above, such *mimetic* violence manifests increasing levels of hostility as "one *gives* twice as good as one gets." *Historical enmity* between groups often spans decades if not centuries. Deep-seated resentment over past wrongs—real or perceived—is nurtured and carried forward from one generation to the next.[67] Hostilities simmer punctuated by seasons of violence (See *Wounded Memory* above). Contributing as well to closed relational systems are aspirations of statehood and sentiments relating to the sacredness of land and an oft-inviolable destiny of its people. *Ethno-nationalism* in particular shapes identity around land *and* space—a place to live, move and act—to becoming land *as* place. Identity becomes historically rooted in the idea of a homeland.[68] Among other identity markers known to contribute to *ethno-nationalism*, language, religion and culture are predominant. *Scapegoating* occurs when two or more groups are reconciled at the expense of a third party. The identified group is deemed responsible for disrupting or threatening life for the majority. Once the scapegoated are expelled or destroyed, tensions are relieved and the majority groups coalesce into a more harmonious whole.[69] Redekop adds,

> The hatred directed toward the scapegoat unites members of the community. They forget their antagonisms, and the violent emotions that they have had for one another are projected onto the surrogate victim. Everyone becomes united in desiring the same negative—the destruction of the scapegoat.[70]

Hegemonic structures manifest in the dialectic between the dominant (*self*) and subjugated (*other*). Few have written more passionately than Paul Farmer about its oppressive socioeconomic structures. His work resonates with the topic at hand in that the conditions created by hegemonic structures invariably inflict severe socioeconomic hardship for the subjugated, something he defines as "structural violence." He elucidates that structural violence is a broad rubric that includes a host of offenses against human dignity, "extreme and relative poverty, social inequalities ranging from racism to gender inequality, and the more spectacular forms of violence that are uncontestedly human rights abuses, some of them punishment for efforts to escape structural violence."[71] Farmer further articulates that where a history exists of such domination, oppressive economically driven conditions markedly increase the probability of acts of violence. State power (the dominant) is most often responsible for human rights violations perpetuating "social and economic inequities that determine who will be at risk for assaults and who will be shielded from them."[72] Rhetoric *of exclusion* is pervasive where closed relational systems have become entrenched. The *other* is deemed beyond any meaningful dialogue and the indisputable cause of the tension and conflict. This becomes the lens through which all communication is viewed. The exclusivity of closed relational systems spawns some of the more ugly aspects of deep-rooted conflict of which demonizing and dehumanizing the *other* are two. In demonizing, evil qualities repulsive to one*self* are attributed to the enemy, for the more the enemy is demonized, the purer *self* becomes, rendering *self*-criticism of no effect.[73] Dehumanization takes that further step. It is a direct attack on the humanity and dignity of the *other*. The outgroup is considered to be sub-human, literally no better than animals or their behavior is crazy and irrational.[74] They are deemed "not worthy of being related to as presenting a likeness of ourselves, [consequently] they need not be empathized with."[75] In closed relational systems—as indicated by the groups of circles off to the side—*human identity needs* are either threatened or unmet. Where violence is a reality, people may become traumatized—the top set of circles—leaving them dissociated, unable to empathize or connect with *others*. Also, not uncommon, are the establishing of entrenched positions—the bottom set of circles—where the conflict is rigidly viewed in a black and white perspective—"us" and "them" (see *Human Identity Needs* above).

Open Relational Systems

Poignant to intervention within conflict zones, or its oft-resultant inter-communal estrangement once open hostilities have ceased, are endeavors designed to lessen tensions enough to open ways of communication and cooperation across ethno-religious boundaries. A helpful way of describing these kinds of overtures is that of *open relational systems.* This is particularly pertinent to the operational experiences of chaplains, as it aids in demonstrating the *mimetic modeling* phenomenon associated with their reconciling role introduced earlier.

Building on the previous diagram, figure 2.8 reduces a presenting conflict environment from the existing tensions between identity groups (represented by Self and Other at the opposite ends of the large double arrow), to that of the alienation that often persists between religious leaders (RL) whose larger identity groups are in conflict (see RLs at the opposite ends of a smaller double arrow directly below that of the first). Note the oblong circle drawn around the religious leaders, pointing to the *closed relational system* (CRS) that engulfs their faith group communities. This suggests that their life experience is not dissimilar to those living in a CRS described above. The curved

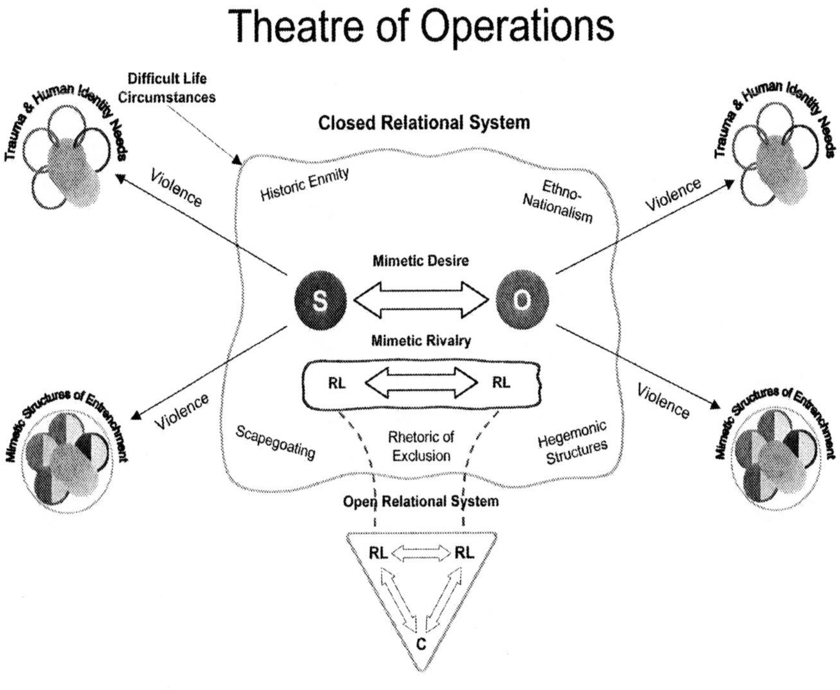

Theatre of Operations

Figure 2.8.   Religious Leader Engagement as an Open Relational System.

dotted lines leading to the triangle below the larger diagram introduces the concept of an *open relational system* (ORS) initiated by the chaplain, represented by the C at the bottom of the triangle. The system of double arrows between the chaplain and both religious leaders, as well as between the religious leaders themselves, identifies the dynamic of *mimetic modeling*. In engaging each of these leaders separately over an extended period of time, the chaplain demonstrates before all concerned an openness and acceptance of the *other*. The modeling of such engendered trust and genuine hospitality is demonstrative of the *openness in the self for the other*, an "interiority" that elicits a similar *re-humanizing* of the *other* in the religious leaders. With incremental successes in individual engagement, in time, formerly estranged faith group leaders may come together for *encounter*, where the *will to embrace* and its *double vision* have occasion to seed, and, hopefully germinate. Such an ORS creates the structure by which *working trust* can lead to further dialogue, the lessening of stereotypes, and opportunity to pursue greater cooperation and understanding. The concepts introduced here will be more thoroughly examined in chapter 4—Religious Leader Engagement—prior to the presentation of the Case Studies. Figure 2.8 will appear again, as the *mimetic modeling* of chaplains via *open relational systems* will be explored in the *ministry* of Imam Sulyeman Demiray among the Sunni and Shia faith group leadership in Kandahar, Afghanistan, amplifying for the reader the theory presented here by way of a documented case study (See Ch. 5, under "Whole of Government Partners: The Ulema Shura" 2006-2007).

Secondary Relational Systems

Filtering through from the external into already conflicted and closed relational systems are secondary relational systems, interjecting such spoilers as *geography*, *kinship*, *ideology*, and *history/memory*, each contributing to increased hostilities. Geographical proximity prominently factors into intractable conflict due to the frequent immediacy of related ethnic groups. Closely linked to geography is kinship. Fraternal bonds fostering a strong sense of connectedness reaching back decades or even centuries in some instances, can lead to collaboration among identity groups that have been separated by arbitrarily drawn borders. Easy access, due to close proximity, often provides occasion for kin close to conflicted areas to 'support' their brothers in arms. Such fraternity is often reinforced ideologically due to commonly held beliefs and a shared vision, creating strong ties. As noted earlier history/memory looms large in conflict. Combatants remember former atrocities while using present hostilities to settle old scores. Persuasive leaders operating out of these four external categories create a toxic influence for the uninformed living in isolated areas. As such, thinking, behavior and, ultimately, identity are influenced by such encounters with the *other*.

At this juncture the more theoretical gives way to the practical, as Praxis is introduced. The elements described here are more accessible and given to more straightforward application. A significant portion of what is to follow is devoted to *Culture* due to the weight it carries for the successful initiatives of interveners. The *Place of Hospitality* speaks of creating the welcoming and secure environment required for *encounter* to occur. Lastly, and related to culture, *Ritual and Symbol* unfurls the multifaceted nature of ritual, the efficacy of symbol with its subliminal messaging for those unable to face present circumstances, and, yet, the prominent and ubiquitous place ritual holds in religion and culture within indigenous societies.

CULTURE COMPETENCY

Kevin Avruch describes culture as being multi-layered with much crosscutting criteria. The operationally experienced would readily identify with his depiction of the various traits and groupings within a given culture. He expands further,

> Individuals are organized in many potentially different ways in a population, by many different (and cross-cutting) criteria: for example, by kinship into families or clans; by language, race, or creed into ethnic groups; by socioeconomic characteristics into social classes; by geographical region into political interest groups; and by occupation or institutional memberships into unions, bureaucracies, industries, political parties, and militaries.[76]

The danger lay in our making sweeping assumptions about people, failing to remember that societies are comprised of individuals, each with their own experience of culture. An encouraging note comes from Louis Kriesberg who contends that people living "within" a given society experience more of a *common culture*, which, in his estimation, aids in de-escalating conflict and starting the journey toward reconciliation. He further states, "People who believe they share the same culture tend to have a decent regard for each other and resist dehumanizing each other."[77] If his observation bears credence, the *common culture* of peoples may help in creating a climate more conducive to reconciliation efforts.

Lebaron and Pillay hone culture further by defining it as the shared or unspoken understandings in a group. They use the analogy of underground rivers of meaning making, "the places where we make choices about what matters and how, that connect us to others in the groups to which we belong . . . a series of lenses that shape what we see and don't see, how we perceive and interpret, and where we draw boundaries."[78] Culture often remains invisible, yet it impacts what one thinks and why one believes it to be important. At the cultural level values and attitudes are influenced, which, in turn, drives our behaviors. Where groups are in conflict, culture functions as an undercurrent that orients how a group navigates through treacherous waters, causing them to gravitate toward some things while avoiding others. [79] Pillay articulates, "Culture lives in the collective—it is the glue that connects us in social groups providing unwritten rules, codes, and boundaries around communication, perception, and meaning-making." [80]

Returning to Avruch, he illumines further the danger of assuming "that everyone shares the same cultural content (images and encodements) to the same degree." [81] He introduces two critical elements relating to cultural content: (1) culture is *sociogenic*—having to do with social groups and institutions; and (2) culture is *psychogenic*—having to do with cognitive and affective processes characteristic of individuals. Simply put, the *sociogenic* dynamic indicates that the sociological location is not the same for everyone in a particular culture. This refers to the variable of class, religious, regional or ethnic backgrounds experienced by the individual. Two individuals cannot experience culture identically, hence the need for "sub-culture" identifiers coupled with the acknowledgment that "culture is socially distributed within a population." [82] The *psychogenic* dynamic of culture reveals that no matter how evenly culture may be defined sociologically individuals internalize culture differently. "[T]he ways and circumstances under which an individual receives or learns cultural images or encodements" [83] certainly contributes to how these are internalized. Who passes on mythical stories from one generation to the next, and how incendiary the narratives become, accounts for the dissimilarity of intensity from one individual to the next. Deep-rooted conflict is cultivated in this manner.

Tatsushi Arai speaks of how culture frames the outer boundaries of our mind's vision, rendering the cultural terrain of outsiders lying beyond one's horizon difficult to recognize. Unfamiliarity moves quite effortlessly to strangeness, making it easy to become polarized between "us" and "them." He attributes the shared memories often transported from earlier times via the use of emotionally laden symbols as an aspect of culture, frequently used to exacerbate conflict. Cultural differences and similarities emerge as divisive or unifying factors. [84] As groups begin to recognize alternative *cultural lenses* to their own, stereotyping emerges quite easily. As such, assumptions are made "that a particular cultural group has specific, immutable characteristics shared by all members, [leaving] no room for nuances, exceptions, or change." [85] Stereotyping is a safety and convenience mechanism, allowing for judgments to be made about the *other*, whereby people decide to engage or disengage in terms of communication, providing a false sense of knowing *others*. [86]

Avruch refers to *cultural clichés* and *culture as causal*—key distinctions as one considers the role of culture in conflict. He elucidates that the cultural representations of images and encodements, schemas and models are not internalized equally by individuals or at the same level. For some, such cultural internalization is more superficial (*clichés*), while for others it registers deeply and highly invested with emotion or affect (*causal*). Herein lies the danger: that which moves one deeply within "can instigate behavior by being connected to desirable goals or end states. The more deeply internalized and affectively loaded, the more certain images or schemas are able to motivate to action."[87] Individuals within groups may trigger a *mimetic* reaction, causing a domino effect on others, mobilizing entire communities. Avruch offers the following illustration of the non-uniform distribution of culture where two hypothetical individuals form a "completely shared sociological placement, [yet] can be differentially internalized." He illumines, "Of two revolutionaries, each sharing the same socioeconomic background and program, the same political ideology, and the same intellectual opposition to the regime in power, only one is motivated (by rage? by hatred? by childhood? by trauma? by what?) to throw the bomb."[88]

Cultural Borrowing: Indigenous Populations as Resources not Recipients

Drawing on his extensive peacebuilding experience in Central-American countries, John Paul Lederach, "calls for a seedbed understanding of culture, as well as conflict."[89] His theory and praxis places cultural sensitivity in company with contextualization, a term encapsulating "how conflict and appropriate responses for constructively responding to conflict are understood and rooted in the social realities—as perceived, experienced, and created by the people in the setting."[90] He acknowledges that, " . . . culture is the soil in which conflict-handling mechanisms sprout and take root."[91] This is of increasing importance to deploying personnel—civilian or military—who, in a matter of 24-48 hours, may find themselves in a vastly different culture than the one they just left. Ron Kraybill adds to this, "Conflict and appropriate responses are of course culturally rooted. What works in one place may be disastrous in another. This means that efforts to develop peacebuilding skills must build on local insights, not inject prescriptions from other places."[92] Any engaging of the indigenous *other* may be thwarted by one's unfamiliarity with local custom and tradition, salient elements of culture. Where engaging religious leaders is in the offing, receptivity to the initiation and continuance of dialogue may depend on this very fact. Rabbi Marc Gopin relates the importance of "caring for the Other, respecting his Otherness, and making a commitment not to invade his culture."[93] He expands further his inference to *cultural invasion* by borrowing from the teachings of the Apostle Paul: "One is in the world of the other culture but self-consciously not of it."[94] At stake is the unwitting offending of an indigenous leader due to a lack of cultural awareness or preparedness.

Following on the above is the egregious presumption that Western ideas hold within them the answers for a given conflict, disregarding rich and untapped peacebuilding mechanisms that the host culture may possess. Lederach contends that "mov[ing] from stagnant cycles of violence toward a desired and shared vision of increased interdependence . . . emerge[s] creatively from the culture and context."[95] For this reason, he continues, "the international community must see people in the setting as resources and not recipients."[96] It is such sensitivity that contributes to Lederach's success, says Gopin. It was the recognition of the totally Christian context of the Latin American encounters that led Lederach to draw on, "Christian prayers before and after those difficult negotiations between enemies . . . critical to creating what [Gopin] calls a bonding *cultural envelope* that surround[ed] the intractability of rational power negotiations, where lives, property, security, and dignity were at stake."[97]

In today's missions, it will be the appreciation of culture and its oft-distinct religiosity that enables personnel to create such *cultural envelopes*. Such encounters are increasingly cross-cultural as theatres of operation recurrently engage more than one ethno-religious group. In displaying respect of the traditions of the *other*, one's credibility is bolstered by expressing genuine interest in who they are as a people and what their future holds for them as a community. Echoing the above notion, Islamic scholar Bassam Tibi interjects that *cultural borrowing* has historically facilitated learning among civilizations proving to be "one of the great sources of enriching [humankind]."[98] He illumines, "Islam does have resources within its history that enables *cultural borrowing*."[99] One builds *trust* and creates close bonds by mining the traditions and teachings emanating from the host culture, incorporating them into peacebuilding endeavors. The subsequent section aids in this understanding both in praxis and theory.

Cultural Strangers: Individualist Ethos or Interdependent Ethos

Raymond Cohen employs the term *cultural strangers*[100] in describing the cultural contrasts between Western and non-European societies. He states that in such contexts one cannot "rely on shared experience of family, church, schooling, community and country. Their national histories, traditions and belief systems may or may not concur."[101] As such, non-Western cultures most often possess a: "communal" or "interdependent" ethos as compared to the more "individualist" ethos of Western society. In high context communities "the collectivist ethic has the welfare of the group and cooperative endeavor as its guiding themes . . . the individual is identified on the basis of group affiliation and individual needs defined in terms of communal interests."[102] When dialoguing in such settings, those intervening will need to tune their ear to "read more between the lines." Communication is more indirect, relying on understandings to give communication meaning. [103] Interpreters are invaluable resources in this regard, alerting personnel of important local cultural nuances.

Whereas the individualist ethos accentuates "freedom, the development of the individual personality, self expression and personal enterprise and achievement as supreme values." [104] In low context situations valued communication is more verbal and direct—contextual meaning is not the focus. Pillay relates, "Words rather than context are relied upon to give communication meaning, and there is less allowance for implied meaning." [105]

Cohen brings to light the cultural subtleties embedded within communication defined as "high" and "low contexts." Albeit, his focus is actual negotiation, the contrasts that he delineates are staggeringly pertinent to cultural sensitivity and awareness in operations. "High context" communication emanates from the "communal ethos," emphasizing the following traits:

> Communally minded persons are vitally concerned about how they will appear to others. . . . Loss of face (humiliation before the group) is an excruciating penalty to be avoided at all costs . . . the members of such societies are highly sensitive to the effect of what they say on others. Language is a social instrument—a device for preserving and promoting social interests as much as transmitting information. High-context speakers must weigh their words carefully.
> Since communal affiliation looms large in any interaction, it is hard for members of a collectivistic culture to deal with a stranger from outside their circle. Where the in-group/out-group division is crucial, confidence can never be assumed; an outsider owes you nothing. Before a frank exchange becomes possible, let alone the conduct of business, a *personal relation must be cultivated. But relations are not simply instrumental; they are, profoundly, ends in themselves.* [106]

Cohen characterizes "Low Context" of more western societies as follows,

> The low-context culture . . . reserves a quite different role for language. Very little meaning is implicit in the context of articulation. On the contrary, what has to be said is stated explicitly. Indirection is much disliked. "Straight-from-the-shoulder" talk is admired. "Get to the point" is the heartfelt reaction to small talk and evasive formulations. People have little time or patience for "beating around the bush" and wish to get down to business and move on to another problem. Why waste time in social trivialities? Doing business should not require the interlocutors to be bosom friends. Clearly, this propensity is associated with individualistic people's relative freedom from group constraints and niceties, and their ability to distinguish between professional and social role-playing.
> Language, then, performs on the whole an informational rather than socially lubricative function. The reverse is the case, because [Low Context cultures] flourish on debate, persuasion, and the hard sell. Subtlety and allusiveness in speech, if grasped at all, serve little purpose. Nor does "face" possess

the crucial importance it has for the high-context culture. An internalized sense of responsibility, rather than a concern with outward appearances, is the rule.[107]

Acquiring a sense of the difference between the 'individualist' culture of the West in comparison to the more communal orientation of the non-Western culture of "interdependence" is crucial to engaging the *other* in dialogue. Given the trend in Operations in recent years, government personnel and aid workers will most likely deploy to conflict zones in the developing world where high context forms of communication will be predominant.

A recent article in *The Guardian Weekly* may be of assistance here. Ewan MacAskill makes reference to the seeming communication difficulties of South Korean Ban Ki-moon, secretary general of the United Nations. At question is Ki-moon's style of leadership, to some, almost invisible. To his staff he is a man who "operates best out of the limelight—what they call quiet diplomacy, private conversations with world leaders"[108] away from television cameras. His predecessor, Kofi Annan, was far more comfortable with the media, raising his profile markedly. Some say, a hard act to follow. Ki-moon's UN under-secretary-general for communications, Kiyo Akasaka, is Japanese and, as such, offers a perspective worthy of reflection. He sees this as a cultural problem of East and West orientations. Akasaka states,

> Asians appreciate Ban's Confucian values, the emphasis on self-effacement, self-discipline and understatement. "To eyes of Asians, his behaviour has been like that of the wise man, the sage in oriental philosophy who does not speak as articulately as you might expect in the leaders of the western world," he said. "I can see that the western world has a different kind of expectation in its leaders, including the element of charisma."[109]

If Akasaka's interpretation is right, this may be a classic example of the communication disconnect that Cohen describes above—high and low contexts with the "communal" emphasis of a high context or Asian ethos conflicting with the low context that accents a more "individualist" or Western ethos. Ban's self-effacing understatement may frustrate the more forthright, get-down-to-business westerner. For the Secretary General, it would appear his style of leadership is consistent with his Asian roots, something for Western minds to ponder.

Interfacing with local leadership—religious or otherwise—an ability to articulate the cultural differences and nuances existing between the Western 'individualist' ethos and the "communal" ethos of their host[110] nation may aid in avoiding any embarrassing moments in communication. Cohen's analysis is of particular significance to peace-building initiatives. Salient to the cultural ethos of "communal" societies is the pivotal theme of relation. Woven into its cultural fabric, dialogue of any consequence orbits around this cultural reality. *Cultural competency* has much to do with giving respect to the *other* and the earning of trust. Those who find themselves caught in the throes of conflict may welcome the *safe space* that trust offers. It may well provide an occasion to speak of the conflict without the guardedness of politically charged situations, a *safe space* to unburden the soul. *Hospitality* is the invitation into that *safe space* where journeying with the *other* truly begins.

THE PLACE OF HOSPITALITY

Conversing over a shared meal is a gesture of hospitality possessing much symbolism in many parts of the world. In Operations, whether within the compound of a participating nation or reciprocated in the home or office of a local indigenous/religious leader, such fellowship engenders trust, kindness and a sense of security.[111] L.E. Klosinski notes that "[e]ating is a behavior that symbolizes feeling and relations, mediates social status and power, and expresses the boundaries of group identity."[112] As D.W. Schriver states, the symbolism of a shared meal may contribute toward creating an atmosphere conducive to the beginnings of reconciliation,

> The act of sitting down to eat is a human gesture of consent to human company; where barriers of social custom or a history of hostile relations have stood in the way of such consent, the mere joint presence of the alienated, now around the same table consuming the same food, can be a powerful symbol of the beginning of negotiation on its way to reconciliation.[113]

Where local leaders have lived in estrangement within the same community, the shared meal offers an image of mutuality, an open relational system of inclusivity. As a structure, the shared meal affords the discursive process an occasion to reframe relationships. For those living in conflict situations, or its residual estrangement, creating a hospitable environment where trust, kindness and safety exist may be for their guests an experience that will remain with them in memory. Paraphrasing Schreiter, trust enables the resumption of human communication. Kindness bears witness that violence may be overcome and put behind them, providing the space for the vulnerability required for the journey toward healing. Safety is the companion of trust for those who have, or presently are, living with threats and danger. Restoring safety creates the space for the bonds of trust to grow. Hospitality also shares a sense of gratuity, a kind of graciousness that is not measured in a *quid pro quo* manner. There is an abundance that invites thinking about new possibilities. Emanating from the gratuitous nature of hospitality is the caution not to make it into something other than what it is. "Hospitality has its own place and its own priority. Part of the experience of its gratuity, then, is that it is not used for any extraneous purposes: it is there for its own sake."[114]

Hospitality becomes more than a carefully crafted technique with designed outcomes; it is in reality a spiritual experience. This is not to suggest that one approach is superior to the other, rather religious communities tend to be more receptive to a spiritual component of the process of reconciliation.

> That ability to remember in a different way does not grow out of a calculating calibration of the wrong and its redress, but from the abundance of life we call grace. That is why *hospitality*, which sets up an environment of *trust, kindness,* and *safety*, is the prelude to *reconciliation*. It helps prepare victims for the welling up of God's healing grace in their lives, for the restorations of their humanity. It is a restoration, not in the sense of returning them to a previous, unviolated state, but in the sense of bringing them to a new place.[115]

Discerning how to extend hospitality in forms that the people understand is critical, e.g., appreciating cultural nuances and local customs. As Schreiter notes, a certain "reconfiguration of the self or of the community in the act of hospitality is important if the hospitality is to be effective."[116] For instance, when facilitating dialogue between religious leaders of opposing identity groups, the trust, kindness and safety engendered by hospitality creates a *mimetic* environment where the *will to embrace* tends to draw the *self* and the *other* toward reconciliation.

Where possible, extending hospitality to community leaders becomes mutually enriching. One learns much from such individuals as an environment of trust develops leading to sincere exchanges. Such hospitality precipitates traditional and cultural events, aspects of the rituals of life for indigenous communities. The symbolism of such structures is significant and most pertinent to the peacebuilding among those struggling with relation with the estranged *other*.

The place of hospitality in the form of the shared meal segues quite naturally into Ritual and Symbol in the Shaping of New Narratives. The subsequent section will analyze ritual and symbol as structural. Granted, such events are more intrinsic to the role of operational chaplains, yet government and aid agency personnel implicated in reconstruction and stabilization endeavors should avail themselves of the inroads that chaplains naturally create within religious communities of indigenous populations: ritual events factor into such considerations.

RITUAL AND SYMBOL IN THE SHAPING OF NEW NARRATIVES

Robert Schreiter and Lisa Schirch contribute heavily to the theoretical development of operational structures that accommodate ritual and symbol. Here ritual and symbol will find institutional force as such *encounters* are envisioned as outcomes adaptable within operational structures. Chapter 5 through 8 will offer practical application of this theory in the form of documented case studies where ritual events—some religious, some cultural— facilitated by chaplains served as collaborative efforts with their Whole of Government partners, an aspect of the Comprehensive Approach. The theory provided here is intended to illuminate these events more fully, offering opportunity for review if so desired.

In his book, *Reconciliation: Mission and Ministry in a Changing Social Order*, Schreiter identifies one's sense of safety and self-hood as two of the underpinnings to overcoming feelings of insecurity and uncertainty in the midst of conflict. He postulates that "symbol-making activity" creates this sense of safety and self-hood. Schreiter describes such pursuits as the "physical features and temporal events in one's life."[117] Physical features are described as what one eats, the shelters one builds and, the clothes one wears, all of which are fraught with meaning and a sense of sameness assuring individuals of identity and how one fits into the scheme of things. He contends that these features of life provide a certain sense of security, enabling individuals to deal with other aspects of life. Such sameness gives shape to the definition of oneself as *self*, a reference point (location/orientation) in the flow of time. The humanitarian assistance provided to those impacted by conflict, becomes a gesture in symbol-making activity. Insecurity associated with a loss of the 'sense of safety' is linked to conflict's undermining of one's physical features of life as described above. The limited provision of food, clothing and sometimes shelter by UN/NATO personnel or more robust assistance programs of NGOs/IOs, aids in rebuilding meaning and sameness, key ingredients to finding one's place again in a world that has become chaotic and confusing.

Temporal events look more to the creation of narratives. These stories not only assist in identifying the *self* in comparison to the *other*, but aid in self-understanding. Culturally, narratives shape who individuals and groups are as a people. Schreiter contends that the calculated destructiveness of ethnic violence attempts to destroy the *other* by rendering their cultural, religious and ethnic symbols and symbol-making activities as meaningless: the destroying of one's "sense of self-hood." Violence toward the *other* is exclusion in the extreme and abject rejection of relation. Engaging in 'symbol-destroying activities' is an overt means of domination and alienation: physical assault, imprisonment, exile, destruction of cultural and religious icons, acts of terrorism, all expressions of hegemony, the sphere of exclusion.[118] Chaplains are increasingly discovering that ritual and symbol have a valued place among conflicted groups in the writing of new narratives. The remainder of this section will deal more specifically with the dynamics of symbol and ritual, and how they may be used effectively. Introduced will be the more pertinent dynamics of symbol and ritual that naturally coalesce with the role of a chaplain as a religious leader functioning in the domain of the religious *other*—an *intra-* or *inter*faith environment.

The Subliminal of Symbol in Ritual

Lisa Schirch rightly contends that the contribution of ritual and symbol to peacebuilding is underestimated and therefore underused. In theatres of operation where 'intra-state' conflict pitches ethno-religious groups against one another, ritual "communicate[s] complicated messages about social ties, shared humanity, and the dangers of using violence to solve problems in a world increasingly marked by failed social relations between identity groups."[119] Schirch defines ritual as: (1) nonreferential symbolic acts in the sense that they "do not directly discuss the people or events at hand, but communicate through symbols, myths, and metaphors that allow for multiple interpretations; (2) rituals often take place in unique spaces . . . set off from everyday life in a variety of ways; and most importantly (3) rituals aim to form (build) or transform (change) people's worldviews, identities, and relations."[120] Schreiter further illumines the capacity for ritual to aid those struggling with the conflictual past,

> We do not understand entirely how ritual works, but its formal character creates a space in which a difficult and conflictual past can be dealt with, and a certain closure can be brought to the experience. Since the past cannot be undone, ritual actions in the present can blunt its power and transform it from something death dealing and victimizing to something transforming and life-giving.[121]

Symbol brings much to ritual due to its functioning at the subliminal level, impressing upon the individual/group new truths or possible realities that are either too taxing to consider in the midst of an ongoing conflict, and therefore resisted, or simply beyond the capacity of the participants to grasp at present. Amplifying symbol, Paul Ricoeur articulates it eloquently, " . . . symbol is the movement of the primary meaning which makes us participate in the latent meaning and thus assimilates us to that which is symbolized without our being able to master the similitude intellectually."[122] Yeats poetically offers an additional lens, "A symbol is indeed the only possible expression of some invisible essence, a transparent lamp about a spiritual flame."[123] The power of symbol in ritual in conflict or post-conflict environments is its conduciveness to communicate tacitly. Transpiring over time, the latent meaning of a given ritual event may aid in the 'dawning' of a new vision of the *other*—a new understanding of the *self* and the *other* germinating within the participant as symbol and ritual draws the *self* and the *other* into a new space . . . a shared space.

Poignant to peacebuilding is ritual's facility to aid communication across cultural divides. As such, ritual events demonstrate the capacity to temporarily suspend social structures and roles, and in so doing "creat[e] a passageway to a new reality in which new social structures, relations, and roles can take hold."[124] Amplifying further, Victor Witter Turner states that through ritual "the possibility exists of standing aside not only from one's own social position but from all social positions, and of formulating a potentially unlimited series of alternative social arrangements."[125]

Shared cultural/religious events offer a venue for cultivating open relational systems where the reframing of relation is facilitated through *encounter*. The ritual and symbol of such events open new windows through which to see. Their "willingness" (embrace) to share in an event serves as a filter, allowing new information about the *other* into their personal space, thus, bringing the humanity of the *other* into view. Perhaps only tacitly, each leaves with an altered perception of the *other*: the beginnings of transcending the conflict and its alienation.

Schirch contends that in pluralistic communities symbols held in common may be used in shared ritual as a way of providing meaning for people.[126] This may be true, however, one must be certain that the usage of a shared symbol does not create unanticipated difficulty. Rabbi Marc Gopin offers the following cautionary note,

> I do not recommend synthesis [of cultural/religious expressions of reconciliation] but rather alternation, unless a cultural symbol is so shared by both groups that a shared ceremony or symbol would not threaten identities on either side. Threat to and confusion of enemy identities is one of the main things to avoid.[127]

Formal and informal ritual events are pertinent to conflict and post-conflict environments. As will be seen, both are effective in the seeding of reconciliation. Both forms of ritual carry significance as they are given to structural adaptation.

Formal and Informal Ritual

Schirch categorizes ritual as "formal" and "informal." Simply defined, in "formal" rituals participants are cognizant of their involvement, whereas rituals of an "informal" nature leaves participants either less aware or unaware of their taking part.[128] It is through ritual events that one's humanity is communicated to the *other*. Through *re-humanizing* a person's adversary new and creative ways of understanding the conflict develop.[129] As structures, shared ritual events "transform the focus of identity and locus of conflict from one identity, such as ethnicity, to a more inclusive, complex, and varied set of identities."[130] Whatever the ritual may be: eating, drinking, dancing, building a structure together, participating in a Shura, or an actual interfaith celebration, identity is transformed in such *humanizing* space. As Schirch suggests, the *self's* understanding of the *other*, or identity, "is defined in context, [where] perceptions of identity change according to both physical and relational situations. . . . A ritual context can help people find common identities and recognize the complex identities each persons holds."[131]

The breadth of the operational ministry of chaplains offers opportunities to benefit from "formal" and "informal"rituals in operational environments. As religious leaders in their own right they are uniquely suited and strategically placed to build relation with local religious leaders and their faith communities through such mediums. Ritual events, be they formal or informal, provide occasion to bring religious leaders together from opposing identity groups into a new dimension of relation. For a period of time the *self* meets the *other* in the liminal space of *encounter*, hopefully leaving with an altered impression of the *other*. Tacitly, stereotypes are challenged and propaganda refuted. Embryonic in nature, seeding reconciliation takes place in such events, operational ministry of strategic import.

Constructive and Destructive Ritual

Offered as bookends to "formal" and "informal" rituals, Schirch broadens ritual to the dimensions of "constructive" or "destructive" depending on their usage.

> Like conflict, ritual is a neutral tool and people can use it for either the betterment or destruction of humanity. [Destructive ritual] delivers oppressive messages and [has] horrific, destructive outcomes [whereas] constructive [ritual] is used to better the lives of the people who use it, without causing harm to others . . . transforming conflict-defined identities . . . forming and transforming relations between groups. [132]

The quintessential "destructive" and "formal" ritual of more recent times was the Serbian yearlong ritual lamentation marking the 600th anniversary of the Battle of Kosovo. Prior to the battle's commemoration in June of 1989, the former, and now late, Serbian President Slobodan Milošević, orchestrated the ritual parading of the remains of the idolized Serbian martyr, Prince Lazar, to towns and villages throughout Serbia and Kosovo. The Serbian defeat and martyrdom of Prince Lazar at the Battle of Kosovo in 1389 at the hands of the Ottomans is an ever-present wound on the Serbian nationalist memory.[133] The ritual procession of Prince Lazar's remains[134] throughout Serbia and Kosovo was met "by huge crowds of mourners dressed in black[135] . . . re-igniting the flames of the Battle of Kosovo and further strengthening [the] collective memory as a tool of entitlement to revenge."[136] Milošević adroitly manipulated this ritual memorial as a means to revive the nationalistic fervor of a greater Serbia, tying what were the perceived aspirations of the Bosnian Muslims to a rejuvenating of the former times of Muslim domination. The destructive nature of this ritual contributed to the Balkan war of the 1990s with significant loss of life and displaced peoples among all three ethno-religious groups.

Constructive rituals, formal or informal, powerfully convey to the *self* and the *other* messages of a different way of being. The symbolism attached may be readily apparent or more subliminal in nature. Regardless, at some level within those in attendance, transcendence becomes reality. Transcendence manifests itself within a structural event of a shared ritual by contravening the tendency within conflict to rigidly center on one aspect of the other's identity.[137] New and altered perceptions of the *other* begin to emerge. Whatever the faith tradition, religious ritual and symbol may present an occasion to connect with local religious leaders in a manner not afforded to other contingent members. As will be seen below, the potency of such ritual events is their capacity to confront local power structures, offering a different view of relation, one of empowerment in mutuality.

Rituals of Inversion

Schirch purports that relation between individuals, and by extension groups, experiences the most harm due to conflict's spiraling *mimetic* nature. The pernicious out of control dynamic of conflict persists mainly because "there are no processes to prevent the destruction of the social and environmental system."[138] Introducing what is termed rituals of inversion, Schirch interjects the "possibility of peacebuilders to either mute the impact of power on social relations entirely or actually turn the power structures upside down, if only for the length of the ritual [thus warranting repetition]."[139] In theatres of operation such time-specific events, although short in duration, occur often. The vision is, as Schirch states, "people in conflict may gain new perspectives and relations through participating in this type of ritual, which may then carry over into non-ritual time and space."[140] The subliminal nature of symbol in ritual is impactful where rituals of inversion are concerned. Witnessing leaders together in the public forum of a ritual event who, due to present or past conflict, would normally not entertain such collaboration presents their respective communities with a different vision. Tacitly, the latent meaning of such events communicates over time the possibility of a new and shared space for communities still caught in the reality or memory of conflict. Chaplains can host intercommunal and, depending on the context, interfaith ritual events that accomplish what Schirch describes here. In rituals of inversion, local religious leaders and people alike are afforded a different vision of what can be—communities where engendered trust and cooperation lead to harmonious living. "Ritual can be a plough that turns over the soil, allowing us to plant new seeds to sustain ongoing growth in a system. It changes our worldviews, identities and social relations."[141]

The intention of this chapter has been to acquaint the reader with various theoretical constructs pertinent to inter-group conflict as it is known today, as well as provide something of a backdrop to the praxis that surrounds the ministry of chaplains in Religious Leader Engagement. Reference will be made to what is offered here throughout the remainder of the book, but primarily in the case studies to come in chapters 5 through 7, an option for further reflection should the reader choose to. Attention will now turn to the Role of Religion in Conflict and Peacebuilding. A candid examination of the ambivalence of religion will offer a more balanced view of religion in conflict and post-conflict environments—its seeming detached utopian themes, frequent extreme expressions and underestimated peacebuilding applications. Some of the world's principal religions will be consulted for their contributions to present religious peacebuilding initiatives globally—in some instances interfaith collaboration.

NOTES

1. R. Scott Appleby, *The Ambivalence of the Sacred: Religion, Violence, and Reconciliation* (Lanham, Maryland: Rowman & Littlefield Publishers, 2000), 69.

2. Terrell A. Northrup, "The Dynamic of Identity in Personal and Social Conflict" in *Intractable Conflicts and Their Transformation*, eds. Louis Kriesberg, Terrell A. Northrup & Stuart Thorson (Syracuse, New York: Syracuse University Press, 1989), 65.

3. Herbert C. Kelman, "Reconciliation From a Social-Psychological Perspective" in *The Social Psychology of Intergroup Reconciliation*, eds. Arie Nadler, Thomas E. Malloy and Jeffery D. Fisher (New York: Oxford University Press, 2008), p. 24.

4. Robert J. Schreiter, *Reconciliation: Mission and Ministry in A Changing Social Order* (Maryknoll, New York: Orbis Books, 1992), 52 (Italics mine).

5. Appleby, 2000, 61.

6. Andrew Clark, "Obama Drawn into Anti-abortion debate" in *The Guardian Weekly*, May 22, 2010, 8.

7. Clark, 2010, 8.

8. See "George Tiller Killed: Abortion Doctor Shot at Church," www.huffingtonpost.com/ 2009/05/31/george-tiller-killed-abor_n_209504.html, accessed 28 January 2010.

9. For a complete "Overview of the Mimetic Theory," see René Girard, *The Girard Reader*, edited by James G. Williams. New York: Crossroad Publishing, 1996, edition printed 2001, 9-29.

10. Vern Neufeld Redekop and Shirley Paré, *Beyond Control: A Mutual Respect Approach to Protest Crowd-Police Reactions* (New York: Bloomsbury Academic, 2010), 117.

11. Vern Neufeld Redekop, *From Violence to Blessing: How An Understanding of Deep-Rooted Conflict Can Open Paths to Reconciliation* (Toronto: Novalis, 2002), 66.

12. Vern Neufeld Redekop, "Deep-Rooted Conflict Theory and Pastoral Counselling: Dealing With What One Sees," *Pastoral Sciences*, 2001, Vol. 20, No. 1, 16.

13. Anthony Storr, *Human Aggression* (New York, 1968) in René Girard, *Violence and the Sacred* translated by Patrick Gregory (Baltimore and London: John Hopkins University Press, 1972), 8. In the same vein, John F. Kennedy wrote of Daniel Webster's famous words during the tense days of 1850 when talk of secession from the Union in various quarters was rife. He opined of what he believed to be his duty, "In highly excited times it is far easier to fan and

feed the flames of discord, than to subdue them; and he who counsels moderation is in danger of being regarded as failing in this duty to his party." Webster, then Senator for Massachusetts, stood in the breach against partisan voices and through seasoned reason and renowned oratory staved off civil war for another decade. John F. Kennedy, *Profiles in Courage* (New York, Harper & Row, 1956), 82.

14. René Girard, *Violence and the Sacred*, trans. by Patrick Gregory (Baltimore, MD: Johns Hopkins University Press, English Translation, 1977), 31, 81.

15. The riots of Bombay in 1993 were the worst spate of violence India had seen for many decades. It was sparked by the destruction of the Baburi Mosque in Ayodhya by nationalist Hindus, which was followed by riots in major centers throughout India. Muslims retaliated by attacking state symbols in areas predominantly Muslim. The *mimetic* nature of the violence soon led to spiralling aggression as Hindu nationalists began holding "victory processions," proudly proclaiming the settling of an old score—the Baburi Mosque having been built on what had originally been a Hindu holy site. For a span of two months Hindu and Muslim gangs throughout the country attacked each other's people and homes. The sustained reciprocal violence left hundreds dead, thousands wounded and as many as 200,000 sought sanctuary in other parts of India. See Julia Eckert, "Reconciling the Mohalla: Politics of Violence and the Strength and Limits of Mediation in Bombay" in *Religion Between Violence and Reconciliation*, Introduction, ed. Thomas Scheffler (Beirut: Orient-Institute, 2002), 366-369; Ashutosh Varshney, Hindu-Muslim riots, 1950-1995: The National Picture in *Ethic Conflict and Civic Life: Hindus and Muslims in India* (New Haven, CN: Yale University Press, 2002, 87-115.

16. Julia Eckert, "Reconciling the Mohalla: Politics of Violence and the Strength and Limits of Mediation in Bombay" in *Religion Between Violence and Reconciliation*, ed. Thomas Scheffler (Beirut: Ergon Verlag Wurzburg, 2002), 308.

17. René Girard, *Deceit, Desire and the Novel: Self and the Other in Literary Structure* trans. by Yvonne Freccero, Original Publican, 1961: Trans. 1965, Paperbacks edition (Baltimore and London: The John Hopkins University Press, 1976), 96-99.

18. Redekop & Paré, 2010, 119.

19. Redekop, 2002, 162.

20. Redekop, 2002, 161-172.

21. Redekop, 2002, 163.

22. Redekop & Paré, 2010, 6.

23. Neufeld Redekop and Paré, 2010, 6.

24. Redekop, 2002, 276.

25. Redekop and Paré, 2010, 124.

26. Neufeld Redekop, 2002, 277.

27. Volf's concept of the *will to embrace* will be introduced in Chapter Four with a full treatment of his theology of exclusion and embrace to follow in Chapter Ten.

28. John Burton, *Conflict: Human Needs Theory*, Introduction (New York: St. Martin's Press, 1990), 2.

29. Burton, 1990, 2.

30. See "Human Identity Needs," Chapter Two in Redekop, 2002, 31-60.

31. Mary E. Clark, *In Search of Human Nature* (London: Routledge, 2002), 377.

32. Robert Schreiter, *Reconciliation: Mission and Ministry in a Changing Social Order* (New York and Newton, Mass: Orbis Books and Boston Theological Institute, 1992), 32.

33. See Schreiter, 1992, 32-34.

34. Ronnie Janoff-Bulman, *Shattered Assumptions: Towards a New Psychology of Trauma* (New York: The Free Press, 1992), 88-89.

35. Janoff-Bulman, 1992, 89.

36. Janoff-Bulman, 1992, 89.

37. See Vamik Volkan, *Blood Lines: From Ethnic Pride to Ethnic Terrorism* (Boulder, Colorado: Westview Press, 1997). Volkan discusses chosen trauma and chosen glories: "Chosen trauma describes the collective memory of a calamity that once befell a group's ancestors . . . bringing with them powerful experiences of loss and feelings of humiliation, vengeance, and hatred that trigger a variety of unconscious defense mechanisms that attempt to reverse these experiences and feelings" (48,82). "Chosen glories influence identity less perva-

sively than chosen traumas, however, because their effect is less complex . . . involving enhanced libidinal attachment, with no need for reversal" (82). For more on Volkan's *chosen trauma* see Vern Neufeld Redekop, *From Violence to Blessing: How An Understanding of Deep-Rooted Conflict Can Open Paths to Reconciliation* (Toronto: Novalis, 2002), 134, 145, 184, 186, 227, 276 & 298.

38. Charles Taylor, *Sources of the Self: The Making of the Modern Identity* (Cambridge, Mass, Harvard University Press, 1989), 34-36.

39. Paul Ricoeur, *Oneself as Another,* (Chicago: The University of Chicago Press, 1992), 3.

40. Clark, 2002, 36.

41. George A. De Vos, "Ethnic Pluralism: Conflict and Accommodation: The Role of Ethnicity in Social History," in *Ethnic Identity: Creation, Conflict, and Accommodation,* eds. Lola Lomanucci-Ross and George A. De Vos (Walnut Creek, California: Altamira Press, 1995), 25.

42. Clark, 2002, 278.

43. Major S.K. Moore, "Toward an Understanding of Deep-Rooted Conflict", course presentation for *Chaplains in NATO Operations,* NATO School, Oberammergau, Germany, 6 May 2003, 15.

44. Paul Ricoeur, 1992, 145.

45. Emmanuel Levinas, *Totality and Infinity: An Essay on Exteriority,* trans. Alphonso Lingis (Pittsburgh: Duquesne University Press, 1969), 21.

46. Levinas, 1969, 14.

47. Rita Rogers, M.D., "Intergenerational Transmission of Historical Enmity" in *The Psychodynamics of International Relationships,* eds. Vamik D. Volkan, Demetrios A. Julias and Joseph V. Montville (Lexington, Toronto: Lexington Books, 1990), 95-96.

48. Raymond Cohen, *Negotiating Across Cultures: International Communication in an Interdependent World* (Washington, D.C.: United States Institution of Peace, 1997), 35-36.

49. John Agnew, "Beyond Reason: Spatial and Temporal Sources of Ethnic Conflicts" in *Intractable Conflicts and Their Transformation,* eds. Louis Kriesberg, Terrell A. Northrup & Stuart Thorson (Syracuse, New York: Syracuse University Press, 1989), p. 47.

50. Protestant William III of England defeated Roman Catholic James II, deposed King of England at the River Boyne to remain the undisputed monarch of the realm on 12 July 1690. See http://www.irelandseye.com/aarticles/history/events/dates/ch5.shtm

51. In 1689 Irish Roman Catholic troops loyal to deposed King James II of England laid siege to the walled city of Londonderry (now Derry) were met with resistance. The gates were bared from Lord Antrim's entry, which began the 105 days siege: 7 Dec 1688-31 July 1689. British ships loyal to William III of England braved constant artillery fire to relieve the town on 30 July 1689 to end the siege. See http://www.libraryireland.com/JoyceHistory/Derry.php.

52. M.C. Kenny, "Ritualized Conflict and Ideological Polarization in Northern Ireland," in *Beyond Ethnic Boundaries: New Approaches in the Anthropology of Ethnicity,* ed. William G. Lockwood, Vol 7 of *Michigan Discussions in Anthropology.* Ann Arbor: Department of Anthropology, University of Michigan, cited in John Agnew, "Beyond Reason: Spatial and Temporal Sources of Ethnic Conflicts" in Kriesberg et al, *Intractable Conflicts,* p. 47.

53. For a full treatment of *chosen trauma* see Vamik Volkan's account of the Battle of Kosovo and its relevance to Serbian history and national ethos. Vamik Volkan, *Blood Lines: From Ethnic Pride to Ethnic Terrorism* (Boulder, Colorado: Westview Press, 1997), 50-80.

54. Mark Gopin, *Holy War, Holy Peace: How Religion Can Bring Peace to the Middle East* (New York: Oxford University Press, 2002), 8.

55. Gopin, 2002, 97. For further amplification see also Notes to pages 89-94, No. 1 of the same volume.

56. Volkan, 1997, 48.

57. Volkan, 1997, 78.

58. Miroslav Volf, *Exclusion and Embrace: A Theological Exploration of Identity, Otherness, and Reconciliation,* (Nashville, TN: Abingdon Press, 1996), 77.

59. Redekop, 2002, 180.

60. Redekop, 2002, 13.

61. Redekop, 2002, 13.

62. Redekop, 2002, 147.

63. John Darby, "Northern Ireland: The Persistence and Limitations of Violence" in *Conflict and Peacemaking in Multiethnic Societies*, ed. Joseph Montville (Lexington/Toronto: Lexington Books, 1989), 155.

64. Redekop, 2001, 20.

65. For expansion on Volf's concept of *differentiation*, see Chapter Ten, *Relation in Creation*, xx.

66. Volf, 1996, 66.

67. A recent example of *historical enmity* would be the mass demonstrations in Paris by Turkish people from across Europe protesting against the French Senate's plans to vote on a bill making it illegal to deny the 1915 mass killing of Armenians by Ottoman Turks. See http://www.youtube.com/watch?v=UkePDjhdlu4, accessed 10 Feb 2012. Accounts of the genocide are a continued source of friction between Turkey and other nations who hold to different historical version. As reported by the New York Times, "Relations between France and Turkey dipped to a nadir as the French Senate approved a bill late Monday [21 Jan 2012] criminalizing the denial of officially recognized genocides, including the Armenian genocide begun in 1915." See "Genocide Bill Angers Turks as it Passes in France," http://www.nytimes.com/2012/01/24/world/europe/french-senate-passes-genocide-bill-angering-turks.html, accessed 10 Feb 2012.

68. Redekop, 2001, 138.

69. René Girard, *The Girard Reader*, edited by James G. Williams (New York: Crossroad Publishing, 1996, edition printed 2001), 12

70. Redekop, 2002, 99.

71. Paul Farmer, *Pathologies of Power: Health, Human Rights and the New War on the Poor* (Berkley and Los Angeles: University of California Press, 2003), 8.

72. Farmer, 2003, 9, 17.

73. Rafael Moses, M.D., "Self, Self-View, and Identity" in *The Psychodynamics of International Relationships*, Vol 1, eds. Vamik D. Volkan, Demetrios A. Julias & Joseph V. Montville (Lexington, Toronto: Lexington Books, 1990), 52.

74. Stephen Ryan, *Ethnic Conflict and international Relations* (Aldershot, England and Burlington, Vermont: Ashgate Publishing Group, 1995), 88.

75. Moses, 1990, 53.

76. Kevin Avruch, *Culture and Conflict Resolution* (Washington, D.C.: United States Institute of Peace Press, 1998), 17-18.

77. Louis Kriesberg, "Comparing Reconciliation Actions within and between Countries" in *From Conflict Resolution to Reconciliation*, ed. Yaacov Bar-Siman-Tov (New York: Oxford University Press, 2004), 94.

78. Michelle Lebaron and Venashri Pillay, *Conflict Across Cultures: A Unique Experience of Bridging Differences.* (Boston and London: Intercultural Press, 2006), 14.

79. Lebaron and Pillay, 2006, 14.

80. Lebaron and Pillay, 2006, 31.

81. Avruch, 1998, 18.

82. Avruch, 1998, 18.

83. Avruch, 1998, 18.

84. Lebaron and Pillay, 2006, 93.

85. Lebaron and Pillay, 2006, 31

86. Lebaron and Pillay, 2006, 31

87. Avruch, 1998, 19.

88. Avruch, 1998, 19.

89. John Paul Lederach, "Journey From Resolution to Transformative Peacebuilding" in *From the Ground Up: Mennonite Contributions to International Peacebuilding*, eds. Cynthia Sampson and John Paul Lederach (New York: Oxford University Press, 2000), 47.

90. Lederach, 2000, 47. (Italics mine).

91. Lederach, 2000, 47.

92. Ron Kraybill, "Reflections on Twenty Years of Peacebuilding" in *From the Ground Up: Mennonite Contributions to International Peacebuilding*, eds. Cynthia Sampson and John Paul Lederach (New York: Oxford University Press, 2000), 42.

93. Marc Gopin, "The Religious Component of Mennonite Peacemaking and Its Global Implications" in Sampson and Lederach, 2000, 241.

94. Gopin, 2000, 241.

95. John Paul Lederach, *Building Peace: Sustainable Reconciliation in Divided Societies* (Washington DC: United States Institute of Peace, 1997), 84. (Italics mine).

96. Lederach, 1997, 94.

97. Marc Gopin, *Holy War, Holy Peace: How Religion Can Bring Peace to the Middle East* (New York: Oxford University Press, 2002), 14 (italics mine).

98. Bassam Tibi, "Islam Between Culture and Politics" (Basingstoke: Palgrave, 2001), 139 cited in *Muslims and Modernity: An Introduction to the Issues and Debates*, Clinton Bennett (London and New York: Continuum, 2005), 70.

99. Bassam Tibi, "The Challenge of Fundamentalism: Political Islam and the New World Disorder" (Berkley, CA: University of California Press, 1998), 202 cited in Bennett, 2005, 70.

100. Raymond Cohen, *Negotiating Across Cultures: International Communication in an Interdependent World*, Revised Edition (Washington, D.C.: United States Institute of Peace Press, 1991), 27.

101. Cohen, 2002, 27.

102. Cohen, 2002, 30.

103. Cohen, 2002, 33.

104. Cohen, 2002, 29.

105. Lebaron and Pillay, 2006, 34.

106. Cohen, 2002, 31-32 (italics mine).

107. Cohen, 2002, 33. For further insight on High and Low Contexts of Communication, see Lebaron and Pillay, 2006, 32-42.

108. Ewen MacAskill, "Invisible man at the United Nations: A leaked memo has questioned Ban Ki-moon's skill at global diplomacy," in *The Guardian Weekly.* 6-12 August 2010, pp. 30-31.

109. MacAskill, 2010, 31.

110. Employing the term *host nation* implies an invitation issuing from a given state(s) to the international community for intervention due to insurmountable internal conflicts. Of significance is the late 20th century shift away from the more classic 'inter-state' conflicts that has dominated warfare to today's 'intra-state' strife between principals within the borders of a sovereign state. With the striking of the landmark document, *The Responsibility to Protect*, it is conceivable that the international community could intervene within the borders of a sovereign state without being invited to do so. Such action would be primarily based on human security issues emanating from a government's inability to arrest violence of genocidal proportions or a government's unwillingness to do so. In such situations the term *host nation* would be rendered inapplicable. *The Responsibility to Protect: Report of the International Commission on Intervention and State Sovereignty.* International Development Research Centre: Ottawa, Canada, 2001.

111. Robert Schreiter, C.PP.S, *The Ministry of Reconciliation: Spirituality and Strategies* (Maryknoll, New York: Orbis Books, 2002), 88.

112. L.E. Klosinski, *The Meals in Mark* (Ann Arbor, Mich.: University Microfilms International, 1988), 58 as quoted by Crossan, 341 cited in Shriver, D.W in An *Ethic For Enemies* (Oxford University Press, New York, 1995), 40 (italics mine)

113. D.W. Shriver, *An Ethic For Enemies* (New York: Oxford University Press, 1995), 40.

114. Schreiter, 2002, 90 (italics mine).

115. Schreiter, 2002, 89 (italics mine).

116. Schreiter, 2002, 89.

117. Robert J. Schreiter, *Reconciliation: Mission & Ministry in a Changing Social Order* (Maryknoll, NY and Newton, Mass: Orbis Books and Boston Theological Institute, 1992), 29-36.

118. Schreiter, 1992, 29-36.

119. Lisa Schirch, *Ritual and Symbol in Peacebuilding* (Bloomfield, CT: Kumarian Press, 2005), 141. (Italics mine).

120. Schreiter, 1992, 17-18. (Italics mine).

121. Schreiter, 2002, 93.

122. Paul Ricoeur, *The Symbolism of Evil* (Boston: Beacon Press, 1967), 16.

123. Quoted in Kermode, "Romantic Image," 109, 113 cited in Charles Taylor, *Sources of the Self: The Making of the Modern Identity* (Cambridge, Mass, Harvard University Press, 1989), 421.

124. Schirch, 2005, 142-143. (Italics mine).

125. Victor Witter Turner, "Dramas, Fields, and Metaphors: Symbolic Action in Human Society," (Ithaca, N.Y.: Cornell University Press, 1974) cited in Schirch, 2005, 143.

126. Schirch, 2005, 94.

127. Gopin, 2002, 196.

128. Schirch, 2005, 22.

129. Schirch, 2005, 93-94.

130. Schirch, 2005, 127.

131. Schirch, 2005, 126.

132. Schirch, 2005, 24-25. Bracketed words offer clarity while remaining consistent with the author's intent.

133. For a complete explanation of the Serbian *chosen trauma* relating to the Battle of Kosovo see VamikVolkan, *Blood Lines: From Ethnic Pride to Ethnic Terrorism*, 2nd Edition, Chapter Four, (Boulder, Colorado: Westview Press, 1997), 30-80.

134. In addition to Vamik Volkan's account, noted Bosnian authority, Michael Sells cites the procession of Prince Lazar's bones, the inference being throughout Serbian populated areas of the Balkans. See "Religion, History, and Genocide in Bosnia-Herzegovina," in G. Scott Davis (ed), *Religion and Justice in the War over Bosnia*, New York: Routledge, 1997, pp. 23-43, http://coursesa.matrix.msu.edu/~fisher/bosnia/readings/sells1.html, accessed 2 Jan 2012; Robert J. Donia (University of Michigan) in his article, Nationalism and Religious Extremism in Bosnia-Herzegovina and Kosovo since 1990, documents the removal of "the earthly remains of Prince Lazar, Serbian hero of the 1389 Battle of Kosovo, from the Serbian Orthodox Patriarchal Church in Belgrade and paraded his remains on a tour of Serbian Orthodox monasteries in Serbia, Bosnia-Herzegovina, Croatia, and Kosovo. The procession served to link the secular and religious cores of Serbianism—Belgrade and Serbian Orthodox monasteries in Kosovo—with peripheral Serb communities in Yugoslavia's 'near abroad'." See http://www.srpskadijaspora.info/vest.asp?id=8713, accessed 2 Jan 2012.

135. R.D. Kaplan, "Balkan Ghosts: A Journey Through History" (New York: Vintage Books, 1993), 38, cited in Volkan, 1997, 67.

136. Kaplan, 1993 67.

137. Schirch, 2005, 154.

138. Schirch, 2005, 154.

139. Schirch, 2005, 154.

140. Schirch, 2005, 154.

141. Schirch, 2005, 148.

Chapter Three

The Role of Religion in Conflict and Peacebuilding

Of import to this discussion is the paradoxical nature of religion and the complexity that it engenders: a component of conflict and, yet, a purveyor of peace. This seeming discordant message of religion is what many observe: "Religion can be engaged for social welfare, justice, nonviolent action, equality, human rights, respect and tolerance, but it can also foster hatred, injustice, violence, intolerance, disrespect, etc."[1] Proponents of religious peacebuilding face similar queries. In her examination of this nascent domain within the field of conflict resolution, Katrien Hertog underscores R. Scott Appleby's contention that the center of gravity of religious peacebuilding is not solely on the pure peace potential of religion, rather it considers the more perplexing space of ambivalence. As the starting point to more beneficial reflection, ambivalence moves the discourse beyond the broader, idealistic literature on religion and peace, which often leaves the impression of being detached from actual conflict. To grapple with the ambivalent role of religion in the reality of conflict makes for a more balanced and constructive analysis of the reality on the ground. Peacebuilder scholar Rabbi Marc Gopin echoes Appleby's call for a more candid treatment of religion's role in exacerbating conflict, a necessary precursor to making application of religion's more peaceful themes. Utopian calls for peace once conflict erupts renders the values of the culture of little use. Needed are mechanisms of constructive conflict, focusing on the ideas, interests and needs of those trapped in the vicious cycle of violence,[2] a phenomenon earlier described as *mimetic.* Broadening the discussion beyond the misappropriation of religious themes known to accompany conflict is the need to consider the "concrete dynamics of how and when religion prevents, condemns, lessens, or overcomes violence."[3] Coming to terms with religion's ambivalence over its role in conflict as well as peace—whatever the reasons—may be the wisest way forward.

This chapter will begin with an overview of religion's resurgence followed by a concise examination of the role of social categorization and boundaries as a means of grappling with the hollowing out of the faith experience that so often precipitates the congealing of 'us' and 'them' attitudes among the "faithful," leading to conflict and acts of violence. Religious extremism will be explored as a driver of conflict, delving into what lay behind its prevalence and efficacy. Presented also will be the variance of faith expression that exists within the religious domain, emphasizing the need for discernment where violence masquerades as a legitimate religious manifestation. Deeper into this discussion religious peacebuilding will be introduced as an emerging domain presently contributing to reconciling efforts among conflicting groups around the world. The advantages of such approaches will be highlighted along with a profile of the traits of religious peacebuilders, who engender trust and confidence among local populations. The closing segment will feature examples of religious peacebuilding endeavors globally from the major faith traditions: Christianity, Judaism, Islam, Buddhism and those of an interfaith nature.

RELIGION'S RESURGENCE

Stretching back decades, Western liberal, Marxist, and secular thinkers have spoken compellingly of religion's retreat from the political and social space to the private sphere, where it would dwindle in influence and relative obscurity. Their rhetoric today tends to "stress the fact that religion has not so much disappeared as it has changed in its dimensions and function."[4] A peacebuilder among the Jewish and Palestinian people for some twenty-five years, Yehezkel Landau summarizes quite succinctly what many in the West fail to grasp with respect to religion's profile in other parts of the world. He states, ". . . religion is a public concern, not just a private pursuit."[5] Further to this, Appleby contends that the West, with its public-private dictum as to the place of religion in society, represents less than one-sixth of the world's population, a "vantage point" that does not provide a privileged platform to make pronouncements as to the depth and place of religious faith in other cultures globally. It is also true that significant numbers of individuals in Western nations would disagree with such assertions.[6] Donald Horowitz touches on the contrast between West and East understanding of *religiosity.* He writes,

The modern Western notion is that religion is voluntary or affiliational, an act of faith. As a delayed result of the Reformation and a direct result of the Enlightenment and the French Revolution the right to choose one's religion was recognized. Religion passed into the realm of affiliations one could enter or leave at will. Even then, most people identified with the religion given them at birth. Outside the West, religion remained an ascriptive affiliation. *For many groups, religion is not a matter of faith but a given, an integral part of their identity, and for some an inextricable component of their sense of people-hood.*[7]

Increasingly, Westerners are coming face to face with societies globally that are suffuse with religion. "In regions of the Middle East, Africa, and South Asia, for example, it is not uncommon for political leaders and government officials to demonstrate (and sometimes exaggerate) the depth of their formal religious commitment."[8] Some scholars openly refer to religion's "recovery" as its 'return from exile' in international relations.[9] Citing religion's resurgence, Hertog provides the following synopsis.

Evidence of religious resurgence became very clear in the Shi'ite-led revolution in Iran, the liberationist movements in Latin America, the emergence of Jewish fundamentalism in Israel, The Christian Right in the United States, Hindu nationalism and Muslim communalism in India, the resurgence of religion in Eastern Europe after the fall of communism, the Islamic revival in the Middle East since the 1970s, Islamist opposition movements in Algeria, Pakistan, Egypt, and Indonesia, and ethno religious conflicts in Sri Lanka, Sudan, Bosnia, Kosovo, or Lebanon.[10]

Arguably, the forceful reappearance of religion in international affairs has created more than a small stir within the halls of power of Western countries where more secularist approaches to resolving conflict are practiced. Calls for the inclusion of religious methods of peacebuilding have begun to surface, interestingly enough, originating from both religious and secular sources.[11] Reticence within diplomatic circles to employ religious actors as credible partners in conflict resolution is longstanding. The all-too-common response from non-religious actors is for an institution that professes much goodness, there appears to be more than a small degree of evil associated with its activities, both historically and in the contemporary context. Notwithstanding the numerous examples of such duplicity in the name of religion, this thinking tends to be reductionist, and, as such, is not always helpful in considering the complexities associated with religion, conflict and peace. David Smock notes that although religion is often an important factor of conflict in terms of marking identity differences, motivating and justifying violence, religion is not usually the sole or primary reason of conflict. "The reality is that religion becomes intertwined with a range of causal factors—economic, political, and social—that define, propel, and sustain conflict."[12]

He contends that religious disagreements must be addressed alongside the above if reconciling differences is to be achieved. Of encouragement is the recognition that many of the approaches to mitigating religious violence are found within faith traditions themselves.

Important as well to this discussion is the function of belief in shaping the response of individuals and groups toward the *other*. Social categorization and the establishing of boundaries between groups are often influenced by religious socialization. In preparing to examine more deeply the antecedents of religiously motivated acts of violence, it behooves us to explore religion's role in creating the "us" and "them" mentality that so often spawns such violence.

RELIGION: SOCIAL CATEGORIZATION AND BOUNDARIES

Claire Mitchell is an Irish sociologist at Queen's University, Belfast, Northern Ireland. Her book *Religion, Identity and Politics in Northern Ireland: Boundaries of Belonging and Belief*[13] is extremely insightful in terms of the complexity of belief and its role in conflict. Albeit, much of her research and findings pertains to the Protestant and Roman Catholic dynamic at play in Northern Ireland, much of what she articulates may be extrapolated to other contexts. In preparing the ground for this discussion, I will paraphrase some of her thinking due to its relevance to religion's role in conflict.

She suggests that we are naturally disposed towards social categorization, which in turn provides the basis for social comparison leading to identity construction. As such, our ability to create meaningful order results in dividing our social world into categories: black/white, friend/enemy, tasteful/ tacky. Such social categorization and comparison leads to the establishing of boundaries that help us delineate what is familiar from what is different. Moral evaluations accompany these boundaries enabling us to determine when difference may be threatening, and in some instances, perhaps worse. Boundaries, as can be expected, relate to the building of community as well, a grouping of people based on social categorization. In ascribing to a community one identifies with others who belong to the same large group that share language, location, given activities, etc. Communities are not necessarily entities in their own right but exist in the minds of groups of people who relate to them: psychological lines that divide people like us from people like them. It may be that in the normal everyday flow of life these boundaries may not seem that pressing. However, it is during times of tension and crisis that such identity boundaries become more rigid, drawing distinctive lines/ walls between "in-groups" and "out-groups." In the world in which we live, we do not select the community to which we belong—we are born into it. Becoming a part of another community or receiving *others* into our own is easier said than done. Existing historical and institutional structures govern largely what aspects of identity will be socially important to us for most of our lives—be that gender, race, religion or nationality.

Mitchell identifies religious affiliation as a determining factor of one's place in the social and political structure—community. She makes the point that for many, religion is much more than a label. Where religion has held historical significance it often continues as a cultural reservoir from which categorizations of the *self* and the *other* may be derived. "In other words, as well as marking out the boundary, religion can give meaning to it . . . provid[ing] the substantive content to differentiate insiders from outsiders."[14] Where conflict is ongoing, these same individuals may seem threatening. "So ideas of religious difference can become embedded in how we perceive ourselves as well as what we think the other group is like. When we think and act in these terms, we reproduce these religious differences."[15] Compounding the social categorization of identity boundaries, religious belief may also legitimize a groups' feeling that their community is superior to that of the *other*. Boundaries ossify when differing beliefs are used as a means of identification.[16] In a very real sense, religious ideas delineate difference while providing moral evaluations of social relationships. Language and imagery become codes conveying belonging, which transmits an identity narrative that does more than tell their story, it also influences people to act in the present.[17] Vamik Volkan identifies such transgenerational transmission as *chosen trauma*: a group's *wounded memory* narrative relating to perceived wrongs committed toward earlier generations, avenged against an enemy in the present deemed connected to such past injustice. [18]

Continuing further, Mitchell delves more deeply into the question of religion's influence by her assertion that religious ideology may be understood to be "concepts that are informed by religious doctrines but that are not concerned with answering spiritual questions," to which the phrase 'believing without belonging' is associated. This suggests that for some, religion may continue to be socially significant due to earlier religious socialization, yet it does not carry over into having strong religious belief or regular practice in the present.[19] Drawing on the work of G. Davie, she underscores the notion of *vicarious religion* which uses the iceberg analogy: religiously speaking, the tip of the iceberg may be all that appears in a given culture, yet "beneath the surface of the water, a wealth of religious ideas and concepts simmer, ready to erupt in times of crisis and hardship."[20] In this vein, the 'religious experience' of the individual may be quite responsive to social and political developments, which can lead to a collective and often dramatic resurfacing of religious sentiment rather unexpectedly.[21]

This brief overview of social categorization and boundary development prepares the way for a closer look into religious extremism as a factor of conflict and some of the possible reasons for its advancement. For some, religious socialization is a distant memory, leaving any active engagement with an authentic faith in the remote past. Lacking the substance of a valid faith experience or any depth of understanding of its creed or tenets, gratuitous violence against the *other* finds footing in the name of religion. Still others, as will be seen, strike out against the "enemy *other*" out of deep religious passion, extremely misguided and without accurate foundation in doctrine or holy writ. This is the dilemma of religion today as it relates to conflict. The following will touch on some of the more confounding inconsistencies associated with the insidious nature of religious extremism and how it is manifest among those otherwise committed to promoting messages far more inclusive of the *other.*

RELIGIOUS EXTREMISM AS A DRIVER OF CONFLICT

In their final report, *Exploring Canada's Relations with the Countries of the Muslim World*, the Standing Committee of Foreign Affairs and International Trade (DFAIT) identify religion as contributing to ideological fault lines for decades to come. Citing a seminal strategy paper from the United Kingdom presented to the British parliament, the writers state,

> The possible confrontations of ideas most likely to affect the UK and other western democracies in the early twenty-first century stem from religion and culture. Religious belief is coming back to the fore as a motivating force in international relations. In some cases it is distorted to cloak political purposes. [22]

Echoing these sentiments, Georgetown University's Bruce Hoffman, author of *Inside Terrorism*, categorically states "the religious imperative for terrorism is the most important defining characteristic of terrorist activity today." [23] Since the early 1990's the only phenomenon to outdistance the increase in numbers of terrorist groups has been the steady growth in the percentage of these groups that hold to religious extremism as their driving force. In 1994, Hoffman states, a third of terrorist groups—sixteen of the forty-nine identified—could be classified as religious in character or in motivation. The following year, the numbers of terrorist organizations purporting to be religiously inspired accounted for nearly half—twenty-six, or 46 percent. Continuing his research into the new millennium, in 2004 religious terrorist organizations remained nearly half of those listed as active terrorist groups—52, or 46 percent of the total, [24] a significant and disturbing trend. In presenting to a gathering of senior U.S. chaplains at the Pentagon [25] Dr. Hoffman was asked how long he thought the West would be dealing with religious terrorism. Without hesitation he responded, "Two generations!" He based this partially on the numbers of disenchanted Muslim youth throughout the world who are easy prey to Islamic extremists coupled with the reality that communication and training for militant groups has never been easier with a ubiquitous Internet that transcends borders and connects continents. Exacerbating these challenges, Hoffman cited the West's seeming inability to influence the present generation of Muslim youth and a chilling absence of a viable strategy to impact, in any significant way, the generation coming up behind them.

Dr. Hoffman's comments are indicative of the sea state change in the nature and complexity of conflict. Mary Kaldor describes how the use of extreme politics based on fear and hatred now factor into conflict's equation: "mass killing and forcible resettlement, as well as a range of political, psychological and economic techniques of intimidation . . . atrocities against non-combatants, sieges, destruction of historic monuments, etc., constitutes an essential component of the strategies of the new mode of warfare."[26] Kaldor underscores the staggering change in statistics—whereas in more conventional conflict the ratio of military to civilian casualties was in the order of 8:1, today's asymmetric warfare is witness to military to civilian casualties of approximately 1:8. The residual effect of these shifting currents has brought a greater complexity to the fore with its accompanying instability and intense quest for workable solutions.[27]

Exacerbating such conflict are extreme expressions of religion. While purely religious conflict is rare, contends Hertog, there is a rise in hostilities with explicit reference to religion. For those implicated, the clash frequently becomes a struggle between good and evil, rendering violence a sacred duty.[28] Today's unprecedented co-optation of religion as a means of deepening existing cultural and political fault lines aids in fueling the justification of militancy and terrorism.[29] Militant extremism motivated by a religious imperative embraces violence as a divine duty or sacramental act. Holding to markedly different notions of legitimization and justification than their secular counterparts, these organizations indulge without compunction in greater bloodshed and destruction than terrorist groups with solely a political agenda. Noting the role of religious leadership, anthropologist Pauletta Otis illumines, "The complexities of conflict may be compounded further when religious leaders who, with their incendiary language, contribute to the congealing of adversarial identity markers, exacerbating the polarization of communities even more."[30] As a vehicle of influence, religion is known for its efficacy, frequently exploited by political leaders prone to supplement their anemic rhetoric with religious ideology as a means to motivate local populations to "extreme patriotism and violent behavior."[31] In reference to the Bosnian war, Appleby makes specific mention of how religion, wed to ethnicity, became an identity marker for violence toward the other. He continues, "Thus, the demonizers relied on religion to provide "primordial" and "age-old" justifications for people intent on hating one another."[32]

Complications mount when opportunistic politicians resort to religious appeal as the principal driver for political action and exclusive political programming.[33] In such instances, the impressionable and uninformed come to experience religion as a combination of misinterpreted sacred texts imparted via clerical authorities claiming to speak for the divine.[34] Today's lexicon now includes the term *sacralizing* to describe such manipulation of religious themes by ambitious leaders, a powerful inducement for engaging in violence against rival ethno-religious groups.[35] Such entanglement of religion with nationalist movements, intones Gerard Powers, is not necessarily a question of nationalism being an alternative to religion. Sadly, it is not always a case of nationalism "entering into the naked public square when and where religion weakens, but they advance mutually, reinforcing one another in the wake of the same dynamics and the same trends, penetrating together into the naked public square."[36] Is it coincidence, he queries, how nationalist reawakenings and religious revivals seem to occur concurrently? From his vantage point of the Middle East tinderbox, Yehezkel Landau adds to Powers' appraisal, ". . . the mixture of religion and nationalism is dangerously combustible."[37]

In recent decades religiously inspired violence has become more pronounced mainly due to a strategy of elevating religious images to the realm of divine struggle, thus creating in the minds of ardent followers the specter of cosmic war. Appleby notes, "Rather than break down barriers, in short, religion often fortifies them. . . . Constructed as inseparable from ethnic and linguistic traits, religion in such settings lends them a transcendent depth and dignity. Extremists thus invoke religion to legitimate discrimination and violence against groups of a different race or language."[38] Harnessing such emotive themes is the mainstay for many waging worldly political battles. Convincing youth to commit horrific acts of violence against vulnerable civilian populations becomes much less arduous when such atrocities are deemed to be "sanctioned by divine mandate or conceived in the mind of God. The power of this idea has been enormous. It has surpassed all ordinary claims of political authority and elevated religious ideologies to supernatural heights."[39] Today, extreme religious expression has given terrorism remarkable power through spiritualizing violence.[40]

The inner dynamics of a religious community are complex as is the individual's experience within that community. Oversimplification and generalizations of religiously motivated violence are not helpful. This premise must serve as a guide to any comprehension of how a religious individual comes to embrace violence as acceptable to their belief system. As Gopin illumines, individuals so inclined become increasingly isolated as their internal dynamic and hermeneutic of engagement with their religious tradition results in opposition and estrangement from family and community of religious origin. Devoid of any guiding religious authority, they gravitate to those sympathetic to their "faith journey." Radical religious leaders feed off of such vulnerable "postulants," integrating them into an existing network of like individuals where seeds of an ideology of religiously motivated violence are sown and cultivated—the result is the harvesting of a communal dynamic of violence. Religious terrorists are often needy individuals who, once banded together, can have a dramatic impact on an entire community. Where power shifts to those religious authorities that embrace these radicalized and violent individuals who look to them as mentors and leaders, the momentum toward violence can be unstoppable.[41] Research continues as to the relationship between conflict and religion, identifying occasions and frequencies. As informative as this may be and given the present climate of religiously motivated violence increasingly on a large scale, questions are emerging as to its utility.

RELIGIOUS UNDERSTANDING

Adjusting the Emphasis of Research

Returning to Powers, he reflects on how quantitative research examines conflict statistically, investigating the degree to which religion factors into such aggression. He reports on a number of reputable quantitative studies that cite religion as a factor in various conflicts, yet principally not a primary or exclusive factor. An analysis by Uppsala University's Department of Peace and Conflict Research is one such study, which parsed religion's implication in conflict where applicable between the years 1989 to 2003. The analyses found:

> (1) 58 percent were conflicts in which religion played no part in either separating the identities of the belligerents or in the claims of the parties to the conflict (e.g., Burundi, Nepal, El Salvador); (2) 20 percent were conflicts in which the parties were separated by a difference in religious identities but without any religious claims at stake (e.g., ITA—British government in Northern Ireland); (3) 11 percent were conflicts between belligerents that belong to the same religious tradition but in which there are religious claims in the conflict (e.g., conflicts among Muslims in Algeria, Egypt and Indonesia over the religious or secular nature of the state; (4) 11 percent were conflicts where the parties were separated by their religious identities and at least one party made religious claims (e.g., Sri Lanka, Sudan, and Kashmir).[42]

According to these findings, only 22 percent of conflicts implicated religion. Powers refers to additional studies that replicate similar findings.[43] Considering terrorism specifically, Daniel Philpot's research indicates that at present 36 percent of terrorist organizations espouse religious ties.[44] Monica Toft's work is among the studies named. Her probing revealed, "that religious civil wars were nearly twice as likely to recur as nonreligious civil wars, and religious civil wars were four times harder on noncombatants than civil wars in which religion is peripheral."[45] Toft's analysis also revealed that, on average, religious civil wars lasted two years longer than internal conflicts that had no religious component.[46]

Following on with Powers' argument, he cites the value of such statistical research in identifying variances among religious traditions and the incidence of conflict, but points to the greater need for measuring the intensity of religious identity and beliefs that enflame conflict. He contends that such quantitative research does not attend to "the complex interaction between religious identity and ethnic, national, racial, class, cultural, gender, and political identities,"[47] something that more qualitative studies address. Conflict infused by skewed religious themes is far more complex and variegated than many would suppose or statistical studies are able to chart. In this vein, the salient factor confronting the international community today is not how religious conflicts compare with other types of conflicts, rather the urgent imperative is to differentiate between religious actors who insidiously stoke violence from those who espouse an authentic faith and, as such, interface positively with local populations, regardless of ethnicity. The greater benefit is to distinguish between extremists and nonextremists, enabling the *tolerant voice* of religion to be audible above the rhetoric and propaganda that fuels conflict.[48] Powers makes his case succinctly, "The challenge, then, is to marginalize religious extremists, not religion."[49] As a proponent of strategic peacebuilding, he positions this logic as integral to more fully comprehending the field of conflict and informing initiatives where religious extremism is a factor. His words serve as a natural segue into the following discussion pertaining to how inauthentic religious expression may take root in religious communities, thus necessitating discernment against that which would masquerade as genuine.

> Strategic peacebuilding insists that we go much deeper than quantitative measures of religion's role in conflict, that we avoid treating religion as an easily categorizable monolith, and that we understand both the negative and positive roles of religion in conflict and peacebuilding. Strategic peacebuilding gives priority to qualitative analyses that take seriously pluralism within and among religious traditions as well as the complex qualitative factors that contribute to either conflict or peace in particular cases. Strategic peacebuilding makes a normative judgment that a political scientist or sociologist of religions might not be willing to make: that an interpretation of a religious tradition or certain religious practices that promote violence and injustice are "inauthentic," whereas those that are a force for peace and justice are "authentic."[50]

Discerning Legitimate Religiosity

Building on Powers' language of "inauthentic" and "authentic" religion, Appleby further examines the antecedents of such incongruent religious expression. Employing the descriptors "strong" and "weak" religion, he cautions, is not done lightly and, as David Little suggests, can "oversimplify,"[51] as will be seen shortly. That said, Appleby's careful differentiation between these two identifiers is insightful when played over against the backdrop of religion's oft-contradictory role of violence against the *other*. He associates "strong" religion with well-developed and secure institutions with "adherents 'literate' in its doctrinal and moral teachings and practiced in its devotional, ritual, and spiritual traditions."[52] This is contrasted with "weak" religion where "people retain meaningful contact only with vestiges of the broader religious worldview and network of meanings and resources, in which they are isolated from . . . educators and spiritual-moral exemplars."[53] With the paucity of such religious formation, "the low-level or virtual absence of second-order moral reflection and basic theological knowledge among religious actors [creates] a structural condition that increases the likelihood of collective violence in crisis situations."[54] It is in such settings that "ethnic, nationalist, secular-liberal, and other worldviews and ideologies have full reign to shape the meaning of those vestiges," as was the case in the former Yugoslavia under decades of communism. Appleby's point is well taken, for religious illiteracy weakens authentic belief, as do "informed interpreters who privilege, exalt, and reify its capacity for violence."[55] He rightly asserts where interpretations of the sacred legitimize intolerance and violence toward the *other*, religion in this light may have an outward appearance of legitimacy yet remain flagrantly flawed. Religious organizations that deny "religion's capacity to promote pluralistic and tolerant political cultures . . . are weak in the normative sense."[56] Karen Armstrong, in *The Battle for God*, speaks quite candidly of authentic faith among the world's religions. She opines,

> [N]o religious doctrine or practice can be authentic if it does not lead to practical compassion. Buddhist, Hindus, Taoists, and monotheists all agree that the sacred reality is not simply transcendent, "out there," but is enshrined in every single human being who must therefore be treated with absolute honor and respect. Fundamentalist faith, be it Jewish, Christian, or Muslim, fails this crucial test if it becomes a theology of rage and hatred.[57]

Expanding on the above, in *Peacemakers in Action*,[58] Little examines the lives and work of a number of religious *peacebuilders* active in various trouble spots around the globe. The following paraphrases his reflection[59] on the recurrent tendency to oversimplify one's understanding of religion's role in conflict and peace. His thesis aids in better grasping the dichotomies presented by Appleby and Armstrong. Little's argument holds that proponents in both camps have a tendency to overgeneralize: (1) those who contend that if one digs deeply enough, invariably connections between conflict, violence and religion will appear, and (2) those who believe real or authentic religion will never be associated with violence, only flawed or distorted versions will. In the first instance, if religion is predisposed to violence in certain situations, this inescapably underscores the notion that the linkage between religion and violence is indeed complex. Concomitantly, to ascribe the violence of some of today's more protracted conflicts as simply being a function of religion is spurious. Easy answers will not do. The need exists to examine the complexity present in conflict while exercising sensitivity. However, he quickly counters, this is not to suggest the implausibility of religion's role in conflict; juxtaposition that heralds back to Appleby's usage of the term "ambivalence." Upon scrutinizing the lives and accounts of these religious *peacebuilders*, Little concludes that the idea of religion serving only to foment hate and destruction was without foundation. From here he turns to the second position—authentic religion could not be associated with violence—with the same openness and candor. He confronts the logic that religious groups committed to following the "bona fide and pristine" teachings of their traditions would never be associated with violence, be that Christian, Jewish, Muslim or any other. The thinking continues that to be devoted to one's religious traditions is to "invariably become instruments of peace and harmony, rather than chaos and destruction."[60]

Earlier sections of this chapter explicitly tie aberrant religious expressions to the tendency toward violence—extremism. Conversely, Little acknowledges that certain religious *peacebuilders* in his study—devout as they may be—have been associated with conflict and violence. These are individuals committed to conciliation and harmony, yet, at times, their desire for peace by peaceful means has heightened tensions. Their nonviolent approaches to addressing injustice are often looked upon with disdain by those opposed to changing existing structures, thus precipitating retaliation. Little explains further that creating such antagonism can be interpreted as being noble. That is to say, some may deem the oversimplification that "good religion brings peace" credible. There are religious *peacebuilders* who embrace the logic that violence resulting from the promotion of peace and justice by peaceful means may be a viable *short-term* goal in subduing oppression and violence in the *long run*. From a moral point of view, so the logic goes, they maintain the high ground. If, for reasons of continued injustice, peaceful means of challenging the "oppressor" brings about retaliation and force, the responsibility of any mistreatment or bloodletting rests with those who resort to such measures.

Redekop's categories of "religious understanding" are also helpful in grasping something of the complexity that the religious experience brings to any given context. The breadth of faith expression ranges from the extremely limited to the abundant with gradations of religiosity in between the two. Where religion is considered to be a factor of conflict, credible analysis must consider how it is manifest, and where religious aquifers may be tapped, holding potential for easing tensions and/or resolving hostilities. His categories offer further clarity as to why some professing to be religious are easily swayed in their perceptions of and actions toward those deemed unlike themselves, while yet others among the faithful embrace such diversity as the embodiment of true religious teaching and values.

Variance of Understanding

Comprehending something of how religious understanding manifests contextually—both individually and collectively—undoubtedly aids in illuminating the complexity that religion presents for those who intervene, be they indigenous or external actors. The following overview speaks to the variance of religions understanding that exists across the spectrum of contemporary faith expressions.

Tacit Only Illiterate Visored Informed Well-versed Reflective

Religious people in any religious tradition have wide-ranging differences of understanding about their own tradition. For some, tradition is influential only at the *tacit* level. They could tell you little about their sacred texts or the meaning of the traditions but knowledge still exists at the tacit level through an experience of our exposure to the religion. Then there are religiously *illiterate*, who know some of the basics and some of the religious markers that set them apart from other groups, but have neither read the texts nor sat at the feet of teachers in the tradition. Religiously illiterate adherents have a religious life based on folk-religion. These people are very susceptible to manipulation by leaders who pick up on a few details about the religion so they can frame a situation religiously in a way that sweeps the illiterate followers in to a military crusade. Some persons are *visored*—they have studied only a narrow aspect of their religion. Some are *informed* and others have studied the religion in some depth. Those with a profound understanding of a religion can place its development into historical context and can think critically about their religious tradition. [61]

Religion's Roots and Legacy

Moreover, in many parts of the world, nationalism is fairly novel and some-what foreign. "Religion and clan," Barry Rubin suggests, "are the primary, tightly entwined roots of ideology and loyalty in the long histories of peoples."[62] He contends that, for some, the nation-state became more of an existential notion that may have existed in practice but conceptually seemed to lack definition or acceptance. Religion, on the other hand, reaches back millennia. These beliefs, in whatever form, developed or adapted through long internal practice, taking the form of an indigenous idea. Rubin further postulates, "nationalist, Marxist, humanist, and secularist ideas are imports that often are viewed with some suspicion, if not hostility." Where longer periods of communal fusion into a nation have been lacking, "these societies continue to see religion, clan, ethnicity, and other such factors as the markers of community identity."[63] Ironically, rather than declining in influence as predicted by many, in certain parts of the world, religion increasingly assumes a stronger public role either as a partner in the processes of state-building or party to revolutionary transformation.[64]

Rubin goes on to point out the lack of strong social institutions in many parts of the world. In these localities the church, mosque or temple, inclusive of leadership (cleric and lay), often occupy an important role in defining values and social goals, with support either to rulers or ties to the opposition. Globally, religious institutions continue to enjoy the greatest presence among the people, and, by extension, pervasive influence.[65] As such, it is becoming markedly more difficult to relegate religion to the margins as irrelevant to strategic thinking.

RELIGIOUS CONTRIBUTIONS TO PEACEBUILDING

A broad spectrum of individuals and organizations—external and indigenous actors—increasingly inter-religious—now collaborate in various venues on a number of levels to bring the irenic attributes of religion to bear on conflict and violence. The impetus of this surge to include religious approaches in resolving conflict—despite the incongruous portrayal religion frequently presents—is the recognition that it possesses social and moral characteristics that often serve as constructive forces for peace and conflict transformation.[66] Where religion is a factor in conflict, those endeavoring to bring structural, economic, political and social change have begun to reflect on these connections.[67] In today's *new wars*, "there is clearly now a greater imperative to dialogue not just to get to know the religious other, but to form bonds of inter-religious solidarity against the hijacking of religions to legitimate violence."[68] Among the approaches under consideration is the need to discern ways to "integrate the wisdom, spirit and techniques of the world's religious traditions into the politics and practice of contemporary conflict management, resolution, and prevention."[69] Instances where leadership has failed to appreciate religion as an element of a presenting conflict have, in some cases, led to unfortunate decisions with disastrous results, culminating in missed opportunities.[70] In societies where, due to conflict, centralized authority has ceased to function all together, religious communities often represent the only institutional and social structure functioning with any degree of credibility, trust and moral authority among the people.[71] The role and training of religious leaders often positions them to better interpret an ongoing conflict. Due to their closeness to the situation, acquaintance with many of the actors and ease with the language and an appreciation of the issues, religious leaders offer an invaluable perspective of the conflict at hand.[72]

Kofi Annan, former secretary general to the United Nations, recognized the unique position religious organizations held in local communities and the potential inroads to resolving conflict they offered globally. In his 2001 Report, *Prevention of Armed Conflict: Report of the Secretary General,* he stated the following,

> Religious organizations can play a role in preventing armed conflict because of the moral authority that they carry in many communities. In some cases, religious groups and leaders possess a culturally based comparative advantage in conflict prevention, and as such are most effective when they emphasize the common humanity of all parties to a conflict while refusing to identify with any single party. In addition, religious groups could mobilize non-violent alternative ways of expressing dissent prior to the outbreak of armed conflict.[73]

Annan clearly identifies religious leaders, living authentically among the people within local communities the world over as a valued resource in conflict intervention. These are individuals *tolerant* of the *other*, possessing moral integrity and courage, cognizant of local culture, and capable of inspiring the people to more peaceful means of resolving conflict. This gives added credence to Appleby's contention that although exploitive leaders frequently appeal to religious identity in order to stir ethnic and tribal division, it is also true that religion may be invoked as a means of transcending differences and unifying rival tribes.[74]

Returning to *Peacemakers in Action,* David Little presents a series of case studies of the activities of a number of religious peacebuilders and organizations from some of the more troubled spots on the globe: Central America, Northern Ireland, Eastern Europe, Africa, the Middle East, Afghanistan and Indonesia. More than a few of these peacebuilders are indigenous religious leaders. Paramount to his overview is the recognition that the indigenous religious leader is one of the more effective resources available to resolving conflict and sustaining peace. Especially intriguing are his observations of what he deemed the central identity of the religious peacebuilder paraphrased here.

Much of their effectiveness lay in the fact that these religious leaders were perceived by the people as a committed neighbor, intimately acquainted with their suffering. Not only did they witness hardship, at times they experienced personal loss as well. Indian and Christian scholar Israel Selvanayagam echoes the above drawing from his experience in multi-faith contexts. Truthful living by religious leaders goes far in creating bonds—where one is "open to admit the struggles and problems of one's own life of faith and being eager to know how others experience and deal with them."[75] The peacebuilders of Little's study exhibited an authentic religiosity: deeply personal and only sometimes institutionally based. Having met these rare individuals, he discerned a honed emotional intelligence demonstrated in their unusual capacity to deeply comprehend what the *other* is experiencing—their aspirations and pain. All of these religious peacebuilders exhibited a visceral reaction to injustice and cruelty with a tangible revulsion toward violence, compelling them to become activists. For the most part these individuals had no formal training in conflict resolution or peacebuilding, rather they drew on their capacity for deep personal awareness, self-reflection, and, sometimes, simply trial and error. The singleness of purpose in their quest for peace permeated their conduct, coupled with a demonstrative intelligence witnessed in the thoughtfulness of their comments and inexhaustible creativity. There was never any question to their dedication—they were there for the long haul.[76] Such resolve engenders trust in leadership and instills hope within people encountering violence. Key to long term sustainability of peace initiatives, Lederach and Appleby articulate that the role of external actors must be understood from the beginning to consist of ". . . ongoing activities and operations that may be initiated and supported for a time by outsiders . . . must eventually become the ordinary practices of the citizens and institutions of the society in question."[77] Indigenous religious leaders may prove to be integral to such processes.

Falling within the domain of what Joseph Montville coined as Track II[78] diplomacy—more commonly referred to as multi-track diplomacy[79] today—a growing number of religious interventionists, individuals and/or organizations, are toiling with religious leaders and their faith communities as a means of bridging alienation and transcending the conflict that consumes their communities. (Track I diplomacy refers more to the classic or traditional role of state-sponsored diplomats, shuttle diplomacy, etc.). The recognition that traditional approaches need to be inclusive of more innovative ways of resolving the perplexing tests of today's *new wars* has emerged among Western nations in particular. Internationally renowned for his mediation and negotiation acumen, I. William Zartman's poignant statement rings true,

Conflict resolution needs all the help it can get. Since parties to a conflict typically are already well entrenched in their conflicting behavior for reasons they have often repeated to themselves to justify their resistance toward the other party, all the knowledge that can be brought to bear in favor of conflict resolution is badly needed and all the hands that can be brought to the task can be helpful.[80]

RELIGIOUS PEACEBUILDERS: AN EMERGING DOMAIN

The watershed publication, *Religion, the Missing Dimension of Statecraft*, by Douglas Johnston and Cynthia Samson (1994), was the first scholarly endeavor to draw attention to the role of religious peacebuilding. Religious leaders, they illumined, were "often better equipped to reach people at the level of the individual and the subnational groups—where inequities and insecurities are often most keenly felt—than are most political leaders who walk the corridors of power."[81] Moral issues and spiritual need fell more naturally within their domain, frequently transcending the boundaries of their own faith traditions.[82] Engaging religious actors as a means of conflict transformation began in earnest in the early 1990's. Hertog heralds Johnston and Samson's research a precursor to religious peacebuilding emerging as a viable domain of practice and study, finding sure footing in 2000.[83] Propelling this work forward were the landmark publications of R. Scott Appleby, *Ambivalence of the Sacred: Religion, Violence and Reconciliation*, and Rabbi Marc Gopin's *Between Eden and Armageddon: The Future of World Religions, Violence and Peacemaking*. From this time forward, insists Hertog, the field rapidly grew in terms of "an expanding body of literature, the dedication of scholars, the establishment of research centers, and the organization of specific disciplines."[84] The sphere of religious peacebuilding merits a broadening conversation as to its efficacy and, now, its necessity. The following is but a sampling of the individual initiatives and organizational endeavors linking religion to effectual and credible peacebuilding efforts.

Christian Peacebuilding

Canon Andrew White, the Archbishop of Canterbury's Special Envoy to the Middle East, is the co-founder of the Foundation for Relief and Reconciliation in the Middle East, an organization working for peace and relief in one of the most complex areas in the world: Iraq, Israeli and Palestinian areas, and the UK.[85] He recently was awarded the 2010 Civil Courage Prize Medal by The Train Foundation in New York. Dubbed the "Vicar of Baghdad," as Rector of Saint George's Anglican Church in Baghdad, he has striven for peace since his arrival in 2003. As a religious peacebuilder, he has labored to reconcile Iraq's disparate religious factions by developed relationships among many of the most senior leaders within the Sunni, Shi'a, Kurdish, Christian and other minority communities. Canon White's initiative resulted in the "facilitation of [an] ongoing inter-religious dialogue in Iraq . . . result[ing] in 2004's Baghdad Religious Accord, the formation of the Iraqi Institute for Peace, a series of conferences among senior Iraqi religious leaders, and 2008's historic joint Sunni-Shi'a Fatwa condemning sectarian violence."[86] This proclamation was the result of an ongoing series of conferences that brought together many different religious groups in Iraq with no other forum for debate and reconciliation.[87] Of significance, U.S. Army chaplain Col. (ret.) Michael Hoyt collaborated with Canon White in successfully establishing the Iraq Inter-religious Council (IIRC), which led to the June 2007, Baghdad Accords. This Accords included the principal religious groups in Iraq and the Iraqi government, one of several case studies coming in later chapters.

The Community of Sant'Egidio, the peacebuilding arm of the Roman Catholic Church, chronicles extensive involvement in peacebuilding efforts in such places as Mozambique (1990-1992), Algeria (1995), Guatemala (1996), Albania (1997), Kosovo (1996–1998), Bosnia-Herzegovina (2000) and Burundi (2001).[88] Of particular significance was Sant'Egidio's implication in the "general peace accord" of Mozambique. The Mozambican negotiations lasted twenty-seven months, with eleven sessions of work. During this period negotiations experienced highs and lows, yet, due to the constructive climate of the talks an enabling trust between the parties emerged. Over the course of time, the choice for a negotiated solution grew stronger until it made irreversible progress. In order to observe and support the Mozambican process several representatives of Western and neighboring governments were invited, as well as a UN delegation. During the negotiations in 1990–1992 between the two warring parties (RENAMO & FRELIMO) and the Mozambique government, religious peacebuilder Andrea Bartoli (now at George Mason University) represented Sant'Egidio at the United Nations. "The general peace accord, signed in Sant'Egidio (Rome) on October 4, 1992, stands as one of the few examples of an African conflict brought to an end through peace talks . . . an example of how a non-institutional reality, the Community of Sant'Egidio, can successfully bring a mediation process to an end with a mixture and a synergy of responsibilities between governmental entities and non-governmental organizations."[89] As a mediator of longstanding with Sant'Egidio, Bartoli remains active in peacebuilding endeavors. The following are among the regions where he has been involved at one level or another in negotiations: Algeria, Albania, Burma, Burundi, The Democratic Republic of the Congo, Guatemala, and Kosovo.[90]

Mennonite Peacebuilding: Mennonite peacebuilders are among the most effective in the world. Names like John Paul Lederach, Lisa Schirch, Vern Neufeld Redekop, Ron Kraybill and Barry Hart, are but a few of the more notable. Mennonites come to peacebuilding with a distinct peace theology coupled with practical peacemaking skills and strategies. Placing much emphasis on building relations within local populations, they become part of communities in conflict for extended periods of time, living among the people, gradually winning their trust. From a peacebuilding perspective, they deem quick solutions as providing temporary relief from conflict but inadequate to ascertain the deeper underlying issues that may lead to more constructive and wider change. Resolving conflict must be more than a set of techniques; it can be a way of being.[91] Mennonite conflict transformation brings clarity to the questions of what needs to be stopped and what do they hope to build. Lederach, Neufeldt and Culbertson in *Reflective Peacebuilding: A Planning, Monitoring, and Learning Toolkit* state it succinctly, "While conflict resolution focuses on de-escalation of conflict and diffusion of crises, transformation allows for an ebb and flow in conflict, and sees the presenting problem as a potential opportunity to transform the relationship and the systems in which relationships are embedded."[92] Complementing and supporting grassroots peace organizations and initiatives within local populations is a Mennonite trait in recognition that peace agreements made by leaders must exhibit ownership from the people if such initiatives are to be embraced and sustained. In his analysis of Mennonite peacebuilding Christopher Mitchell speaks of *withinness* as a common characteristic. That is to say, "engag[ing] in capacity building rather than training (the former implying that knowledge, skills, and above all, the capabilities that are there, in the society awaiting opportunities for use and development); and to the necessity of helping local people to 'give themselves permission' in Ron Kraybill's words, to develop their own methods and models."[93] Mennonites contribute to peacebuilding endeavors the world over. They offer much by way of inspiration and instruction to those aspiring to aid in reconciliation processes.

Jewish Peacebuilding

Oz VeShalom—Netivot Shalom translates "Strength and Peace—Paths of Peace." This Jewish organization was founded in 1975 as an alternative expression to religious Zionism. Envisioned as a bridge between two Israeli constituencies, each with its own vision of an authentic "Jewish state," this movement endeavors to bring together the secular left and religious right—a seismic fault line in Israeli society.[94] It embraces the ideals of tolerance, pluralism and justice as a means to counter more fundamentalist and extremist political positions that place the value of the Land of Israel above human life, justice, and peace. A fair and just society demonstrated in the co-existence between Jews and Arabs, this group holds peace as a central religious value. As a religious body advocating equality for all, *Oz VeShalom—*

Netivot Shalom attracts interest from many within secular Israeli society and beyond. Education and activism are its main strategies in promoting support for the peace process and political rights for Palestinians. Programs are offered for youth, students, educators and families coupled with protest activities on human rights issues, co-existence for Jews and Arabs, and issues of particular religious relevance.

Another effective Jewish peacebuilding organization is the Israeli *Rabbis for Human Rights (RHR)*. This is a rabbinical association, of no political affiliation, comprised of Reform, Orthodox, Conservative, Reconstructionist and Renewal rabbis and students. Of singular importance to RHR is the Jewish tradition of human rights, specifically relating to minorities. Their emphasis is to give voice to the stranger, those vulnerable within society and to defy silent complicity. Where injustice exists for Israeli or Arab alike, these Rabbis bring such grievances before the Israeli public all the while pressuring authorities to redress such wrongs. RHR addresses human rights issues throughout the Middle East.

Probably one of the more heartwarming instances of peacebuilding originating in Israel is that of Yehezkel and, then-wife, Dalia Landau's journey of *Open House*.[95] This interfaith peacebuilding account brings together all three of the Abrahamic faith traditions. Following the war that led to the 1948 creation of the Jewish state, multitudes of Jews flocked to Israel's shores. Among them was Dalia, who, at age one, immigrated to Israel with her Bulgarian family in 1948. Like many newly arrived Jewish families they were settled in a ready-to-occupy home in Ramale—an "Arab house." Following the establishing of the Israeli state, confiscated Palestinian homes were classified as "abandoned houses" and, consequently, available for Jewish families emigrating from other parts the world. As Landau recounts the story, after the Six-Day War of 1967 the original owners of the property—having settled in the West Bank city of El-Bireh—came to visit. After a period of time and several visits to each other's homes, the Landau and Al-Khayri families began to bond. Each called the house and garden "home."

Eventually, Dalia learned that the Al-Khayri family did not leave the house voluntarily, but were forcibly evacuated by the Israeli authorities, a decision driven by the Arab world rejection of the 1947 United Nations partition plan. Acknowledging the reasons of their leaving Ramale, and sensitive to their ties to the home, the Landau's entered into discussions with the Al-Khayri family concerning the future of what was home to both families. Together they formed "Open House," based on the commitment to *mishpat* (justice) and *tzedakah* (compassion). The home of these two families has come to symbolize Israel/Palestine as the homeland of two nations. As can be appreciated, Dalia's decision to dedicate her childhood home to educational projects fostering reconciliation between these two peoples has been acclaimed internationally. In sharing her story at interfaith conferences around the world, Dalia shares her belief that to achieve reconciliation those involved in the process must take three steps: "(1) to acknowledge the harm done by one's own side to the other side; (2) to apologize for the hurt and injustice inflicted; and (3) to make amends for past actions by acts of repentance and rectification, now and into the future." These practical guidelines for peacebuilding, believes Dalia, may be applied to the macro-level of negotiations and peacebuilding gestures between groups.

As reported in Yehezkel Landau's publication, "Healing the Holy Land; Interreligious Peacebuilding in Israel/Palestine," (*Peaceworks* 51, United States Institute of Peace), the interfaith dimension of this Jewish/Muslim initiative was expanded to include a third Abrahamic partner as well. Michail Fanous, born into a devout Christian family with deep roots in Ramale, serves on the Ramale City Council. He has been the Executive Director of Open House since its founding, with Landau acting as its International Relations Director up until more recent times. These three families have worked together to actualize the Abraham/Ibrahim promise of Genesis 12:3: "through you all the families of the earth shall be blessed."[96]

Islamic Peacebuilding

Qamar-Ul Huda is an Islamic scholar affiliated with the United States Institute of Peace, functioning as the Senior Program Officer in their Religion and Peacemaking program. His specialties lie in Islamic theology, intellectual history, ethics, and peacemaking. This section on Islamic peacebuilding will draw principally from his work and that of his colleague David Smock. Edited by Huda, *The Crescent and Dove: Peace and Conflict Resolution in Islam* is as cogent as it is prescient, as one considers the challenges, yet, opportunities, that Islamic peacemaking and peacebuilding hold for future endeavors. The following paraphrases Huda's thinking.[97]

Huda begins by clarifying for Western minds that peacemaking and conflict resolution are new mediums for Islamic religious leaders. Compounding this is the sense that such approaches are Western and, therefore, foreign to Muslim culture and values, a point not to be taken lightly. The perception is that conflict resolution is a secular approach, which does not take religious components into account. A further complication is that when religious peacemaking models are introduced, emphasis is placed on non-violence, reconciliation and dialogue, belief and practices more Christian in orientation. Most noted that training undertaken in peacemaking was helpful, yet the models and methodologies used in interfaith activities were not indigenous to their culture, an impediment to progress. Insufficient numbers of trained facilitators in religious peacemaking activities worked against such initiatives. Usually this was tied to funding issues, too few experts trained in the field, and the inability to institutionalize such strategies locally.

Integral to achieving peace through change, cites Huda, "peace trainers must select methods, approaches, and tactics that are rooted in a range of theories about how peace can be achieved in an Islamic context."[98] Encouraging religious leaders to shape approaches from their own traditions, while drawing on the larger field of conflict resolution, can enhance local ownership of peacebuilding initiatives, thus lessoning the stigma of external involvement. Huda is adamant that workshops among Islamic religious leaders must move beyond the usual discussions of "open communication, interfaith dialogue, religious pluralism, tolerating other opinions, and the basics of conflict resolution [to] such tools as skills transmission and enhancement."[99] Skills training of this nature will allow Islamic religious leaders "first, to evaluate, negotiate, and mediate the conflict, and, second, structurally change their situation."[100] Essential to implementing peacebuilding strategies among Muslim religious leaders, Huda suggests the following: "organization management, understanding the source of the conflict, mediation and negotiation, strategic planning for intervention and transformation, acquiring knowledge of all parties involved, understanding the art of engagement, and training in the complexities of building sustainable peace."[101] He cites imams/mullahs as crucial players where mediation is necessary between communities and individuals or between communities and government officials. What's more, he highlights the significance of Islamic educators who often provide social, economic, and religious support. These teachers and administrators often take on a mediation role in times of crisis, often deciding on interfaith dialogue programs or interfaith-reconciliation peacemaking projects.

Unfortunately, Islamic peacebuilding is a topic that does not get much of the spotlight due to the rhetoric and competing forces of more radical expressions of Islam, which clamor for media attention as a means of spreading their message. Once delving into the peacebuilding domain of Islam, it's quite amazing to learn of the many and varied peace initiatives there are all over the globe that simply go without notice or mention by mainstream media. David Smock and Qamar-ul Huda offer a rather impressive survey of Islamic peacebuilding in their Special Report, *Islamic Peacebuilding Since 9/11* from the United States Institute of Peace. Coalescing from a number of sources, they state that the fundamental Islamic principles of non-violence and peacebuilding include the following,

> [T]he pursuit of justice; doing good; the universality and dignity of humanity; the sacredness of human life; equality; the quest for peace (individual, interpersonal, communal, regional, and international) peacemaking via reason, knowledge and understanding; creativity; forgiveness; proper deeds and actions; responsibility; patience; collaborative actions and solidarity; inclusively; diversity; pluralism and tolerance. [102]

Referred to here are some of the Islamic initiatives and organizations highlighted in Smock and Huda's report. Interfaith dialogue to promote peace dates from the mid-1990s in a number of locales globally. Mentioned earlier, the *Bishops-Ulama Forum* in the Philippines assisted in bringing the Philippine government and the Moro National Liberation Front together in achieving a peace agreement. In Jordan, the *Jordanian Interfaith Coexistence Research Centre* (JICRC) sponsors research and dialogue to promote values of peaceful coexistence and mutual respect between different religions. Since 2007, the Muslim initiative "*A Common Word Between Us and You*" has received wide approval globally. A collaborative effort of 138 Muslim scholars, clerics and intellectuals, this document draws from Islamic teaching in declaring the common ground between Islam and Christianity. One of the more important interfaith conferences to date was initiated by King Abdullah of Saudi Arabia in 2008. Sponsored by the Saudi-based *World Muslim League*, this Madrid-based conference drew religious scholars from Sunni and Shiite Muslim traditions, Jews, Christians, Hindus, Buddhists and Shintoists. Again, the *Centre for Religious Dialogue* in post-war Bosnia regularly sponsors Muslim-Christian dialogue as a means to ease the lingering tensions of the open conflict of former times across ethno-religious lines. As a Muslim non-governmental organization, the *Wajir Peace and Development Committee* in Kenya continues to support community infrastructure and educational development. During Kenya's recent spate of violence, arms smuggling displacement and kidnappings, this NGO spearheaded the formation of the *Women for Peace Nonviolent Movement*, an interfaith and interethnic group working for peace.

In Thailand, the *Asian Muslim Action Network* brings together Muslim scholars and peacemakers focusing on human rights, ethnic and religious intolerance, peace education, globalization, and youth leadership training. They offer a one-month training program for those working in the peacebuilding domain through their School of Peace Studies and Conflict Transformation. Established in 1957 and now functioning in twenty-five countries, the *Aga Khan Development Network* (*AKDN*) brings relief to some of the world's poorest communities in the form of education, health, and rural and economic development. *AKDN* is a Muslim organization of the Ismaili, a Shiite sect. Islamic and non-Islamic communities alike have benefited from their advanced approach to microfinance, first-class hospitals, and extensive housing projects.

Buddhist Peacebuilding

Sarvodaya Shramadana Movement: This is a peacebuilding movement in Sri Lanka rooted in the Buddhist and Gandhian philosophical tenets and traditions. Seminal to these is the belief that everything is interconnected and the interdependence of all that exists carries with it the sense that "suffering of others is like one's own and the violence committed by others is like the violence one commits oneself . . . one's inner peace and peace of mind contribute to outer peace."[103] As such, conflict results from a self-centered understanding of one's world, which, in turn, alters understanding, feelings and relationships, precipitating confusion and conflict with reality. Buddhist approaches offer ways and means of coping with conflict by changing psycho-spiritual processes. Key to such change is meditation as it unlocks meaning-building mechanisms within those caught in the cycle of conflict.[104]

Reaching back fifty years, the *Sarvodaya Shramadana Movement* networks throughout more than 15,000 villages with an emphasis on comprehensive and nonviolent social transformation. The movement's activities include "peacebuilding, conflict resolution, appropriate technology and programmes for children at risk, elders and those with disabilities all the while emphasizing a holistic approach to social mobilization through empowerment of people beyond mere economic development."[105] As a religious movement dedicated to precluding and mitigating conflict, much attention is given to the "common people," identifying the importance of personal relationships that take into account the cultural and spiritual life of individuals and communities. This is made tangible "by build[ing] around their lives certain symbols, customs, beliefs and superstitions, human feelings, simple household economies, informal social and economic formations and a whole range of religious practices."[106] Addressing basic human needs is a central tenet to creating harmony among the people: a clean environment inclusive of access to potable water, clothing, food, housing, health care, energy requirements, education, communication facilities, and a focus on cultural and spiritual needs. Leadership inspires communities to cultivate integrity and solidarity among their people by developing self-sustaining efforts irrespective of caste, religion, race or party-political considerations.

Interfaith Peacebuilding (Christian/Muslim)

The Interfaith Mediation Centre in Nigeria: Imam Muhammad Ashafa and Pastor James Wuye are Nigerians from nearby communities in the Kaduna district of northern Nigeria. Former leaders in the ethnic and religious conflicts of opposing, armed militias that ravaged their region in the 1990's, they were both dedicated to defending their respective communities. Both of these men have experienced great loss: Pastor James lost his hand and Imam Ashafa's spiritual mentor and two close relatives were killed. These two religious leaders have had an impact worldwide since laying down their arms and embracing forgiveness. They presently are co-directors of the Muslim-Christian Interfaith Mediation Centre located in their hometown. Together they are leading peacebuilding initiatives across Nigeria and, most recently, in conflict stricken areas of Kenya. Their faith-based organization is yet another example of a grass roots initiative to rebuild communities torn apart by conflict—a message of hope for the world from an unexpected quarter. Their acclaim has led to sharing their story in some of the western world's greatest capitals: London, Washington, Ottawa, and others.

The *Mindanao Peacebuilding Institute*[107] (MPI) in the Philippines is another current account of interfaith peacebuilding. Documenting their work, Maryann Cusimano Love of the Catholic University of America currently researches developments that exemplify a convergence of military members, religious leaders, and NGO peacebuilding efforts. MPI has facilitated the coming together of the *Roman Catholic Bishops of Mindanao* and leading members of the *Muslim Ulama League of the Philippines* in interfaith dialogue. Leaders within the Philippine military at the general and flag officer level have undergone training in peacebuilding and, with the assistance of MPI, have created a peacebuilding program for the Forces at large known as "Culture of Peace." Filipino military chaplains are now receiving the same formation. In 2007 the Bishops-Ulama Mindanao Week of Peace was held, centering on "The Soldier as Peacebuilder" as the central theme. Implicated in this initiative was the Philippine army including BGen. Ferrer and his soldiers' experience of peacebuilding. Underscoring the efficacy of such efforts within communities, BGen. Soria states,

> I have seen how my learning's from Mindanao Peacebuilding Institute worked effectively in trying to settle disputes among feuding Muslim clans. At first getting families together who are practically at war against each other was quite difficult, particularly when blood has already been spilt. Under such circumstances the animosity has already made the conflict a protracted one of "rido" or vengeance. It must be considered always that elders and other respected key leaders in the community have important roles to play. In all aspects, respectful dialogue plays a crucial role in clarifying issues attendant to the conflict, leading the conflicted parties in dialogue using non-violent communication skills to arrive at a non-violent solution to the conflict. The Catholic Relief Services/Mindanao Peacebuilding Institute training sets the concrete guidelines and practical roadmaps to engage the communities, parties in conflict, and the influential persons in arriving at a peaceful solution to "rido."[108]

MPI is a collaborative endeavor of the Catholic Relief Services, the Mennonite Central Committee and the Catholic Agency for Overseas Development, combining efforts and resources to bring together peacebuilders and practitioners from forty countries. "The intensive training in areas such as religious peacebuilding, conflict transformation, community-based peacebuilding and other themes increases people's skills, drawing on the shared knowledge of both the participants and the facilitators. At the heart of the learning and sharing, the MPI builds upon people's commitment and strengthens their capacity, as well as that of their organizations, to build a more peaceful and just world."[109] Mennonite peacebuilder, John Paul Lederach of the Kroc Institute at the University of Notre Dame, Indiana, is heavily invested in the training as well.

Informative to this study, the MPI initiative involves the armed forces of the Philippines—the Filipino army in particular. Indigenous Roman Catholic Bishops and Muslim Imams have joined together in the collaborative activity of training armed forces personnel, inclusive of chaplains, in hands-on conflict resolution/transformation skills to assist in resolving longstanding conflict among Muslim groups—an interfaith initiative. The discussion soon to be engaged in has as its central thrust the role of chaplains facilitating reconciling endeavors among such communities.

In preparation for the coming deliberation on the strategic peacebuilding of chaplains among religious communities in conflict and post-conflict environments, this chapter has examined the complexity and oft ambivalence of religion. Considered was the misuse of religion in inspiring individuals and groups to violence, yet, when lived out authentically, its capacity to stir *others* to reach across ethnic boundaries to those desirous of transcending conflict, at times, inclusive of the *enemy other*. Further to this study, religious extremism was acknowledged as a reality exacerbating contemporary conflict, but more importantly, attention was given to discerning some of the possible reasons behind such contradictory behavior. Social categorization and boundary development were deemed contributing factors to the range of religious experience feeding into the overt behaviors performed in the name of religion—good, bad or indifferent. Finally, the discussion broached the emerging domain of religious peacebuilding among conflicting groups where religiously motivated violence is a dynamic of the presenting hostilities. Emphasizing the poignancy of such approaches, a number of examples of religious peacebuilding organizations were drawn from Christian, Jewish, Muslim, and Buddhist faith traditions inclusive of interfaith projects globally. As integral as external actors are to cultivating and nurturing the shoots of peace that break through the hard crust of conflict, local and regional indigenous actors are the pivotal players to sustaining the strategic initiatives of religious peacebuilding.

In theatres of operation, an overture by a military chaplain to local/regional religious leaders of indigenous populations may be framed as civic engagement. As such, Religious Leader Engagement becomes a means of facilitating a number of activities potentially aiding disparate religious communities engulfed in the larger conflicts of their respective identity groups. One consideration, among many, is the acknowledgment that the greater preponderance of deploying chaplains are from Western nations and, at this juncture in time, are in need of a more in-depth understanding of indigenous populations and the group dynamics that transpire amid these often divergent communities.

Keeping in mind the preceding discussion, the next chapter will introduce the role of Religious Leader Engagement (RLE) for operational chaplains. As a form of strategic peacebuilding, RLE becomes a means of engaging religious leaders and their communities in dialogue and collaborative activities. Initiatives of this nature build networks and establish partnerships among community leadership of large segments of local populations—not always an easy proposition for interagency (Whole of Government) entities who are often viewed as 'secularists' by faith group leaders in more theocratic societies. Where cleavages persist along ethno-religious boundaries, civic engagement (agency) of this nature may be seen as *instrumental* reconciliation, an approach worthy of consideration where conflict may be ongoing or in situations of post-conflict reconstruction.

NOTES

1. Katrien Hertog, *The Complex Reality of Religious Peacebuilding: Conceptual Contributions and Critical Analysis* (Lanham, Maryland: Lexington Books, 2010), 18–19.
2. Marc Gopin, *Between Eden and Armageddon: The Future of World Religions, Violence, and Peacemaking* (New York: Oxford University Press, 2000), 126–127. The term *mimetic* is interjected is here to reinforce Gopin's reference to the cyclic nature of violence. See the explanation of *mimesis* as a phenomenon of violence discussed in chapter 2.
3. Hertog, 2010, 19.
4. Hertog, 2010, 75.
5. Yehezkel Landau, "Healing the Holy Land," *Peaceworks* No. 51 (Washington, D.C.: United States Institute of Peace, 2003), 11.
6. R. Scott Appleby, *The Ambivalence of the Sacred: Religion, Violence, and Reconciliation* (Lanham, Maryland: Rowman & Littlefield, 2000), 3.
7. Donald A. Horowitz, *Ethnic Groups in Conflict* (Berkeley: University of California Press, 1985), 50 (italics mine).
8. Appleby, 2000, 3.
9. See Petito Fabio and Pavlos Hatzopoulos (eds). *Religion in International Relations: The Return from Exile* (New York: Palgrave Macmillan, 2003) cited in Megan Shore, *Religion and Conflict Resolution: Christianity and South Africa's Truth and Reconciliation Commission* (Surrey, England and Burlington, VT: Ashgate, 2009), 23.
10. Hertog, 2010, 7.
11. See Liora Danan and Alice Hunt, *Mixed Blessings: U.S. Government and Engagement with Religion in Conflict Prone Settings* (Washington, DC: Centre for Strategic and International Studies, 2007), http://csis.org/publication/mixed-blessings; USAID, *Religion, Conflict & Peacebuilding: An Introductory Programming Guide.* *http://12.238.75.62/search?q= Religion%2C+Conflict+%26++Peacebuilding&btnG=Search&entqr=0&ud=1&sort= date%3AD%3AL%3Ad1&output=xml_no_dtd&oe=UTF-8&ie=UTF-8&client=default_ frontend&proxystylesheet=default_frontend&site=lpa_collection*; R. Scott Appleby and Richard Cizik, Engaging *Religious Communities Abroad: A New Imperative for U.S. Foreign Policy* (Chicago: The Chicago Council on Global Affairs, 2010), http://www.thechicagocouncil.org/Files/Studies_Publications/TaskForcesandStudies/Religion_2010.aspx.
12. David Smock, *Religion in World Affairs: Its Role in Conflict and Peace*, Special Report 101(Washington, D.C.: Unites States Institute of Peace, 2008), 3.

13. Claire Mitchell, *Religion, Identity and Politics in Northern Ireland* (Aldershot, England & Burlington, VT: Ashgate 2006), 12.

14. Mitchell, 2006, 15.

15. Mitchell, 2005, 15.

16. Mitchell, 2006, 16.

17. Mitchell, 2006, 96. See R. Samuel and P. Thompson, *The Myths We Live By* (London: Routledge, 1990).

18. Vamik Volkan, *Blood Lines: From Ethnic Pride to Ethnic Terrorism*, (Boulder, CO: Westview Press, 1997), 43-44.

19. Mitchell, 2006, 91. See G. Davie, *Religion in Modern Europe: A memory mutates* (Oxford: Oxford University Press, 2000).

20. Mitchell, 2006, 92. See G. Davie *Religion in Britain since 1945: Believe without belonging* (Oxford: Blackwell, 1994).

21. Mitchell, 2006, 92.

22. "UK International Priorities: A Strategy for the FCO," United Kingdom, Foreign and Commonwealth Office, Crown Copyright, December 2003, 15 cited in Bernard Party, M. P. Chair, *Exploring Canada's Relations with the Countries of the Muslim World* (Report of the Standing Committee on Foreign Affairs and International Trade: Ottawa, Canada, 2004), 2.

23. Bruce Hoffman, *Inside Terrorism: Revised and Expanded Edition* (New York: Columbia University Press, 2006), 82.

24. Hoffman, 2006, 86.

25. Chaplains Workshop on Religion, Conflict and Peace at the Pentagon, hosted by Georgetown University's Berkley Center for Religion, Peace & World Affairs and National Defense University's Institute for National Security, Ethics and Leadership, Washington, D.C., 24-25 March 2010.

26. Mary Kaldor, *New and Cold Wars: Organized Violence in a Global Era*, 2nd Edition, Introduction (Stanford, California: Stanford University Press, 2006), 8-9.

27. Peter Gizewski and LCol Michael Rostek, "Toward A Comprehensive Approach To CF Operations: The Land Force JIMP Concept" in *Defence R&D Canada: Centre for Operational Research and Analysis*, DRCD CORA TM 2007-60, September 2007, 5.

28. Hertog, 2010, 10-11.

29. R. Scott Appleby and Richard Cizik, *Engaging Religious Communities Abroad: A New Imperative for U.S. Foreign Policy* (Chicago: The Chicago Council on Global Affairs, 2010), 17.

30. Pauletta Otis, "Religion and War in the Twenty-first Century," in *Religion and Security: The New Nexus in International Relations*, eds. R. A. Seiple & D. R. Hoover (Lanham, Maryland: Rowan and Littlefield Publishers, 2004), 20; Appleby adds, "Rather than break down barriers, in short, religion often fortifies them...Constructed as inseparable from ethnic and linguistic traits, religion in such settings lends them a transcendent depth and dignity. Extremists thus invoke religion to legitimate discrimination and violence against groups of a different race or language." R. Scott Appleby, *The Ambivalence of the Sacred: Religion, Violence, and Reconciliation* (Lanham, Maryland: Rowman & Littlefield, 2000), 62.

31. Marc Gopin, *To Make the Earth Whole: The Art of Citizen Diplomacy in an Age of Religious Militancy* (Lanham, Maryland: Rowan and Littlefield Publishers, 2009), 37-38.

32. Appleby, 2000, 63.

33. Mario Apostolov, *Religious Minorities, Nation States and Security: Five Cases from the Balkans and Eastern Mediterranean* (Aldershot, Hampshire, England: Ashgate Publishing Ltd., 2001), 13

34. Hoffman, 2006, 83.

35. Appleby, 2000, 60.

36. Srdjan Vrcan, "Religious Factors in the War in Bosnia-Herzegovina" in *Religion and the War in Bosnia*, ed. Paul Mojzes (Atlanta, Georgia: Scholars Press, 1998), 124.

37. Landau, 2003, 11.

38. Appleby, 2000, 62.

39. Mark Juergensmeyer, *Terror in the Mind of God* (Berkeley, Los Angeles, London: University of California Press, 2000), 146, 216.

40. Juergensmeyer, 2000, 217.

41. Marc Gopin, *Between Eden and Armageddon: The Future of World Religions, Violence and Peacemaking*, (New York: Oxford University Press, 2000) 58-59.

42. Isak Svensson, "Fighting with Faith: Religion and Conflict Resolution in Civil Wars," *Journal of Conflict Resolution*, 2007 51: 932-934 cited in Gerard Powers, "Religion and Peacebuilding" in *Strategies of Peace: Transforming Conflict in a Violent World*, eds. Daniel Philpot and Gerard Powers (New York: Oxford University Press, 2010), 319.

43. Powers states, "Only 8 of 49 militant sects (out of 233 communal groups) in the early 1990's were defined solely or mainly by their religious beliefs. Ted Robert Gurr, *Minorities at Risk: A Global View of Enthnopolitical Conflicts* (Washington, D.C.: United States Institute of Peace, 1993), p. 317." Powers, 2010, 349 (Note 14).

44. Bruce Hoffman's research has already been cited regarding the rise of religiously inspired terrorist groups, findings that Daniel Philpot draws on in his analysis. In his Endnotes, Powers adds, "Today, based on the Terrorism Knowledge Base, Philpot finds that 95 of 262 (36 percent) of known terrorists groups are identifiably religious. The knowledge base is presented by the National Memorial Institute for Prevention of Terrorism and can be found at http://www.tkb.org/Home.jsp. 'Explaining the Political Ambivalence of Religion,' *American Political Science Review* 101 (August 2007): 520."

45. Monica Duffy Toft, 'Getting Religion: The Puzzling Case of Islam and Civil War,' *International Security 3* (Spring 2007), 116."

46. Duffy Toft, 2007, 116.

47. Powers, 2010, 320.

48. Powers, 2010, 320.

49. Powers, 2010, 320.

50. Powers, 2010, 321.

51. David Little, *Peacemakers in Action: Profiles of Religion in Conflict Resolution* (New York: Cambridge University Press, 2007), 429

52. Appleby, 2000, 77.

53. Appleby, 2000, 77.

54. Appleby, 2000, 68–69.

55. Appleby, 2000, 77.

56. Appleby, 2000, 77.

57. Karen Armstrong, *The Battle For God* (New York: Ballantine Publishing Group, 2000), 322.

58. For continuity sake, the term "peacebuilder" will be substituted for Little's usage of "peacemaker," terms often employed interchangeably.

59. Little, 2007, 429–437.

60. Little, 2007, 433.

61. Vern Neufeld Redekop, *From Violence to Blessing: How an Understanding of Deep-rooted Conflict Can Open Paths to Reconciliation* (Toronto: Novalis, 2002), 136.

62. Barry Rubin, "Religion and Internal Affairs," in *Religion, the Missing Dimension of Statecraft*, eds. Douglas Johnston and Cynthia Sampson (New York: Oxford University Press, 1994), 22. Rubin cites Africa, the Middle East and Asia in particular where religion continues to reverberate while for many countries national identity is still largely a function of religious affiliation. In the Middle East "one's community is either Sunni or Shiite Muslim, Alawite, Druze, Christian (Roman Catholic, Maronite, Copt, Eastern Orthodox, or Greek Catholic), or Jewish." There is the Islamic revolution in Iran, Lebanon's civil war with its religious factions, Pakistan's Islamic focus, not to mention the Islamic resurgence in many of the breakaway states of the former USSR in eastern Asia. Religion has become a rallying point in Sudan, India, Malaysia, Indonesia, and elsewhere. One cannot forget the religious cleavages of Northern Ireland nor the former Yugoslavia that have contributed to the exacerbation of conflict. See Rubin's entire article for further elaboration, 20–34.

63. Rubin, 1994, 22.

64. Rubin, 1994, 23.

65. Rubin, 1994, 24.

66. Cynthia Sampson, "Religion and Peacebuilding," in *Peacemaking in International Conflict*, eds. I. William Zartman and J. Lewis Rasmussen (Washington, D.C.: United States Institute of Peace, 1997), 275.

67. Judy Carter and Gordon S. Smith, "Religious Peacebuilding" in *Religion and Peacebuilding*, eds. Howard Coward and Gordon S. Smith (Albany, New York: State University of New York Press, 2004), 280.

68. Robert Schreiter, "The Theology of Reconciliation and Peacemaking for Mission," in *Mission—Violence and Reconciliation*, eds., H. Mellor & T. Yates (Sheffield, 2004), 25 cited in *Peace and Reconciliation: In Search of Shared Identity,* eds. Sebastian C. H. Kim, Pauline Kollontai and Greg Hoyland (Hampshire, England and Burlington, VT: 2008), 37.

69. Carter and Gordon, 2004, 280.

70. Carter and Gordon, 2004, 280.

71. Cynthia Sampson, 1997, 275.

72. Andrea Bartoli, Christianity and Peace in Howard Coward and Gordon S. Smith eds., *Religion and Peacebuilding* (Albany, New York: State University of New York Press, 2004), 158.

73. Kofi A. Annan, *Prevention of Armed Conflict: Report of the Secretary* General, A/55/985-S/2001/574, United Nations General Assembly, Fifty-fifth Session, 2001, Agenda Item 10, para 147. http://www.reliefweb.int/library/documents/2001/un-conflprev-07jun.htm

74. Appleby, 2000, 61.

75. Israel Selvanayagam, "Truth and Reconciliation: An Interfaith Perspective from India," in *Peace and Reconciliation: In Search of Shared Identity,* eds. Sebastian C. H. Kim, Pauline Kollontai and Greg Hoyland (Hampshire, England and Burlington, VT: 2008), 44.

76. Little, 2007, 5–9.

77. John Paul Lederach and R. Scott Appleby, "Strategic Peacebuilding: An Overview" in *Strategies of Peace: Transforming Conflict in a Violent World*, eds. Daniel Philpot and Gerard Powers (New York: Oxford University Press, 2010), 23.

78. M. J. Zuckerman, "Can 'Unofficial Talks Avert Disaster? Defining Track II: Meet Joseph Montville" in *The Carnegie Reporter*, Vol 3. No 3, 2005. http://carnegie.org/publications/carnegie-reporter/single/view/article/item/136/, accessed 31 Jan 2001.

79. Multi-track diplomacy is a term coined by Louise Diamond referring to an approach to peacebuilding "involving as many different tracks as possible when implementing projects [designed to promote conflict transformation]. This way, even when doing social peacebuilding work, [people are involved] from government, media, or other social institutions, which provide a link between the structural peacebuilding and political peacebuilding processes. Just as conflict transformation and peacebuilding are understood in terms of systems change, multi-track diplomacy takes a systems approach to understanding the nature of international peacebuilding." Together, Diamond and Ambassador John Macdonald expanded on what Joseph Montville termed Track II diplomacy to include the following domains: conflict resolution professionals, business, private citizens, the media, religion, activism; research, training, and education; and philanthropy, or the funding community. See The Institute for Multi-Track Diplomacy, http://www.imtd.org/publications/occasional-papers/building-peace-and-transforming-conflict-multi-track-diplomacy-in-practice/, accessed 16 Mar. 2012. See also Louise Diamond and John MacDonald, *Multi-track Diplomacy: A Systems Approach to Peacebuilding* (West Hartford, Connecticut: Kumarian Press, 1996).

80. I. William Zartman, "Toward the Resolution of International Conflicts" in *Peacemaking in International Conflict: Methods & Techniques*, eds. I. William Zartman and J. Lewis Rasmussen, (Washington, D.C.: United States Institute of Peace Press, 1997), 14.

81. Douglas Johnston, "Introduction: Beyond Power Politics" in *Religion, the Missing Dimension of Statecraft*, eds. Douglas Johnston and Cynthia Sampson (New York: Oxford University Press, 1994), 4.

82. Johnston, 1994, 4.

83. Hertog, 2010, Introduction, xv.

84. Hertog, 2010, Introduction, xv.

85. The Foundation for Relief and Reconciliation in the Middle East, http://frrme.convio.net/site/PageServer?pagename=homepage, accessed 28 Feb 2011.

86. Civil Courage Prize, http://www.civilcourageprize.org/honoree-2010.htm, accessed 28 Feb 2011.

87. Barbara Becker, 2010. Canon Andrew White Wins 11th Annual Civil Courage Prize. http://www.religionwriters.com/canon-andrew-white-wins-11th-annual-civil-courage-prize, accessed 28 Oct 2010.

88. Community of Sant'Egidio and Peace, http://www.santegidio.org/en/pace/documenti.htm>, accessed 20 Oct 2010.

89. War, Mother of All Poverty: Mozambique, http://www.santegidio.org/en/pace/pace3.htm>, accessed 20 Oct 2010.

90. Curriculum Vitae of Dr. Andrea Bartoli, Drucie French Cumbie Chair of Conflict Analysis and Resolution and Dean of the School for Conflict Analysis and Resolution, George Mason University, Arlington, Virginia, p. 3.

91. Hertog, 2010, 91.

92. John Paul Lederach, Reina Neufeldt and Hal Culbertson, *Reflective Peacebuilding: A Planning, Monitoring, and Learning Toolkit* (Notre Dame, IN and Bangkok, Thailand: Kroc Institute for Peace Studies and Catholic Relief Services, East Asia Regional Office, 2007), 17.

93. Christopher Mitchell, "Mennonite Approaches to Peace and Conflict Resolution," in *From the Ground Up: Mennonite Contributions to International Peacebuilding*, eds. Cynthia Sampson and John Paul Lederach (New York: Oxford University Press, 2000), 224.

94. Yehezkel Landau, "Peacebuilding in Israel/Palestine: A 25-Year Retrospective," in *Waging Peace: A Two-Part Discussion of Religion-Based Peacemaking*, Washington National Cathedral, November 2003, 11-14. See also, Oz VeShalom-Netivot Shalom, Objectives and Principles, http://www.netivot-shalom.org.il/, accessed 12 Apr 11; About the Movement, http://www.netivot-shalom.org.il/, accessed 12 Apr 11.

95. Landau, 2003, 11–14.

96. Yehezkel Landau, "Healing the Holy Land," *Peaceworks* No. 51 (Washington, D.C.: United States Institute of Peace, 2003), 42.

97. Qamar-ul Huda, "Enhancing Skills and Capacity Building in Islamic Peacemaking" in *Crescent and Dove: Peace and Conflict Resolution in Islam*, ed. Qamar-ul Huda (Washington: United States Institute of Peace, 2010), 213-14,

98. Huda, 2010, 218.

99. Huda, 2010, 220.

100. Huda, 2010, 220.

101. Huda, 2010, 220.

102. David Smock and Qamar-ul Huda, *Islamic Peacebuilding Since 9/11*, Special Report 218, (Washington, D.C.: United States Institute of Peace, 2009), 8. See also *Muslim Peacebuilding Actors in the Balkans, Horn of Africa and the Great Lakes Regions*, Salam" Institute for Peace and Justice, Washington, D.C. www.salaminstitute.org.

103. Hertog, 2010, 93.

104. Hertog, 2010, 93–94. These concepts are gleaned from John A. McConnell, *Mindful Meditation: A Handbook for Buddhist Peacemakers*. Thailand: Buddhist Research Institute & Mahachula Buddhist University, 1995.

105. Sarvodaya Shramadana Movement, http://www.savodaya.org/about, accessed 11 April 2011.

106. See http://www.sarvodaya.org/about/philosophy/collected-works-vol-2/common-man, accessed 11 April 2011.

107. Mindanao Peacebuilding Institute, http://www.internationalpeaceandconflict.org/forum/topics/mindanao-peacebuilding, accessed 28 Sept 2010.

108. Maryann Cusimano Love, 2010. Partnering for Peace in the Philippines: Military and Religious Engagement. A non-published paper presented at the Chaplains Workshop on Religion, Conflict and Peace at the Pentagon, hosted by Georgetown University's Berkley Center for Religion, Peace & World Affairs and National Defense University's Institute for National Security, Ethics and Leadership, Washington, D.C., 24–25 March 2010.

109. Mindanao Peacebuilding Institute, http://www.internationalpeaceandconflict.org/forum/topics/mindanao-peacebuilding>, accessed 28 Sept 2010.

Chapter Four

Religious Leader Engagement

An Emerging Role for Operational Chaplains

The previous discussion focused on the reality of today's religious extremism as a factor of conflict and the role of religious peacebuilding as a possible counter to the spread of such radically inspired violence. As a prelude to Religious Leader Engagement (RLE), a number of examples of religious peacebuilding organizations from the main faith traditions were provided as a means of acquainting the reader with this associated approach to conflict resolution—an aspect of multi-track diplomacy.[1]

The role of chaplains engaging the leaders of religious communities is not a new phenomenon in operational environments. Encounters of this nature have occurred over the decades wherever chaplains have deployed with troops, regardless of nationality. In one form or another, RLE has been a successful aspect of civic engagement in active conflict zones, in peace support operations, with its emphasis on reconstruction and stabilization, and in post-conflict environments where brokered cease-fires led to mission mandates enforcing fledgling peace agreements between former belligerents. Among academics committed to examining inter-group conflict, much emphasis is placed on post-conflict reconstruction, an essential element to achieving sustainable peace. These are valid concerns given the tendency for intervening nations in theaters of operation to extract their forces as soon as practicably possible. The cessation of overt conflict is by no means an indication that tensions between the principals have been resolved. Simmering divisions often undermine progress made. Sustaining stability a nation has sweeping implications on a number of fronts, presently the focus of the

Comprehensive Approach introduced in the introductory chapter (Ch. 1, Introduction, The Comprehensive Approach). Weight must be continually placed on post-conflict reconstruction as a means of solidifying gains made and rebuilding societies.

Having served for more than two decades in uniform, this author has witnessed a shift from more traditional forms of conflict reminiscent of the cold war era to what was earlier identified as *new wars* or *wars amongst the people*: *inter*state warfare as compared to that of *intra*state. Today's reality is such that *new wars* have ushered in changes in how conflict and violence manifests. Old paradigms have been challenged as the international community has struggled to come to terms with these *new wars*.[2] Much of the inspiration for this writing finds its origin in the operational experience of Bosnia-Herzegovina, 1993 and Afghanistan, 2006, both countries in the throes of open conflict at the time. The shaping of RLE has been a shared journey of a number of military chaplaincies, Canada and the United States being paramount among them. Bearing this in mind, any stressing of RLE in conflict situations in the following is not intended to lessen the saliency of efforts in post-conflict environments, as engagement among the religious communities of societies endeavoring to leave conflict behind is critical to achieving sustainable peace. Sadly, in more recent times, bringing convulsing societies to the post-conflict stage has been an arduous and elusive enterprise. Unfortunately, leaving a country once the fighting is over, yet, before the peace is truly won, has been more often than not the case.

Reflecting further on the contemporary context, societal implosion due to the stressors of intergroup conflict is not uncommon. A number of countries continue to strain under the burden of protracted insurgencies committed to undermining any form of centralized democratic governance—a significant challenge to Western nations endeavoring to stabilize these nascent democracies. Creating an environment of interdependence among such conflicting groups is considered to be a precursor to reconciliation. Increasingly, indigenous leaders ascribing to more tolerant and inclusive attitudes are viewed as partners in the peace process owing to their pervasive influence within their own communities and their ability to reach out to their like-minded counterparts across ethnic and religious lines. This is especially relevant in the face of rising religious militancy.

More specifically, this chapter will introduce the Operational Ministry of chaplains, both internal to the troops and external among the religious communities of indigenous populations. A precursor to RLE, Religious Area Analysis will be discussed as an effective means of analyzing the religious terrain of an Area of Operations (AO) and advising command of its salient features. RLE will be presented in full detail, articulating its functionality within the military context and principal features—encounter and collaborative activities leading to enhanced trust and cooperation among estranged communities. Albeit, the emphasis here will focus more on chaplains engaging religious leaders at various levels, RLE is not limited to the religious domain. Regardless of whom the chaplain engages—religious or other community leaders—all encounters are defined as RLE by virtue of the chaplain's involvement.

ADMONITIONS FROM OTHERS

The Chicago Council on Global Affairs Task Force is a leading independent, nonpartisan organization committed to a continuing discourse on global issues pertaining to policy formation, leadership dialogue and public learning.[3] Pivotal to their deliberations is the recognition that religious communities globally are central to developing assistance, promoting human rights, caring for the environment and pursuing peace in troubled parts of the world.[4] Given the likelihood of radical religious groups continuing as agitators in future conflict, the Task Force acknowledges the unique contribution of faith group leaders and their communities as advocates of a more proactive approach to lessening such adverse effects. These leaders represent hundreds of millions of people throughout the world whose identities are defined by religion. Their most recent publication, *Engaging Religious Communities Abroad: A New Imperative for U.S. Foreign Policy* (2010), calls for authentic engagement with the *tolerant religious voice* as a means of advancing stability and development, an effective approach to countering the strengthening influence of religious extremism. They propose the following,

> The task force believes that the best way to counter religious extremism is through more authentic engagement with religion and religious communities. Authentic engagement is the most effective way to support and further empower the progressive and benevolent elements within societies and cultures shaped by religions. It entails engaging religious communities on their own terms, listening carefully to their concerns and fears, and entering into substantive dialogue about how to realize their legitimate aspirations.[5]

Identifying the *tolerant voice* among religious leaders is key to initiating such dialogue, establishing networks, and creating partnerships. These are faith group leaders—community leaders—desirous of moving beyond conflict, thus transcending the presenting hostilities and intransigence that continue to pit their respective identity groups against each other. Known as "middle-range actors,"[6] religious leaders enjoy the confidence of the grassroots while moving freely at the higher levels of leadership within their own communities without feeling constricted by strictures that often dictate decision-making processes for its political leaders.[7] Paraphrasing John Paul Lederach further, by virtue of their affinity with the people, faith group leaders are familiar with the daily lives and circumstances of those at the grassroots, yet are not hampered by survival needs themselves. Nor are those of the tolerant voice prone to seeking positions of power—political or military. Key to their influence are the kinds of relationships they develop within the community: professional, institutional, formal or simply friendships and acquaintances they have made due to their role in the public realm. Of greater consequence to these deliberations, as *middle range actors* (see *The Tolerant Voice* in this chapter), local religious leaders often have established ties with their counterparts across the lines of conflict. They are cognizant of those of kindred spirit—a foundation upon which to build.[8] Echoing Lederach, Rabbi Marc Gopin relates, "Religious moderates and peacebuilders are the ones who can counteract the corrosive effects of religious militancy because they have the capacity to entice religious people into the larger community of humanity."[9]

In addition to the above, a growing number of secular organizations recognize the potential role for religious actors in the resolving of conflict. Among them is the Washington-based think tank, the Centre for Strategic and International Studies (CSIS). Their admonition is to engage a broader range of leaders in conflict-prone parts of the world, specifically identifying religious leaders and faith-based groups as potential partners integral to resolving contemporary conflict where the manipulation of religious fervor has become a factor.

> Programs should seek a fuller range of religious representatives abroad and engage with less traditional—and possibly less welcoming—religious leaders and audiences, recognizing not only "religious moderates" but also "religious conservatives" as opinion leaders and possible drivers of change . . . government should enable increased partnerships with previously excluded faith-based groups abroad, actively pursuing them as partners in facilitating inter- and intra-faith dialogue.[10]

The United States Agency for International Development (USAID) echoes similar sentiments. The Toolkit (2010), *Religion, Conflict & Peacebuilding: An Introductory Program Guide*, states, "These actors play an important role in many societies as a key stakeholder in communities where they are often trusted more by individuals than secular government actors . . . increase[ing] the likelihood of expanding support for peace."[11] Given the right conditions and support, chaplains may facilitate encounter among the religious leaders of estranged communities, leading to altered perspectives and the re-*humanizing* of the other.

AN EXPANDING HERMENEUTIC OF PEACE FOR CHAPLAINS

Religious traditions constantly face new questions and contextual challenges summoning ardent reflection with respect to sacred texts and belief, leading to new self-understanding and orientation toward the world in which people live. Each religious community remakes itself in light of their present circumstances, something that continues from one generation to the next. In the extreme, the vagaries of war influence such *hermeneutical* processes for faith groups confronted with its banality and the evil it unleashes on all concerned, regardless of loyalties. As such, groups look to their central stories, institutions, traditions, texts, rituals, precepts and values in a quest to grasp what it means to be a community of faith confronted with situations of extreme violence and how best to live out that faith in light of such realities. R. Scott Appleby notes, "the legal, theological and spiritual resources of a religious tradition . . . are relevant only to the extent that they shape religion as it is lived on the ground, where text and tradition transform, and are transformed by, the concrete realities of daily life."[12] It behooves religious leaders, scholars and theologians to "seek the good between the inherited wisdom and the specific contemporary situation."[13]

As a multifaith community, military chaplaincy represents numerous religious traditions, each with its own understanding and interpretation of belief based upon the sacred texts and teachings of their particular tradition. At the core of this interfaith collaboration resides a *hermeneutics of peace* that recognizes peace and justice as a sacred priority by peaceable means where possible.[14] Religious leaders in uniform, these men and women of faith often witness the horrific acts of violence and its effects known to conflict and post-conflict environments, manifest in the tragic loss of life and livelihood, often accompanied by the staggering movements of refugees in search of safety. It is circumstances in time and space such as these that challenge one's belief and time-honored traditions, precipitating new self-understandings of chaplaincy. Demonstrative of this expanding *hermeneutics of peace* is the *impulse* among chaplains to draw on the understanding, imagination and requisite values of their collective faith traditions to aid conflicting groups in *re-humanizing* the *other*. *Hermeneutically*, this *impulse* to engage indigenous populations is visible in its many forms among those struggling to rebuild their lives either in the midst of conflict or in its wake. From the humanitarian assistance of earlier times—something that continues today—to building relations with the religious *other(s)* through dialogue—thus spanning the divide of estranged communities (*encounter*)—to the subsequent *collaborative activities* that engender trust and cooperation between estranged groups, chaplains continue to engage the religious *other* as *agents of peace*.

THE OPERATIONAL ROLE OF CHAPLAINS

Appreciating something of the role of chaplains in operations is deemed helpful preparation to a more in-depth discussion of Religious Leader Engagement. Figure 4.1 provides an overview of the diversity of ministry carried out by chaplains in operational settings globally.

The term Operational Ministry describes the overall role of chaplains in Operations: in support of the troops and among local indigenous populations. The primary purpose for a chaplain's presence with a deploying contingent is to administer the sacraments and to provide pastoral support for the troops— designated as *Internal Operational Ministry* in figure 4.1. It has always been and must continue to be the principal focus of deploying chaplains. Also depicted in the diagram is the recommended *External Operational Ministry* that sees the future role of chaplains' extended to the strategic realm of advising Commanders in terms of Religious Area Analysis (RAA) of an Area of Operations (AO). In addition, as clerics in uniform, engaging local and regional religious leaders, such civic engagement engenders trust and establishes cooperation within communities, benefiting mission mandates— the domain of Religious Leader Engagement (RLE).

Figure 4.1.   Operational Ministry of Military Chaplains. © Major S.K. Moore, PhD.

THE CHAPLAIN AS A CREDENTIALED RELIGIOUS LEADER IN OPERATIONS

Unique to chaplains is their status as religious leaders in their own right. More than any other contingent member, they share common ground with their local counterparts. As practicing spiritual leaders, chaplains understand the rigors of a religious discipline and are intimately familiar with leading faith communities, one of the main reasons why indigenous religious leaders reach out to them. Hence, due to this common bond, it is not unusual for chaplains to be sought out by local religious leaders. As spiritual leaders, chaplains are deemed *trusted* individuals—*people of the book* according to tenets of Islamic teaching. Thus, faith group leaders often look for an exchange on the spiritual plane, as that is their way of life. An added dimension to such rapport is the oft-held *perception* by indigenous leaders of the developing world that Western leaders are secularist, and, consequently, a threat to their faith and way of life. Consequently, the tendency by the religious is to avoid engaging "Westerners" be they military or civilian. Chaplains are often able to bridge to these influential communities, breaking the way for meaningful dialogue with other mission members—military or civilian.

Also of note, the chaplain's orientation is one of peace versus that of perceiving the *other* as enemy with its emphasis on maneuvering groups to advantage. The aim is to engage those religious/community leaders who are desirous of transcending conflict; those who would join together with even the *enemy other* across ethnic lines in search of ways to move beyond the divisive alienation that denies greater security for their people and undermines a brighter future for their collective youth. Noted in the upcoming Case Study Two, is Canadian Forces (CF) Muslim chaplain, Capt. Imam Suleyman Demiray, facilitated a meeting of the leading Mullahs[15] to discuss community needs with the leadership of the Kandahar Provincial Reconstruction Team (2006). Recalling the anxiety of the council, these leading religious leaders of Kandahar Province were distressed with their inability to stem the tide of their young boys streaming into the radical madrasas operating in the border districts of western Pakistan. They were hopeful that help could be found to construct madrasas where a more moderate Islam could be taught to the upcoming generation.

As credentialed clerics, the training and orientation of the chaplain better enables him/her to grasp the religious impulses of local communities that, if supported, may mitigate conflict and ameliorate relationships between alienated groups and toward international troops. Chaplains become a *safe space* for religious leaders to share their story, an important aspect of the reconciliation process. The integrity of such exchanges must be respected. Preceding the discussion on RLE an additional development in the domain of *external operational ministry* must be highlighted. Increasingly, chaplains are called upon to advise commanders on the religious terrain of an AO. Training in Religious Area Analysis is now underway in the U.S. Army Chaplaincy and has recently become a part of the Canadian Forces Chaplain Branch curriculum as well.

ADVISING COMMAND: RELIGIOUS AREA ANALYSIS[16] (RAA)

The intent of RAA in operations is to determine the basis for what people do and why they do it with respect to religion. As a capability, deploying chaplains increasingly possess the skills to accumulate and categorize information relating to the religious practices and traditions of indigenous populations within an AO. This information will be gathered from as wide a range of resources as practicably possible in the amount of time allotted prior to deployment. In a very real sense, this remains a living document once *networking* among local religious leaders and their communities becomes a reality.

Coupled with advanced theological training, analysis of this nature positions chaplains to better interpret the nuances of religious belief that often escape detection—something that could be very costly to a mission. In grasping something of the meaning and reality of the faith perspective, chaplains are more apt to appreciate how the belief system of the grassroots person may color their response to given mission initiatives, plans of action, troop movements, etc. The nature of command often necessitates sending troops into the way of harm. As such, the availability of all information pertinent to the decision-making process is critical. Advising commanders of the possible pitfalls or backlashes of given courses of action with respect to religious communities is a crucial aspect of the role of chaplains.

Chaplain Mike Hoyt, Col. (retd.) U.S. Army, tells of a situation in Iraq where orders were to secure an area that had recently been cleared of belligerents. To protect the local neighborhoods a curfew was imposed and roads were sealed off to prevent any further infiltration of insurgents. In the Commander's mind, the local communities needed to be more inaccessible, resulting in his decision to render certain streets off limits. Unfortunately, and with no malice of intent, the curfew was imposed indiscriminately without adequate consideration of the religious practices of the local people. Adding to the movement restrictions was the issue of access to water for ablutions, no longer conveniently located next to a particular mosque in question due to an explosion that disrupted water services. People were obliged to do ablutions elsewhere before attending evening prayers at the mosque, the nearest water source now in a restricted area. In imposing a curfew and movement restrictions the commander believed his security measures would improve life for the local Iraqis. In effect, he created undue hostility toward the

American presence by unwittingly withholding the essentials to their religious practice: admission to their mosque at the appointed evening prayer times and access to water for the purifying ritual of ablutions prior to prayer. The *networking* related to RAA heightened Hoyt's awareness of the present situation for the religious communities and his training as a chaplain equipped him to grasp the nuances the commander's orders held for a local community pertaining to the ritual practices of their faith—a way of life for conservative Islamic communities. Adjustments were made.

For this reason *networking* among religious communities in an AO is an integral aspect of RAA as chaplains engage faith group leaders. Engendering *trust* soon develops into the chaplain/religious leader encounter becoming a *safe space* for these community leaders to share their concerns and aspirations. RLE activities will naturally flow out of the RAA conducted by chaplains. In this sense one is built upon the other—both are necessary to the full scope of engagement among local religious communities.

As chaplains become more intentional with respect to engaging religious leaders in AOs, what were once *ad hoc* experiences of strategic peacebuilding will increasingly become the norm. Where conflict or its residual effects leaves religious leaders and their communities estranged, chaplains are finding occasion to facilitate dialogue and promote cooperation among those desirous of change—initiatives conducted under commander's authority and in his explicit intent. (For a comparison between RAA and the Intelligence Preparation of the Battlefield [IPB], see chapter 10).

KEY LEADER ENGAGEMENT (KLE)

The suggestion that the chaplain's role in Religious Leader Engagement in Operations needs further examination and development is moot. Notwithstanding, more than any other contingent member, the chaplain has a unique bond with local religious leaders. Their role as spiritual leaders offers a natural conduit to engaging faith group leaders in dialogue. Civic engagement in the form of strategic peacebuilding among religious communities holds much promise for international missions. The capacity of chaplains to build bridges into these communities holds strategic import for mission mandates.

Considering the importance of civic engagement from a strictly doctrinal perspective, National Defence (Canada) publication (08), *Land Operations*, stipulates that ". . . a wide range of capabilities and activities are required in order to influence and affect systems and actors, including the indigenous population, in order to realize operational objectives."[17] Of import here are actors within 'indigenous populations' as centers of gravity, a term defined as ". . . strengths that create effects; therefore, they are better defined in terms of people—individuals or groups—that can create effects."[18] Land Forces newly released *Counter-Insurgency Operations* manual states, "In all cases, the indigenous population is the *primary* centre of gravity because no insurgency can survive amidst the hostile terrain of an unreceptive public."[19] "Public opinion," "public will" and "strength of national purpose" are all factors of the abstract and moral perspectives of centers of gravity.[20] Reenforcing this thinking, Wilson et al. write, ". . . people and ideas are the essence of why wars are fought and for how long."[21] More poignant still to our deliberations here, Allan English illumines, "the real centre of gravity is a shared religious/ideological goal where common purpose and zealotry replace military equipment and command structures."[22] Charismatic religious leaders are identified as having the capacity to shape moral opinion in the public domain—significant centers of gravity within local populations.[23]

As a harbinger of things to come, engaging the *tolerant voice* among local religious leaders as centers of gravity segues naturally into the operational domain of Key Leader Engagement (KLE). KLE presents as an Influence Activity (IA) used at Commanders discretion. It may be defined as "the conduct of a deliberate and focused meeting with a person of significant importance in order to achieve a desired effect."[24] Religious communities within indigenous populations—and the inherent influence of their leaders among the people—are worthy of consideration. A modification of KLE, Religious Leader Engagement (RLE) stands as an enhanced capability that will prove to be of strategic import to Commanders in the field due to its contribution to creating stability. Albeit, not speaking of religious leaders in particular, Jeanne F. Hull's cogent comment reference to American KLE resonates well with the ideas presented here: "Rather than expend considerable resources attempting to take over insurgent strongholds and controlled areas by force, it would be more efficient for counterinsurgents to find means by which the host-nation and insurgent organizations can find common ground and, ultimately, reconcile with each other."[25] If today's intractable conflict is to move toward resolution, all viable levers must be applied, including religion's oft-dismissed message of peace. However, it must be stated, the prospects of RLE aligning with IA creates unease among chaplains, as such an association may potentially jeopardize the protected status of chaplains as non-combatants. (For a discussion on the notion of *intent* and the first order effects of RLE in comparison to IA see chapter 10, Influence Activities). Clear doctrinal guidance is needed to assist chaplains when engaging local religious leaders as members of KLE teams.

Established earlier as a leading authority in intractable conflict, Terrell A. Northrup elucidates further that in time eventual shifts in the perception of the *other* touches on identity. She contends, although not a panacea for change, where intractable conflict between groups persists, the possibility for improvement is increased if the dynamics in relation with the oppositional *other* occur.[26] Embryonic in today's operational environment, the vision is for tomorrow's chaplains to collaborate with their Whole of Government (interagency) partners to impact the dynamics of relation among religious communities within indigenous populations.

RELIGIOUS LEADER ENGAGEMENT (RLE)[27]

The Chicago Council on Global Affairs Task Force underscores as the core objective of religious engagement to be networking and the building of partnerships that would increase in value over the long run. Here, understanding and respect are deepened where actors may otherwise remain wary of each other, thus engendering the trust and confidence that enables the advancement of shared interests and objectives.[28] The Task Force cites as well that such cooperation among local religious leaders and their communities over the long-term may function as "shock absorbers," preventing the manipulation or abuse of religion to escalate conflict or tensions.[29]

Perhaps an imposing diagram at the outset, figure 4.2 unpacks in stages in actual presentation. For purposes here it illustrates more clearly how RLE

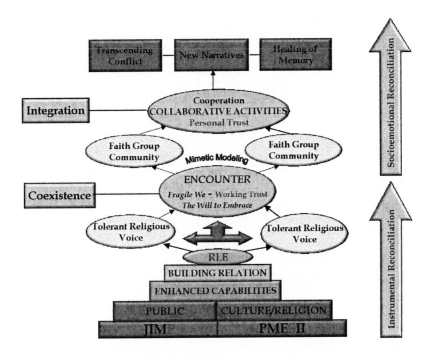

Figure 4.2.   Religious Leader Engagement. © S.K. Moore, PhD.

factors into mission mandates. In moving through the various facets of this diagram, the primary focus will be on the chaplains' role of civic engagement among religious communities as it relates to networking, partnering and peacebuilding (facilitation) where conflict or its residual effects have left communities estranged. References will be offered to present military doctrine, predominantly from the Canadian context, yet similar to that which exists elsewhere among allied nations, as has been seen with Key Leader Engagement (KLE).

JIMP

The RLE construct finds its origins in the public space of the JIMP principle, ". . . an [Army] descriptor that identifies the various categories of players (e.g., organizations, interest groups, institutions) that inhabit the broad environment in which military operations take place."[30]

The environment that JIMP defines is that of the Comprehensive Approach in Operations: (1) "J" represents Joint or the combined nature of operations where the marshaling of different military elements are used in a complementary fashion to accomplish the mission; (2) "I" stands for Interagency, which is the Whole of Government domain—government departments and agencies collaborating in nation building efforts; (3) "M" or Multinational speaks to international will—numbers of nations coming together under the auspices of the UN, NATO or other coalitions, bringing to bear all of their combined resources to create stability and effect change where needed, and; (4) "P" or the Public space hosts to a number of organizations and activities in Operations, but, as has already been underscored, the indigenous population therein is without question the most consequential. This contrasts with U.S. Army doctrine, which employs the acronym JIIM: Joint, Interagency, Intergovernmental, and Multinational.[31] Noted above, within CF doctrine, Interagency encompasses Intergovernmental interface. The striking difference, of course, is the JIMP emphasis on the Public Space and its poignancy with respect to the potential strategic role of indigenous populations (domestic publics), more importantly, the all-pervasive religious element frequently known to operational environments globally. As figure 4.3 indicates, RLE falls within the Public domain of Operations. Chaplains are able to contribute much due to their ability to move freely within religious circles.

PMESII

Concomitant to JIMP is another aspect of doctrine referred to as PMESII. This acronym delineates the breadth of interests in a given campaign: Politi-

Joint Interagency Multinational Public

Aim: To achieve desired effects

Joint

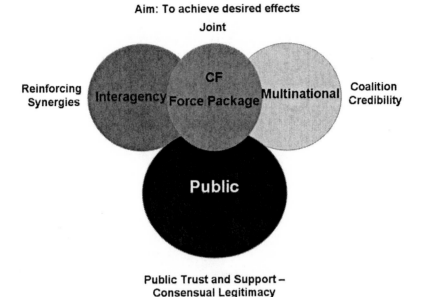

Reinforcing
Synergies

Coalition
Credibility

Public Trust and Support –
Consensual Legitimacy

CF operations must be viewed in a JIMP context, where a CF force package operates with multinational and interagency partners to attain unity of purpose and effort in achieving desired effects, all while considering the requirement for public trust and support both domestically and internationally. Public consent will confer legitimacy to the operation.

Figure 4.3. *Schematic of Joint Interagency Multinational Public Concept.* Used by permission, CF Dept of Army Doctrine (DAD).

cal, Military, Economic, Social, Infrastructure and Information. The Social sphere of PMESII runs in tandem to the Public Space of JIMP, for indigenous populations are host to both *culture* and *religion*, salient aspects of the Social sphere. Religious communities factor significantly within culture—again, a domain familiar to operational chaplains.

ENHANCED CAPABILITIES

The complexities of contemporary conflict will extend well into the future as will the interagency environment created as a force multiplier to counteract the sweeping societal effects of prolonged insurgency—intractable conflict. Due to the strategic import of interfacing with indigenous populations, RLE will continue to gain traction as a means of engaging communities. As chaplains' competencies advance, their ability to establish meaningful dialogue and working trust with local religious leaders will prove to be an added asset to the interagency environment, the "I" of JIMP. An *enhanced capability*, RLE opens doors and creates opportunities that otherwise would remain inaccessible to other Whole of Government[32] partners.

Advancing "new capabilities" in theatres of operations is a needed aspect of mission readiness and success. Engaging in dialogue and building relation among religious leaders is not new to chaplains. Otherwise known as "the ministry of presence," chaplains engage the *other* as a matter of course in *ministry*. In this sense, honing RLE is a furthering of skills inherent to the chaplains' role. As spiritual leaders, chaplains enjoy a natural rapport and share common ground with their co-religionists, hence the previously noted phrase—*people of the book*—citing the religious commonalities of the Abrahamic faith traditions: Judaism, Christianity and Islam. This is not to limit activities to monotheistic cultures. As a capability, RLE may be generalized to other contexts globally regardless of the presenting faith tradition. Significant also, civic engagement among religious communities engulfed in the greater conflicts of their respective identity groups is not ministry to be taken lightly. Not all chaplains are equipped or theologically predisposed to effectively engage local religious leaders across religious boundaries. Added to this are the presenting complexities of intractable conflict, a dimension that must be considered. Whether in conflict or post-conflict environments, instances of *encounter* and/or *collaborative activities* have led to conflict transformation among estranged religious communities suggesting continued investment in additional skills beyond present levels of chaplaincy training would be wise. If Command is to support such chaplaincy initiatives, and actors within the Interagency environment are to recognize them as legitimate interlocutors offering the necessary requisite skills, a demonstrable capacity to do such must be evident: *Enhanced Capabilities*. As RLE continues its development, it is conceivable that future operations will see select chaplains embedded within PRT-like organizations, collaborating with their Whole of Government partners in engaging religious leaders and their communities.

BUILDING RELATION

With respect to engaging the *other*, John Paul Lederach writes, "Who we have been, are, and will be emerges and shapes itself in a context of relational interdependency."[33] Again, he emphasizes, "The centrality of relationship provides the context and potential for breaking violence, for it brings people into the pregnant moments of the moral imagination: the space of recognition that ultimately the quality of our life is dependent on the quality of life of *others.*"[34] Engaging the *other* is all about building relation. Often a prominent local religious leader is a voice of reason within their community and frequently among other faith groups, as they move across ethno-religious lines easily. Carter and Smith conclude that, "Religious leaders can encourage disputants to turn their attention to the future, to the society and to *relationships* that must be rebuilt. They can help disputants change their thinking, their actions, and their *relationships* to facilitate genuine transformations."[35]

RLE must be viewed as the beginning of a relationship with local religious leaders—it is not a one-time event. Civic engagement of this nature is not an end in and of itself but should be viewed as one in a series of engagements over an extended period of time as relation develops. The intention for RLE is to see *networking* become *partnering* as friendship deepens. Be that advancing opportunities for programming for our interagency partners within religious communities or facilitating dialogue between estranged religious leaders whose communities have experienced conflict, the temptation is often to expect immediate results. Once a given initiative is identified, the role for the chaplain would remain one of *trusted friend* to the religious leaders but would segue to becoming *facilitator* as Whole of Government members are introduced to the leadership. Out of necessity, the chaplain would remain connected to any such endeavor. Building sufficient levels of trust will require time. The objective of such engagement is not to look for "quick fixes" or "bandage solutions" that will unravel if constant "life support" is not there. The long view must be considered as the most effective approach to achieving lasting results.

Indian scholar Ashutosh Varshney[36] postulates that the degree of integration between certain Hindu and Muslim communities in India that led to establishing the transformative *inter*communal Peace Committees was not a short-term process.[37] The level of trust that bonded Hindu-Muslim relations in the face of *exogenous shocks* emanating from violence elsewhere was realized through cooperation over an extended period of time. The integrity of the chaplains' engagement with local religious communities must be recognized as holding strategic value, in and of itself, and, therefore, be preserved. Co-opting such processes for other purposes must be resisted.

The element of trust will be discussed further in the upcoming section on *Encounter*. However, a word here on the subject is seen as constructive by virtue of its significance to building relation with religious leaders of *tolerant voice*, the topic of the next section. In this vein, the integrity of the process, and that of the individual, factor centrally to *trust* building. If chaplains are to engender trust among local religious leaders where the environment is one of distrust for the *other*, projecting an image of trustworthiness that directly correlates to one's actions is essential. In any dialogue, following through on commitments, no matter how small, quickly becomes the standard of measurement. Lewicki and Tomlinson's defining of *calculus-based trust* comes into play here—continuing in dialogue may depend on perceived benefits as compared to the potential costs of discontinuing communication, hence, appearing untrustworthy.

THE TOLERANT VOICE OF RELIGION: MIDDLE RANGE ACTORS

Identifying the *tolerant voice* among religious leaders is key to initiating dialogue. These are faith group leaders—community leaders—often desirous of moving beyond conflict, thus transcending the present hostilities and intransigence that are pitting their respective identity groups against one another. Known as *middle-range actors*, they enjoy the confidence of the grass roots while moving freely at the higher levels of leadership within their own communities. Their ease of movement affords them relationships that are professional, institutional, some formal, while other ties are more a matter of friendship and acquaintance, hence a high degree of social capital within communities.[38] More notable still, "middle-range actors tend to have pre-existing relationships with counterparts that cut across the lines of conflict within the setting . . . a network or relationships that cut across the identity divisions within the society."[39]

Religious leaders are undoubtedly among the more dominant centers of gravity within indigenous populations—*middle range actors* who, in non-Western societies, where the lines of separation between faith and the public space are markedly less defined, are often revered individuals at community and regional levels. Such esteem owes its origins to the almost seamless nature existing between religious communities and local culture and, at times, politics. Having conducted extensive research in religious leader liaison by operational chaplains, United States Navy chaplain, George Adams, offers the following with respect to relation,

> Since the human relationship is a key ingredient in the resolution and healing of deeply rooted conflicts, it is highly beneficial in stability operations for conflicted groups to be given opportunities to establish constructive relationships. Activities that allow opposing parties to be together and come to know one another facilitate in the humanization of the other side. Generally, a positive relationship with another person contributes an enormous amount toward preventing future violence against that individual; that is, it is more difficult to commit violence against someone you hold in high regard than against someone you view as an adversary.[40]

Lieutenant-General (retd.) Sir Rupert Smith of Britain states that contemporary conflict tends to be timeless. The operational objective has become more to *win the will of the people*, which leads to opponents adopting more of a guerrilla warfare approach. This, in turn, creates greater complexity, making it far more demanding to reach a condition where a strategic decision can be made and solutions found.[41] Iraq and Afghanistan have embroiled the international community in protracted conflict, reinforcing Smith's contention that the post-conflict phase of missions has become exceedingly difficult to attain. Where the *will of the people* is the center of gravity, those of *tolerant voice* within religious communities may offer a way forward. Rabbi Marc Gopin believes that even in the most damaging conflicts there remain those individuals who resist passing on the violence, rather they see it as a clear sign of the futility and evil of violence itself. He calls us to seek ways of supporting these rare individuals who potentially represent a way forward for fractured fraternities that leave their communities estranged.[42]

A caveat to the above is that although the emphasis is on engaging the *tolerant voice* of religion, dialogue should not be confined to them alone. The fluidity and unpredictability of conflict may give rise to situations where those involved in the conflict may choose to speak with religious leaders as a conduit to entering into discussions. A chaplain could find him/herself implicated or on the periphery of such engagement. This is not to suggest that chaplains become negotiators. However, they could *facilitate* bringing those with expertise in such matters to the table where meaningful dialogue could begin between principals to the conflict.

MIMETIC MODELING: CREATING OPENNESS TO THE OTHER

Mimetic modeling will be presented here in brief due to its importance to the process of encounter. (For more on *mimetic* theory see chapter 2). In keeping with the explanation of figure 4.2, the *mimetic modeling* of the chaplain is initiated when dialogue among estranged religious leaders begins. The reality of conflict zones is that faith group communities are often inextricably entangled in the larger conflicts that engulf them. Entrenchment and estrangement from the religious *other* are some of the more prominent residual effects, often known to the domain of post-conflict reconstruction. Alienation of this nature remain as *inter*communal fissures barely sealed, rupturing easily with little provocation.

Recalling the *mimetic* effect, it is one of seemingly mirroring the desires and behaviors of the *other.* In chapter 2 conflict and violence were seen to escalate due to the spiraling *mimetic* effect of reciprocal violence—the lust for revenge eliciting the desire to strike back, often with greater force than the original injury. *Mimesis* may also be experienced in a positive light. The earlier example of the young recruit desirous of emulating the demeanor of the self-disciplined and honorable member of the Directing Staff was a case in point. Such *mimetic* behavior extends to the chaplains' realm as well. In theatres of operation, it is via the chaplain's *mimetic modeling* of trust, acceptance, tolerance and hospitality among alienated religious and community leaders that a gradual engaging of the estranged *other(s)* occurs—something that previously neither religious leader could have entertained.

Where the desire exists within the religious *other* for a reconciling of differences and a return to coexistence/relation, movement toward such interdependence may emerge. Instances where entrenchment is such that enmity and bitterness prohibit communication, it is conceivable that the *mimetic modeling* of the chaplain with each group individually may challenge old perceptions, creating willingness for dialogue. It is journeying in relation with the religious *other* that chaplains are able to promote such possibilities that become catalytic in nature.

ENCOUNTER: THE WILL TO EMBRACE AND THE FRAGILE WE OF WORKING TRUST—COEXISTENCE AND INSTRUMENTAL RECONCILIATION

It is in *encounter* that the rigidity of long held stereotypes and the constant barrage of propaganda begin to lose their strength. Through the chaplains' *mimetic modeling* of the acceptance of the *other* and a genuine desire for their collective well-being, the desire for the same has a chance to take root and, in some instances, begin to well up within the estranged leaders. The *will to embrace* is that first step toward the *other*, where against a backdrop of tremendous hurt and destruction, one comes to recognize the good in a gesture extended by the *other*. In so doing a fissure of openness towards the *other* begins to emerge.[43]

Here, as Fumitaka Matsuoka[44] describes, in a gesture of openness, *self* pulls back from the edges of *self's* identity boundary to make room for the *other*. Such encounters are likened to an "antechamber" where the participants come to what is defined as the liminal experience of mutual participation or mutuality if you will. Liminal space may be understood as the approaching of a "threshold" of something new; an experience of the other that is "barely perceptible." The *self's* granting access to the *other* within the *self's* cultural boundaries leaves an altered and lingering impression of the estranged *other* once the encounter is concluded. Miroslav Volf's *double vision* emerges here: In an encounter one does not simply see the *other* from one's own perspective but begins to view one*self* from the perspective of the *other*—one sees one*self* through the eyes of the *other*.[45] Hence, the closed relational systems that characterize conflict—alienation, estrangement and open hostility—begin to give way to open relational systems where the mutuality of interdependence is manifest in more openness to see beyond entrenched stereotypes and a willingness to engage the *other*—a *re-humanizing* of the *other* (the *will to embrace*).

The possibility of future cooperation is built on such exchanges. As trust develops between religious leaders and their communities, damaging effects of intercommunal violence may be lessened among groups due to the channels of communication established across ethnic lines via the religious community leadership. Collaborative activities among faith groups may be one approach to initiating such co-operation.

Reuben Baron believes that the complexities of today's conflicts require new group dynamics that utilize processes such as "tipping points," where small changes can have large effects. Greater attention must be given to the "self-organization" that often rises from "grassroots" movements among visionary community leaders. Higher order structures may respond positively to such local interaction patterns. [46] Wisely selected superordinate goals pertinent to the needs of conflicting groups facilitate the *re-humanizing* of the *other* making way for the "fragile we." In contexts where conflict is ongoing or still fresh in memory, civic engagement—*encounter*—is the best we can hope for as a beginning. Civic engagement that engenders integrative processes is one approach among others to aid in creating and sustaining *inter*-communal structures that will rebuild conflict-stricken communities. Baron offers additional insight on how such community building may be affected.

TRUST DEVELOPMENT

Yeats wrote, ". . . peace comes dropping slow." [47] Such is the work of reconciliation. Where religious communities are estranged due to being engulfed in the larger conflict of their respective identity groups, as Baron states, "trust seeking can be a collective motivation; people interested in peace will seek to find a situation where . . . "working trust" will occur." [48] Here the goal becomes one of gradually bringing religious community leaders together in *encounter*, a delicate process of dialogue leading to the establishing of what practitioners refer to as the *fragile we* , a situation . . . where *us* versus *them* gives way to *we* at least in certain contexts." [49] As progress in relations improves, *working trust* emerges—a prerequisite to "motivat[ing] people to engage in difficult and effortful cooperative problem solving." [50] It is the repeated acts of co-operation in achieving common instrumental goals that see such trust emerge, an indispensable element of reconciliation, bringing conflicting communities closer to *coexistence.* Social psychologists refer to such collaboration as *instrumental reconciliation.* [51] Salutary to any overture toward the religious leadership of local faith communities is the element of trust. The capacity to grasp something of its dynamics and development is an essential component to its engendering.

Social psychologists Thompson and Gill of Defence Research and Development Canada (DRDC) have conducted research in the domain of organizational trust and the Comprehensive Approach for several years.[52] The objective of their work in the development of inter-departmental trust is to benefit deploying personnel called upon to collaborate in the taxing conditions known to international missions. With colleagues Febbraro and Piasentin, they are now applying their research to chaplains building trust among indigenous religious leaders. Due to its distinct relevance to the topic at hand, their recent publication, *the Role of Trust in the Religious Engagement Capability: Key Considerations for the Canadian Forces Chaplain Branch* will primarily be drawn upon here.

Where individuals and/or groups are endeavoring to put divisive conflict behind them, initial levels of trust often depend on what benefits exist for continuing in the relationship. This is often weighed against the potential costs that may be incurred for being untrustworthy once dialogue has begun—benefits and costs are carefully calculated. Ergo, key to trust development is how one assesses whether another is trustworthy.[53] Each of the four dimensions of trust featured in figure 4.4, holds significance for RLE, especially true in cultures with which one is unfamiliar: (1) competence—domain-specific expertise and/or skills, e.g., some sense that one possesses the

Trust: Local Culture

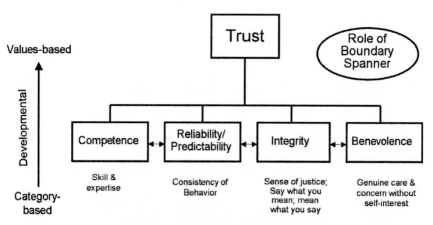

Facilitating trust: superordinate goals & shared
understanding of roles, responsibilities & constraints

Figure 4.4.   The Dimensions of Trust. Used by permission—Defence Research and Development Canada (DRCD).

knowledge, skill, and competency to follow through on commitments; (2) predictability—consistency in thought and action, e.g., the *other* acts as expected; (3) integrity—the possession and expression of a set of guiding principles that are based on decency, truthfulness, fairness, and justice; and (4) benevolence—genuine care and compassion for *others* without self-interest.[54] Evident here, one is concerned enough about the *other's* well-being to, at a maximum, advance their interests and, at a minimum, not impede progress made. As trust builds, so, too, will the recognition of the *benevolence* in the *other.* "Honest and open communication, delegating decisions, and sharing control indicate evidence of one's benevolence."[55]

As would be expected, trust deepens over time. Figure 4.5 depicts trust development in increasing gradations from: (1) *category-based* trust, in which roles and/or credentials similar to one's own/group are identified; (2) *interest-based* trust, where increased co-operation (instrumental reconciliation) is rewarded with taking the risk of incremental small steps, each gesture creating more confidence than the last; and (3) *values-based* trust that strengthens over an extended period, as values held in common aid in deriving meaning from what has become an established relationship.[56]

Thompson et al. articulate below how trust moves from its initial stages to becoming more established.

The Development of Trust

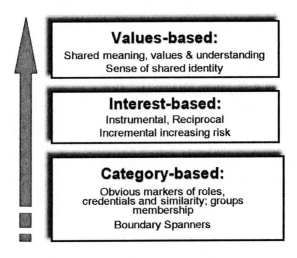

Figure 4.5.   The Development of Trust. Used by Permission—Defence Research and Development Canada (DRDC).

Beyond its initial stages, trust develops based on the personal character and attributes of another. Trust often begins in small gestures with increasing risks taken over time, should one's initial trust in another be rewarded. At this point the exchange of tangible benefits by both parties that meets each other's needs is often most important. However, the need to consistently see an immediate mutual exchange of tangible benefits (referred to as the *reciprocity norm*) with every exchange becomes less important as trust becomes established. Trust becomes increasingly rooted in a growing perceived value similarity and shared outcomes, and at times in a growing sense of shared identity.[57]

Adding to the role of the chaplain, these authors suggest that in interactions with others one is most likely to base trust on the *categories* that others most obviously represent, best understood as a range of additional qualities that the *other* possesses. "In the case of RLE, simply knowing that someone is a chaplain, for instance, suggests certain domain knowledge and expertise and a level of integrity and benevolence that is associated with the role, distinct from the attributes of any particular individual."[58]

The term *boundary spanners*[59] comes into play to describe the role of a local leader—religious in this instance—individuals prone to taking the initial steps of trust development. A synonymous term with *middle-range actors*, again, these are persons predisposed to building rapport, establishing relationships and knowledge-development, accompanied by an understanding with respect to cultures, norms, etc. among diverse groups.

Trust development and seeding reconciliation nourish one another, as perceptions of the *other* are reframed. Researchers in Northern Ireland attest to a lessening of the alienating effects of segregation due to the cultivation of *cross-community trust* resulting from increased contact between Protestant and Roman Catholic communities. The dimensions of trust, as articulated above, would have factored predominantly into its development across the hardened boundaries of such communal isolation.

[S]egregation sustains the conflict by fostering mutual ignorance, suspicion, and distrust and by maintaining prejudice and negative stereotypes. Thus, encouraging cross-community contact has been an important strategy adopted by policy makers in Northern Ireland to build cross-community trust.[60]

Initiatives of this nature have a beginning. *Boundary spanners* from within their respective communities often are imbued with enough *moral imagination* to take the risks necessary to make overtures across seeming impenetrable communal divides: ". . . the capacity to imagine and generate constructive responses and initiatives that, while rooted in the day-to-day challenges of violence, transcend and ultimately break the grips of those destructive patterns and cycles."[61] Extending such gestures are sufficiently authentic, yet create cognitive dissonance as an unsolicited and altruistic deed may raise questions regarding previously held assumptions.[62] The cost of rhetoric concerning good intentions is little. The relationship-building process with the estranged *other*, on the other hand, suggests "doing things and sharing things, both as moral acts in and of themselves and as symbolic acts that convey to the enemy a conciliatory intention that is not merely words but something that has been concretized as deed."[63]

The consensus among these psychologists was that chaplains are particularly well-positioned in terms of role, training and personal attributes to cultivate trust development in an RLE context. Reinforcing the benevolence associated with such engendered trust necessitates maintaining a clear vision that the purpose of the RLE-related activities is to help facilitate the creation of conditions conducive to groups building trust and generating solutions that connote local ownership.

COLLABORATIVE ACTIVITIES: TOWARDS PERSONAL TRUST AND INTEGRATION

In circumstances where security and opportunity have been favorable, commanders have authorized chaplains to undertake more intentional *peacebuilding* activities among religious communities. Padres have brought religious leaders together who, due to existing tensions, have been incommunicado for a number of years. Dialogue and, in some instances, collaborative activities have resulted, affording occasions to seed reconciliation. Such cooperation among local religious leaders and their communities over the long-term may function as "shock absorbers," preventing the manipulation or abuse of religion to escalate conflict or tensions.[64]

The predominant feature of *collaborative activities* is the *peacebuilding* nature of supra-ordinate goals. These are jointly agreed-upon objectives that benefit both communities, yet neither group can accomplish alone, achievable only through *inter*communal cooperation. With thorough needs analysis—an evaluation process facilitated by the chaplain involving the local religious leadership and military/civilian program developers—a shared project with the right fit may be selected. As such, nascent integration takes root. Through cooperation of this nature, an identity more inclusive of the *other* begins to develop. It is in such an atmosphere that conflict is transcended, new narratives are written and the healing of memory begins.

An increasing number of social psychologists are now researching in the domain of intergroup reconciliation—a timely and propitious enterprise, given the seismic shift in how contemporary conflict often manifests. The intent here is not to suggest that chaplains replicate the kinds of collaborative activities between groups cited in much of their literature; rather, the aim is to discern the similarities and parallels between what they offer and the

potential opportunities presented to a growing number of chaplains in operations. Of particular note is the work of Reuben M. Baron. He advocates a
"bottom-up" approach to the reconciliation process rather than placing the
entire emphasis on the more traditional approach of "top-down," e.g., negotiating with the high-level leaders. Much success has occurred when "bottom-up"attempts at the small-group level have brought together middle- or
lower-level leaders (middle range actors/boundary spanners) for face-to-face
consultations.[65] From his perspective, transformation occurs more at the
interface between individual-level and group-level processes. He further articulates that a *circular causality* between the "bottom-up" and "top-down" is
needed if reconciliation is to be lasting—progress among individuals and
small groups must be embedded within structures, requiring the aid of higher
level leadership. Bar-Tal and Bennink concur, ". . . although the reconciliation process may begin either with the leaders or the grassroots it must
always proceed top-down and bottom-up simultaneously."[66] They contend
that leaders are crucial due to their role of negotiating peaceful resolutions to
conflict and leading reconciliation processes.

Baron posits that "bottom-up" reconciliation is often the most effectual,
"social networks" creating "individual local interactions." In other words, as
individuals interact, social networking evolves, influencing greater numbers.
Social networking, in turn, gives rise to a "group structure." He describes this
as self-organization, or, more simply put, a cross-section of people joining
together in common cause. Individuals drawn to a common cause ultimately
are impacted, an "influencing of the parts" in Baron's parlance. This is very
typical of "grassroots" initiatives. In a conflict scenario, the "parts" would
correspond to a loosely formed group of individuals representative of the
ethnicities implicated in the hostilities—a result of social networking. Finally, such changed "parts" come to influence the "whole" through a process
known as minority influence—the "whole" being whatever "body" represents the interests of the collective groups.

His following example poignantly illustrates the transformative power of
a "bottom-up" initiative. The 2006 award-winning film documentary *Encounter Point*[67] (the true story about everyday leaders who refuse to sit back
as the Israeli-Palestinian conflict escalates) brought to light an Israeli-Palestinian phenomenon emerging from the pain and suffering associated with the
continued Middle East unrest. *Encounter Point*, a movement by the same
name, has seen scores of grieving Israeli and Palestinian families come together in mutual support; all having suffered the loss of loved ones in the
ongoing intifada. Last count there were nearly 500 involved in this grassroots
movement. The impetus to their banding together was the mutual dissatisfaction with their "within group" support groups that were focused more on
assigning blame than searching for ways to create peace. These families were
desirous of reconciliation, not revenge, something they could not achieve

alone. Baron makes the point, *"Thus, at times it is adaptive to build bridges across intergroup boundaries."*[68]

More pertinent still, *Encounter Point* has become "a peace-oriented su-pra-ordinate[69] group emerg[ing] out of the local self-organization."[70] In this example, enough distraught Israeli and Palestinian families became dissatis-fied by the dearth of adequate support within their own communities that they reached across communal boundaries to connect with those experienc-ing similar pain—"individual local interactions." The expanding "social net-works" resulted in a "group structure" as they banded together or, as it was in this case, an *encounter group*. Because the "parts were sufficiently influ-enced," e.g., the families from both communities, the "whole was altered" by the creation of something new out of the parts—a supra-ordinate group com-prised of families from both communities, dedicated to the cause of *inter*-communal peace and reconciliation. As a movement, *Encounter Point* is very much in the public view, winning acclaim at home and abroad. What must not be lost sight of is that it began at the "grassroots"—"bottom-up" not "top-down."

An additional aspect of "bottom-up" movements is the amount of trust that may develop across community lines. It is not unusual that unofficial, lower-level channels of communication and cooperation come to the fore when official levels have become mired down. Baron uses the term *ambient* trust to describe an atmosphere of trust that may exist among the people in general. At times leaders can instill such confidence in the electorate that good will on both sides of a conflict percolates to the surface, creating greater than normal levels of support. He ties engendering trust to cooperative en-gagement with the *other*; where "trust at both ends of cooperation [may become] a bridge to the reconciliation process,"[71] e.g., extended seasons of collaboration create opportunities for building trust. Whereas some contend that trust is a prerequisite for cooperation, he suggests that it may also be a product of collaborative activity.[72] Establishing trust may also be a way of beginning emotional healing, a level of reconciliation necessitating a higher level of trust: it moves beyond the stage of monitoring if commitments are being honored (co-existence), to "resembl[ing] the trust of friends or family," commonly referred to as *inter-personal* or simply *personal trust*. Through continued interaction old attitudes are replaced by new perceptions of the *other*, an internalization that "over time" leaves its mark on identity. Al-though old frictions may rear their head—eventualities over which one has no control—the ties forged through such intercommunal collaboration leaves those involved less vulnerable to situational changes.[73] Such deepened trust develops over the long run leading to the transcendence of conflict, the writing of new narratives and, hopefully, an eventual healing of memory. In time, integration becomes such that former enemies come to embrace a larger more inclusive identity where apology and forgiveness free them from threats that each presents to the identity of the *other,*[74] something called *socioemotional reconciliation.*[75]

A caveat, Baron rightly cautions that trust can be compared to "an investment with potential rewards and costs," e.g., "it is easier to achieve trust than it is to restore trust once it is lost."[76] The emphasis here is not so much the addressing of past wrongs as it is beginning the writing of new narratives together through increased association as a way of moving forward. As cooperative interdependence leads to other forms of integrated civic engagement one hopes that the painful edges of historical memory will be dulled.[77]

As a people's movement, *Encounter Point* clearly demonstrates the dynamics of a grassroots activity beginning with just a handful of concerned citizens possessing the desire to transcend conflict in pursuit of a more promising future together with those, who in former times, would have been classified as members of the enemy community. The previous case studies of the operational ministry of chaplains reflect similar dynamics, albeit on a lesser scale. Collaborative activities across communal lines leading to unprecedented cooperation have, and continue to be, facilitated by chaplains. Instances of *inter*faith dialogue have led to public celebrations inclusive of the faith group leaders of the implicated identity groups in conflict, an activity that could be replicated in post-conflict reconstruction where tensions continue to simmer between/among groups. Such public displays of unity offer to the people a vision of themes of peace, justice and mutuality that are faithful to the Holy texts known to all faith traditions. Articulated earlier, such rituals of inversion have a way of turning a present power structure on its head, offering a different vision to the people of what could be, e.g., seeding reconciliation.

Noted earlier, transcending boundaries that divide is also often a concern among religious leaders stemming from their passion for the well being of their youth and what future may lay ahead for them. With the guidance of their Whole of Government partners, chaplains may facilitate the development of more long-term programming to address such concerns. Peacebuilders in other contexts speak of cooperative initiatives having revolved around the renaming of a building, street or a park in commemoration of the suffering on both sides of a conflict. A project of this nature implicates people from the communities touched by the conflict, providing a means to move from entrenched positions to begin the work of envisioning a shared future together. Given time and resources, much could be accomplished in designing context-specific programming for implementation among religious communities where appropriate.

Added to this is the possibility of a chaplain facilitating the creation of what is referred to as a *peacebuilding constituency.*[78] Noted previously, ease of accessibility to local religious communities provides opportunities to identify religious leaders open to reconciling initiatives—middle range actors. In addition, interfacing with the various civilian organizations (NGOs, IOs) gives occasion to determine what skills and capabilities these organizations bring. Listening to local leadership opens a window to assessing needs. Peacebuilders have been known to hold *peacebuilding clinics*, where the organizations present are able to match their expertise and contributions to identified needs among various communities that otherwise would have gone undetected. Concomitant with such endeavors is the provision of support to ongoing indigenous peacebuilding activities in an AO. Identified as legitimate, chaplains can facilitate bringing the much-needed resources to bear on local initiatives that coincide with mission objectives.

INTERDEPENDENCE AS INCREMENTAL RECONCILIATION

Rabbi Marc Gopin suggests that a new way of understanding conflict resolution and reconciliation is in the offing; a notion applicable to many areas of the world where religious leaders/peacebuilders are endeavoring to make a difference. He introduces the concept of "transformational increment[s] of change that can be seized upon as the basis for steady, measurable change, even when structural paradigm shifts prove elusive for decades or even generations."[79] The complexities of the human community will always remain a challenge, leaving peacebuilders at times stymied with their seeming ineffectiveness. Those engaged in such endeavors must keep before them that every gesture, every movement in improved relations, however small, is a success in and of itself. Gopin contends that, given the right circumstances, such positive change impacts human social life with a steady accumulation of positive increments of change. He has coined the term "incremental conflict resolution," which for the purposes of this discussion will be defined as "incremental reconciliation." As a rule, religious leaders do not have training in conflict resolution but—due to their orientation toward peace, justice and often an innate ability to communicate—have made timely contributions toward the resolution of conflicts. He posits that incremental reconciliation should be judged "one increment at a time and *then* move resolutely with each increment toward lasting change that indeed addresses the deep roots of conflict through paradigm shifts in attitudes, behaviors, and world views."[80]

The Rabbi cautions peacebuilders not to confuse "long-term ends with short-term tasks."[81] This is sage counsel for a difference exists between first order goals and those of higher order. In a conflict or post-conflict environment, the former—civil dialogue, cooperation, working trust, i.e., peaceful coexistence—is "evaluated on its own merit without any regard as to how events unfold in the long-term," a situation which may sustain a degree of unpredictability. High order goals look to what may be accomplished over the long-term: "justice, the satisfaction of basic human needs, and the creation of a peaceful society that is egalitarian."[82] Realizing such profound objectives often takes decades if not a generation or more.

Conflict resolution expert, Lisa Schirch, is actively involved with the U.S. military in building a "Civil Society-Military Dialogue" in Afghanistan. With respect to "time horizons," she states, "the challenge is to design short-term programming that contributes toward long-term goals and to design long-term programming that supports short-term objectives."[83] Olivera Jovanovic, Serbian Orthodox theologian and Senior Advisor for the Inter-Religious Council in Bosnia-Herzegovina, espouses similar logic regarding the peacebuilding activities of the council in Sarajevo. Her twelve years of experience with inter-confessional dialogue (Bosniak [Muslim], Croat Roman Catholic, Serbian Orthodox and Jewish) has convinced her that impacting concrete steps are the most practical approach to lasting and improved relations in post-conflict Bosnia. In her mind, reconciliation remained an admirable goal but was a process requiring many years of patient labor measured in concrete and tangible efforts that promote mutuality.[84] The saying is true that "it is the darkest just before dawn." Whatever the decided strategies for change, the ethos for peace will always find their center in *relation*; the interdependence of integrated societies finds its impetus here. For it is in their cumulative effect that lasting change will be realized.

RELIGIOUS COMMUNITIES: PROMOTING LOCAL OWNERSHIP AND BUILDING LOCAL CAPACITY

A recurring theme for leadership continues to be the lack of a clear "exit strategy" once personnel and resources have been committed. The cultivation of local ownership from an early stage in the mission is an underutilized approach in building local capacity. Of note in the Helsinki conference, *Comprehensive Approach: Trends, Challenges and Possibilities for Cooperation in Crisis Prevention and Management*, was an overemphasis on waiting to engage relevant international actors in peacebuilding efforts to the neglect of integrating local actors at an early stage.[85] In fragile states, where infrastructure and services have been interrupted and the corruption of political figures is far too common, top down structures frequently have difficulty gaining traction in local communities. Consideration must be given to the employment of religious organizations as credible local actors readily available to aid in the rebuilding of much-needed infrastructure and services. Returning to the Chicago Task Force's *Engaging Religious Communities Abroad: A New Imperative for U.S. Foreign Policy*, the authors emphasize that, "Religious institutions, because of their structure and experience, can and often will fill the vacuum created by the absence, erosion, or collapse of state authority over some or all of its territory."[86] In societies suffering from the strain of conflict or its residual effects, citizens will begin searching for alternative means of service delivery: one such means is the religious sector. An added advantage that religious institutions bring is that they function well at the grassroots level optimizing networking among the people. Religious centers function as the hub of many cultures, most often viewed by local communities as trusted organizations—an available means for building local capacity.

The task force (2010) emphatically states, that authentic engagement "entails engaging religious communities on their own terms, listening carefully to their concerns and fears, and entering into substantive dialogue about how to realize their legitimate aspirations."[87] Cementing such gains made must be viewed over the long-term and calls for "collaborative processes that enhance the likelihood of favorable and enduring outcomes within a particular environment."[88] More than any other contingent member, the chaplain is in a position to engage local religious leaders. The common ground of the spiritual plane is a natural precursor to authentic engagement. Essential to consideration, activities of this nature—the results of which may be more challenging to measure in the short term—in the aggregate can have considerable significance for people's lives.[89] The key here is for the chaplain to be familiar enough with the interagency environment, when engaging in dialogue, that needs may be identified, opening the way for other agencies to effect change within entire communities that otherwise might remain at a distance to such overtures. Foreign Affairs Canada (DFAIT) "promotes dialogue and reconciliation with communities, vulnerable groups and conflicting parties"[90] as an aspect of their Global Peace and Security Program. A chaplain with enhanced skills could contribute where religious communities are implicated. Given time and resources, much could be done in designing context-specific programming for implementation among religious communities where appropriate. Given their profile among the people, future operations may benefit from the integration of willing moderate religious leaders into operational strategies. Where hostilities have resulted in alienation and estrangement of communities, building relation through continued dialogue and collaborative activities with such prominent community leaders may in time serve to ameliorate relations among estranged peoples. Religious communities will undoubtedly remain centers of gravity within indigenous populations well into the future. Religious leaders in their own right, chaplains are ideal candidates for RLE, a strategic asset for commanders.

The following five chapters will move from the more theoretical to RLE in application. Case studies featuring the *external operational ministry* of chaplains from Canada, France, the United States, Norway and New Zealand, closing with an inspirational discussion regarding the newly established Chaplaincy of the Bosnia-Herzegovina Defense Forces. Showcased will be the experiences of these chaplains as they engaged religious and community leaders according to the situation and presenting need. The theory and praxis from previous chapters will be brought to bear in graduations as the reader is transported to Bosnia, Kosovo, Iraq and Afghanistan through these documented operational anecdotes spanning two decades. For ease of reference, citations pointing to the more in-depth treatment of the theoretical constructs of earlier chapters will be provided within the case studies.

NOTES

1. See chapter 1, Introduction, endnote 4.
2. See chapter 1, Introduction, *The Contemporary Context*.
3. *Engaging Religious Communities Abroad: A New Imperative for U.S. Foreign Policy*, Report of the Task Force on Religion and the Making of Foreign Policy, R. Scott Appleby and Richard Cizik, Cochairs, Thomas Wright, Project Director (Chicago: The Chicago Council on Global Affairs, 2010), flyleaf.
4. Appleby and Cizik, 2010, Foreword.
5. Appleby and Cizik, 2010, 23.
6. John Paul Lederach, *Building Peace: Sustainable Reconciliation in Divided Societies* (Washington, D.C.: United States Institute of Peace Press, 1997), 41–42. See also Douglas Johnston and Cynthia Sampson, eds., *Religion, The Missing Dimension of Statecraft* (New York: Oxford University Press, 1994); Douglas Johnston, ed., *Faith-Based Diplomacy: Trumping Realpolitik* (New York: Oxford University Press, 2003); Marc Gopin, *Between Eden and Armageddon: the Future of World Religions, Violence, and Peacemaking* (New York: Oxford University Press, 2000).
7. Lederach, 1997, 41–42.
8. Lederach, 1997, 41–42.
9. Marc Gopin, *To Make the Earth Whole* (Lanham, Maryland: Rowman and Littlefield, 2009), 57.
10. Liora Danan and Alice Hunt, *Mixed Blessings: U.S. Government Engagement with Religion in Conflict-Prone Settings*, A Report of the Post-Conflict Reconstruction Project, Introduction (Washington, D.C.: CSIS Press, 2007), 52. See http://csis.org/files/media/csis/pubs/070820_religion.pdf. For additional reflections from this Report, see chapter 8, The Potential Role of Indigenous Peacebuilders within the Whole of Government Environment.
11. USAID, *Religion, Conflict & Peacebuilding: An Introductory Programming Guide*, http://www.usaid.gov/our_work/cross-cutting_programs/conflict/publications/docs/Religion_Conflict_and_Peacebuilding_Toolkit.pdf., accessed 15 May 2010.
12. Scott Appleby, "Retrieving the Missing Dimension of Statecraft,' in *Faith-based Diplomacy: Trumping Realpolitik*, ed. Douglas Johnston. (Oxford: Oxford University Press, 2003), 239-40 cited in Katrien Hertog, *The Complex Reality of Religious Peacebuilding: Conceptual Contributions and Critical Analysis* (Lanham, Maryland: Lexington Books, 2010), 81.
13. Hertog, 2010, 82.
14. Informed by David Little, *Peacemakers in Action: Profiles of Religion in Conflict Resolution* (New York: Cambridge University Press, 2007), 438.
15. Mullah refers to an Islamic religious leader in Asia, whereas Imam is more commonly used in other parts of the world. The Ulema Shura is a government appointed council of leading Islamic scholars tasked with the oversight of religious affairs for a provincial jurisdiction. Ideally, this council works in concert with the Director of Religious Affairs, a portfolio of the Governor's Cabinet.
16. The description of Religious Area Analysis (RAA) provided here is drawn from a number of sources provided by the United States Army Chaplain Center and School at Fort Jackson, South Carolina. The CF Chaplain Branch is working in consultation with their American counterparts in implementing this aspect of chaplaincy training. The first serial of what will become an annual RAA course was taught to CF chaplains on the Chaplain in

Deployed Operations course at the CF Chaplain School and Center (CFChSC), Canadian Forces Base (CFB) Borden during the fall of 2011.

17. *Land Operations*, B-GL-300-001/FP-001 (209-01-01) (Ottawa: DND, 2008), p. 5–24. See https://info.publicintelligence.net/CanadaLandOps.pdf.

18. *Land Force: Counter-Insurgency Operations* B-GL-323-004/FP-003 (Kingston, ON: Army Publishing Office, 2008), 508.6 b (1), 5–11. See http://info.publicintelligence.net/CanadaCOIN.pdf.

19. *Land Force: Counter-Insurgency Operations*, 2008, 511.7, 5–16 (italics mine). Again, the authors reinforce the strategic import of local populations to COIN operations, "Generally, within a COIN campaign, strategic centres of gravity are populations and their support of the campaign. The population of the region or nation in question is a centre of gravity over which the insurgents and the COIN elements will fight for support." COIN is the abbreviation for Counter-Insurgency Operations. *Land Force: Counter-Insurgency Operations* 508.6 b. (3), 5–11. See http://info.publicintelligence.net/CanadaCOIN.pdf.

20. "Canadian Forces Operations" B-GG-005-004/AF-000 (18 Dec 2000), 3-2 cited by Colonel Craig King, "Effects Based Operations: Buzzword or Blueprint (Kingston, Ontario: Canadian Defence Academy Press, 2005), in *The Operational Art, Canadian Perspectives – Context and Concepts*, eds. Allan English, Daniel Gosselin, Howard Coombs, and Laurence M. Hickey (Kingston, Ontario: Canadian Defence Academy Press, 2005), 318.

21. G.I. Wilson, John P. Sullivan, and Hal Kempfer, "4GW Tactics of the Weak Confound the Strong," Military.com (8 September 2003) http://www.military.com/NewContent/0.13190.Wilson090803.00.html, cited by English, "Operational Art in the Canadian Context," in English, Gosselin, Coombs and Hickey, 2005, 53.

22. Allan English, "The Operational Art: Theory, Practice, and Implications for the Future," in English, Gosselin, Coombs, and Hickey, 2005, 53.

23. *Counter-Insurgency Operations*, 2008, 508.6 b, (1), 5–11, see http://info.publicintelligence.net/CanadaCOIN.pdf.

24. Land Force Doctrine Note 2-09 Key Leader Engagement (KLE) – Approval Draft, Oct 2009, 1.

25. Jeanne F. Hull, *Iraq: Strategic Reconciliation, Targeting and Key Leader Engagement -* Summary (Carlisle, PA: Strategic Studies Institute, U.S. Army War College: 2009), 5.

26. Terrell A. Northrup, "The Dynamic of Identity in Personal and Social Conflict" in *Intractable Conflicts and Their Transformation*, eds. Louis Kriesburg, Terrell A. Northrup and Stuart J. Thornson (Syracuse, New York: Syracuse University Press, 1989), 70.

27. RLE is a capability under development within the CF. At the time of this publication approved CF policy and doctrine for RLE were in process. The following is offered as a working definition recognizing that additional nuancing may have occurred. "RLE is a Command-led, uniquely chaplain conducted ministry activity: (1) to enhance the understanding of the religious dimension within an Area of Operations (AO); (2) to establish trust and build relationships with indigenous religious leaders, and; (3) in support of peace and the resolution of conflict among indigenous populations." Religious Leader Engagement Seminar War Game, Canadian Army Command and Staff College, Fort Frontenac, CFB Kingston, 16-20 April 2012.

28. Appleby and Cizik, 2010, 51–53.

29. Appleby and Cizik, 2010, 51–53.

30. Peter Gizewski (Strategic Analyst), LCD OR Team, and LCol Michael Rostek (DLCD-Land Futures), "Toward A Comprehensive Approach To CF Operations (see figure 4.3): The Land Force JIMP Concept" in *Defence R&D Canada: Centre for Operational Research and Analysis*, DRDC CORA TM 2007-60, September 2007, 8.

31. JIIM Lessons Learned Report (Joint, Interagency, Intergovernmental, Multinational), OIF and OEF Joint Context and Knowledge Training Gaps, No. 07-24, May 2007 Center for Army Lessons Learned, Fort Leavenworth, Kansas. www.google.ca/search?q=JIIM&ie=utf-8&oe=utf-8&aq=t&rls=org.mozilla:en-US:official&client=firefox-a#q=US+Army+and+JIIM&hl=en&client=firefox-a&rls=org.mozilla:en-US:official&prmd=ivns&ei=d_AkTYeOKs6Qswax1rHdAg&start=10&sa=N&fp=825210affd154cf0

32. Whole of Government and Interagency are synonymous terms, both descriptors of the operational space in which government departments and agencies, international organizations (IO), non-governmental organizations (NGO), and private volunteer organizations (PVO) operate.

33. John Paul Lederach, *The Moral Imagination: The Art and Soul of Building Peace* (New York: Oxford University Press, 2005), 35.

34. Lederach, 2005, 35.

35. Judy Carter and Gordon S. Smith, "Religious Peacebuilding: From Potential to Action" in *Religion and Peacebuilding*, eds. Harold Coward and Gordon S. Smith (Albany, New York: State University of New York Press, 2004), 297. (Italics mine).

36. Ashutosh Varshney's seminal research, published in *Ethnic Conflict and Civic Life: Hindus and Muslims in India*, contends that where communities in India were more integrated civically across ethnic lines, the propensity toward violence was less when *exogenous shocks* impacted the community—an ethnically/religiously induced crisis within a populace free of conflict, emanating from outside. Peace Councils were *inter*communal groups of concerned individuals within neighborhoods who came together to address problems of prejudice, civic tensions, and religious rituals in order to foster communal harmony, as a means of countering communal antagonism rooted in the sentiments of hatred. His examination of six cities—three more ethnically integrated compared with three more segregated—offers critical insight in terms of conflict transformation. He asserts where Hindu/Muslim tensions spilled over into violence elsewhere in the country, the more civically integrated urban centers were able to contain its spread—either outbursts were quelled in short order or they didn't happen at all. The depth of civic engagement had much to do with maintaining the peace as it promoted more integrative structures, which held additional relational benefits, hence, a peace dividend for the community when the contagion of violence originating externally threatened to metastasize locally. In communities where daily *inter*communal activity and communication was less evident ethnic segregation became the norm. During periods of internal strife elsewhere in India, these localities were more susceptible to violence spreading to their communities, a *mimetic* phenomenon. See Ashutosh Varshney, *Ethic Conflict and Civic Life: Hindus and Muslims in India* (New Haven, CN: Yale University Press, 2002).

37. For more on Peace Committees, see Chapter Eight, Endnote 32.

38. Lederach, 1997, 41–42.

39. Lederach, 1997, 42.

40. George Adams, CDR, CHC, USN, "Chaplains as Liaisons with Religious Leaders: Lessons from Iraq and Afghanistan," in *Peaceworks*, No. 56 (Washington D.C.: The United States Institute of Peace, 2006), 32.

41. Rupert Smith, *The Utility of Force: The Art of War in the Modern World* (London: Penguin Books, 2006), 289–292.

42. Gopin, 2000, 270.

43. See Miroslav Volf, "Embrace" in *Exclusion and Embrace: A Theological Exploration of Identity, Otherness, and Reconciliation* (Nashville, TN: Abingdon Press, 1996), 99–165. Chapter 10 will be devoted to Volf's theological themes and their applicability to the conflict environment.

44. Fumitaka Matsuoka, "A Reflection on 'Teaching Theology from an Intercultural Perspective,'" *Theological Education* 36, no 1 (1989), 35–42 cited in Robert Schreiter, *The New Catholicity: Theology Between the Global and the Local* (Maryknoll, N.Y.: Orbis Books, 2000), 40-41.

45. For more on Volf's "double vision" see Chapter Three, Part 3 "Reconciliation as Embrace," dissertation of Major S.K. Moore entitled, *Military Chaplains as Agents of Peace: The Theology and Praxis of Reconciliation in Stability Operations* (Ottawa, Canada: Saint Paul University, 2008), 117–143.

46. Ruben M. Baron, "Reconciliation, Trust, and Cooperation: Using Bottom-Up and Top-Down Strategies to Achieve Peace in Israeli-Palestinian Conflict" in *The Social Psychology of Intergroup Reconciliation*, eds. Arie Nadler, Thomas E. Malloy and Jeffery D. Fisher, (New York: Oxford University Press, 2008), 284.

47. William Butler Yeats, "The Lake Isle of Innisfree," http://www.eecs.harvard.edu/~keith/poems/Innisfree.html accessed 25 July 2010.

48. Baron, 2008, 286.

49. Baron, 2008, 279.

50. Baron, 2008, 286.

51. Arie Nadler and Nurit Shnabel, "Instrumental and Socioemotional Paths to Intergroup Reconciliation and the Needs-Based Model of Socioemotional Reconciliation" in *The Social Psychology of Intergroup Reconciliation*, eds. Arie Nadler, Thomas E. Malloy and Jeffery D. Fisher, (New York: Oxford University Press, 2008), 41.

52. M. M. Thompson & R. Gill. "The role of trust in whole of government missions" in *Mission critical: Smaller democracies role in global stability operations*, eds. C. Leuprecht, T. Jodok, & D. Last, (Montreal & Kingston: McGill-Queen's University Press, 2010), 225–244.

53. Roy J. Lewicki and Edward C. Tomlinson, "Trust and Trust Building" in *Beyond Intractability*, eds. Guy Burgess and Heidi Burgess (Boulder, Colorado: Conflict Resolution Consortium, 2003), http://www.beyondintractability.org/essay/trust_building/, accessed 26 July 2010; R.J. Lewicki & C. Wiethoff. "Trust, Trust Development, and Trust Repair" in *The Handbook of Conflict Resolution*, eds. M. Deutsch & P.T. Coleman, (San Francisco: Josey-Bas Publishers, 2000), 86–107.

54. See also C. McLeod. *Trust, The Stanford Encyclopedia of Philosophy* (Spring 2011 Edition), ed. Edward N. Zalta, http://plato.stanford.edu/archives/spring2011/entries/trust; T.R. Tyler & R.M. Kramer. "Whither Trust" in *Trust in organizations: Frontiers of theory and research* (Thousand Oaks, CA: Sage Publications, 1996).

55. Lewicki and Tomlinson, 2003.

56. T.R. Tyler & R.M. Kramer. "Whither Trust" in *Trust in organizations: Frontiers of theory and research* (Thousand Oaks, CA: Sage Publications, 1996); M. Yakovleva, R.R. Reilly & R. Werko. "Why do we trust? Moving beyond individual to dyadic perceptions" in *Journal of Applied Psychology*, 95 (1), 2010, 79–91.

57. Megan Thompson, Ritu Gill, Angela Febbraro & Kelly Piasentin. "The Role of Trust in Religious Leader Engagement," Defence Research and Development Canada, 3772-12og04, 30 April 2012, 4 (2–12).

58. Thompson, Gill, Febbraro & Piasentin, 2012, 3 (2–10).

59. S. Currall & T. Judge. "Measuring trust between organizational boundary persons" in *Organizational Behavior and Human Decision Processes* 64 (2), 1995, 151–170; P. Williams. "The competent boundary spanner" in *Public Administration* 80, 2002, 103–124.

60. Miles Hewstone, Jared B. Kenworthy, Ed Cairns, Nocole Tausch, Joanne Hughes, Tania Tam, Alberto Voci, Ulrich Von Hecker, and Catherine Pinder, "Stepping Stones to Reconciliation in Northern Ireland: Intergroup Contact, Forgiveness, and Trust" in *The Social Psychology of Intergroup Reconciliation*, eds. Arie Nadler, Thomas E. Malloy and Jeffery D. Fisher (New York: Oxford University Press, 2008), 212. See also Fiona Bloomer and Peter Weinreich, "Cross-community Relations Projects and Interdependent Identities" in *Researching the Troubles: Social Science Perspectives on the Northern Ireland Conflict*, eds. Owen Hargie and David Dickson (Edinburgh and London: Mainstream Publishing, 2003), 141–162.

61. Lederach, *The Moral Imagination*, 29.

62. Gopin, 2000, 78.

63. Gopin, 2000, 79.

64. Appleby and Cizik, 2010, 52.

65. Baron, 2008, 283.

66. Daniel Bar-Tal and Gemma H. Bennink, "The Nature of Reconciliation as an Outcome and as a Process" in *From Conflict Resolution to Reconciliation*, ed. Yaacov Bar-Siman-tov (New York: Oxford University Press, 2004), 27.

67. See http://www.justvision.org/encounterpoint; http://www.justvision.org/home, accessed 11 May 2011.

68. Baron, 2008, 280.

69. A supra-ordinate group may be understood to be an *inter*communal body achieving in collaboration what either community could not attain on its own. Supra-ordinate goals reflect such *inter*communal aspirations.

70. Baron, 2008, 280.

71. Baron, 2008, 287.

72. R.M. Kramer and P.J. Carnevale, "Trust and intergroup negotiation" in *Intergroup Processes*, eds. R. Brown and S Gaertner (Malden, MA: Blackwell, 2003), pp. 432–450 cited in Baron, 2008, 287.

73. Herbert C. Kelman, "Reconciliation from a Social-Psychological Perspective" in *The Social Psychology of Intergroup Reconciliation*, eds. Arie Nadler, Thomas E. Malloy and Jeffrey D. Fisher (New York: Oxford University Press, 2008), 25.

74. Nadler and Shnabel, 2008, 44–45.

75. "The *goal of reconciliation* can be the creation of a conflict-free environment in which two separate parties coexist or the formation of one *integrated* social unit of which the former adversaries are two parts that share a "we" feeling (i.e., *separation* and *integration*, respectively). If the goal of reconciliation is separate coexistence between the former enemies instrumental reconciliation is enough. It restores trust to the relations between the two former adversaries who wish separate coexistence in a conflict-free environment. Socioemotional reconciliation is consistent with the goal of integration. It seeks to restore each of the parties' worthy identities through the apology-forgiveness cycle thereby freeing them from the threats that each presents to the identity of the other. It therefore allows the former adversaries to share a larger and more inclusive identity." Arie Nadler and Nurit Shnabel, "Instrumental and Socioemotional Paths to Intergroup Reconciliation and the Needs-Based Model of Socioemotional Reconciliation" in Arie Nadler, Thomas E. Malloy and Jeffery D. Fisher (eds.), *The Social Psychology of Intergroup Reconciliation*, eds. (New York: Oxford University Press, 2008), 44.

76. Baron, 2008, 287.

77. Ashutosh Varshney, *Ethnic Conflict and Civic Life: Hindus and Muslims in India* (New Haven, CN: Yale University Press, 2002), 131. See also Robert Schreiter, *Reconciliation: Mission and Ministry in a Changing Social Order* (New York and Newton, Mass: Orbis Books and Boston Theological Institute, 1992), 32–34.

78. See Lederach, 1997, chapters 6 and 7.

79. Gopin, 2009, 67.

80. Gopin, 2009, 64.

81. Gopin, 2009, 64.

82. Gopin, 2009, 64.

83. Lisa Schirch, The Civil Society-Military Relationship in Afghanistan in *Peacebrief* (Washington, D.C.: United States Institute of Peace), No 56, Sept 24, 2010, 4.

84. The Inter-Religious Council in Bosnia-Herzegovina is an NGO that comes under the umbrella of The World Conference of Religions for Peace, headquarted in New York and has been operating since 1996. I conversed with Olivera Jovanovic 25 and 26 Oct 2009, while visiting the Bosnian Defence Forces Chaplaincy—an inter-confessional body comprised of Muslim (Bosniak), Roman Catholic (Croatian) and Orthodox (Serbian) chaplains.

85. *Comprehensive Approach: Trends, Challenges and Possibilities for Cooperation in Crisis Prevention and Management* Based on Comprehensive Approach Seminar 17 June 2008 Helsinki, Articles from International Actors and from National Delegations, Work of the CAS Research Team and Expertise of the Crisis Management Initiative (Ministry of Defence: Helsinki, Finland, 2008), 26–27.

86. Appleby and Cizik, 2010, 35.

87. Appleby and Cizik, 2010, 23.

88. Land Operations, p. 5–14. See https://info.publicintelligence.net/CanadaLandOps.pdf.

89. Gopin, 2009, 66.

90. The Global Peace and Security Program (GPSP), Foreign Affairs and International Trade Canada, 10 August 2010 http://www.international.gc.ca/START-GTSR/gpsp-ppsm.aspx.

Part II

Case Studies from the International Military Chaplaincy Community

THE CASE STUDIES

In the following case studies theory and praxis come together in the operational anecdotes of chaplains from a number of countries: Canada, France, the United States, New Zealand and Norway. These individual studies feature different times and places as well as the distinctive experiences of chaplains that mark them as unique. Spanning two decades, missions implicating the United Nations (UN), the North Atlantic Treaty Organization (NATO) and Coalition Forces in four theatres of operation are drawn on: Bosnia-Herzegovina, Kosovo, Iraq and Afghanistan. The type of mission varies from peacekeeping in Kosovo, wider peacekeeping in Bosnia, counter-insurgency operations (COIN) in Iraq to the reconstruction and stabilization emphasis of the Provincial Reconstruction Teams (PRT) of Afghanistan. As diverse as the operations, so too are the RLE experiences of the individual chaplains: the ritual event of an interfaith celebration inclusive of all three faith groups during the Bosnian war (CAN); the ritual breaking of bread together with Muslim and Orthodox religious leaders implicating high ranking politicians in Kosovo (FR); the ritual event of the Ulema Shura in the Kandahar PRT facilitated by a Muslim chaplain (CAN); the striking of the Baghdad Accords bringing together representatives of all faith groups, top Iraqi leaders, U.S. government departments, and the NGO and diplomatic communities (US); the development role of building educational infrastructure in the Bamyan Province PRT, Afghanistan (NZ); and lastly, collaborating with the Faryab Province PRT team in facilitating dialogue with the Afghan religious community (NOR). Given the focus of this entire book—reconciliation in conflict and post-conflict environments—an appropriate manner to complete the case studies will be to consider the journey of the Religious Directors of the Bosnian Defense Forces. Theirs' is a living story of hope for those still engulfed in conflict. The extensive analysis presented will convincingly demonstrate the breadth of RLE as an operational construct, as its inherent dynamics may be effectively generalized from one context to another within Command structures and Whole of Government configurations alike.

Chapter Five

Canada in Bosnia and Afghanistan

Early Days:
An Interfaith Celebration in a War Zone (1994)

The following case study is based on actual events that occurred in the Bosnian theatre of operations during the war (winter/spring, 1993), as experienced by this author. The benefits of *trust building* among the religious leadership of ethno-religious communities in a conflict environment will be brought forward. In this instance, the combined efforts of chaplains from consecutive rotations aided conflicting groups in capturing a renewed vision of the humanity of the *other*. This study will provide context for the key theoretical component of *mimetic* structures and the application in praxis of *ritual and symbol*, with reference to lesser themes throughout. Conflict's *mimetic* dynamics will speak to the escalating nature of violence among groups, providing greater appreciation of its role in intensifying conflict. Unique to this operational anecdote will be the inclusion of the more positive role of *mimetic modeling*. Here the expressed desire of chaplains for the well-being of the *other*, across ethno-religious lines, cultivated within these religious leaders, living in divisive times, an openness toward dialogue—the *will to embrace* the estranged *other*. Praxis will complement theory as *ritual and symbol* are introduced in the unprecedented *ritual event* of an Interfaith Celebration for Peace among alienated faith group leaders and their communities in the midst of overt conflict. Illuminated also will be how, under commander's authority and in his explicit intent, the engendered trust earned by these chaplains led to unparalleled collaboration, symbolically signalling to their respective ethno-religious communities that the future lay not in fighting but in fraternity. Known today as Religious Leader Engagement (RLE), this case study will examine its strengths and identify some of the weaknesses of its employment.

PADRES MOORE AND EUGENIO: BOSNIAK AND CROAT FAITH COMMUNITIES

In the spring of 1993 Padre Steve Moore deployed with Canadian Forces (CF), 2nd Battalion of the Royal Canadian Regiment Battle Group (CAN-BAT II)[1] from southern Croatia to the outskirts of Sarajevo, a city very much at war. The mission was that of the United Nations Protection Force (UN-PROFOR).[2] The main body of the Battle Group resided in the town of Visoko with more than a company in Kiseljak, communities on the edge of the capital—the first rotation of Canadian troops to this region (Roto 0).[3] The Area of Operations (AO)[4] encompassed a populace representative of all three ethno-religious groups: Serbian Orthodox, Croat Roman Catholic and Bosniak Muslim. At the outbreak of hostilities, feeling vulnerable to the Bosniak-Croat majority, the Serbian community vacated Visoko, leaving it to the Croats and Bosniaks. Typical of the war, who was fighting whom at any particular time remained rather fluid. In this region at that juncture of the war, Croat and Bosniak forces were siding together against the Serbs.

Upon learning through the Bosniak interpreters that the newly arrived Canadian Contingent to Visoko had with them two Christian "priests," an invitation to dialogue was immediately issued from Imam Asim Azdahič, an imam responsible for the supervision of sixty mosques in the greater Visoko area. The prescient nature of this gesture eventually came to light, as Azdahič revealed himself as one desirous of peace and reconciliation. In the Imam Association conference room of their downtown offices, five senior imams conversed with Padres Moore and Eugenio over refreshments for an entire afternoon. Muslim hospitality was extended with openness, accompanied by a tour of the famed Sherefudin White Mosque[5] of Visoko. The imams were inquisitive of life in the West, in particular, the fervency of Christian belief and praxis.

Unfortunately, hostilities were such that overtures toward the Serbian Orthodox were not possible at this time. However, regular visits to both Roman Catholic and Muslim faith communities were complemented with the sharing of humanitarian assistance as it became available from Canada via convoy from the port of Ploče, on the Dalmatian Coast of Croatia. As always, care was taken to be impartial. *Merhemet* (Red Crescent) was particularly appreciative of the clothing and non-perishable food items. Hospitality was extended to the leadership of both faith communities to visit the CANBAT II compound to meet the Commanding Officer, take a tour of the contingent chapel and to share in a meal among the troops. Imam Azdahič graciously accepted and invited us to his own home to meet his family and for refreshments.

During the remaining months of the rotation, visits became more frequent. Relations warmed, as did the engendered trust between the Canadian chaplains and both the Franciscan and Muslim communities. Imam Azdahič openly shared his intense longing to return to more amiable times when Bosniak, Croat and Serb lived as neighbors, sharing the same streets, stores, parks and councils. He acutely felt the separation and alienation that fractured relation brings. This genuine expression of the *will to embrace* (see ch. 4, Encounter; ch. 11, The Will to Embrace—A Balance to Strict Justice) bore witness to his nascent desire to initiate renewed relation with the *other*, thus *transcending* the present conflict. Over against a backdrop of tremendous hurt and suffering, Imam Azdahič chose to see the *humanity* of the *other*. His parting words to this author prior to redeploying to Canada were to tell the West of their story, that they were a peace-loving people who did not want to be at war with their neighbors. Demonstrative of the *tolerant voice of religion* (see ch. 4, The Tolerant Voice of Religion: Middle Range Actors), Azdahič called for reason where there was chaos, an opening of the *self* to the religious *other* where there had only been *exclusion*: isolation and alienation.

MIMETIC RIVALRY IN THE ESCALATION OF CONFLICT

Conflict itself is complex and, as such, elicits responses that demonstrate both the depth and breadth necessary to grasp something of its essence and, yet, approach potential solutions. *Mimetic structures* represents one of the more foundational concepts to comprehending the inner workings of deep-rooted conflict. Once assimilated, one begins to recognize *mimetic* dynamics, not just in conflict, but in everyday life for it is an aspect of the human condition. (For greater expansion on the *mimetic* theory presented here, see ch. 2, Mimesis: The Reciprocal Nature of Escalating Violence and endnotes).

The *mimetic* effect is often referred to as a contagion[6] due to its contribution to the escalation of violence. For those living with *mimetic* rivalry, it doesn't matter what one achieves or acquires, what does matter is that what one gets is the same or better than the *other*[7] (see ch. 2, Mimetic Rivalry). Such rivalry was evident in Visoko adversely affecting the economy. Industry had greatly diminished due to the fighting, resulting in a weakened dinara (Bosnian currency). In 1993 many families were subsisting on the equivalent of 10 to 15 Deutschmarks a month,[8] the desired currency at the time. Clothing items such as children's footwear[9] were in great demand and farming became problematic due to the indiscriminate mining of fields and the fear of sniper fire. Farmers came to fear harvesting their crops. Many fields were left unattended, leaving much-needed yields to rot. The provision of food became an everyday challenge for Bosnian families. With resources in such scarce supply, preoccupation with what the *other* possessed or received became a natural consequence. Resentment towards another group was often exacerbated when humanitarian aid was delivered to an opposing village or town. It was not uncommon to see in the Canadian compound United Nations High Commission on Refugees (UNHCR)[10] trucks having recently returned from a humanitarian convoy to a "UN Safe Haven" with bullet-riddled bodies and pocked windshield's held together with duct tape. Events of this nature soon became reciprocal.

This author recalls witnessing such *mimetic* rivalry firsthand while delivering humanitarian aid to the Croat community that had come in through Canadian supply lines. The Serbian community had vacated Visoko for safer territory at a much higher elevation overlooking the town. They displayed their discontent with their former neighbors quite regularly by lobbing mortar rounds into the town. Serbian snipers stealthily penetrated the town limits firing on unsuspecting citizens. During a visit with Father Paulo, the local Franciscan priest (Croatian), he recounted one of his close calls with a sniper by pointing out the bullet hole in his study wall just above his head where he sat studying at the time of the shot. It was during the same visit, while unloading a number of tri-walls[11] of clothing and non-perishable food items from a large UN vehicle (white with black lettering), two mortar rounds landed several hundred meters from the truck in the courtyard. Sentries at the Serbian location were watching and decided to send a "message." It had its desired effect. The small section of Canadians with their interpreter in tow quickly departed. The advancement of one frequently leads to a reaction in the *other*. Such acts of aggression are soon avenged—the reciprocity typical of *mimetic* rivalry.

MIMETIC VIOLENCE IN RECIPROCATION

Prior to the Canadians deploying to the outskirts of Sarajevo in the spring of 1993, *mimetic violence* was particularly discernible in the deliberate attacks by the Serbian military on iconic vestiges of Bosniak culture (see ch. 2, Mimetic Violence). As Michael Sells reports, the spring of 1992 saw a systematic campaign of cultural eradication, a blatant attempt to strike at the heart of the Bosniak identity in Sarajevo.[12] The National Library of Bosnia-Herzegovina was shelled from positions on the mountainside directly in front of it. Over a million books, more than a hundred thousand manuscripts and centuries of historical records of Bosniak culture were incinerated. Also targeted was the Oriental Institute in Sarajevo, which archived the largest collections of Islamic and Jewish manuscripts in the Balkans. Destroyed were more than five thousand Persian, Arabic, Ottoman Turkish and Adzamijski (Slavic in Arabic script) manuscripts. Added to the toll were the National Museum and numerous mosques. The destruction of many of the cultural institutions of Sarajevo that preceded the arrival of CANBAT II was intentional and methodical, a practice that spread to other areas throughout Bosnia. True to *mimetic* form, movement for the people of Sarajevo became constricted and precarious with the onslaught of the relentless sniper fire. During the siege many lost their lives simply trying to find food and fuel to keep their families alive.

It was into this environment in the regions surrounding Sarajevo in 1993 that the Canadians and others deployed. Animosity and alienation were deeply felt sentiments in Visoko tangibly displayed. Although the Croats and Bosniaks were on friendly terms at that time, the Serbian community left en masse at the commencement of hostilities. Evidence of ethnic cleansing was not difficult to find. The Serbian Orthodox church down the street from the famed White Mosque bore evidence of the ongoing conflict. A gaping hole through the sidewall left by a tank round, revealed a ransacked interior. Damaging or destroying cultural, often religious, landmarks of the opposing ethno-religious groups had become standard procedure, anything to spur the *other* to leave an ethnically mixed community and assure that they would never return. Interspersed throughout local neighborhoods were former Serb houses mined from within, leaving a heap of brick, mortar, and splintered timbers spewing out onto sidewalks. It was not uncommon to see an ethnic insignia crudely painted on what was left of an exterior wall—the perpetrators proudly laying claim to the destruction, assuring the unwelcome owners would never return. These are the scenes and sentiments that welcomed the Canadian contingent in the early winter of 1993.

MIMETIC STRUCTURES OF VIOLENCE PERPETUATING CONFLICT

When patterns of violence become entrenched to the degree that the aim is to control, hurt, diminish or otherwise do violence to the *other*, the escalating violence seemingly takes on a life of its own—a distinct driver of conflict. At this stage the *mimetic* nature of "giving as good as one gets, and then some" becomes normative. In such instances, conflict begins to shape identity and as *mimetic structures of violence* emerge (see ch. 2, Mimetic Structures of Violence). People find themselves doing things that under normal circumstances they would never do. As Redekop relates, ". . . when subject to these structures, [individuals] construct a framework within which their own violence is justified."[13] Where *mimetic structures of violence* become entrenched, preoccupation of eliminating the *other* is often all that matters: it does not have to make sense.

Mimetic structures of violence may be seen as layers of misunderstanding and patterns of behavior and reaction developing over time to create a sedimented effect of mutual reinforcement. In greater Visoko, violent structures were manifest in different ways: violence *controlled* the freedom of movement between certain of these communities, e.g., the Serbian villages were behind the front lines; the *force* of violence had inflicted economic hardship on all as the Serbs felt compelled to leave everything behind and relocate to safer environs among their own. In so doing, the violence of *extraction* ruptured families and life-long friendships in what had been for decades integrated communities, inclusive of extensive intercommunal marriage known to Yugoslavian culture; violence *diminished* the dignity of all concerned as individuals and communities succumbed to behaviors and activities that would normally never occur; *hurting* the *other* physically and emotionally became commonplace; the *curse* of violence had become prevalent in that extended hardship bred an orientation of wishing evil on the *other*; and the passive *refusal of help* as individuals found it increasingly easier to allow suffering when the means of its alleviation were close at hand.

PADRES GUAY AND PICHETTE: INCLUDING THE SERBIAN ORTHODOX

The subsequent rotation of Canadian troops brought Roman Catholic Padres Jean-Pierre Guay (priest) and Yvon Pichette (pastoral associate) of the 2nd Battalion of the Royal 22e Regiment (2nd R22R)[14] to Visoko. In Split, Croatia, Padre Moore had but a brief conversation with Padre Pichette as segments of their two contingents literally crossed paths in rotation. He was informed of the interest in intercommunal dialogue demonstrated by Imam Asim Azdahič and Father Paulo. In the coming months, Guay and Pichette expanded the dialogue to include the local Serbian Orthodox priest, Miroslav Drincič, thus making contact with the regional leadership of all three major faith groups of the suburbs of Sarajevo and regions farther west. These chaplains facilitated the *networking* among the religious leadership of these ethno-religious communities beyond what had begun during the previous rotation, clearly illustrating the strategic value of continuity in operational ministry—a point to be revisited later in this study.

The Chaplain Support Plan submitted to the Commander of the Land Forces Quebec Area succinctly outlines the goals for their Religious Leader Engagement among the three faith communities—a ministry strategy also approved by LCol. Desjardins, the contingent commander. Their strategy clearly emphasized the need for nurturing *trust* in building relation among the local religious leaders and their respective faith communities. As outlined in their report, they desired to:

- Understand the situation relating to the various communities of faith of persons residing in central Bosnia, and their humanitarian needs;
- Develop partnerships with the spiritual leaders of the communities;
- Attempt to find common ground between the factions by way of small iterative steps; and,
- [Engage in] intercommunal prayers for peace. [15]

In support of this vision, visits were made to the various Franciscan and Muslim leaders of Visoko and Kiseljak, and, more significantly, to the Serbian Orthodox priests of Zenica and Kraljeva. As relation moved beyond introductions, Father Guay's empathic listening enabled these leaders to share the pain of their war-ravaged communities and fractured fraternity, stories all strikingly similar. [16] It is through the *place of hospitality* (see ch. 2, The Place of Hospitality) that the sense of a *safe space* was created, enabling sharing to occur, and a companion to *trust* for those who are living in the midst of conflict. Here hospitality is demonstrated in its gratuity and graciousness. It is extended for no other reason but to create a space and an occasion to begin seeding reconciliation. *Trust* grows out of such displays of hospitality (see ch 4., Trust Development).

Their private sharing and public participation in prayer services with all three faith group leaders and their communities inspired Guay and Pichette to propose an Interfaith Celebration for Peace including these leaders and members of their respective faith communities. Erudite individuals, they immediately fathomed the symbolic significance of such an interfaith celebration to the long road toward *reconciliation* that lay before them and their communities. At the suggestion of Guay, each cleric agreed to offer a symbol from their faith tradition to present to the assembled, representing the richness of each religious confession. These symbols were to dwell permanently in the modular tent that served as the chapel for CANBAT II, testifying to the mounting good will among these leaders despite the conflict, past and present. Individual relation building between the chaplains and the religious leaders engendered the beginnings of trust among these clerics, trust enough to join together in a symbolic event for the greater good of all of their collective peoples, regardless of faith tradition or orientation of their respective political leaders. The following is an excerpt from the celebration liturgy including a description of the symbols offered as gestures of good will and fraternity. [17]

Spiritual leaders from central Bosnia, coming from various religions represented here today, will exchange treasured symbols, each representing the confession of their religious faith.

First, the Imam Asim Azdahič, Muslim cleric, President of the Islamic Community of the region, will give Padre Guay the Islamic symbol, which will
always reside in the tent of the chapel in our community of Camp Visoko.

Silence and Islamic recitation.
The Orthodox priest Miroslav Drincič, in charge of the Zenica parish for the
last 22 years, presents an icon of the Virgin Mary, Mother of God; Let us recall
the importance of the Gospa throughout the world, and particularly in the last
twelve years at Medjugorje. [18]

Orthodox chant.
Tomorrow, 4 October, celebrates St. Francis of Assisi in Italy, and the Francis-
cans have grown the Christian communities all over the former Yugoslavia.
Srebrenica erected its first chapel 700 years ago. Twice already, Assisi was the
meeting location for the spiritual leadership of the world where they prayed for
peace. Father Paolo de Visoko presents us the effigy of St. Francis. This will
serve as an important symbol among us as a model artisan of peace.

Prayer of St. Francis from the Blue Book.
Padres Guay and Pichette present a crucifix as a symbol of our communion
recognizing the communities of believers that reside in Bosnia. It is also a
symbol of our journey among them.

Crucifix

Comments by Major Guay.

Also, poignantly symbolic of the hope that remained for war-torn Bosnia was
the intentional involvement of children from the participating faith communities, life-giving signs of the future. The celebration continued:

Children place baskets on the table.
The children bring flowers.
Songs
Comments: As long as there are children, there is hope, regardless of the
suffering and the obstacles . . . as long as there are roses and lilies in Bosnia,
there will be a sign of life that will always be growing. Let us see and hear the
children sing about life and peace.

Such occasions give amplification to both the possibility and efficacy of
speaking with one religious voice, "so that others may hear a voice of unity,
rather than a partisan voice, especially in an area where the ethnic and relig-

ious fault lines are so closely aligned,"[19] aiding the resolution of conflict via the emergence of religious pluralism.

These religious leaders came to *trust* Padres Guay and Pichette as men of faith who manifested genuine concern for their well-being and that of their people. Such nurturing of *working trust* made way for renewed *mutuality*,[20] fostering the reframing of relation between the Serbian Orthodox priest and his Croat and Muslim counterparts. The *mutuality* of the *self* and the *other* brought into view greater receptivity, moving the Serbian Orthodox priest, and by extension his community, away from their isolation toward greater inclusivity with the *other*.

RITUAL AND SYMBOL[21]

As a symbol-making activity, events such as the Interfaith Celebration for Peace potentially create a sense of safety and selfhood for those experiencing the insecurity and uncertainty associated with conflict. In some small way this event gave occasion to address the injustice of a conflict that had shattered communities and to offer an opportunity to begin the hard work of reaching across the divide that had resulted. The following synopsis will amplify for the reader how *symbol and ritual* communicates to the participants on multiple levels.

As a *formal ritual*, (see ch. 2, Formal and Informal Ritual) all involved were cognizant of the significance of participating in this celebration within the Canadian compound. This was a bold step for these religious leaders for the division between the Croat/Bosniak alliance and the Serbian community were stark and real. At some level, an approaching of the *re-humanizing* of the *other* transpired. Accomplished here, at least for the duration of the interfaith celebration, was a shift in the focus of identity and locus of the conflict away from an obsession with one's ethnicity to a more inclusive vision of mutuality. This ritual event stressed their common identities as the spiritual leaders of their respective communities, not without influence among political leadership, and in some sense caretakers of culture and narrative. Salient as well, this celebration was a *constructive ritual*. Its main objective was to better the lives of those involved, transforming identities defined by the conflict and providing occasion to re-establish broken relationships. The intent of Padres Guay and Pichette was to present a message of a different way of being to communities living in estrangement and open conflict. These religious leaders had come to grasp the significance of the opportunity that had been afforded them to speak before this gathering of their peoples with a voice of unity—a call that had fallen silent since the outbreak of hostilities.

As a *ritual of inversion*, (see ch. 2, Rituals of Inversion) local citizens witnessing this event experienced, at least for a time, a different view of what had become fractured ethnicity. The grip of local power structures (*mimetic*) on social relations among these communities in a sense became muted, thus tipping them on their head as it were, if only for the duration of the ritual event. One cannot underestimate that which is communicated tacitly. During this period of conflict, witnessing the religious leaders of all three faith groups worshiping together may have been more than a rare glimpse of fraternity. Subliminally, such events sow seeds of openness to the possibility of creating the much-needed shared space for their communities in the midst of such overt conflict (see ch. 2, The Subliminal of Symbol in Ritual).

MIMETIC MODELING

Mimetic structures need not always be a negative force. *Mimesis* also manifests positively. *Mimetic* desire reaches beyond imitating the behavior of the *other* or wanting what the other possesses. It also may encompass a desire for the "interiority" of the *other* (see ch. 2, Mimetic Modeling: Creating Openness to the Other). *Modeling*, or exemplifying, trust, acceptance, tolerance, and hospitality before individuals or groups caught in the grips of ruptured and alienated relationships, becomes *mimetic*. It nurtures the desire for such subjectivity—the internalizing of similar sentiments—*mimetic modeling*. Dialogue with the Orthodox priests ceased with the commencement of hostilities. The *mimetic modeling* of inclusivity and acceptance of the religious *other* by Guay and Pichette, regardless of ethnicity, cultivated desire within each leader for the same. Visiting these clerics individually, sharing privately with them, and participating in prayer services when appropriate, modeled before them the *will to embrace* the *other* (see ch. 4, Encounter). Such mutuality enabled a reframing of relation between the Serbian Orthodox priest and his Croat and Muslim counterparts where the isolation of independence was weighed against the inclusivity of interdependence with the *other*. Together, these leaders realized that security for their peoples was to be found in relation, not alienation. As such, they recognized the higher good at work in their midst and chose to grasp the opportunity it presented to transcend that which had created such division for their respective peoples. For a period of time, the mimetic structures of violence that had totally consumed these communities were eclipsed by *mimetic structures of blessing*: that desire for the well-being of the *other*, with its ever-expanding options oriented toward life saw the beginnings of movement away from estrangement to renewed relation—a catalytic effect emanating from the intervener's desire for their well-being (see ch. 2, Mimetic Structures of Blessing).

The inclusiveness of the interfaith celebration temporarily suspended the social structures and roles that had perpetuated alienation and conflict. A "double vision" of sorts emerged where not only did one see the *other* through new eyes but saw oneself through the eyes of the *other* (see ch. 11, The Reframing of Relation). Of particular note was the presentation of icons from each faith community left to reside together in the Camp Chapel, a glimpse into the liminal space of the reframing of relation and unity. Transcending the inherent symbolism of the individual icons was the intentionality of the three religious leaders to consider the worldviews and identity of the *others*. A dimension of symbol and ritual in peacebuilding is the depth of meaning subliminally imparted by an event that may initially evade the participant's ability to articulate. Nonetheless, enshrouded in symbol, the seed of truth at some level takes root, slowly germinating over time. [22]

RE-ENFORCING THE HUMANITY OF THE OTHER

Reinforcing their shared humanity was Padre Guay's utilization of an expansive hand-painted mural that served as a backdrop to the makeshift chancel area: the symbol of a mature tree with large branches, full foliage and exposed roots. His accompanying commentary is as follows,

> This tree represents all the roots of the same God, from which a unique life has given the world each and everyone of you. Regardless if we are Muslim, Jewish, Orthodox Christian or of all other protestant or catholic religions, we form the trunk together. The trunk is represented here today by the prayer of this unified family who pray to the same God so that each of our gifts, that each of our traditions, each of our lives may grow like these leaves in the sun which shines of the same life, and of the same faith. [23]

Guay's emphasis on the common heritage of the Abrahamic faith traditions was yet another unifying message of kinship and rootedness, reinforcing the humanity of the *other*, pluralism, and unity, something that had been distorted by the war. He reminded his listeners of the identity of the *other* aside from that of the conflict. The shared celebration contravened the tendency of the conflict to rigidly center on one aspect of the *other's* identity. [24] Accentuating the vital importance of open ethno-kin connections for future generations was the intentional presence of their youth. Regardless of religious orientation, religious/cultural *ritual* and *symbol* present to operational chaplains an occasion to connect with local religious leaders in a manner not afforded to other contingent members. In theatres of operation such time-specific events, although short in duration, occur often. The vision of transcendence is for renewed relation in ritual to "carry over into non-ritual time and space." [25] It is through such collaboration that the writing of new narratives begins—incremental events that become the substance of *instrumental reconciliation.*

CONCERNS

As hopeful as this interfaith celebration was in a very dark time for Bosnian society in the greater Visoko area, one must consider the detractors present. Padre Guay related an initial concern at the lateness of Imam Azdahič arriving for the event. The liturgy had begun by the time the Imam appeared, requiring adjustments to accommodate him. Following the celebration it was learned that his tardiness was the result of an altercation with some of the other imams who did not want him to participate due to the presence of the Serbian Orthodox priest, Father Drincič. This poses a complex question. It is not uncommon for those desirous of transcending a given conflict to reach across a communal divide to one of like mind of an opposing group. The danger lies in moving beyond the boundary of one's own community to meet the *other* in a neutral space, acceptance among one's own people may be jeopardized. With such initiatives, as meaningful and well intentioned as they may be, care must be taken not to create a precarious situation for one who is courageous enough to look to a future based on mutuality rather than division.

The reader must also appreciate that these events were *ad hoc* in nature. For Moore and Eugenio, the initiation of dialogue by Imam Azdahič and its ensuing conversations were totally unanticipated. Guay and Pichette arrived with a plan to promote reconciliation among these conflicting ethno-religious communities if opportunity was afforded. This one-time-event was a tangible step toward mutuality, bolstered by the progress of an earlier rotation. Sadly, any lasting effect within these communities was not realized. For activities involving *ritual and symbol* to have the desired effect, they must be repeated, intentionally building on earlier events. In today's operational environments, planning that spans a number of rotations is needed, lengthier tours for those engaged in peacebuilding and conflict transformation activities, with extended handovers as one Padre re-deploys home.

WHOLE OF GOVERNMENT PARTNERS: THE ULEMA SHURA (2006–2007)

Case Study Preface

This case study will be devoted to the operational ministry of Imam Suleyman Demiray, a Canadian Forces (CF) chaplain, who, in 2006–2007, worked among the Sunni and Shia faith communities in Kandahar, Afghanistan,[26] while serving with the International Security Assistance Forces (ISAF),[27] a NATO-led[28] Coalition Forces mission. Imam Demiray is a Sunni Muslim of Turkish extraction, now a naturalized Canadian citizen and officer of the Queen. This author deployed to Afghanistan with the express purpose of chronicling Demiray's contribution to the mandate of the Kandahar Provincial Reconstruction Team (PRT).[29] His collaborative role as a Muslim chaplain in the PRT with Gavin Buchan, then Foreign Affairs Canada (DFAIT)[30] Political Adviser (PolAd) for Regional Command (RC) South, an area representative of the province of Kanhaharwas, and continues to be at the writing of this book, unprecedented. Buchan, a seasoned diplomat, initiated cooperation with Demiray with the view to engaging the Sunni and Shia faith communities of Kandahar Province. With his guidance, the Imam succeeded in making inroads into the Islamic community, which aided the PRT in gaining access to the religious leadership of Kandahar. How to engage this influential body within Afghan culture had eluded Buchan for some time. Demiray presented that opportunity. Characteristic of a collaborative comprehensive approach (CA), the level of civic engagement achieved among the religious scholars of Kandahar region enhanced the Advisor's ability to establish much-needed dialogue and pursue strategic goals, specific to mission objectives.[31] Critical to any initiative among the indigenous population, Buchan and Demiray were careful to proceed under the commander's authority, executing their plan in his explicit intent. CF Brigadier General David Fraser, Commander RC South, was in full support of Imam Demiray's role with the PRT staff. Fraser acknowledged to this author the good will his ministry had generated among the local religious communities, ultimately enhancing security for troops and the local populace alike.[32]

This case study will take the reader more deeply still into theoretical constructs dealing with intergroup conflict. *Intractable conflict* has become a distinguishing feature of the 21st century. Threat to one's core identity—individual or group—stands as a salient facet of contemporary conflict. The stages of its development are notable in Afghanistan and factor into this study. Building on the role of identity in intractable conflict, *human identity needs* will be examined for their relevance in linking the beliefs, desires and emotions of individuals and groups with the overt actions and motivations often associated with conflict. The aim is to provide the reader with a shorthand method of discerning how identifying need satisfiers may move groups toward more openness and cooperation. *Open and closed relational systems* will further delineate the dynamics contributing to the rigid exclusivity in relation that defines intergroup conflict. Most often, it is through the intervention of another that a softening of entrenched positions is experienced. Facilitating such *encounter* precipitates the beginnings of an *open relational system*, as will be seen in the *ritual event* of the Ulema Shura in the Kandahar

PRT. Where deemed fitting and for the purposes of continuity, theory introduced in the earlier case study will be touched on here.

The Context

During the spring of 2006 Imam Suleyman Demiray was posted to the Canadian PRT in Kandahar, Afghanistan, an affiliation that stretched well into the summer months. In terms of the Comprehensive Approach (CA), Demiray's contribution represents a "first look" into the potential supportive role of a religious peacebuilder alongside other partners in a PRT-like organization. Gavin Buchan, PolAd to the PRT, initiated this *ad hoc* arrangement. Demiray, the Commander of RC South, the Chaplain Branch, and, more importantly, ISAF Cmdr., Lieutenant General Sir David Richards (UK), shared his vision.[33] The CF approach was to assign chaplains to the PRT due to the numbers of troops and civilian staff (300 plus) committed to its mission. Added to this was the level of danger associated with its programming. Demiray's arrival was in part a departure from this model. He remained faithful to providing pastoral support to those in need. Moreover, there were no terms of reference to follow for an Imam assigned to work with government personnel with the express purpose of identifying and engaging the religious leadership of the Islamic faith communities of Kandahar. This was new terrain for Command, the CF Chaplain Branch and Foreign Affairs Canada (DFAIT). As will be seen, Buchan astutely drew on the attributes that Imam Demiray possessed in his capacity as a Sunni Muslim Imam. Opportunities to connect with local and regional religious leaders were afforded that otherwise would not have occurred.

Both military leadership and government personnel recognized afresh the distinct advantages of incorporating Religious Leader Engagement (RLE) into strategic thinking and planning for a more integrative approach to present and future operations. For the Chaplain Branch itself, the benefits of Demiray's contribution to the mission—more particularly, the interagency environment of government departments and agencies—was evident. Of concern, were the parameters of the chaplain's involvement, which, on occasion, fell outside the cognizance or supervision of senior chaplains at the operational and strategic levels. These were indeed early days for RLE. Demiray's involvement in 2006 and his subsequent return visits to Afghanistan in 2007[34] to continue with the work begun while attached to the PRT was well outside any frame of reference for chaplain's involvement. As important as his activities among the Islamic faith communities of Kandahar were, his collaboration with other Whole of Government actors stands as a prescient example of the place RLE potentially holds within the CA. Concomitant with Demiray's contribution were similar initiatives from other nations, as will be seen in upcoming case studies. Further discussion arising from Demiray's unique involvement will be forthcoming deeper into this study—the place of faith traditions other than Christianity and civilian religious peacebuilders being among them. Attention will now shift to the actual events interspersed with theoretical descriptors.

Together, Buchan and Demiray set about endeavoring to determine who the key players were within the religious community, and who among them would be open to their overtures. They needed time to listen to their concerns in order to identify their issues, if they were going to be of any assistance to them, which would, in turn, hold benefits for the mission. Buchan likened working on his own with the religious community to trying to open an envelope wearing boxing gloves;[35] to be effective one needed the tools. He looked to Demiray to bring understanding of the religious context inclusive of the subtleties of the roles played by individual strands of the faith. In his words, "Suleyman took the initial opening and tried to build an understanding of who was who and figure out what their issues were and how we could use that to engage more effectively."[36] A series of diagrams will aid the reader in following Imam Demiray's activities with the PRT staff and among the Sunni and Shia faith group leadership in Kandahar City and Province.

Figure 5.1 depicts the two major initiatives that became the focus of the Demiray-Buchan collaboration. Confusion over the Ulema Council's role with that of the Director of Religious Affairs for Kandahar Province immediately became apparent. This will be discussed under the heading, *Engaging the Director of Religious Affairs*, deeper into the Case Study but needs to be identified now. The Shia absence from the Ulema Council will be clarified now.

Buchan readily understood that in Afghanistan religion was pervasive, an aspect of identity and a part of daily life for the people. He also recognized that the insurgents were co-opting religion as a means of motivation; quite literally they were using the religious community as a battleground. During his 13 months in Kandahar, the Taliban assassinated a number of Kandahar's religious scholars who they perceived to be a threat to their influence. In 2004, the Senior Mullah of the Kandahar Ulema Council (Sunni) was murdered. The Shia community comprised between 10 and 15 percent of the Kandahar city population. Prior to Buchan's time, they had maintained repre-

Figure 5.1. Identifying the Issues: Shia Absence on Ulema Council.

sentation on the Ulema Council. Unfortunately, Shia participation had not occurred since the death of the leading Sunni Mullah, leaving their faith community in isolation with little voice in the affairs of the greater religious community of Kandahar Province for a period of more than two years at that point. A resultant lessening of communication between the faith groups leadership had occurred. As a political advisor it was crucial for Buchan to know who mattered, who actually set the tone, who was influential and who held what views. Imam Demiray brought with him the distinct advantage of an innate ability to access the religious community of Kandahar.

Intractable Conflict

In situations of intractable conflict, emotional distance, for whatever reason, between groups often leads to real or perceived notions of *threat* (see ch. 2, Intractable Conflict). The lack of communication between the Sunni and Shia religious leadership left these groups dangerously susceptible to propagandists who stood to benefit from any 'misunderstanding' that might contribute to increased cleavage between these faith communities. Paramount to the Kandahar PRT was the need to balance such messages of *distortion* that would only intensify any growing sense of alienation between the Sunni and Shia communities, or, for that matter, dispel unfavorable messages depicting them as Crusader's bent on changing their faith and way of life. In more tribal cultures, such as Afghanistan, the threat of violence at the hands of Sunni militants is a constant in the lives of Shia Muslims, emanating from historical enmity over religious and doctrinal differences.[37] Evidence of the beginnings of *rigidification* were noticeable in Kandahar but had yet to ossify into entrenched positions of the 'us' and 'them' that often precede the violence associated with the negation of the *other*. A growing estrangement had evolved between the Sunni and Shia religious leadership of Kandahar, however, room existed for a reconciling of differences and a re-establishing of ties. Imam Demiray noted a willingness on the part of the Shia leadership to rejoin the Ulema Council and openness among the Sunni to see them return.

During this same time period (2006–2007), the *rigidification* and *collusion* of intractable conflict could be better observed with the all or nothing stakes that prevailed between the Taliban and the Kabul government. On the one hand, Taliban identity, and their perception of the rightful voice of a pure Islamic way of life, stood out against the Karzai government's message of democracy, prosperity and freedom for the Afghan people. These unbending positions stood as virtual ramparts upon which the "reason to be" (identity) found footing and around which all else availed. Furthermore, *collusion* translated into maintaining tensions and advancing violence that ultimately defined identity—the black and white perspectives of the Taliban's extremist position.

As noted in the Preface, human identity needs serve as a veritable prism through which to observe conflict. Likened to refracted light, identity needs reveal the complexion and layered effect of the beliefs, desires and motivation of individuals and groups caught in conflict. Identifying these needs and grasping something of their role in either sustaining or resolving conflict may be of benefit to those endeavoring to mitigate its violence.

Human Identity Needs

Elucidated earlier, where perceived or actual violence has transpired, reciprocal aggression results from *mimetic* behavior intensified by threatened human identity needs: meaning, connectedness, security, action and recognition. When all, or a combination of these needs are at risk, people withdraw behind group identity boundaries (*security*) where they feel safe in the face of real or perceived threat, frequently leading to relocating geographically among one's own (see ch. 2, Security). Identifying with one's kin, to the exclusion of the *other*, was exacerbated in Kandahar Province due to the absence of Shia representation on the Governor-appointed Ulema Shura. Evidence of the need for emotional security, they pulled back behind the lines of their identity group, as detachment from the predominant Sunni led to greater isolation. Too, historical enmity (see ch. 2, Wounded Memory) had worsened between these faith groups in recent years due to the cases of reciprocal ethnic cleansing in other parts of Afghanistan,[38] lessening a sense of *security* for the minority Shia. As Ahmed Rashid notes of the Hazaras—a Shia tribe to the north—to the Sunni Taliban were considered "*munafaqeen* or hypocrites and beyond the pale of true Islam."[39] Sunni tribesmen slaughtered thousands of Hazara men, women and children in Kabul (March 1995),[40] a massacre that was avenged (*mimetic*) by the Hazaras in Mazar-e-Sharif in 1997 with the butchering of several thousand captured Pashtun Taliban.[41] Menacingly, people are reminded of unsettled scores from the past by those all to willing to revive, distort and manipulate for personal gain. As one person intoned, "Everyone knows where the hatchet is buried." For the Shia of Kandahar, memories of such recent atrocities so close at hand would not have been far from the surface, naturally intensifying the human identity need for *security* and its heightened emotional state.

In addition, it is during times of conflict that groups are drawn to those who are "like them" for it is with those who share the same narratives (*meaning*) that a much-needed sense of belonging is reinforced (see ch. 2, Meaning). Threat to *meaning* for the Shia was tantamount to an attack on "self-hood." Shia narratives of life and culture were under constant threat in the hostile Afghan environment where the Sunni Taliban melded into indigenous everyday life. This sense of *connectedness* between these Islamic communities had dissipated significantly in Kandahar. Bonding within their own community, alienation of the Shia religious leadership from their Sunni counterparts ruptured the human identity need of *connectedness* between them. In such situations feelings of separation, alienation, ostracism and humiliation are common.

Fears of being acted upon against one's will (*action*) create a sense of vulnerability (see ch. 2, Action). It is reasonable to think that the sheer numbers of Pashtun Sunni,[42] of whom many were Taliban, would have contributed to a sense of incapacity to act or protect oneself. Intense resentment towards the *other* abscesses as a group's sense of worth is brought into question, sometimes to the point of violence. Where overt conflict is manifest, additional factors exacerbate tensions. Where the *other* does not meet one's perception of the *self* with a reasonable acknowledgement of the value the human identity need of *recognition* a sense of rejection ensues. It is difficult to say how overt any rhetoric of *exclusion* may have been against the Shia. That said, a simmering resentment at their exclusion from the Ulema Shura was evident to Imam Demiray (see ch. 2, Recognition).

A strategic objective of the ISAF leadership was to ameliorate relation between Sunni and Shia communities while mitigating the effects of their increasingly entrenched positions (see ch. 2, Mimetic Structures of Entrenchment). Kandahar City and Province—cradle of the Taliban movement—could ill-afford a *rigidification* of an entrenched intra-faith isolation of the religious leadership that would contribute to a broadening of the existing conflict between the Taliban insurgents and the Afghan government forces supported by its allies (see ch. 2, Intractable Conflict).

RITUAL OF THE SHURA: MEETING THE SUNNI MULLAHS OF THE ULEMA COUNCIL AT THE PRT— SPRING 2006

Imam Demiray's initial partnering with the PRT team was as Chair of a Shura[43] of the provincially appointed Religious Council of Ulema (Islamic Scholars) of Kandahar on 15 April 2006. Hosting a Shura for the Ulema Council of scholars within the PRT holds much significance. As a *formal ritual* within Afghan culture, the Shura offered an occasion for PRT staff to respectfully engage these religious leaders in a manner to which they were accustomed (See ch. 2, Formal and Informal Ritual). This should not be seen as an attempt to co-opt a cultural and religious medium, rather as an example of *cultural borrowing* (see ch. 2, xx). What better way to reach out to the local Mullahs but via the familiar to them? Acknowledging the value of local traditions and customs reinforces the reality that indigenous groups are indeed reservoirs of truth, justice and peace, not simply recipients of Western understanding with its preconceived answers to their difficulties. In building relation with the Mullahs, the engendering of trust, as well as hearing and sharing ideas and information, were wrapped in the *cultural envelope* of the Shura (see ch. 2, Cultural Competency, Cultural Borrowing: Indigenous Populations as Resources not Recipients). Present were Demiray, LCol. T. Doucette (Commandant of the PRT), Gavin Buchan (PolAd), and LCol. Fletcher (Command Chaplain of Chief of the Land Staff [Army]) who was visiting from Canada at that time. Buchan recognized Fletcher's presence as an opportunity to engage the local religious leaders, something that had evaded him up to this point. In Fletcher's words,

> The motivation behind it [Shura] was really Mr. Buchan's, from Foreign Affairs Canada: he wanted to have this happen . . . [he] was absolutely adamant that they take advantage of the opportunity of my being there, as he referred to me as sort of the senior Mullah of the Army. . . . Now the truth is I was not the card; the card we had to play was Imam Demiray, as they were very interested in meeting with him. [44]

The unique dynamic was that of having an Imam in uniform in their midst. Having served with the diplomatic corps in a number of countries, a seasoned Buchan was cognizant that in more theocratic societies Westerners were often deemed as secularists. Any overtures to the Islamic religious leadership on his part would have likely been viewed through this lens. As propaganda goes, in their minds the foreigners on their soil could not be trusted; from their perspective they were there to change their ways and expose their youth to Western decadence and immorality. [45] As a Sunni Imam, Demiray had instant credibility. He was at ease in making overtures toward the Islamic faith community of Kandahar Province, something that was reciprocated by the leadership of the Ulema Council of Kandahar Province. Demiray states, "The purpose of this Shura was to provide opportunity for dialogue with local scholars in order to understand their perspective on the situation in Kandahar, and to establish the reasoning among the religious leadership for the presence of ISAF forces and the PRT in the area." [46] Any authentic engagement must begin with sincerely listening to the needs of the *other* and then doing whatever possible to aid in meeting those needs, program objectives and funds permitting. *Trust* is earned and *cooperation* given by such means (see ch. 4, Trust Development). Buchan recalls this first meeting with the Islamic scholars.

> We invited them, they all came, it was a large group of fifteen or sixteen religious leaders sitting cross-legged on the floor and it wasn't immediately a connection. I have a very vivid memory of the senior Mullah who chairs the Ulema Council in Kandahar saying, "So, you tell us that it's a good thing that you are here in Afghanistan. You tell us that it's a good thing that our women

can now walk the streets without having to be accompanied by their husband
or uncle! Who says these are good? Who says democracy is a good thing?
Who says this concept of women's rights is a good thing?" And I'm sort of
sitting there back on my heels going, "Okay, this is going to take a while." But
it was a starting point and this has to begin with understanding who is who. If
you hope to comprehend the myriad of struggling factions among the population then you have to have an understanding of who matters, who actually sets
the tone, who is influential and who holds what views. For someone working
in this context, it's as fundamental an issue as a conventional approach. [47]

This Ulema Shura was the first time the leading Sunni Mullahs of Kandahar
Province were able to voice their grievances to ISAF representatives—a
strategic gap to be avoided in cultures where religion's role is central to
leadership and people alike. Of grave concern to them was the plight of their
youth. For years they had watched their adolescent boys leave Afghanistan to
study the Koranic scriptures in the madrasas of Pakistan where they became
easy prey for Taliban recruitment. These Mullahs were intent on establishing
local madrasahs [48] under their supervision as a means to counteract the radical 'scholarship' of Mullahs in the region of the North Western Frontier
Provinces just across the border in Pakistan. Their first request was for
government and/or foreign assistance to build a number of madrasahs and
help in developing a suitable curriculum. [49] Secondly, as a government sponsored and funded religious body, these Mullahs protested their being ex-
cluded from government decision making, particularly with regard to foreign
aid projects. [50] Strained relations between the provincial government leadership and the Ulema Council was evident—to what degree the Minister of
Religious Affairs contributed to this would come to light later. From Buchan's perspective, how effective the PRT could be in facilitating such
changes was a matter for other's to decide. Notwithstanding, the Ulema
Council had been heard and the beginnings of relation based on mutual *trust*
and *cooperation* had begun, opening a window for further deliberation.
Where *encounter* (see ch. 4, Encounter) is concerned, one must be mindful
that much transpires at the subliminal level of consciousness. Experiences of
acceptance, hospitality and kindness continue to resonate long after engaging
the *other*. Born out of isolation, misconceptions and stereotypes of the *other*
begin to lose their influence as a result of such engagement.

   For Buchan and Demiray, the relational breach between the Sunni and
Shia clerics in Kandahar was of the utmost concern, as relations had not
ossified to the degree of becoming intractable. Once the context was understood more clearly, the concern quickly became to create the *space* where
encounter could precipitate *collaborative activities*——conditions conducive
for the restoration of relation. The isolation of leadership and subsequent
segregation of their communities was a state of affairs highly susceptible to
the menacing influence of radical elements—something to be avoided if at

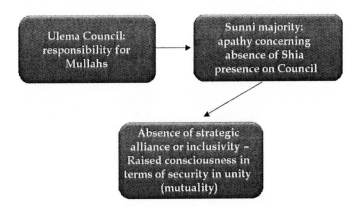

Figure 5.2. **Raising Consciousness of Security in Unity: Sunni/Shia Collaboration.**

all possible . . . not always easy in Afghanistan. In need of renewal was the *working trust* between these religious leaders that would move the "us" and "them" mentality to one of the *fragile we*—mutuality. In effect, what Imam Demiray proposed, and eventually facilitated among these religious scholars, was an *open relational system* where more constructive interdependence could begin its restoration. As will be seen, Imam Demiray *mimetically modeled* before the Sunni and Shia leadership a genuine desire for their well being and a tolerance and acceptance of the *other*, becoming the catalyst to bridging the relational chasm that had developed between them.

It must be clarified that establishing relation with the Sunni and Shia faith communities is in no way deemed as an occasion to revisit any unpleasantness that may issue from their shared history in Afghanistan. Their bringing these two faith communities out of their respective solitudes is viewed as a positive step toward mutuality in renewed relation—an *open relational system*. It was far more propitious to see the Sunni and Shia leadership in dialogue, however limited, where understanding would have opportunity to grow, than to leave these groups in isolation where the contagion of suspicion of the *other* was free to spread among their respective communities. Relational systems of this nature may be viewed as *mimetic structures of blessing* (see ch. 2, Mimetic Structure of Blessing) in the sense that conflict may be precluded in the building of relation with the *other* bringing the *self* and the *other* into a new space relationally. Mutuality *embraced* here may *mimetically* influence *other(s)* elsewhere.

RELATIONAL SYSTEMS: ENGAGING THE SHIA FAITH
COMMUNITY IN KANDAHAR—SUMMER 2006

From a theoretical perspective, a *closed relational system* (CRS) was at play between the Sunni and Shia faith communities in Kandahar. Although, the situation had not erupted into hostilities, as has been the case in the sectarian violence in Iraq, in 2006 the Sunni and Shia faith group leadership were living in isolation and had been for an extended period of time due to the absence of the Shia presence on the Ulema Shura. CRS contributes to intractable conflict taking root, inter-group dynamics more than familiar to tribal Afghanistan. (For a more complete treatment of CRS see ch. 2, Relational Systems). To better situate CRS for the reader insights particular to Afghanistan will be sited. Figure 5.3 below is provided for easy reference to both *closed* and *open relational systems* (ORS).

Sadly, Afghans can relate to *difficult life circumstances* more than most—a people having experienced war in one form or another for more than thirty years.[51] Where groups are caught up in a closed relational system, rhetoric of

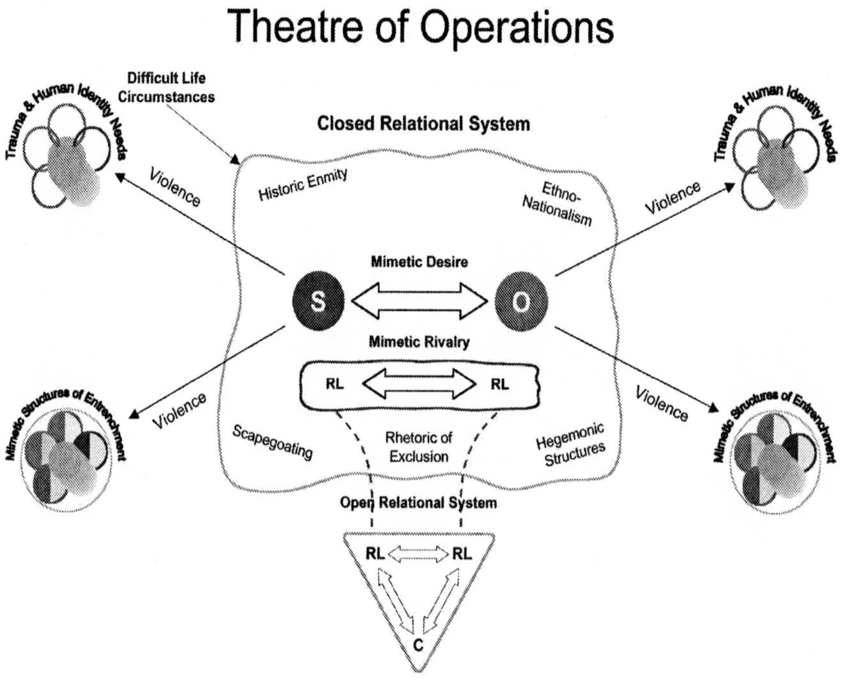

Figure 5.3. *Open Relational System* of Chaplains' (C) engaging local religious leaders (RL).

exclusion becomes normative. The *other* is viewed through a skewed lens that has developed—in some instances nurtured—over time, tainting communication and behavior. Noted previously, the religious and doctrinal differences between the Sunni and Shia Islamic traditions continue to stoke the embers of *historical enmity* (see endnote 37), at times boiling over into lethal reciprocal violence. The antecedents of Pashtun *ethno-nationalist* aspirations date back to the 1940's calling for the establishment of Pashtunistan.[52] The Taliban passion to establish an Islamist state under their version of Sharia Law (see endnote 51 for a description and related references) stands as a more recent occurrence of such aspirations. Afghan tribal society is no stranger to *scapegoating*, with instances emanating from Sunni-Shia "cooperation." In Mazar-e-Sharif in 1997 an unlikely alliance was forged between the Sunni Uzbeks and the Shia Hazaras against the invading Taliban from the south.[53] Here a common enemy enabled them to put aside any historical enmity that may have existed between them as Sunni and Shia, relieving any such tensions—at least for a while—as together the foe is vanquished. Again, for the Afghan, Taliban rule was tantamount to living under a *hegemonic structure* of severe proportions. Such a structure may be seen in the oppressive nature of the Taliban rule in Afghanistan. Their extreme interpretation of Sharia Law[54] manifested in domination that impacted virtually every facet of life, especially harsh on the rights of women. The circles off to the right and left of the main diagram represent the impact closed relational systems may have on human identity needs. The intensity of conflict impacts the need for *security* for individuals and groups to such a degree that entrenched positions between them emerges as a means to secure the essentials for survival. Where extended periods of conflict persist, trauma may become a reality for some, as human identity needs are perpetually threatened or denied (see ch. 2, Trauma and Human Identity Needs). It is into such environments that government and military personnel deploy. Attention will now turn to *open relational systems* (ORS) facilitated by Imam Demiray.

In figure 5.3 above, Sunni and Shia faith group leaders are represented by RL (Religious Leaders) in the diagram. The double arrow separating them depicts their isolation within a *closed relational system*; estrangement often resulting from ethno-religious communities engulfed in the larger conflicts of their respective identity groups. Through Demiray's engagement (represented by C for chaplain) with each RL, an *open relational system* emerged (bottom triangle). In engaging the religious leaders of each group separately, he *mimetically modeled* (see ch. 2, Mimetic Modeling: Creating Openness to the Other) openness and acceptance of the *other,* raising the prospects of *encounter* between these religious leaders where there had been none. Where entrenched estrangement creates alienation, initiating ORS enables the re-humanizing of the *other* to begin. Here double vision becomes a factor as the

Sunni and Shia Mullahs begin not only to see the *other* anew, they begin to see themselves through the eyes of the *other*—a different perspective.

To both the Sunni and Shia faith communities of Kandahar, Demiray *mimetically models* the *will to embrace* by his willingness to move towards a healing of their breached interconnectedness. Such is transcendence—rising above the discernable divide of conflict to reach across existing boundaries to the *other*. In Redekop's terms, *mimetic structures of blessing* appear in the relational openness and expansion of the *self* toward the *other*. Options become life-oriented rather than conflicting, creativity and generosity begin to eclipse the will to confront. Blessing manifests in the hope of a more peaceful and prosperous future for all—the *fragile we* of *working trust.*

Of import, *secondary relational systems*[55] factor into this analysis: *geography, kinship, ideology*, and *history/memory*. These become spoilers intruding from the exterior into already conflicted and closed relational systems. The Pashtun are the largest ethnic group in Afghanistan, by far the predominant ethnic presence within the Taliban (see endnote 52). The arbitrarily drawing of the Indian-Afghan border in 1893 by the British, the Durand Line,[56] *geographically* divided the Pashtun population in two. A Pakistani-Afghan border since 1948, the immediacy and porosity of the border offers unopposed movement for their Pashtun Pakistani brethren. The obvious *kinship* adds to the complexity for the Afghan government, as the human identity need of *connectedness* conjures up fraternal bonds reaching back centuries. In such circumstances, related groups look for occasion to "support their cousins" in difficulty. Such depth of fraternity is readily reinforced *ideologically*, as commonly held beliefs and a shared vision create formidable ties. Sadly, *history* and *memory* render a focus on past deeds. The chosen trauma (see ch. 2, Wounded Memory) of identity groups keeps former atrocities in the forefront of consciousness of those waiting to settle old scores. In Afghanistan *secondary relational systems* are never far away; the Sunni enjoy the support of their Pashtun brethren in Pakistan while the Shia look to Iran.[57]

It was at this juncture that Buchan and Demiray introduced the *superordinate goal* of a collaborative activity focusing on what they could best accomplish together—cooperation pertaining to a bottom up grassroots initiative (see ch. 4, Collaborative Activities: Towards Personal Trust and Integration. After much discussion over a period of weeks the Shia leadership was sufficiently convinced that Sunni and Shia concerns were mutual. Their common cause for the youth of their respective communities and the desire for their voice to be heard in government became the catalytic motivator in uniting them in this endeavor.

In July of 2006 Shia Mullahs met with provincial government officials, Imam Demiray and certain Sunni Mullahs within the PRT compound for exploratory discussions relating to such collaboration. Greatly encouraged,

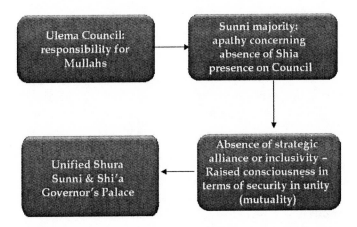

Figure 5.4.   A Unified Sunni/Shia Ulema Council: Governer's Palace, Kandahar.

the Shia leaders testified to looking forward with anticipation to a renewed Shia presence as participating members of the predominantly Sunni (Pashtun) Ulema Council of Kandahar.[58] The first Sunni and Shia Ulema Shura took place in the Governor's Palace in Kandahar City before the summer of 2006 finished where they jointly discussed their mutual concerns. This common journey of interdependence represents a vision that must not be lost from view. A provincial government/regional structure, the Ulema Council of Sunni and Shia Islamic scholars became the "top down" mechanism by which this "grass roots/bottom up" initiative found footing—in Reuben Baron's language, *circular causation.*[59] With full authority and in the explicit intent of Command, this Muslim chaplain collaborated with his *interagency* partners in a *peacebuilding* endeavor, thus contributing to the mission mandate. A *working trust* had given rise to renewed *collaboration*, bringing the Shia leadership out of their isolation. Religious Leader Engagement of this nature re-enforces peaceful *coexistence* between ethno-religious groups while promoting *integration.* Such initiatives create the conditions for *continued dialogue* and deeper *personal trust* to take root—*instrumental reconciliation.* These incremental steps give place to the *writing of new narratives* as the *will to embrace* enables and empowers leadership to *transcend* that which divides. In time, the past may be revisited and the work of the *healing of memory* begun. One hopes, a harbinger of better things to come.

ENGAGING THE DIRECTOR OF RELIGIOUS AFFAIRS —
KANDAHAR PROVINCE

Soon after his arrival to the PRT, the Political Advisor directed Imam Demiray to make contact with the Director of Religious Affairs (DRA) for the province of Kandahar. Albeit, this represents engagement from the tactical level, it underscores potential roles for chaplains embedded in the Interagency (Whole of Government)—environment, a function more suited to a religious leader. Figure 5.5 below provides a sequential overview of Imam Demiray's engagement with the religious communities of Kandahar Province and the DRA at the provincial level, followed by an explanation of these events.

During his first visit with the DRA Demiray discerned that the director was serving on an interim basis awaiting his position to be made substantive by the governor. In subsequent visits he learned that a degree of role confusion existed between the DRA and the Ulema Council in terms of the oversight responsibility for mosques and their Mullahs. As a government appointed religious body, the Ulema Council deemed their role to be one of cleric oversight—to communicate with and give direction to the local Mullahs. They described his responsibilities as being those of infrastructure management, whereas the DRA saw his role as being more sweeping than mosques and madrassahs. He contested that his job description also included supervising the local Mullahs. Understandably, there was a degree of friction between these two bodies. As a result a growing sense of disconnectedness

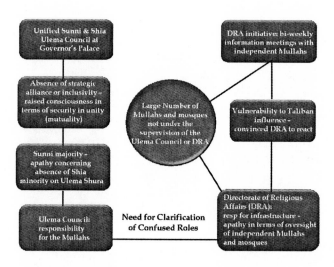

Figure 5.5. Religious Community & Government. Unified Ulema Council & Director of Religious Affairs Initiative.

among the Mullahs of the Ulema Council from the Provincial Government had emerged.

By virtue of his easy association among the religious communities of Kandahar City, Demiray discovered that there were more than a few independent mosques that came under the jurisdiction of neither the Ulema Council nor the DRA. Devoid of oversight, these mosques were often funded by a local patron and were vulnerable to "outside influences." The supervision of these mosques became a concern to both Demiray and the PRT Political Advisor, apprehensions that were raised with the DRA. The Imam went to great lengths to impress upon the DRA of the urgency of engaging these Mullahs due to their susceptibility to Taliban infiltration. Bi-weekly information meetings with these independent Mullahs were initiated and held at the Governor's Palace. When Imam Demiray left Afghanistan, these meetings were still convening.

In addition to bringing the Shia presence back on the Ulema Council, Imam Demiray endeavored to facilitate dialogue between this provincial government body and the DRA office in the hopes of clarifying their roles. Bringing the DRA and local independent Mullahs together for initial consultations was another significant initiative. Regular consultation with Gavin Buchan as the PRT Political Advisor was a part of this process, inclusive of consultation with and producing regular reports for the chain of command.

OBSERVATIONS AND CONCERNS

This is not to suggest that challenges do not remain. Imam Demiray represents a "one of" in terms of incorporating religious peacebuilding into the mandate of a PRT. As a religious leader in uniform, his contribution stands as one of the few collaborative endeavors to date of engaging local and regional religious leaders with the view to reconciling differences. Within the Canadian context in Afghanistan, it is the only one. The case of the resurgence of religion as a factor of conflict has already been made. Co-opting and distorting its messages by unscrupulous leaders are a ready means to ignite the passions of the unsuspecting for political aims. Where religious leaders of tolerant voice are open to overtures for dialogue and cooperation across identity boundaries, attempts must be made to shore up such aspirations. In environments where religion factors significantly into the culture and the conflict, an interagency approach devoid of a religious element is, unfortunately, myopic. Demiray's experience represents an occasion upon which to build future engagements. Government personnel of western nations are sincere and effective in their efforts to make a difference for populations endeavoring to recover from what are frequently nothing short of horrific circumstances. Every lever is applied in an effort to build trust among the people so as to effect change. Engaging the tolerant voice of religion is one such lever opening up an extremely influential sector within indigenous societies.

INDIGENOUS RELIGIOUS PEACEBUILDERS

Chapter 10 will deal with this topic in more depth. However, a word here is warranted. For some, Demiray's impact as an Imam raises the question of whether chaplains are the only qualified personnel to conduct RLE activities. This author has maintained that chaplains are well suited for such engagement due to their unique status as religious leaders in their own right and their familiarity with the military milieu. It has often been the case that indigenous religious leaders request dialogue with the chaplain of a local contingent, as was my experience during the Bosnian war. As clerics in uniform, these men and women comprehend military structures and are comfortable bridging to local religious communities via their leadership. It appears to be a natural fit. However, to limit RLE activities exclusively to chaplains would not be in the best interests of mission mandates. Where radical faith expressions misrepresent religious belief and practice, misleading otherwise peaceful populations, leadership must seriously consider employing every available means to counter such rhetoric and its destructive impact. Employing religious peacebuilders—ideally indigenous to the local population—as interagency partners in future operations represents a positive step to addressing an otherwise inaccessible and influential sector of indigenous culture and society. For further discussion, see ch. 10, The Potential Role of Indigenous Peacebuilders within the Whole of Government Environment).

EMPLOYING LIKE-FAITH RELIGIOUS LEADERS

In addition, the involvement of Imam Demiray raises the issue of employing like-faith religious leaders in a theatre of operation where the principal religious expression is not that of Christianity. By far, the majority of chaplains from Western nations deploying to operational venues are Christian, many of whom have little or no exposure to the religious *other*. Over the last decade, operational environments have been primarily Islamic, Iraq and Afghanistan in particular. Inserting Muslim chaplains into these environments raises the likelihood of less suspicion and greater openness to engagement among the religious leadership and people of these countries. A witness to the reception and effectiveness of Imam Demiray, Brigadier-General David Fraser (Commander Regional Command South,[60] ISAF Afghanistan 2006) expressed to this author, "Whatever country you're in, whatever the presenting religion, if it's Muslim, Hindu, Judaism or whatever, it behooves us that we have the right pastoral support that can actually fit into that society's culture. Tell your Chaplain General to recruit more religious leaders from groups other than Christian."[61] Fraser, of course, was citing the present model of a double-hatted role whereby one would perform pastoral duties while engaging local religious communities—a template that may need to be revisited as RLE-type activities become more mainstream, raising the prospects of specialist-training.

LIMITATIONS OF AD HOC AND PERSONALITY DRIVEN APPROACHES

Another chronic limitation to initiatives that are more of an *ad hoc* nature, as this was, is the capacity to maintain momentum where projects are more personality driven. Under commander's (Fraser) authority and in his explicit intent, Buchan incorporated Demiray into the PRT plan of engaging the indigenous population as a means of advancing the mission mandate. This is not to insinuate that their ingenuity and vision detracted from mission objectives. To the contrary—this is how new concepts are born. The deficiency recounted to this author by Imam Demiray was the lack of continuity from one rotation to the next.[62] Without structures in place to support such endeavors among the religious leadership it became increasingly difficult to sustain the effort. Fraser recognized the inroads that had been made into the Sunni and Shia Islamic communities and resolved that these successes be sustained. His intention was to replace Demiray with an Imam from one of the NATO partner nations. In the interim, and with Chaplaincy approval, Demiray agreed to return to Kandahar a number of times over the course of the following year in an attempt to solidify the gains made while waiting for a replacement. Unfortunately, the vision was not realized. Another Imam was not forthcoming. Interest began to wane. As it goes in operations, the focus often shifts from one rotation to the next, as do the priorities. Initiatives that held such promise months earlier die on the vine. The institutionalizing of RLE as an operational construct will do much to bring to bear the support of operational elements designed to build on and sustain such advancement. By endorsing RLE as a capability under development, the Canadian Forces Army and Chaplain Branch together are taking appropriate measures to integrate such engagement into training and operational structures. Training now emerging will equip chaplains to recognize and facilitate peacebuilding activities among religious communities where estrangement has given rise to conflict, a topic to be revisited in more depth in chapter 10. As U.S. Navy Chaplain Phil Gwaltney states, "The ideal would be to assign chaplains with the capabilities to design and sustain RLE efforts over time by synchronizing initiatives with theater objectives, building a Concept of Operations that looks out 3 to 5 years and establishes measurable goals, and communicates the effects of our advice and engagements."[63]

SECURITY ISSUES FOR INDIGENOUS LEADERS

The previous case study raised concerns for the personal safety of religious leaders in conflict or post-conflict environments courageously engaging chaplains. Such activities carry a degree of risk for those implicated. Although guarantees of safety never exist where prying eyes and cell phone cameras are ubiquitous, deeper into his tour Imam Demiray began meeting with Islamic leaders at the Governor's Palace in Kandahar City. The Ulema Council of Islamic Scholars is a government-sponsored body under the supervision of the Directorate of Religious Affairs, providing religious leaders a legitimate reason to visit the palace.

COOPERATION VS. CO-OPTATION

Intimated earlier also was concern for the parameters of Imam Demiray's involvement, which, on occasion, fell outside the cognizance or supervision of senior chaplains at the operational and strategic levels. This underscores the necessity for the creation of doctrine and policy for RLE activities. During that same time period, an enthusiastic service member related to then CF Chaplain General Stan Johnstone, in Afghanistan on an official visit, that Imam Demiray was "their greatest weapon." Believing his words to be of encouragement to the Chaplain General, it re-enforced all the more that these were indeed uncharted waters. This raises the specter, although teeming with potential for good; the temptation for "others" to co-opt such a capability looms large. Either collaborating with military members or in an Interagency environment, by its very nature to invoke potential misuse, the application and function of RLE as an operational capability must be clearly delineated—hence the need for policy and doctrine. This will be discussed in more detail in chapter 10.

It is encouraging to note that an Office of Religious Freedom[64] has opened at Foreign Affairs Canada, counterpart to the Office of International Religious Freedom (IRF) at the United States Department of State. One of the objectives of IRF is to sponsor reconciliation programs in disputes where groups are divided along lines of religious identity.[65] These are encouraging signs. In conflict and post-conflict environments, RLE within Whole of Government formulations may hold lessons as to the value of employing religious peacebuilders indigenous to a given society. Imam Demiray's experience serves as a lens through which to view the impact of a religious leader of like faith to a local populace. This is not to rule out chaplains functioning as facilitators, establishing those first contacts with local religious leaders and building much-needed trust. Embedding indigenous peacebuilders within a chaplain team or PRT-like organization (Interagency) may prove to be an overlooked and underused asset to achieving mission mandates. Identifying such individuals and grooming them to either be inserted in an RLE activity when greater expertise beyond that of the chaplain is needed or accompanying contingents on tour may be prudent building blocks to consider putting in place. From an inter-governmental perspective, those given to more diplomatic endeavors may find such well-schooled individuals of immense assistance in advancing their efforts as well. An additional deliverable of an indigenous peacebuilder with language and faith commonalities to a host society would be their capacity to create the *peacebuilding architecture* within an indigenous community essential to sustaining the gains made once international goals are achieved and forces are extracted.

NOTES

1. CANBAT II (1,500 troops) operated under a mandate from the UN Security Council to provide escort protection for humanitarian aid convoys destined for UN Declared Safe Havens in southern Bosnia and similar protection for contracted civilian workers endeavoring to revive the infrastructure of Sarajevo: electricity, water, sewage. The Princess Patricia Canadian Light Infantry (PPCLI) comprised the main body of CANBAT I, a Battle Group having deployed earlier to southern Croatia where fighting had subsided but tensions remained high with pockets of sporadic outbursts.

2. The Bosnian theatre of operations was but one of several in the former Yugoslavia. Canadian Forces personnel served in Croatia and Kosovo with brief stints to Macedonia. Canadian troops served with the United Nations Protection Force (UNPROFOR, 1992–95), and with NATO-led forces, i.e. Stabilization Forces (SFOR, 1995-present), Implementation Forces (IFOR, 1995-present) and, Kosovo Forces (KFOR, 1999-present).

3. The first deploying contingent to a new Area of Operation (AO) is always considered Roto 0 as opposed to Roto 1, which would in fact be the replacing contingent.

4. An Area of Operation (AO) is one of a number of geographical areas within a theatre of operations designated to the contingent of a member nation. It becomes their mission responsibility to secure and stabilize the AO while fulfilling the mandate as understood and directed by Command.

5. The Sherefudin White Mosque of Visoko, Bosnia-Herzegovina is world renowned for its architectural design, recipient of the Aga Khan Award for Architecture, 1983. "Commending the mosque for its 'boldness, creativity and brilliance', the jury found it 'full of originality and innovation (though with an undeniable debt to Ronchamp), laden with the architect's thought and spirit, shared richly with the community, and connecting with the future and the past.'" See http://archnet.org/library/images/one-image.jsp?location_id=1649&image_id=14216.

6. The concept of contagion originates in Girard. He states, "being eminently contagious desire follows the most unexpected paths in order to spread from one person to another." Again, it is in the crescendo of *mimetic* intensity, *self* (subject) rivaling the *other* (model) for the much-sought object, that "one 'catches' a nearby desire just as one would catch the plague or cholera, simply by contact with an infected person." See René Girard, *Deceit, Desire and the Novel: Self and the Other in Literary Structure* trans. by Yvonne Freccero, Original Publican,

1961: Trans. 1965, Paperbacks edition (Baltimore and London: The John Hopkins University Press, 1976), pp 96-99.

7. Vern Neufeld Redekop, from *Violence to Blessing: How and Understanding of Deep-rooted Conflict can Open Paths to Reconciliation*, Toronto: Novalis, 2002, p. 68.

8. The economic situation of local families was made known via the Bosniak interpreters, who were paid fair wages for their work—a small fortune by comparison to incomes in general at that time. For information on Bosnian currency at that time see http://www.daggarjon.com/Currency_Bosnia_&_Herzegovina.php.

9. In responding to the parting request of Imam Azdahič, this author mounted a humanitarian campaign in the Maritime provinces of Canada and parts of the State of Maine, U.S.A. in 1994 where 17,000 pairs of children's shoes, sneakers and rubbers were collected and shipped via four sea containers to refugee camps in Croatia and Bosnia-Herzegovina. McCain's Food International sponsored the program Boots for Bosnia and the British NGO, Feed The Children, was the distributor.

10. See http://www.unhcr.org/cgi-bin/texis/vtx/home.

11. Tri-walls were large rectangular cardboard containers designed to be fork-lifted on pallets, easily shipped by sea container or transported by truck.

12. Michael A. Sells, *The Bridge Betrayed: Religion and Genocide in Bosnia* (Berkley, California: University of California Press, 1996), 1–3. See also Paul Mojzes, *Yugoslavian Inferno: Ethnoreligious Warfare in the Balkans* (New York: Continuum Publishing Company, 1995) and Paul Mojzes (ed), *Religion and the War in Bosnia* (Atlanta, Georgia: Scholars Press, 1998).

13. Vern Neufeld Redekop, "Mimetic Structures of Violence and of Blessing," in *Theoforum*, Vol. 3, No. 3, 2002, P. 313.

14. For a concise overview of the history of the French Canadian infantry regiment from the province of Quebec in Canada, the famed Van Doos (an anglicized version of the French *vingt-deuxième*), see http://www.ameriquefrancaise.org/en/article-465/Royal_22e_Regiment.html.

15. Maj J.P. Guay and Capt Y. Pichette, *Chaplain's After Action Report,* 2nd R22R Battle Group, Annex B, 1630–1, October 1993, p. B–1.

16. Telephone conversation with Major Jean-Pierre Guay, Deputy Area Chaplain, Headquarters, Land Forces Quebec Area, Montreal, Quebec, 16 Sept 2005.

17. Guay and Pichette, *Chaplain's After Action Report*, Annex B, 9, Oct 1993.

18. Medjugorje is a small village in Bosnia-Herzegovina where, since 24 June1981, the Blessed Virgin Mary has been appearing and giving messages to the world. Six individuals (known as visionaries) of the village have been receiving messages from the Blessed Virgin Mary. In general terms the message is, "I have come to tell the world that God exists. He is the fullness of life, and to enjoy this fullness and peace, you must return to God." *Gospa* is Serbo-Croat for *Lady*, as in *Our Lady of Medjugorje.* See http://www.medjugorje.org/overview.htm, accessed 26 Jan 2012.

19. Rabbi Arnie Resnicoff, former Command Chaplain, United States European Command (USEUCOM), US Navy, presently Special Assistant to SECAF and CSAF for Values and Vision, Pentagon, Washington, D.C., email, 6 Oct 2005.

20. *Mutuality* may be understood as the *self* experiencing the *other* in reciprocal connectedness, enhancing identity for both. Its essence is love and respect for the dignity and humanity of the *other.*

21. The theory presented here with respect to ritual and symbol originates with the following publication: Lisa Schirch, *Ritual and Symbol in Peacebuilding* (Bloomfield, CT: Kumarian Press, 2005).

22. See ch. 2, "The Place of Ritual and Symbol in the Shaping of New Narratives".

23. Guay and Pichette, *Chaplain's After Action Report,* Annex B, 1, Oct 1993.

24. Schirch, 2005, 154.

25. Schirch, 2005,154.

26. The World Food Programme (United Nations) provides a thorough description and overview for Kandahar Province: Geography; Demography and Population; Current State of Development in the Province; Agriculture and Rural Development; Education; Health; Social

Protection; and additional information. See http://www.foodsecurityatlas.org/afg/country/provincial-Profile/Kandahar, accessed 12 Aug 2012.

27. See http://www.isaf.nato.int/.

28. NATO - The North Atlantic Treaty Organization. See http://www.nato.int/cps/en/natolive/index.htm.

29. "Provincial Reconstruction Teams were designed to spread a peacekeeping effect without creating a large peacekeeping force. They are the grease, not the wheel. . . . The policy is to establish PRTs in locations [helping to] stabilize the region by extending the reach of the central government and facilitating increased reconstruction efforts. As a location becomes more secure, the PRT [shifts] from brick and mortar reconstruction efforts to governmental capacity building and focus on such tasks as security planning for elections, DDR (disarmament, demobilization, and reintegration), police mentoring, and so forth" (Michael J. Dziedzic and Colonel Michael K. Seidl, "Provincial Reconstruction Teams and Military Relations with International and Nongovernmental Organizations in Afghanistan" in *Special Report*, United States Institute of Peace, No 147, September 2005, 8). The reasoning behind the PRTs development suggests that in the contemporary context of intractable conflict, the international community has rightly recognized that "genuine security remains a fundamental prerequisite for achieving stability and development", something that "cannot be provided by military means alone." Required is the multifaceted approach of "good governance, justice and the rule of law, reinforced by reconstruction and development" (The London Conference on Afghanistan, *Building on Success: The Afghanistan Compact*, London, England, 31 Jan-1 Feb 2006, 3).

30. Dept of Foreign Affairs and International Trade: DFAIT (within the Canadian Government).

31. Interview with Gavin Buchan, Ottawa, Ontario, 9 Nov 2009.

32. Telephone interview with BGen David Fraser, recently returned Commander of Regional Command South, ISAF, 30 Jan 2007.

33. Once it was learned that the Canadians had an Imam in uniform at the main base at Kandahar Air Field (KAF), Lieutenant General Sir David Richards (United Kingdom), then Commander of the International Security Assistance Forces (ISAF), flew Captain Imam Demiray to Kabul for dinner and an exchange of ideas. Richards was extremely interested in his perspective as an Imam of the challenges that lay before them in the Islamic nation of Afghanistan. This transpired just prior to Imam Demiray taking up his duties at the Kandahar PRT. See the following web sites for profiles on Lieutenant General Sir David Richards: http://english.peopledaily.com.cn/200605/05/eng20060505_263205.html; http://www.worldleaders.info/david-richards/.

34. At the request of Regional Command South, during the year (2007) following his initial tour (2006) of duty, Capt Imam Demiray returned to Afghanistan on four occasions, each of three weeks duration.

35. Buchan interview, Ottawa, 2009.

36. Gavin Buchan, Panel presentation transcript: "The External Ministry of Reconciliation Paradigm: Chaplains Engaging Local Religious Leaders in the Whole of Government Environment of Operations" at the *Generative Dialogue* held at Saint Paul University, Ottawa, Canada, 6-8 June 2010. See http://www.amiando.com/eventResources/Z/8/QKbKAoBUrZkeyZ/Generative%20Dialogue%20Ottawa-Report.pdf;

37. "The differences between these two main sub-groups within Islam initially stemmed not from spiritual differences, but political ones. Over the centuries, however, these political differences have spawned a number of varying practices and positions which have come to carry a spiritual significance." Questions of leadership reach back to Islam's beginnings and the death of the Prophet Mohammed. "Sunni Muslims agree with the position taken by many of the Prophet's companions, that the new leader should be elected from among those capable of the job. This is what was done, and the Prophet Muhammad's close friend and advisor, Abu Bakr, became the first Caliph of the Islamic nation. . . . The Shia Muslims believe that following the Prophet Muhammad's death, leadership should have passed directly to his cousin/son-in-law, Ali. Throughout history, Shia Muslims have not recognized the authority of elected Muslim leaders, choosing instead to follow a line of Imams which they believe have been appointed by the Prophet Muhammad or God Himself." From this early division differences in leadership,

religious practices and texts have evolved. See http://islam.about.com/cs/divisions/f/ shia_sunni.htm, accessed 12 Feb 2012.

38. For discussion relating to reciprocal (*mimetic*) violence between the Sunni and Shia see: Ahmed Rashid, *Taliban* (New Haven: Yale Nota Bene, 2001), 55-80; Hafizullah Emadi, *Culture and Customs of Afghanistan* (Westport, Connecticut: Greenwood Press, 2005), 47-48; M. J. Gohari, *The Taliban Ascent to Power* (Oxford: Oxford University Press, 2000), 102-04.

39. Ahmed Rashid, *Taliban* (New Haven: Yale Nota Bene, 2001), 69.

40. Hafizullah Emadi, *Culture and Customs of Afghanistan* (Westport, Connecticut: Greenwood Press, 2005), 47–48.

41. M. J. Gohari, *The Taliban Ascent to Power* (Oxford: Oxford University Press, 2000), 102–04.

42. The Taliban draw from the majority Pashtun ethnic group, which accounts for some 40 per cent of Afghanistan's 20 million people. The Taliban initially revived dreams of Pashtun nationalism, as the Pashtun ruled Afghanistan for approximately 300 years but in recent decades had lost out to other smaller ethnic groups. See Ahmed Rashid, *Taliban* (New Haven: Yale Nota Bene, 2001), 2; See also Louis Dupree, "Chart 6: Ethnic Groups in Afghanistan," in *Afghanistan* (Karachi, Pakistan: Oxford University Press, 1973), 59–64.

43. Shura is an Arabic word which literally means *consultation* and as a basic Islamic principle calls upon Muslims, usually under a system of proportional representation, to gather and, through debate, [shape opinions and offer direction for the betterment of the Ummah]. See http://www.alislam.org/topics/khilafat/Shura.pdf. In this instance, the Religious Council of the Ulema Shura is a government-appointed (provincial) body of Islamic scholars for the purpose of: (1) overseeing religious life for the Islamic community; (2) through consultation discern the finer points of Koranic doctrine as applied to the lives of the faithful; (3) engage in mosque oversight; and (4) advise the Governor and his officials on the application of Islamic principles, deliberating when necessary on contentious points of Islamic belief and practice.

44. Interview with LCol John Fletcher, Command Chaplain to the Chief of the Land Staff, National Defence Headquarters, Ottawa, Canada, 24 May 2006.

45. Interview with Gavin Buchan, Ottawa, Ontario, 9 Nov 2009.

46. Interview with Capt Imam Suleyman Demiray, Kandahar Provincial Reconstruction Team, Afghanistan, 5 July 2006.

47. Buchan, *Generative Dialogue*, 2010.

48. "Madrasah, in Muslim countries, an institution of higher education. The *madrasah* functioned until the 20th century as a theological seminary and law school, with a curriculum centred on the Qurān. In addition to Islāmic theology and law, Arabic grammar and literature, mathematics, logic, and, in some cases, natural science were studied in *madrasahs*. Tuition was free, and food, lodging, and medical care were provided as well. Instruction usually took place in a courtyard and consisted primarily of memorizing textbooks and the instructor's lectures. The lecturer issued certificates to his students that constituted permission to repeat his words," http://www.britannica.com/EBchecked/topic/356072/madrasah, accessed 3 Aug 2012. Of course, the above is not representative of the madrasahs operating in the North-West Frontier Province of Pakistan at the time of this Shura (2006) in Kandahar. In the late 1980s as many as 33,000— mostly unofficial—madrasahs operated in the border areas. The tribal code of the Pashtunwali, heavily influenced by the Wahabbi creed, was taught to the Talib (young students—boys). For a more thorough treatment of the radical madrasahs of the Taliban, see Ahmed Rashid, *Taliban* (New Haven: Yale Nota Bene, 2001), 22–4, 27–7, 31–8, 72, 83–4, 88–91.

49. Demiray, 2006. Capt Demiray states that the Council of Ulema looked to ISAF Forces, of which the PRT is a part, to persuade the Karzai government to permit the establishment of these religious schools, as well as assist in anyway possible with their establishment/construction.

50. Demiray, 2006. On this point, Imam Demiray stated that there had been progress in this area since the 15 April 2006 meeting of the Shura at the PRT.

51. The Soviet invasion of Afghanistan lasted from 1979–89, precipitating entrenched guerrilla warfare with the Mujahideen. See http://www.globalsecurity.org/military/world/afghanistan/cs-invasion.htm. Following the Soviet exodus, the Mujahideen—comprised of a number of tribes and clans—preceded to engulf the country in a devastating civil war as groups vied for

power. See Stephan Tanner, *Afghanistan: A Military History from Alexander the Great to the Fall of the Taliban* (New York: Da Capo Press, 2002), 275-79; Martin Ewans, *Afghanistan: A Short History of Its People and Politics* (New York: HarperCollins Publishers, 2002), 168–82. Overcoming the Mujahideen chaos fell to the Taliban who were initially deemed as saviors restoring order. These 'liberators' soon established an oppressive regime of Sharia Law based on the ultra-conservative Salafist Wahhabi teachings leading to a tyranny of another kind for the unsuspecting Afghans. See Ahmed Rashid, Part 1, "History of the Taliban Movement" and Part 2, "Islam and the Taliban," *Taliban* (New Haven: Yale Nota Bene, 2001), 17–128; Stephan Tanner, "The Rise of the Taliban" in *Afghanistan: A Military History from Alexander the Great to the Fall of the Taliban* (New York: Da Capo Press, 2002), 271–88. The al-Qaeda attacks on New York and Washington led to the invasion of Afghanistan. For a digital chronology of the war in Afghanistan, see U.S. War in Afghanistan, Tracking a War (1999 to pres) *Council on Foreign Relations*, http://www.cfr.org/afghanistan/us-war-afghanistan/p20018.

52. The Pashtun of Pakistan reside in Balochistan, the North West Frontier Province (NWFP) and in seven tribal agencies of the Federally Administered Tribal Areas (FATA). During the years of 1946–47 a surge of nationalism arose among the Pashtun leadership for the establishment of an independent Pashtunistan. Support existed within Afghanistan for its creation, but at no time did this translate into a desire to see the boundaries redrawn to include the Afghan Pashtun—the borders of an independent Pashtunistan would have been comparable to those of the NWFP. For more on the Afghan border question see Raja Anwar, *The Tragedy of Afghanistan: A First-hand Account,* translated from the Urdu by Khalid Hasan (London and New York: Verso, 1988), 30–31; Francis Fukuyama, *Nation Building: Beyond Afghanistan and Iraq* (Baltimore, MD: John Hopkins University Press, 2006), 143

53. The Mazar-e-Sharif account aids in illuminating scapegoating traits: what draws groups together toward a common enemy, how difference factors into the violence, how victims are powerful yet vulnerable, and the scapegoat's illegitimacy. Despite their differences, the Uzbek and Hazara ethnic groups—Sunni and Shia respectively—came together in an uneasy alliance to combat the occupying Taliban in Mazar-e-Sharif. In true scapegoat fashion, these tribesmen rose above their inherent differences to focus on a common foe, effectively putting aside their potential for inter-communal conflict by turning their violence on their mutual enemy...for the immediate crisis at hand. See M. J. Gohari, *The Taliban Ascent to Power* (Oxford, England: Oxford University Press, 2000), 102-04.

54. The following description of the Taliban regime is indicative of a *hegemonic structure* where the dominant subjugates a people. Under the oppressive Taliban, the Department of the Promotion of Virtue and Prevention of Vice enforced their version of Sharia Law. Women were to be separated from the men at all costs due to the inability of some men to behave properly around them. Women were forbidden to work including Western humanitarian aid organizations, aside from the medical domain. While men were forced to grow long beards, women were forced inside, living the vast majority of the time in their homes with windows blackened, virtually living out of sight. They were also subjected to restricted movement; a woman could not appear in public without being accompanied by a male relative. To do so was to be put at risk of certain reprisal. The *burkha* remains to this day a symbol of oppression in Afghan society where Taliban numbers are in force. Women resisting these arcane restrictions were beaten publicly by the Taliban "clothes police" whose mandate it was to patrol city streets in search of "malcontents," enforcing their version of Sharia law. Areas of Afghanistan and Pakistan under Taliban control today are subjected to these draconian measures and more. Under the Taliban, the education system collapsed with scores of schools being closed including the university in Kabul. More than 250,000 boys and girls were forbidden an education. See Ahmed Rashid, "A Vanished Gender: Women, Children and Taliban Culture," in *Taliban* (New Haven: Yale Nota Bene, 2001), 105–16.

55. See chapter 2, Secondary Relational Systems, xx.

56. See Jayshree Bajoria, "The Trouble with the Afghan-Pakistani Border: Durand Line" in *Council on Foreign Relations*, 20 Mar 2009, http://www.cfr.org/pakistan/troubled-afghan-pakistani-border/p14905#p3. For maps of the Durand Line, see http://www.google.ca/search?q=Durand+Line&hl=en&client=firefox-a&hs=Ka9&rls=org.mozilla:en-US:official&

channel=s&prmd=imvnsb&tbm=isch&tbo=u&source=univ&sa=X&ei=9xFBT-XpJ5C_gAfv2-GICA&ved=0CEIQsAQ&biw=1232&bih=597.

57. Ahmed Rashid, *Taliban* (New Haven: Yale Nota Bene, 2001), 74, 92, 203.

58. Telephone conversation with Capt Imam Suleyman Demiray, 1 Feb 2007.

59. See Chapter Four, Reuben Baron: Grassroots initiatives—Trust and Cooperation,

60. In 2006-07, 6,000+ ISAF (NATO) troops were committed to Regional Command South (RC South), a geographical area covering Helmed and Kandahar Provinces.

61. Telephone conversation with BGen David Fraser, recently returned Commander of Regional Command South, ISAF, 30 Jan 2007.

62. Telephone conversation with Imam Demiray, 22 Feb 2012.

63. Email conversation with Chaplain CAPT Phil Gwaltney, Pacific Fleet Chaplain, United States Navy, 21 Dec 2010.

64. See   www.international.gc.ca/media/aff/speeches-discours/2011/2011-034.aspx?lang=eng&view=d, accessed 20 Feb 2012. By way of clarification, Foreign Affairs Canada is known as the Department of Foreign Affairs and International Trade (DFAIT).

65. See http://www.state.gov/j/drl/irf/index.htm, accessed 20 Feb 2012.

Chapter Six

France in Kosovo

Breaking Bread Together and Building Trust:
An Apology

The case study presented here represents the unique operational experience of a French chaplain in a specific space in time in Kosovo. Michel de Peyret is a Roman Catholic priest with extensive exposure to the Balkans. His first tour of duty with the NATO-led[1] mission to Kosovo began with a Parachute Brigade attached to the Franco-Spanish Tactical Group in Bosnia-Herzegovina based out of Mostar[2] in 2003. Aspects of his duties took him from the Croat-Bosniak sector through the Serbian sector to Sarajevo on a regular basis, affording him a certain familiarity with this theatre of operations in the Balkans. As will be seen, this initial tour to the Balkans stood him well for his two subsequent tours to Kosovo, the focus of this study.

The following account is in no way intended to gloss over the longstanding difficulties existing between the Serbian and Albanian peoples in this region of the Balkans. Documented earlier were the residual effects of the Ottoman era and its domination of the Serbian nation—a political and regional rift that historically has also exposed religious fault lines between Muslims and Christians (See ch. 2, Wounded Memory). The Serbian nationalist memory of the Battle of Kosovo is representative of the antecedents of such strained relations.[3] Limitations exist to this study, as it is not possible at the time of this writing to ascertain the impact or sentiments of the K-Serbian and/or K-Albanian[4] communities regarding these events at that time. The reader is invited to appreciate Chaplain de Peyret's contribution for what it was: a genuine and, perhaps, prescient account of what may occur when a chaplain catches a vision for reconciliation between estranged groups, supported by an engaged Command structure. In particular, the *place of hospitality* will be presented as a means of *trust development*, initially with the Sisters of Devič Monastery, but primarily by *breaking bread together* with religious leaders of Kosovo—Serbian Orthodox, Albanian Muslim, and Roman Catholic—hosted by Command, followed by a *shared meal* where these same religious leaders came together with the political leadership of Kosovo. Additional themes will be presened as deems applicable.

FIRST DEPLOYMENT IN KOSOVO (MAY–SEPTEMBER 2004)

In May 2004, Chaplain de Peyret deployed to Kosovo with the 2nd Armored Brigade[5] of the French army, part of the larger Multinational Brigade North East[6] under the command of General Etienne Lafontaine of France. This took de Peyret to Novo Selo, a camp located between the capital, Pristina, and the town of Mitrovica.

Just two months prior to Chaplain de Peyret's arrival in Kosovo (March 2004), violence broke out in a small village close to Mitrovica, spreading across Kosovo. Allegedly, three Albanian boys, in an effort to escape the pursuit of a marauding group of Serbs, jumped into the Ibar River and drowned. The investigation later revealed that the incident was complete conjecture.[7] Miroslav Volf correctly opines that where not enough reason exists to hate the *other*, there are always those who will rewrite histories or fabricate injuries in order to manufacture hatreds.[8] Unfortunately, as is often the case, mob mentality took over creating *exogenous shock*,[9] as hostilities spread from one community to another like a contagion, another example of the *mimetic* nature of violence. Large groups of the majority Albanian population soon began hunting Serbs to take revenge. Where enclaves of Serbs lived, villages were attacked and set on fire. After three days of rioting, NATO[10] troops of Kosovo Forces (KFOR) brought the mayhem under control, with the end result of 19 Serbian deaths and thousands of homeless. The areas near Prizren in the Southwest (under German command) and Mitrovica in the Northeast (under French command) were particularly virulent and difficult to control. Crowds targeted Serbian cultural and religious sites and symbols: churches, monasteries, cemeteries, and scores of homes.

MAKING CONTACT

It became immediately apparent to Chaplain de Peyret that complicating any overtures to the Serbian community was their discernable loss of confidence in the KFOR forces. In their minds, either the NATO forces were unaware of what was about to transpire, or they were simply unwilling to intervene thus protecting them from their attackers. With the support of Command, de Peyret moved quickly to reconnect with the Serbian religious authorities, beginning with the local Orthodox priest in Mitrovica. The rioters had burned his church and if it were not for French troops, he too would have suffered at their hands. Everything was lost, either through looting or the fire. When the chaplain finally met the visibly shaken priest, he had taken shelter offered by French chaplains and was receiving emergency first aid. He made regular visits to see the Orthodox priest as well as accompany him to the building site of the new church under construction.

Of gravest concern to the Orthodox community, and the most significant symbol of failure by KFOR, was the destruction of the monastery of Devič, deep in Albanian territory. It had been plundered and burned, leaving French troops no choice but to evacuate the nuns, due to continued Albanian violence and looting. Once the hostilities subsided, the Sisters obtained permission to return to their monastery to inspect the damage. According to de Peyret, his first visit to the monastery became a lesson in humility. He presented himself as a Roman Catholic priest with the French forces to the Serbian Orthodox Sisters, cognizant of the fact that the KFOR forces had been unable to protect them. As a man of God, he stood with them and by them in their devastation, requesting what he might do to help. Recent events had eroded their faith in KFOR, the French in particular, to provide security for them. They were rather wary of the overtures of this French chaplain. In their minds, they were awaiting martyrdom. They agreed to a return visit provided he would take them to investigate the damage to their cemetery.

In a few days, Chaplain de Peyret returned bringing with him three additional French chaplains—two Roman Catholics and a Protestant—immediately settling into the task of clearing away the debris and cleaning. Re-establishing the lost *trust* was critical to ongoing relations in the sector between KFOR and the Serbian community. At the end of the day's work, he proposed that they return to continue cleaning the ruins of the monastery. The Sisters warmed to the idea of French soldiers aiding in the process, an initiative to which the brigade commander agreed enthusiastically. Intuitively, de Peyret created a situation where those interested in peace could collectively move toward establishing *working trust*. Such trust arises from *interdependence* with others, where achieving that which holds value for one group is made possible through the *benevolent* efforts of others . . . reaffirming one's faith in humanity when reasons to believe otherwise exist. In this instance, the relational trust between the French and this religious order began to strengthen, becoming more resilient as it matured. Basic in nature, *working trust* is seen emerging in the Sister's attempt to focus less on the conflict and more on the benefits of continuing the relationship with the French. Once engendered, strengthening trust depends much on the *integrity* of the individual. Chaplain de Peyret exemplified *integrity* by the consistency of his actions, credibility of commitment . . . and the congruence of his word and deed. Additionally, trust in the French increased due to the recognition of de Peyret's *reliability* to follow through on his commitments, a benefit of his close affiliation with the French Command (see ch. 4, Trust Development). Trust is easier to achieve than it is to regain once it is lost. This meant resisting the temptation of making promises that could not be kept and coming through on what realistically could be delivered.

The news of the ongoing work at the monastery had quite an impact on the local populace—not only for the Serbian community but for the K-Albanians as well, who realized that the KFOR forces would do what they could to ease the state of degradation and improve relations. Chaplain de Peyret proposed to the commander that soldiers participate regularly in the clean up, with priority given to those who rarely left the base camp at Novo Selo due to their employment. Approval was received to spend one day every three weeks at the monastery. By the end of the rotation the number grew to more than sixty French, succeeding in making the monastery livable again. As a sign of their *restored trust*, the Sisters of Devič revealed to Chaplain de Peyret where they had hidden their treasured icons and paintings from the looters.

Word of the work by the French at Devič reached Monsignor (Mgr..) Teodosije, the Serbian Orthodox bishop at the monastery of Decanis. The bishop wanted to see the restoration for himself, as it was his intention to inform his colleagues of the work of KFOR. He intentionally traveled to Devič to meet Chaplain de Peyret on one of the scheduled workdays, an encounter that proved to be of strategic importance for the future.

APPLYING RELIGIOUS LEADER ENGAGEMENT (RLE) AS A MODEL: PART ONE—DEVIČ MONASTERY

As is often the case, chaplains implicated in Religious Leader Engagement with indigenous populations exhibit an amalgam of an expanding hermeneutic of peace and strategic thinking—an inclusivity of the *other* that becomes a value-added for Command (see ch. 4, An Expanded Hermeneutics of Peace). Chaplain Michel de Peyret fits this description. With respect to *internal operational ministry* among the troops, he was careful to attend to his duties as a chaplain in whatever capacity—sacramental, pastoral and administrative. Yet, he was intrinsically drawn to a ministry of healing and reconciliation, identifying not only with the suffering of the *other* but also the breach that remained between faith communities due to an historical enmity[11] that had been exacerbated in the recent bout of violence.

Grasping something of the *human identity needs* at play in this case study will aid in better comprehending some of the underlying dynamics of this account. The violence between the K-Serbian and K-Albanian communities underscores the interdependence of the *self* and the *other* thrown over for a willful independence that deemed the Orthodox as the enemy *other*, preferring segregation, or, better still, a land totally devoid of the alien *other*. The fabricated account of violence toward K-Albanian children—a common ploy of those intent on inciting hostilities—brings the human identity needs of *connectedness* and *security* to the fore immediately. The alleged attack on their community, an affront to identity, caused the K-Albanians to band together (belonging) to retaliate against the perceived threat from what quickly became the "hostile" *other* (see ch. 2, Connectedness). Sensing their *security* endangered, the Serbian community had little recourse but to retreat within the boundaries of their identity group for protection from what was later proven to be an unprovoked and vicious onslaught. The obvious threat of physical security (life) was soon compounded by the loss of food, shelter and clothing, as rioters destroyed K-Serbian cultural and religious landmarks, as well as scores of Serbian homes wherever they were found[12] (see ch. 2, Security). The loss of such welfare needs created the significant exodus of K-Serbians that streamed toward neighboring mother Serbia—a major concern for containment. The human identity need of *meaning* comes into view as justice questions emerge of what is deemed fair and reasonable expectation of the behavior of others in response to one's well-intentioned actions (see ch. 2, Meaning). They had been accused of a treacherous act of aggression without any thought of verifying the veracity of the information. The K-Albanians seemingly fell to the default position of thinking the worst of their K-Serbian neighbors. The negative element of *action* is evident within the K-Serbian community as "choice" is denied them—in effect, "no choice" is imposed upon them, as they had little alternative but to be *acted upon* by the groundswell of overwhelming K-Albanian violence (see ch. 2, Action). Deprived of dignity, the K-Serbian people are denied *recognition*—the congruence between what one deems as grounds for recognition and what is acknowledged from the *other* (see ch. 2, Recognition). The Sisters of the monastery at Devič poignantly demonstrate the trauma of having one's human identity needs undermined: abandonment in that they believed the KFOR forces had not come to their aid; a sense of alienation for they felt rejection by the majority K-Albanian community; sadness at their plight, coupled with vulnerability, anger and questioning.

In addition to *Human Identity Needs*, *Relational Systems* emerge as integral to this study with its emphasis on *mimetic modeling*. *Open relational systems* are evident on several levels in the activities of Chaplain de Peyret. During his initial tour (2004) he *networked* among the Serbian Orthodox Sisters at the ravaged monastery at Devič. Whatever relation existed between the Orthodox community and the K-Albanians prior to the rioting, an expanding breach was evident now between them, demonstrative of a rigid *closed relational system* (see ch. 2, Close Relational Systems) where hostility was palpable, communication became adversarial and, in most instances, dangerously non-existent . . . relational exclusivity. Such communication is indicative of intractable conflict, where *distortions* are placed on another's version of events as a means of redefining it to suit one's own agenda, precipitating a *rigidity* of positions (see ch. 2, Intractable Conflict). The K-Serbian community testified to having lost all confidence in the KFOR forces that, from their perspective, either were caught off guard by the surge in violence or were simply unwilling to intervene. By offering himself as a cathartic *safe space* for the Sisters to share their tortured story, de Peyret effectively created an *open relational system*, facilitating the beginning of the restoration of *trust* between the Sisters and the French—a key element of interdependence (see ch. 2, Open Relational Systems). *Kindness* is evident not only in listening to their plight, but also in actively repairing the monastery and providing escort to verify the condition of their cemetery where many of their order were buried (see ch. 2, The Place of Hospitality). As an *open relational system,* Chaplain de Peyret's ministry was catalytic in that he *mimetically modeled embrace.* Despondent, the Sisters awaited what they believed to be sure martyrdom. In the face of tangible anguish and resentment, this chaplain reached across political, ethnic and religious lines to *embrace* them.

In a very real sense, the *will to embrace* comes to the fore as *space* is *created* in the *self* for the *other*, inclusive of their pain. *Mimetic modeling* (ch. 2, Mimetic Modeling: Creating Openness to the Other) in de Peyret is evident in that his vision and passion were infectious, eliciting a desire from three of his chaplain colleagues to assist in the repair and cleaning of the monastery. The ComKFOR soon authorized one day every three weeks, opening the way for French troops to participate, a number that grew to sixty by the end of his tour. Noted as well was de Peyret's pastoral sense for his troops throughout the mission—he involved those whose duties confined them to the camp, thus providing them an opportunity to join in ministry "outside the wire." His labors with the local religious community did not eclipse his concern for his own. *Mimetic structures of blessing*, explained below, countered the violent forces that bred misunderstanding and reactionary patterns of behavior known to feed spiraling hostility. *Blessing* at the monastery of Devič found at its center the well being of the *other*, which empowered the Sisters to hope again; creative and life-oriented, they were presented with an expanding option that could not have been envisioned earlier—French troops repairing their beloved monastery; and a spirit of generosity that naturally created greater abundance, inspiring others to participate (see ch. 2, Mimetic Structures of Blessing). Trust restoration is evident in their willingness to disclose the location of their hidden icons, safely stored from the rioters bent on their destruction. Chaplain de Peyret's ministry led naturally to *partnering* with his own troops in aiding the stressed Serbian Orthodox community. These efforts may be viewed as *peacebuilding* activities of a humanitarian nature, creating *working trust* between not only the Sisters of Devič monastery, but also Mgr. Teodosije, the local Orthodox Bishop who became a prominent figure during Chaplain de Peyret's second tour to Kosovo.

ARRIVAL OF THE NEW COMMANDER OF KFOR (COMKFOR)

Early in 2004, Lieutenant-General Yves de Kermabon, Commander of the Army (French Defence Forces), became ComKFOR designate for the next rotation, assuming command in September 2004. His prvious role as Deputy ComKFOR a few years prior prepared him well for his new assignment. He and de Peyret met for the first time during one of his reconnaissance visits to Kosovo prior to taking command of the mission. As is the norm for consecutive rotations, there are usually a number of weeks of overlap as the incumbent commander relinquishes his duties to his successor. During these weeks, Lieutenant General de Kermabon attended mass presided by Chaplain de Peyret at KFOR Headquarters in Film City camp, one of the districts of Pristina. By the end of September, de Peyret's tour finished, at which time he returned to France with the soldiers of the 2nd Armored Brigade.

SECOND DEPLOYMENT IN KOSOVO (APRIL–AUGUST 2005)

Unbeknown to Chaplain de Peyret, already slated to join a French contingent deploying to Afghanistan in 2005, Lieutenant General de Kermabon had already requested de Peyret's superiors in Paris to reassign him to Kosovo to take on the role of KFOR theatre chaplain.[13] It was the first time that this position was to be held by a French citizen or a Roman Catholic priest. The challenge was real.

Upon his arrival, the general briefed de Peyret on the specifics of his new duties. He noted that the religious dimension of the operation needed to take into account the local and regional religious authorities. The commander was cognizant of his peacebuilding endeavors among the Orthodox community the previous year in the territory of the North-East Multinational Brigade, and now looked to de Peyret to replicate similar peacebuilding initiatives among the religious communities for the whole of Kosovo.

EXECUTION OF THE MISSION

As KFOR chaplain, de Peyret bore the responsibility for the sacramental and pastoral support of the personnel at the KFOR Headquarters at Film City camp. In addition to these duties, it fell to him to supervise the KFOR chaplains attached to the various units, pastoral and administrative oversight he did not neglect. Albeit, given the specific mandate by Lieutenant General de Kermabon, he concentrated much of his energies on the creation of bonds with the religious authorities. In his monthly meetings with the 32 KFOR chaplains, it became apparent where the interest lay for such engagement.

Gaining a foothold within the religious communities of Kosovo meant establishing a strategy. Chaplain de Peyret recognized that engaging the Albanian Muslim community would be key to any kind of dialogue. His strategy was to approach the Mufti Ternava, spiritual leader for the Muslim community for Kosovo, prior to contacting the various local Imams. However, it made better sense to him to begin with that which was familiar—the K-Albanian Roman Catholic community.

Establishing dialogue and cooperation with the Albanian Roman Catholics[14] was facilitated by a request from Lieutenant General de Kermabon to personally begin worshiping with the local Roman Catholic parishes, an overture to which Mgr.. Marco Sopi, bishop of Prizren, was most amicable. A devout Roman Catholic, the general recognized the importance of worship and the value of moving among the people of local civilian parishes as opposed to remaining within the confines of the KFOR Headquarters. His intention was to worship somewhere locally two to three Sundays a month. de Peyret identified the twenty-four Roman Catholic parishes within the diocese of Prizren, corresponding geographically to the territory of Kosovo, arranging meetings with all the priests and the majority of the parochial councils. Each Sunday attendance in a local parish by ComKFOR was preceded by a visit by Chaplain de Peyret for planning purposes. The General participated in the celebrations by way of short prayer followed by a brief address to the people. It was not unusual to witness between two and three thousand people in attendance. Striking was the fact that young people were the majority, testifying to the vitality of this Albanian Catholic community. The people responded to de Kermabon, inviting him to a number of special celebrations: first communions, first masses of young priests, and pilgrimages.

With inroads made among the Roman Catholic community, Chaplain de Peyret turned his energies to the Serbian Orthodox. The riots of March 2004[15] were still fresh in the minds of the broader K-Serbian community. As is often the case, ethnic conflict frequently entails destroying cultural identity markers that hold meaning—a means of demoralizing the *other*, a much-practiced prerequisite to driving the *other* out regardless of venue. In Kosovo, the predominantly Orthodox Serbian community, suffered from this in particular. K-Albanian violence targeted Serbian places of worship, monasteries, cemeteries and the known homes of K-Serbian residents. Resentment persisted against the French and German KFOR troops in particular for what was perceived to be their inability/inaction to protect the K-Serbian community. de Peyret was cautious to avoid engaging religious leaders with nationalist leanings, so as not to be co-opted by those seeking opportunity to distort the good intentions of KFOR for their own purposes. Prudence was essential.

With the assistance of headquarters staff, a list was drawn up of Orthodox clerics known for their openness to inter-communal liaisons—religious leaders with whom he could engage in confidence. Mgr. Teodosije topped the list, a man reputed for his spirituality and intellect. Chaplain de Peyret visited the bishop's monastery of Decani, where he received a cordial welcome due to their earlier encounters. The renewed good will between them was reinforced by Mgr. Teodosije's invitation to celebrate Easter with them at the monastery in Decani.

The mandate from ComKFOR to engage the religious leadership and communities of Kosovo was strategic in nature, and, as such, necessitated participating in the KFOR Headquarters briefings where the chaplain gave progress reports. These were both daily briefings with his immediate chain of command, as well as the larger Saturday briefings inclusive of headquarters personnel and other department heads. At these briefings de Peyret gave an overview of his weekly activities: religious leaders met, sites visited and, more importantly, an explanation of religious events of a particular faith community such as a festival, pilgrimage, inauguration and what impact, if any, these events might have on day-to-day operations. Devoting a portion of his daily routine to visiting, he soon met all the principal actors of the religious sector (see ch. 4, Religious Area Analysis).

Bridging the chasm between these two ethno-religious communities created by the recent violence meant initiating a process of gradual rapprochement—an incremental approach of successive steps to increased engagement. Visiting the destroyed religious sites with the Serbian Orthodox religious leaders, facilitating their reconstruction, and participating in the religious festivals that celebrated their restoration became transformative moments. Nascent trust restoration through the *benevolence* of the French fostered among certain of the Orthodox leadership the capacity to approximate the re-humanizing of the alienated *other—mimetic modeling.*

BREAKING BREAD TOGETHER

At the invitation of Lieutenant General de Kermabon in late July 2005, and in a more solemn way, in early August, two lunches were hosted at KFOR

Headquarters bringing together the highest religious authorities of Kosovo. This initiative emerged after learning that neither of the bishops, Serbian Orthodox or Roman Catholic, nor the Muslim mufti—the leaders of the three faith traditions of Kosovo—had ever been seated at the same table. The possibility of a shared meal began to germinate. It was determined that the "neutral" ground of KFOR Headquarters would be the more appropriate genre to host the luncheon.

Each religious leader was met in turn, starting with the President of the Islamic Community of Kosova, Mufti Ternava (Muslim), Serbian Orthodox Bishop, Mgr. Teodosije (Orthodox) and, finally, Roman Catholic Bishop, Mgr. Marc Sopi. Invitations were issued with the understanding that there would be no publicity of the event. All three religious authorities agreed to come, each accompanied by an "assistant." The July lunch began with a degree of discomfort due to the unforeseen late arrival of Mgr. Teodosije. Once there, the Serbian Orthodox Bishop offered his apologies for his tardiness, explaining that he had just returned from Belgrade, which made it difficult to arrive at the agreed upon hour.

At the outset, the atmosphere was a bit stilted with no one wanting to be the first to speak. Benefiting from the silence, Mgr. Teodosije rose, requesting the floor. There, solemnly, before the assembled, he addressed Mufti Ternava, declaring that he was sorry for any wrong his people may have caused for the Albanian community. The bishop then explained the reason for his trip to Belgrade was to consult with his fellow Serbian Orthodox bishops regarding the meal they were now sharing and what he proposed to say. Not only did he receive approval from his brethren, they further requested him to offer the same sentiments on their behalf as well. The intensity of the moment was palpable in the small dining room—total silence. The mufti slowly rose to his feet, moved by what he had just heard. Grasping the bishop's hand in his, he presented him with his business card, a symbol of good manners and a gesture of good will in Kosovo. He then earnestly exclaimed that if there were ever anything that he could do for him, it would give him great pleasure to be of assistance. No one moved, awestruck by what they had just witnessed—an offered apology and an acknowledgment of the good will behind such a gesture, something almost unimaginable in a region where the intermingling of religion and nationalism has historically added to the complexity of relations (see ch. 4, The Will to Embrace).

The following day, Kosova Prime Minister Bajram Kosumi and UNMIK (United Nations Interim Mission in Kosovo) deputy chief administrator, Larry Rossin, were hosted at KFOR Headquarters by Lieutenant General de Kermabon,[16] a meeting that had been scheduled for some time. Innocently, ComKFOR inquired if they had any idea who he had entertained for lunch the previous day. Upon learning the names of his guests, the two higher representatives of the political powers were without words. It seemed impossible to them that these three leading religious figures of Kosovo would ever agree to sit at the same table, much less talk in terms of apology. At the completion of their business, ComKFOR called Chaplain de Peyret, asking him to organize a second luncheon, on the same model, including Prime Minister Kosumi and United Nations representative Rossin. On August 8, 2005, the three religious leaders representing Roman Catholicism, the Serbian Orthodox and the Islamic community in Kosovo came together for the second time that summer at KFOR Headquarters in Pristina with the political dignitaries.

> According to the KFOR Information Office, Catholic Bishop Mark Sopi, Islamic Community of Kosova [BIK] President Mufti Ternava and Serbian Orthodox Bishop Teodosije were glad to take part in the "fruitful and very positive meeting," this time in the presence of the highest representatives of UNMIK and the Kosova Provisional Institutions of Self-Government [PISG]. The lunch allowed for mutual recognition and the direct exchange of information. All the participants agreed that tolerance is a common religious value and that Kosova needs goodwill for the establishment of a multiethnic and tolerant society. The religious leaders also stressed the need for dialogue between their communities and condemned the use of violence, saying that violence cannot be employed as a means of communication. On 16 June, the COMKFOR [KFOR Commander] invited the three religious representatives to lunch—the first initiative taken since the riots in March 2004. The three representatives voiced their confidence that meetings like this one will continue in the future, facilitating mutual recognition and restoring confidence among their communities. [17]

The willingness of the religious leadership to convene again was due in part to the progress in relations and budding goodwill that had emerged from their first shared meal the month prior. The luncheon was completely official and in the presence of the press—an incremental step toward improved *inter*-communal relations in Kosovo. Rabbi Marc Gopin suggests that those engaged in such peacebuilding endeavors must keep before them that each individual gesture, every movement in improved relations, however small, is a success in and of itself. He further connotes that, given the right circumstances, such positive change impacts human social life with a steady accumulation of positive increments of change. Such "transformational increment[s] of change," says Gopin, "[may] be seized upon as the basis for steady, measurable change, even when structural paradigm shifts prove elusive for decades or even generations" [18] (see ch. 4, Interdependence as Incremental Reconciliation).

APPLYING RLE AS A MODEL: PART TWO—THE SHARED MEALS

Chaplain de Peyret's second tour in Kosovo is of particular interest to the subject matter brought forward here, as it illustrates the benefits of RLE as an aspect of the Comprehensive Approach. His endeavors among the three faith traditions offers further credence to the notion of institutionalizing RLE as an operational construct, something that is coming to fruition in the Canadian context.[19] RLE is undeniably embryonic in nature, yet, as a capability, offers tangible steps in facilitating greater interdependence between groups that may be more challenging to engage for those employing more secular approaches to resolving conflict.

Lieutenant General de Kermabon (ComKFOR) discerned early on that the indigenous population within the public[20] space was a notable center of gravity for mission success. Increasingly, commanders are recognizing the significance of religious communities within indigenous populations as groups holding much influence societally. As important as de Peyret's *internal* role of sacramental, pastoral and administrative support was, as Theatre chaplain, the *external* role of engaging the leadership of Kosovo's religious communities was an imperative of the mission mandate—engagement under commanders' authority and in his explicit intent. It was due to this underlying priority that sharing a meal *inter*communally emerged as a possibility. Lieutenant General de Kermabon reinforced its strategic merit by attending mass regularly in local Albanian Roman Catholic parishes. Salient to his role, Chaplain de Peyret participated in briefings at the highest levels where he reported of his engagement with the religious communities, citing pertinent points relating to religious life among the indigenous population of strategic value to other elements of Command (see ch. 4, Religious Area Analysis). As vital as other approaches are to resolving conflict, it must be acknowledged that de Peyret's identity as a priest factored significantly into the success enjoyed among these leading religious figures of Kosovo.

Immediately apparent is the continuity that Chaplain de Peyret brought to the 2005 mission, having served the year prior in Kosovo. The rapport and trust previously established with Mgr.s Teodosije (Serbian Orthodox) and Sopi (Albanian Roman Catholic) were of immense value in bringing RLE to the higher plane of the shared meal(s), leaving Mufti Ternava (Albanian Muslim) the only remaining religious leader with whom to engage. In reaching out to all of these leaders, de Peyret is seen to *mimetically model* the *will to embrace* (see ch. 2, Mimetic Modeling: Creating Openness to the Other), extending the hand of fellowship in a display of acceptance and desire for the well-being of the *other*, regardless of faith orientation or history. In so doing he *re-humanized* the *other* in the eyes of the religious leaders, lessening resistance to contact and dialogue. These esteemed religious leaders were *middle-range actors* in Kosovo very much in touch with the grassroots, yet having access to some of the higher levels of political leadership (see ch. 4, The Tolerant Voice). As was seen by the reaction of the political leaders visiting Lieutenant General de Kermabon, their stature in Kosovo society was not lost on them. Mgr. Teodosije in particular stands out as a religious leader of *tolerant voice*, one of those rare individuals who, desirous of *transcending* conflict, is predisposed to reaching across ethnic boundaries to initiate dialogue with the religious *other.*

Understandably, given the recent spate of violence, relations were strained between the Orthodox and Muslim communities,. As such, a *closed relational system* existed between these groups where communication, much less cooperation, was absent. Chaplain de Peyret's overtures were catalytic, in that he created an *open relational system* (see ch. 2, Open Relational Systems) by inserting himself into the dynamic, a third party if you will. The good will that his gestures engendered elicited a similar willingness (*mimetic*) from each of the leaders to come together for what appeared to be the first meeting of its kind in recent memory. The shared meal initiated by de Peyret is demonstrative of the *place of hospitality* where a *safe space* is provided for individuals to meet and share their story—*kindness* that kindles *trust.* Concurrently, the shared meal was a culturally significant *ritual* event. Informal and constructive, breaking bread together carries with it the sense of a gesture of consent to human company, an image of mutuality (see ch. 2 The Place of Hospitality). For these religious leaders, consuming the same food together around the same table held within it the subliminal message that the barriers of social custom and hostile relations can be overcome (see ch. 2, Ritual and Symbol).

Initially, the dynamics of *encounter* in such situations go undetected, yet lasting results are often traced back to such early beginnings. The power of *encounter* lay in how stereotypes brought to such meetings begin to lose their staying power, as something of the *other* is left in the *self* upon the completion of the meeting. Here *double vision* enabled these religious leaders not only to see the *other* more clearly, but also to view themselves from the perspective of the *other* (See ch. 4, Encounter). Unexpected was the *apology* offered by Mgr. Teodosije to Mufti Ternava on behalf of the Orthodox ecclesial leaders in Belgrade for the wrongs committed against the Albanian Muslim population in the past. Equally moving was the spirit in which Mufti Ternava received it. More poignant still, a ritual of inversion infused this gathering. As a specific-time event, the shared meal did more than mute the impact of power on existing social relations, the apology made by Mgr. Teodosije virtually turned the power structures on their head, even if it was just for the duration of the meal (See ch. 2, Rituals of Inversion). No one anticipated such a gesture of good will. This meal was *transformative* as the writing of a *new narrative* began among these leaders—a step was taken toward the *healing of memory,* an incremental process.

Evidence of a *re-humanizing* of the *other* and a reframing of relation among these leaders can be detected in their willingness to meet again, this time for lunch with the prime minister and a senior United Nations representative, an early example of the comprehensive approach in action: the highest level representation of the Kosova government, the United Nations as an international organization, military Command structures and the leading religious leaders of the ethno-religious communities of Kosovo. The stipulation attached to the first meal was for strict privacy to be invoked. The second meal had no such condition; rather they openly shared their fellowship before the press, presumably as a witness of fraternity for their respective peoples—a *mimetic structure of blessing* had emerged with its life-giving, open and expanding options for mutuality in relation. Salutary to this nascent integrative endeavor—Whole of Government to some—is the recognition that state and international leaders were brought to the table with some of Kosovo's most influential religious leaders facilitated by Chaplain de Peyret, acting in collaboration with his Interagency partners, under the authority of Lieutenant General de Kermabon, ComKFOR, and in his explicit intent: Religious Leader Engagement as *peacebuilding*.

NOTES

1. "UN Security Council Resolution (UNSCR) 1244 was adopted on 10 June 1999 and on 12 June, the first elements of the NATO-led Kosovo Force, or KFOR, entered Kosovo. By 20 June, the withdrawal of Serbian forces was complete. KFOR was initially composed of some 50,000 men and women from NATO member countries, Partner countries and non-NATO countries under unified command and control. By early 2002, KFOR was reduced to around 39,000 troops. The improved security environment enabled NATO to reduce KFOR troop levels to 26,000 by June 2003 and to 17 ,00 by the end of 2003. . . . Today, some 5,500 troops from the NATO-led Kosovo Force (KFOR), provided by 30 countries (22 NATO and 8 non-NATO), are still deployed in Kosovo to help maintain a safe and secure environment and freedom of movement for all citizens, irrespective of their ethnic origin." See http://www.nato.int/cps/en/natolive/topics_48818.htm, accessed 1 Apr 2012.
2. Mostar is a city of southwestern Bosnia-Herzegovina founded in the 1400's, historically comprised of Bosnian Muslims, Serbs and Croats and was under Ottoman rule for four centuries. The war in the early 1990's was devastating for Mostar, inflicting much physical and economic damage, leaving the population greatly depleted. A federation was forged between the Bosnian Muslims and Croats in 1994, bringing an end to the hostilities. Today there are no Serbs in the city, with tensions still existing between the Muslim and Croat populations. The Muslims live on the devastated eastern bank of the Neretva, and Croats on the less damaged western bank; travel is restricted between the two sides of the city. See http://bad-zakm.tripod.com/history.htm, accessed 1 Apr 2012. The Croats destroyed the famed Bridge of Mostar, a UNESCO world heritage site, during the war. It has since been restored. "The reconstructed Old Bridge and Old City of Mostar is a symbol of reconciliation, international co-operation and of the coexistence of diverse cultural, ethnic and religious communities." See http://whc.unesco.org/en/list/946, accessed 1 Apr 2012.
3. See chapter 2, Sections Wounded Memory and Constructive and Destructive Rituals under Ritual and Symbol. Note as well the Endnotes that identify sources giving an account of the 12th century Battle of Kosovo and its impact on more recent events leading up to the Bosnian war.

4. K-Serbian and K-Albanian are abbreviations for the Serbian and Albanian peoples of Kosovo.

5. An Armored Brigade is normally comprised of three battalions (400-600 troops each depending on the mission) of Infantry supported by armored vehicles such as tanks.

6. "Multinational Brigade Northeast: HEADQUARTERS: Nova Selo and Mitrovica - Responsible for: Northern Kosovo Lead Nation: France. Contributing Nations: Belgium, Denmark, Estonia, Greece, Luxembourg and Morocco." See Kosovo: A Protectorate in Trouble by Paul Workman, CBC News | May 25, 2004. http://www.cbc.ca/news/background/balkans/workman.html.

7. "On March 17, [2004] at least 33 riots broke out in Kosovo over a 48-hour period, involving an estimated 51,000 protesters. Nineteen people died during the violence. At least 550 homes and 27 Orthodox churches and monasteries were burned, and approximately 4,100 persons from minority communities were displaced from their homes. . . . The violence was sparked by a series of events, notably sensational and ultimately inaccurate reports that Serbs were responsible for the drowning of three ethnic Albanian boys. Other catalysts included anger among ethnic Albanians over the blocking of the main Pristina-Skopje road by Serb villagers to protest the shooting of a Serb teenager by unknown assailants, and a March 16 demonstration organized by groups of veterans and others linked to the disbanded Kosovo Liberation Army who protested the arrest of former KLA leaders on war crimes charges." See "Kosovo: Faith of NATO, U.N. to Protect Minorities," *Human Rights Watch*, http://www.hrw.org/news/2004/07/26/kosovo-failure-nato-un-protect-minorities, accessed 1 Apr 2012.

8. Miroslav Volf, *Exclusion and Embrace: A Theological Exploration of Identity, Otherness, and Reconciliation* (Nashville, TN: Abingdon Press, 1996), 77.

9. The term *exogenous shock* originates with Ashutosh Varshney's seminal research published in *Ethnic Conflict and Civic Life: Hindus and Muslims in India.* Varshney describes *exogenous shock* as ethno-religious violence spreading from one center to another where the populace had been free of conflict. In essence, a wind-blown spark from a nearby fire landing on dry ground, creating a second blaze. He contends that where communities in India were more integrated civically across ethnic lines, the propensity toward violence was less when *exogenous shocks* impacted the community—an ethnically/religiously induced crisis within a populace free of conflict, emanating from outside. His longitudinal study of six cities spanning a period of some 50 years—three more ethnically integrated compared with three more segregated—offers critical insight in terms of conflict transformation. He asserts where Hindu/Muslim tensions spilled over into violence elsewhere in the country, the more civically integrated urban centers were able to contain its spread—either outbursts were quelled in short order or they did not occur at all. The depth of *inter*communal civic engagement had much to do with maintaining the peace as it promoted more integrative structures, which held additional relational benefits, hence, a peace dividend for the community when the contagion of violence originating externally threatened to metastasize locally. In communities where daily *inter*communal activity and communication was less evident ethnic segregation became the norm. During periods of internal strife elsewhere in India, these localities were more susceptible to violence spreading to their communities, a *mimetic* phenomenon. See Ashutosh Varshney, *Ethic Conflict and Civic Life: Hindus and Muslims in India* (New Haven, CN: Yale University Press, 2002).

10. North Atlantic Treaty Organization.

11. See section entitled, *Constructive and Destructive Ritual* under the heading *Ritual and Symbol in the Shaping of New Narratives,* chapter 2

12. See http://www.youtube.com/watch?v=ZOBIROAPY9k for a graphic pictorial account of the Kosovo rioting on 17 March 2004.

13. This position carried with it the responsibility of the oversight of all of the chaplains for the multi-national forces (32), including regularly briefing the Commander on his activities and/or any concerns that may have arisen regarding the troops or the local population. He also attended the Commander's Orders Group, which would have had representatives from all of the nations implicated in the overall mission.

14. Albanian Roman Catholics consist of 3 percent of the population of Kosovo. See https://www.cia.gov/library/publications/the-world-factbook/geos/kv.html, accessed 1 Apr 2012.

15. See endnote #7.

16. "Kosovo's religious leaders stress "need for dialogue" at lunch organized by KFOR." Asia Africa Intelligence Wire. 2005. *accessmylibrary*. (April 1, 2012). http://www.accessmylibrary.com/article-1G1-134985280/kosovo-religious-leaders-stress.html.

17. "Kosovo's religious leaders stress "need for dialogue" at lunch organized by KFOR." Asia Africa Intelligence Wire. 2005. *accessmylibrary*. (April 1, 2012). http://www.accessmylibrary.com/article-1G1-134985280/kosovo-religious-leaders-stress.html.

18. Marc Gopin, *To Make the Earth Whole* (Lanham, Maryland: Rowman and Littlefield, 2009), 67.

19. On 24 June, 2011, in Ottawa, Ontario, Canada, the Army Capabilities Development Board of the Canadian Forces endorsed Religious Leader Engagement (RLE) as a capability under development for expeditionary, humanitarian and domestic operations. With the support of the Canadian Forces Army and Chaplain Branch, RLE is presently moving through the capability development process designed to prepare chaplains to do ministry with local religious communities in conflict.

20. Public space is an aspect of JIMP doctrine within the Canadian Forces, an Army descriptor of the comprehensive approach. "In essence, the term joint, interagency, multinational and public (JIMP) is a descriptor that identifies the various categories of players (i.e., organizations) that inhabit the broad environment in which military operations take place. To Be "JIMP-capable" entails the adoption of an approach to operations both domestic and international that allows such players to effectively interact. Most importantly, it involves a belief in the requirement to adopt a comprehensive approach to problem solving that involves the holistic consideration and, ideally the coordination of all relevant players." See http://www.army.forces.gc.ca/DLCD-DCSFT/archived-eng.asp?eng_filepath=/DLCD-DCSFT/pubs/landops2021/Land_Ops_2021_eng.pdf&fra_filepath=/DLCD-DCSFT/pubs/landops2021/Land_Ops_2021_fre.pdf&eng_FileTitle=Land%20Operations%202021&fra_filetitle=Operations%20terrestres%202021.

Chapter Seven

The United States in Iraq

An Integrated Approach to Forging Alliances: The Iraq Inter-Religious Council Accords

Highly strategic in nature, much of what the preceding three studies have brought forward culminates in this case study. The integrative measures applied to Religious Leader Engagement (RLE) by Chaplain (CH) Mike Hoyt and Canon Andrew White in Iraq during the period of 2007 to 2008 amplify the significance of conflict transformation[1] to such interventions. Their collaborative initiative stands as a prescient example of the contribution RLE potentially brings to the Comprehensive Approach as an emerging operational construct. The reader is encouraged to be conscious of this lens as this account unfolds. Due to the significance of this achievement and the manner in which it is brought forward here, CH Hoyt's rendering of the events as he saw them will be presented in its entirety followed by the application of theory and praxis as explicated in this book. In this author's opinion, to do otherwise would detract from the integrity of Hoyt's thorough and passionate recounting of this multifaceted (Whole of Government) approach to seeding reconciliation among the religious leadership of a nation convulsing from intensive sectarian violence. Following his contribution, pivotal themes previously highlighted will be brought to bear: relational systems, *mimetic* structures, human identity needs, encounter, and ritual and symbol. Additional supportive points will be cited throughout the analysis where deemed applicable with the appropriate references. CH Hoyt begins his account with an overview of the Iraqi situation at that time, which serves as a preface to his

narration of how the Baghdad Accords were realized and, of singular importance, its continuing influence.

BACKGROUND

The complexities of Iraq's political, cultural and religious challenges in 2006
and 2007 cannot be overerstated. The American independent task force
known as The Iraq Study Group (ISG) observed:

> [A]ttacks against US, and Coalition, and Iraq Security Forces (ISF) are persis-
> tent and growing. October 2006 was the deadliest month for US forces since
> January 2005 with 102 Americans killed. Total attacks in October 06 average
> 180 per day, up from 70 per day in January 06. Attacks against ISF in October
> 06 were more than double in January 06. Attacks against civilians in October
> were four times higher than January 06. Some 3000 Iraqi civilians are killed
> every month. [2]

Living and ministering in the midst of such chaos was reality for Hoyt during
this period. His studied analysis and first-hand experience offers the following depiction.

It was almost a self-fulfilling chain of events. Since the collapse of the
Saddam Hussein regime in April of 2003 Iraq national structure was invented
and managed through temporary adjustments with little to no political staying power. Advances occurred through the dogged determinism of the dedicated Coalition forces, the permutations of political entities, and the endu-
rance of the Iraq population. In three years, Iraq passed through a Coalition
Provisional Authority, temporary Iraq Governing Council, an interim
government, to a newly elected permanent government. The effect was three
prime ministers, a misunderstood Constitution, elections boycotted by 40
percent of the Iraq population (Sunni), and a Council of Representatives
voicing the concerns of less than 50 percent of the electorate and shrouded in
layers of prejudice, public distrust, and subjected to frequent deadly attacks.

The national budget was ineffective. Public utilities were sporadic and
broken. The military and law enforcement dismantled. All means of travel
became an adventure between militia and criminal extortion checkpoints and
a shooting gallery. Security was a combination of vigilante, mercenary, sanctioned terror, and Coalition force activities. The brave Iraqis trying to achieve
normalcy were rewarded for their success by murder, family kidnappings,
torture, and intimidation. Layered on top of all of this were persistent combat
activities, criminal violence, retaliation, and raids conducted by Al Qaeda in
Iraq (AQI), foreign fighters, ISF, and Coalition forces. Things were rarely
worse short of return to full-scale war. Progress, when it occurred, did so
only through the heroic efforts of sacrificial politicians, diplomats, military

and security forces, tribal sheiks . . . and one other extremely influential group, religious leaders.

There were three primary power brokers in Iraq; the government of Iraq (GOI), Coalition Forces (known as Multinational Forces-Iraq or MNF-I), and religious leaders (clerics). It should be noted that the religious leaders also include vast arrays of influence through organized para-military groups (militias) and political fronts (voting blocs and social compacts). The ebb and flow of influence among these three created a simultaneous power vacuum on any given day that played itself out on the populace and in the abodes of power. It was also evidenced on the streets and in the mosques of Iraq (and sometimes across the Middle East). In December 2006 the ISG report observed: "The fundamental cause of violence in Iraq is the absence of national reconciliation."[3] Shortly after being elected, Prime Minister Nouri al Maliki announced a multi-step national reconciliation plan oriented on conferences with tribal, civil, religious, and political leaders, as the centerpiece of the forming GOI. The plan stalled as the GOI tried to remain solvent. The question was how to go about it in a maelstrom.

THE NEED FOR NATIONAL RECONCILIATION

Iraq national reconciliation required a willingness on the part of sworn enemies to negotiate a set of enduring compromises no single power broker was either willing or able to bring about. Something needed to be found that appealed to all three in enough authority that each could leverage the results. The illusive solution depended upon the degree of risk matched to the level of integrity each could muster to empower results without diluting them to serve narrow interests. All reconciliation work requires risk management, money, security, reputation, tradition, futures, and faithfulness.

Two central questions in reconciliation are: "how does one manage a sense of loss?" and "how does one animate charity in an environment of hostility, suffering, and selfishness?" Both of these questions reach into the root of human social compacts and transcendent motivations. Someone must be willing to take the first step (risk), build for good in the ruins of evil. Reconciliation must include, among other things, a theological approach because in the end, it is a personal matter of the motivations and beliefs of the heart. The outcomes of reconciliation require the personal comprehension of such concepts as: forgiveness, justice, charity, sacrifice, hope, faith, good and evil. It is not achieved on a balance sheet, or a won-lost record. It occurs in the soul and works its way out through institutions, investments, will power, and humility. Neither can reconciliation be reduced to a program. It is a process of contrition stretched across an iron will yielded to sustainable peace, dignity, and purpose.

THE ROLE OF RELIGION IN RECONCILIATION

People make reconciliation possible or keep it distant. On February 12, 2006, and throughout the following weeks after the bombing of the Shia holy site the Askariya Shrine[4] in Samarra (the golden mosque bombing), teenagers chanted in the streets across Iraq, "We are the soldiers of the clerics. We await the orders of our preachers!" The senior Shia Grand Ayatollah (there are five), Grand Ayatollah Ali Sistani spoke for the rest declaring, "If its (the GOI) security institutions are unable to provide the necessary security, the faithful are able to do that by the will and blessings of God."[5] Islam refers to itself as a community (*ummah*) claiming a certain set of historical beliefs crystallized in the life of the Prophet. Islam perceives itself as a society, local and international. It carries its own sense of justice and moral aptness (*qist and statements, public and private during the Iraqi Religious Council (IIRC) initiative October 2006-May 2007.ma'ruf*); legal method (*Shari'ah and minhaj*); judicial consensus and rulings (*Ijma and fatwa*); and sacred text and Prophetic authority (*Qur'an and hadith*) to mention a few.[6]

The great richness and diversity of the Muslim mosaic called Islam projects a social fabric of the religion that expects and demands a type of comprehensive solution including every aspect of power, politics, neighborliness, personal piety, and living conditions. Iraqis saw their life circumstances as inseparable from their religious confessions and thus revered the words, methods, and leadership of their clerics as part of their personal and public expression of Islam. In other words, in Iraq, everything may not be about religion but every enduring solution requires a religious accommodation. "If the religious leaders do not play a part in this (political actions), it will not be solved," sentiments echoed by Sheikh Al Alani, Senior Iraq Sunni cleric.[7] Thus any hope for reconciliation, national-tribal-individual must consider and be presented from credible religious authority or it will fail. The Western (American-led) view that religion should remain a chiefly private matter out of the public sphere proved a decisive irritant to the progress of reconciliation. The avoidance of religion was not without cause, as the problems were immense. However, marginalizing religion and prominent religious actors inspires activism and deepens religious divides.

Religion also presented itself as the chief antagonist to peace and a portrayer of violence (see ch. 3, Religious Extremism as a Driver of Conflict). There were numerous fatwa's declaring all coalition forces as evil and worthy of destruction. Of course, the most notorious is the Bin Laden Fatwa issued 24 February, 1998, which carried the indictment "to kill the Americans and their allies—civilians and military—is an individual duty for every Muslim who can do it in any country..."[8] Some clerics openly encouraged the killing of as many Americans as possible as an act of religious obedience. The retaliation of Shia on Sunni communities after the Samarra bombing was ruthless. On the same day, 20 Sunni mosques were attacked and destroyed along with their attending clerics. Sunni inmates were taken from their cells and executed on the spot. There was plenty of bloodletting under the guise of religious "permission." Marauding bands of highly volatile, well-equipped Sunni and Shia militias became major "opposing forces" to both the GOI and MNF-I. Indeed religion looked as bad as it looked good but the very fact that religion was uniformly appealed to is what all the power brokers had to face. Reluctantly, defiantly, or timidly a path to reconciliation ran through a religious track and someone needed to engage with a plan.

The GOI was hobbled in the process of religious engagement because it was perceived by the Sunni as "impure therefore unworthy" and actively prejudiced against anything non-Shia. The clerics were their own worst enemy by their inflammatory rhetoric and selective outlandish behavior. The Coalition Forces were fighting an insurgency couched in religious axioms. The ISF owed its recruiting and manning successes to the encouragement of clerics manipulating security conditions in their local area to gain status and find employment for their mosque followers. Once again there were no clear "winners" to engage in reconciliation with the possible exception of a United Kingdom citizen, Anglican vicar, Canon Andrew White.

CANON ANDREW WHITE

Canon White served as the Archbishop of Canterbury's Special Envoy in Iraq since 1998. His personal Christian testimony and genuine love for all Iraqi people earned him unprecedented access and respect by all sides of the Islamic and other religious communities. During the Coalition Provisional Authority[9] (CPA) days, his advice and counsel helped at the national level. It was his influence that garnered critical cleric support to turn out the popular vote in the Constitutional referendum and again in the various national election processes. White suffered beatings for his faithfulness under the Hussein regime, endured death threats, and remained a forgiving symbol of personal charity and engagement. Both the Iraq Institute of Peace, which he helped to found, and his own non-governmental organization, The Foundation for Relief and Reconciliation in the Middle East (FRRME), *were* well known and respected.

Most of the elected and appointed Iraqi GOI officials, the Ambassador staffs working out of Baghdad (Germany, Denmark, Italy, UK, US) and a few American and Coalition officers, knew Canon White. His was a voice for reconciliation demonstrated by his desire to continue the work PM Ibrahim al Jafari appointed him to do in February 2006; form an Iraq religious leader council. However, the frequent change of GOI leaders, the insurgency, the civil violence, and the preoccupation of the US State Department and

MNF-I leadership on other matters coalesced to keep the initiative from moving forward. Still, Canon White built and maintained all the necessary religious leader contacts and access. All that he lacked was a method, means, and convincing message that could penetrate GOI and MNF-I religious intransigence.

CHAPLAIN MIKE HOYT

A new American army chaplain began his tour in Iraq in June 2006 as the MNF-I Command Chaplain, a strategic role that carried with it the responsibility for all US forces in Iraq and the technical point of contact for all US matters relating to the delivery of religious support to the force. The MNF-I Chaplain also served as the point of contact for the Coalition Force Chaplaincies, and the personal staff chaplain for the MNF-I staff and the commander, General George Casey and, later, General David Petraeus. The chaplain, Colonel Mike Hoyt, had twenty-six years in the army and a lot of experience working on complex multi-service and coalition commands and staffs. Army Chaplain Rob Myer introduced Canon White to CH Hoyt in June 2006. White's extensive network and insatiable love for the Iraqi people presented a gracious opportunity to make a difference. Hoyt and White began a friendship of mutual pastoral support which would lead through a fifteen month effort and three national level reconciliation events.

The immediate problem to overcome in the GOI and on the ground was religious antagonism. Any positive outlook for a religious initiative was eclipsed by the shadows of violent sectarianism and calls to radical *jihad.* Conditions were right for a breakthrough but neither the GOI or MNF-I could devote the time or energy to 'another' thing. All efforts were focused on holding a fragile government together, quelling sectarian violence, and fighting an insurgency. Things on the religious front were at a strategic impasse. The risk for failure was too severe to chance; so was the risk for maintaining the status quo.

Large-scale military efforts occur within a very deliberate and complex set of priorities and objectives. These issues are expressed in a campaign plan. A campaign plan surveys the national instruments of power (Diplomatic, Information, Military, Economic) and aligns national and coalition ways and means to achieve a vision and an end state. The MNF-I campaign plan focused on broad areas of strategic interest like: Governance, Security, Economics, Communication, and Transition. Any plan to achieve reconciliation must support campaign plan lines of operation to receive credible attention and resources and affect lasting change.

COLLABORATION: HOYT AND WHITE

CH Hoyt began meeting with Canon White throughout July while he studied the problems of violence, sectarianism, and assessed GOI and MNF-I commitment to pursue a religious track.

That same month Canon White began involving CH Hoyt in weekly personal meetings between himself and Iraq's National Security Advisor Dr Mowaffaq Al Rubaie. The meetings discussed a wide range of Andrew's work with FRRME and then began to focus on a specific track to host a high-level religious reconciliation conference. Canon White and Dr Rubaie built a delegate list of prospective senior clerics and Hoyt worked on the methodology to create the linkage for religious reconciliation through the campaign plan to the MNF-I senior leadership. Canon White had the contacts. CH Hoyt had to frame the issues in the parlance of military diplomatic interests while bringing distinctly religious credibility into operational reality (see ch. 10, The Potential Role of Religious Peacebuilders to the Whole of Government Environment).

A major concern for religious peacebuilding is the need to maintain its religiosity. Remaining authentic to the high principals of religious expression and dedicated to working within the framework of religion is imperative. Instrumentalism—the co-opting of religious initiatives for other purposes—undermines its integrity, value and effectiveness. Persons working in the field of religious peacebuilding have much to offer processes of reconciliation where religious communities are a factor. Personnel from other government departments and agencies must take these principles into consideration when collaborating with religious peacebuilders (see ch. 10, Instrumentalism).

A test to reconciliation efforts is finding clear benefits to encourage each party to support a religious reconciliation track, e.g. *superordinate goals* (see ch. 4, Collaborative Activities). In this case MNF-I needed a reduction of attacks, tapering of military requirements and the implementation of Iraqi lead solutions. The GOI needed to achieve national unity and improve the popular perception of national decision making and attenuating coalition presence. The religious leaders needed a tangible link affirming the relevancy of Muslim interests to the GOI and the legitimacy of religious leaders in the rebuilding of Iraq society. The task at hand was intentionality. Find the connect points to advance the end state without dragging religion through some preconceived checklists or outcomes to stylize a religious result.

Finally, the entire process needed to move in a positive direction that thematically shaped a sustainable Iraq political, social, military, and religious environment. CH Hoyt and Canon White agreed on four overarching outcomes: deny terrorism, denounce sectarian violence, display democratic values, and demonstrate religious cooperation. Armed with this approach, Hoyt presented a plan to the MNF-I leadership. General Casey gave him permission to proceed as best he could and trusted him to work out the details and keep him informed. CH Hoyt coordinated the religious reconciliation initiatives through two MNF-I staff organizations: the Office of National Unity and the Office of Strategic Effects. Over the next fifteen months the reconciliation efforts grew to include coordination with a host of coalition, GOI offices, private security firms, private Iraq companies, embassies, and foreign governments. Eventually the U.S. Department of Defense and the Office of White House liaison, U.S. members of Congress, the UK Foreign Secretary's office and even the prime minister of Great Britain would become involved in the effort.

THE IRAQ INTER-RELIGIOUS COUNCIL (IIRC)

The pathway to conducting a national religious reconciliation initiative was presented as an ongoing process. Canon White was fond of saying, "This is not a one off event. It is a deliberate process over time involving any number of meetings uniquely focused on religious procedures, methods, and outcomes" (see ch. 4, Interdependence as Incremental Reconciliation). The end state the GOI and MNF-I agreed to support was, "religious understanding and leadership cooperating to prevent terrorism and support GOI sovereignty." The inter-religious council was to serve three simultaneous purposes: ameliorate hostilities by providing the platform for warring factions to safely debate their issues, begin GOI political interface, and affirm religious contributions to social and national unity.

The MNF-I commanding general approved of the plan in mid-August of 2006. Chaplain Hoyt and Canon White briefed the plan to Dr. Rubaie who agreed to put the plan before the prime minister. They both also met continually with Iraq Council of Representative members, a former Iraq ambassador and key political advisors, several influential religious sheik's in Baghdad, and the U.S. Iraq ambassador's staff. In mid-September Prime Minister Maliki hosted a private meeting with Dr. Rubaie, White and Hoyt in order to convey his full support for a November 2006 meeting of senior clerics to form the Iraq Inter-religious Council (IIRC) in order to begin the work of national religious reconciliation.

Detailed planning of an agenda and the mechanics of recruiting key leaders continued over the next two months. The chief problem became one of funding. Although the prime minister supported the IIRC, the Iraqi minister of finance refused to release the funds and the November and a rescheduled December conference were postponed. A series of national reconciliation initiatives became political fodder for party opposition leaders in the Maliki government and the IIRC funding became a casualty of the power debate.

Appeals through the U.S. Administration produced a separate funding solution through the office of the Secretary of Defense, which led to the conference being rescheduled by Dr. Rubaie for 27 February through 3 March 2007.

Meanwhile Iraq's six-month-old permanent government struggled to assert itself as a national political force. Under intense pressure to solve Iraqi problems independent of perceived outside pressures, PM Maliki announced in January 2007 all-important meetings concerning Iraq would now occur inside Iraq, despite the horrific security concerns that had forced such venues to neighboring countries. One week before the February IIRC conference was scheduled to occur in the UK, the conference was again cancelled because it did not meet the new 'in Iraq' expectation. This was the third consecutive failure of the IIRC initiative; the third time all the delegates had to alter timetables, security and travel plans, and tell their respective constituents to hold on to their hopes yet again. Patience, money, and most important, credibility were running very thin.

In March of 2007, the IIRC new schedule was announced for mid May at the Al Rasheed Hotel in Baghdad. The security complexities of this were so immense as to be all but impossible. Nearly all of the delegates were clerics living in some form of exile either outside of Iraq or barricaded in their own *muhalahs* under death threats and family intimidation. It appeared the politics of Iraq might again trump the religious potential. The key Sunni leaders began to signal their refusal to attend. The idea of three government invitations, all withdrawn, and then a fourth in Baghdad, the most dangerous location for any meeting of this nature, was more than they would support. The complexities also increased as the Sunnis, continually unsupportive of the Shia-leaning Maliki government, believed the GOI untrustworthy regarding reconciliation.

EXTERNAL SUNNI LEADERSHIP

The lack of Sunni participation would doom the IIRC. To avoid this end Canon White was asked to serve as the interlocutor for the GOI. Additionally, the Sunni religious sheiks insisted on speaking with the "top religious leader of the Coalition forces." The Sunnis perceived the MNF-I as the power broker in Iraq, could not trust the GOI, and wanted to speak with a person of faith they could "trust" as a fellow cleric in order to convey their grievances.

Canon White set up the series of meetings and CH Hoyt secured the complicated permissions to travel to a neighboring Arab country to meet with the senior Sunni Iraq religious leaders. For three days the council met and spoke of the values of faith, sacred writings, trust, honor, justice, politi-

cal process, religious toleration and mutual forgiveness, and eventually reconciliation. Hoyt and White remained at the center of these discussions either
as observers or invited speakers. The meeting concluded with a renewed
confidence in old and newly found friendships, increased esteem towards
Canon White and a willingness to continue the dialogue for reconciliation.
One week later the Sunni's agreed to attend the May 07 Baghdad conference.

It is a tribute to the sorely tried religious leadership that they remained
open enough in mind and spirit to pursue reconciliation in spite of political
rebuffs. It is also noteworthy that these men were willing to overcome considerable personal obstacles to pursue a transcendent goal. The cleric's referred to MNF-I as the "occupiers" and the exit of the coalition forces was a
key platform of the reconciliation agenda. Yet these men invited a non-
Muslim Christian minister from the "occupying force" to speak and dialogue
with them about the religious principals of faithfulness and reconciliation.
The matters of faith and personal character in representation of one's faith
were honored as pivotal to the concepts of religious reconciliation. As stated
earlier, it is ultimately a heart issue. For this group of religious leaders,
controlling large portions of Iraq civil life and function, the government,
politics, and military power could not compel cooperation. Reconciliation
begins and ends with people who can be trusted because they themselves are
servants of a higher sacred truth. Religious authenticity and credibility
counted the most.

A HISTORIC ACCORD: BAGHDAD, JUNE 2007

The IIRC May event was postponed and rescheduled for a fifth and final time
for June 07. It occurred in June, in Baghdad, amid a phenomenal planning
and security effort that remains one of the most complex civilian, government, and military cooperative efforts in Iraq to date. Fifty-five delegates
attended and crafted an historic accord that set the conditions to bring sectarian violence to an all-time low, initiate militia cease-fires, and commence
dialogue between terribly wounded and estranged religious sects, leaders,
and neighborhoods. The IIRC achieved a number of critical precedents. The
IIRC[10] was the largest and most diverse council of religious leaders to meet
in Iraq in thirty-eight years, representing every religious group, geographic
region and ethnicity in Iraq.

The agreement was the first of its kind to receive the personal endorsement of the prime minister during a private meeting with key delegates.
Sayyid Dr. Fadel Al Shara, his personal representative and Advisor on Religious Affairs, was the first to affix his signature to the Accord. It was also the
first broad-based religious accord to recognize the government of Iraq and
call for integration and action by the Iraqi government on all previous and

future tribal or religious formal conferences to achieve reconciliation. The accords were the first Iraqi religious document to publicly renounce Al Qaeda by name, and declare the spread of arms and unauthorized weapons as a criminal act. Crucially, the document provided a way ahead for committed public action by religious leaders to denounce violence, deny terrorism, demonstrate support for democratic principles and the Constitution, and display national unity. Pragmatically, the IIRC in June of 2007 was a hybrid accomplishment of patience, coordination, planning, and cooperation. It was a nongovernmental organization facilitated (FRRME), MNF-I executed, US government funded, multi-embassy supported, government of Iraq national reconciliation peace initiative. It also did not come without a terrible cost. One week after the IIRC concluded ten of the delegates fell victim to assassination because of their role in furthering peace.

CAIRO, APRIL 2008 AND THE SUBSEQUENT FATWA

In the complicated world of Iraq in 2007 social, religious, or political success was always rewarded with murder, intimidation, injury, or extortion. There was no easy road to victory. The news of the IIRC mission remained unheralded because emphasis placed people in direct danger. A follow-up conference with the top Muslim leaders of the world occurred in Cairo, Egypt[11] in August. CH Hoyt and Canon White met with the world leaders of the Shia and Sunni to map out a strategy for implementing the Baghdad IIRC accords and continuing the dialogue over time. The meeting generated the personal commitments of the Iraq Shia and Sunni senior clerics to work towards issuing an unprecedented joint *fatwa* concerning peace and religious tolerance for all. The *fatwa* became reality in April of 2008. The IIRC has since downsized into a smaller body called the High Religious Council of Iraq.[12] It meets on a regular basis and is heavily engaged in limiting violence, renouncing reprisals and terrorism, and seeking sustainable government accountability to the highest ideals of transparency and religious accountability.

LESSONS LEARNED

What is to be learned from all of this experience? A predilection with the separation of church and state fails to address the political and social realities of nearly 70 percent of the world's political structures. A minimalist view of religion creates a considerable vulnerability in today's areas of military activity and is out of step with much of the world's communal and political framework.

The inability to predict outcomes or control religious actors raises the risks in political and military planning. Working in the domain of religion requires a degree of subjectivity, ambiguity, and options built upon the potentials of trust and promise. Potential and promise are difficult to measure in the objective process of military decision-making and effects-based outcomes. That same unpredictability also offers the tantalizing choice to boldly try new initiatives to secure a peace, reconcile enemies, unite societies, or embolden legitimacy.

Religious planning encompasses issues of statecraft, interagency cooperation, command expectations, resource allocation, worldviews, humanitarian action, religious priorities, multinational and coalition positions, host nation perceptions, and institutional training and professional skill. This is not simple.

Authenticity is actualizing the dogma and the design in a religion that makes life flow for its adherents. The *strategic religious planner* harmonizes as much as possible military outcomes compatible with the salient spiritual truths that manifest themselves in cultural norms, behaviors, laws, and expectations. A population that can normalize activities (military, political, legal) within their authentic religious practice is much less vulnerable to extremism, insurgency, and antagonistic sentiments. Authenticity is keeping the main thing (religion) the main thing.

Sustaining religious credibility is the lingering measure of continuing religious success. Credibility is linked to example (personal and corporate) and is the single most required and overlooked trait to conduct religious engagements. Religious leader engagements are personality vulnerable, meaning not everyone can do them. Adversaries and advocates evaluate the actions, behaviors, and intents of each other through a religious worldview. Strategic religious engagement demands intentionality and 'religious' credibility in the conduct of operations to sustain momentum. Persons involved in religious engagements meet based upon their assessments of credibility as measured by: actions, truth, and respect. Pursuing a religious track without the time, resources, and total commitments necessary to achieve an integrated strategic purpose is more damaging than no use at all.

The key to any religious dialogue or activity is protecting the discipline of religion as the focused domain of effort. Trivializing religion guarantees irreligious results. Religious dialogue, achievements, or councils cannot become staff gimmicks. Religion managed out of its context makes the results irreverent and therefore irrelevant. The challenge lies in translating authentic religious understanding and actions into measurable effects while protecting the integrity of religion as a distinct and integrated part of any enduring human solution. The dangers are presenting religion as some re-invented version of social-political or military art. This should not be underestimated. Religion is neither neutral nor idle among its followers. When religion is not honored it is perceived as attacked. When religion is attacked people die, politics crumble, societies fracture, and military campaigns culminate until things are made right.

ANALYSIS: RELIGIOUS LEADER ENGAGEMENT AT THE STRATEGIC LEVEL OF OPERATIONS

It must be stated at the onset of any offered analysis, the RLE demonstrated here is the single most significant collaborative endeavor to date integrating combined military, government and religious resources. This endeavor brings to light the much sought after cohesiveness of the Comprehensive Approach as introduced in the opening chapter of this book—a porthole through which to view the Whole of Government environment of operations. A caveat to this extraordinary anecdote is the reality that chaplains deploying with nations considered to be *middle powers*, such as Canada, commit far fewer troops to an Area of Operation (AO) than the United States, recognized as a *great power.* The size and scope of the American presence in intenational missions affords them broader responsibilities, and, consequently greater access to national levels of military, government and civil authority—inclusive of religious authority. As theatre chaplain,[13] Hoyt conducted his external ministry at the *strategic* level of operations, affording him access to regional and national leadership on several planes. As a rule, such a role is not the purview of chaplains from smaller contingents, where approaches among local communities are more the norm, or the *tactical* level. Essential to the development of RLE was the coordination of such ministry among multinational partners.

From the perspective of *intractable conflict*, these faith group leaders and their communities had moved through its various stages. Overtures to the Sunni religious leadership living in exile by CH Hoyt are not intended to lessen how the Shia community experienced conflict. *Threats* to core constructs relating to group identity had become a reality to which both Sunni and Shia could attest. In this particular instance, Sunni clerics were cited. Here a sense of loss had become unit forming, as they banded together in a nearby country from where they could monitor events at home. Where conflict "drives one out of one's land," often held sacred to identity, *distorting* the motives and the actions of the *other* at times becomes a default position. Invalidating the *other* becomes a means of affirming one's own identity. Hardened positions crystallize as increasingly impermeable constructs are put into place. Such *rigidification* makes change that much more difficult to entertain, much less achieve. Communication ceases. Complete attention focuses on illegitimatizing the *other*, as one's own "boundaries" are made secure. *Collusion* settles in once conflict takes on a life of its own, as criticisms and rejections become the modus operandi for both sides. It was into this vortex that CH Hoyt and Canon White ventured to go. A change in the dynamics of relation was the key to unlocking this seemingly impenetrable door of isolation—something that they believed was attainable (see ch. 2, Intractable Conflict).

With the authorization of his commander, in his explicit intent, and in the face of repeated setbacks and obstacles, CH Hoyt worked collaboratively with Canon White to bring together a confluence of principals and initiatives in the creation of the Iraqi Inter-Religious Council (IIRC). Together they marshaled significant military support: White's faith-based NGO (FRRME), aspects of both domestic and indigenous governments, members of the diplomatic community and, more importantly, the key religious leadership of Iraq. The United Nations would refer to this endeavor as an *Integrative* Mission[14] where a number of organizations coalesce around a given operational objective, pooling their collective resources to bring about a jointly agreed upon outcome.

As striking as CH Hoyt's movement among government and diplomatic circles was, his engagement with the leading religious leaders of Iraq was more so. The dynamics were such that the Iraqi Sunni religious elite, a number of *whom* were living in exile, inherently distrusted the Shia religious headship, convinced they enjoyed favored status with the GOI. From their perspective, MNF-I was the power broker in Iraq. Salutary to this discussion is the request that originated from these Sunni clerics living in exile to speak with a *person of faith* that they could *trust*, one representative of MNF-I. Canon White and CH Hoyt made their way to the rendezvous point outside of Iraq. As Hoyt previously noted, the three days of discussions centered on "the values of faith, sacred writings, trust, honor, justice, political process, religious toleration, mutual forgiveness and, eventually, reconciliation," dialogue that kept both Hoyt and White at its center. Prior to discussing the dynamics of their three-day visit, an appreciation of the *relational systems* and *human identity needs* at play is in order.

RELATIONAL SYSTEMS

Between 2006 and 2007 the relational systems at work in Iraq were as fluid as they were complex. The *closed relational system* (see ch. 2, Closed Relational System) operating among the three major power brokers—the MNF-I, the GOI and the Iraqi religious leadership—oscillated between the rigidity of entrenched positions to altering stances as a means of leveraging events to advantage. Recollections from earlier times, emanating from historic enmity among the religious traditions continually fed suspicion and alienation (see ch. 2, Wounded Memory). At its core was the negation of the *other*, which fed the conflict. Fueling this *closed relational system* further was the perceived dominant Shia Iraqi government, re-enforcing a sense of subjugation among the Sunni.

Secondary relational systems factored into the dynamics of the Iraqi conflict due to its regional implications (see ch. 2, Secondary Relational Systems). *Geographically*, Iraq is part of the Arab world where strong bonds of *kinship* exist among nearby Sunni and Shia populations. *Ideology* looms large as Western democratic approaches brush up against constant calls for more theocratic systems of government. Mentioned above, where a *history* of conflict exists, stoking the embers of memory soon ignites dormant sentiments—*chosen trauma*. All of these elements were at work in Iraq and continue today. CH Hoyt's overture to the exiled and estranged Sunni religious leaders depicts an *open relational system* (see ch. 2, Open Relational Systems). As a third party he brought a different perspective to their entrenched positions that continued to alienate these clerics from their Shia counterparts. Together, he and Canon White disrupted these rigid patterns by exhibiting a concern for their well-being, an acceptance and tolerance for the *other* and an invitation to constructive dialogue.

HUMAN IDENTITY NEEDS

The dissatisfaction of *human identity needs* (see ch. 2, Human Identity Needs: Meaning; Connectedness; Security; Action; Recognition; and Being: An Integrated Sense of Self) is evident with the Sunni religious leaders as well. Living in exile, a palpable concern for their physical safety emanated from their need for *security*. The requirement for collective continuity where people see themselves as members of a group is reflective of *connectedness*. When fundamental needs are threatened, individuals turn to groups most likely to preserve them. These Sunni clerics sought *security* among their own outside of Iraq where their sense of belonging was re-enforced. The fulfillment of *meaning* is associated with an understanding of what is a fair and reasonable expectation of the *other*—something the Sunni believed was lacking in their relation with the Shia leadership. Perceptions of being treated unfairly conjures up feelings of injustice. These Sunni clerics fled due to a threatened sense of safety and selfhood. The human identity need of *action* was mixed. They chose to live in exile to prohibit being "acted upon" by the Shia yet, were left with a limited capacity to "act," as they forfeited a measure of their ability to influence events inside Iraq, a constant irritant. Finally, *recognition* for these Sunni religious leaders was greatly diminished. Recognition entails an appreciation by others for one's identity and associated values. Lacking here was congruence between what the Sunni had determined to be grounds for recognition and any acknowledgment from the *oth-*

er. It is noted that the Hussein regime placed the Sunni minority (35 percent of Iraq) in the ruling class position over the Shia majority (65 percent of Iraq). Much Sunni resistance stemmed from the experience of loss of status, real power, and government endorsement.

ENCOUNTER

Integral to *encounter* between CH Hoyt and the Sunni religious leadership living in exile was Canon White's involvement—a known and trusted Christian leader of long-standing among the Iraqi religious leadership. *Partnering* with him as founder of The Foundation for Relief and Reconciliation in the Middle East (FRRME)[15], created the synergy of effort necessary to launch this endeavor. Known as the "Vicar of Baghdad," his years in Iraq had earned him credibility as a non-Muslim religious leader who genuinely cared for the Iraqi people, regardless of faith or ethnicity. The engendered *trust* he enjoyed earned him "open-door status" among Iraq's diverse religious leadership. As a *middle-range actor* his contacts among the religious, government and diplomatic communities, were unparalleled. Key to such *working trust* is the *integrity* of the individual. For more than a decade, Iraqis had witnessed White's commitment to standards of fairness, consistency of action, and the congruence of his word and deed. Coupled with his *reliability* to follow through on his commitments and his genuine *benevolence* toward all Iraqi people, regardless of creed, this Anglican priest had become a trusted friend to faith group leaders throughout Iraq—a more in-depth relationship established over time described as *personal trust*. The openness among the Sunni religious leaders to CH Hoyt's audience with them had much to do with Canon White's confidence in him (see ch. 4, Trust Development).

The *will to embrace* is exhibited in Hoyt and White's readiness to meet with the Sunni religious leaders, an acknowledged good seen to hold their well being at heart. Adding to the complexity, Hoyt was non-Muslim, a Christian cleric representing for many Iraqis what was the "occupying force" of their homeland. His genuine concern for the healing of the open wounds that perpetuated estrangement among the faith groups of their country, *mimetically* elicited a positive response from among these exiled religious leaders (see ch. 2, Mimetic Modeling). It is a genuine gesture of good will extended toward the *other* often over against a backdrop of tremendous hurt that is acknowledged for its authenticity. In the *will to embrace* the risk of opening up the *self* to the *other* is tested. Hoyt underscores the *transcendence* exhibited here in his reference to the many political rebuffs these Sunni clerics had received and the considerable personal obstacles they had to overcome in order to pursue a reconciling of differences—transcending conflict for the greater good. In a sense, this *encounter* took place in the space of *mutual hospitality.* Trust, kindness and security were manifest both in the gesture of the invitation for the Christian leaders to "come" to a location where the Sunni leadership felt safe, and their reciprocal willingness to "go." There, Hoyt and White bore witness that violence could be overcome, creating a space for the bonds of trust to grow. There was an abundance about their time together that invited thinking about new possibilities (see ch. 2, The Place of Hospitality).

Metaphorically, these Muslim leaders pulled back from their identity boundaries to make room for this Christian chaplain to enter their *inner space,* as it were, in authentic engagement. It is the porosity of identity boundaries—a permeable membrane of sorts—that allows for such exchange and, ultimately, altered impressions of the *other.* Over the course of the three days, both of these Christian leaders immersed themselves in discussions with their Islamic counterparts concerning "the religious principles of faithfulness and reconciliation." *Encounter* of this nature tacitly impacts perceptions and pre-conceived notions of the *other.* One not only comes to view the *other* differently but more importantly, begins to see one*self* through the eyes of the *other—double vision.* This historic and marathon meeting concluded with "renewed confidence in old and newly found friendships." As *encounter* goes, in parting, something of the *other* remains in the *self.* It is true; such seeding of reconciliation offers an occasion to reframe old patterns and ways of being, as the movement toward the *re-humanizing* of the *other* initiates the writing of *new narratives.* It is in such encounter that the arduous journey of the *healing of memory* begins (see ch. 4, Encounter). The following week, the Sunni delegation confirmed their presence at the table in Baghdad to begin discussions of reconciliation—*working trust* had been established.

Another dimension of *encounter* that must not be overlooked is the mode of communication during these extensive discussions. Both CH Hoyt and Canon White adapted well, giving deference to the *interdependent ethos* that infuses meaningful dialogue in the Middle-Eastern context (see ch. 2, Cultural Strangers: Individualist or Interdependent Ethos). The contrast between this more *communal* approach to dialogue and relation building, as compared to the prevailing Western style that places great emphasis on self-expression, personal enterprise and achievement would have represented a clash of values. The 'roll up your sleeves, get down to business and let's make a deal' method often accompanying the *individualist ethos* would have met with resistance, undermining the process. Paramount to these religious leaders was the welfare of the group, its guiding themes and communal interests. Illumined, too, were the spiritual values that buttressed their aspirations and concerns for their people. Searching questions were posed to CH Hoyt of his Christian understanding of faithfulness and reconciliation as compared to their own. Was this Christian leader who stood in their midst credible? Was his faith authentic? Would he be true to his word? Would the IIRC maintain a fiduciary process? Not least among the dynamics at play was the cultivation of *relation*: a gradual coming to professed *interdependence* earned through transparency and integrity. An *interdependent ethos* does not view friendships as *instrumental*: they are, profoundly, ends in and of themselves.

RITUAL AND SYMBOL

Cultural envelopes may be defined as cross-cultural encounters between different ethno-religious groups that facilitate *encounter* all the while respecting the traditions of the *other* (see ch. 2, Cultural Envelopes). Where an oppressive environment of intractable conflict persists, the distinctive *rituals* known to other faith traditions often accommodate a space for *inter*-communal engagement and dialogue. The above Islamic-Christian exchange depicted here was one such *cultural envelope* aided by what could fall within the definition of a Shura *ritual*—the cultural mechanism throughout the Islamic world, comprised of various community leaders, most commonly employed as a means of transmitting information and resolving community disputes. That said, this was not an ordinary Shura. CH Hoyt did not identify this esteemed council of Islamic scholars as an Ulema Shura. However, in other settings, it is quite likely that this gathering of senior clerics would merit such distinction. Of note, is how the chaplain was received as a religious leader. Stepping into their world via this cultural and religious *ritual* may also be viewed as *cultural borrowing*—availing oneself of the cultural richness of another tradition as a means of facilitating dialogue and learning among peoples (see ch. 2, Cultural Borrowing). Such sensitivity recognizes the *other* as a resource rather than a recipient.

As in the majority of the case studies presented here, subliminally, the *ritual of inversion* was at work in this meeting of Islamic clerics. The Christian leader in their midst, representing MNF-I, presented an entirely different frame of reference. From a Christian perspective he expounded the merits of reconciliation for all Iraqi people (see ch. 10, Christian Chaplains and the Rudiments of Islamic Peacebuilding). For the duration of their time together, Hoyt's presence and position—as the spiritual leader of the U.S./Coalition forces—helped to *reframe* their perception of the present Iraqi situation. Together, these Christian clerics, just for a short period of time, turned the existing power structures on their head. Over the next week these themes continued to resonate with these Sunni religious leaders living in exile, bringing them to collectively determine to take the risk of trusting these Christian leaders and this unprecedented opportunity to take a step of faith toward peace. He *mimetically modeled* the *will to embrace* (see ch. 2, Mimetic Modeling: Creating Openness to the Other; ch. 4, Mimetic Modeling: Creating Openness to the Other)in his intense desire for the well being of the

Sunni faith community and his vision of their living integratively among their Shia brethren.

COLLABORATIVE ACTIVITIES

In RLE the aspiration is to see the *working trust* of *encounter* between/ among religious leaders evolve into *collaborative activities* where relation among communities has occasion to deepen to a level approaching friendship, often referred to as *personal trust* (see ch. 4, Collaborative Activities: Towards Personal Trust and Integration). CH Hoyt's early meetings regarding the creation of the IIRC with Canon White and Iraqi National Security Adviser Dr. Mowaffaq Al Rubaie set this in motion. This committee was designed to include the communities of all the religious and ethnic groups in Iraq. More poignant still, is the case in establishing *superordinate goals*— aiding the diverse and fractious religious groups of Iraq to accomplish together what they could not achieve individually—*facilitation*. The necessity of such synergy of effect among mission partners stands as one of the few achievable approaches to resolving the complex issues facing Western governments today emanating from conflict-prone societies around the world—a collaborative approach to improved relations known in social psychology as *instrumental reconciliation*.

Stated earlier, the three simultaneous purposes of the IIRC were: "ameliorate hostilities by providing the platform for warring factions to safely debate their issues, begin GOI political interface, and affirm religious contributions to social and national unity." It is evident from these goals, the only way each individual group could hope to achieve such peaceful and respectful relations with the *other*, inclusive of engaging the government in respectful discourse, was to cooperate in the process. Comprised of fifty-five members of all the major religious and ethnic groups in Iraq, the IIRC met for the first time in June of 2007. In contexts of intractable conflict, accomplishments of this nature are measured incrementally, as individuals determine within themselves to rise above present circumstances (transcendence), and move to establish relation with the *other* in beginning the journey toward *coexistence* that, one day, may lead to *integration*.

Surrounded by spiraling violence (*mimetic structures of violence*), the IIRC represents the beginning of a *new narrative*—a *mimetic structure of blessing* with its open and expanding options, that are life-giving, creative and generous (see ch. 2, Mimesis: The Reciprocal Nature of Escalating Violence; Mimetic Desire; Mimetic Rivalry; Mimetic Violence; Mimetic Structures of Violence; Mimetic Structures of Blessing; and Mimetic Modeling: Creating Openness to the Other). Its expansive nature is demonstrated in the life-giving energy that served as an impetus to the historic Cairo meeting and subsequent joint *fatwa* that witnessed world leaders of the Shia and Sunni commit together to peace and tolerance for all. Were there sacrifices? Tragically yes. Spoilers take their terrible toll. Encouraging, in the midst of the sporadic violence continuing in Iraq today, is the realization that the effects of this process of reconciliation remain. The High Religious Council of Iraq—a modified version of the IIRC—continues the commitment to "limiting violence, renouncing reprisals and terrorism, and seeking sustainable government accountability to the highest ideals of transparency and religious accountability." With the ongoing support of the Foundation for Relief and Reconciliation in the Middle East (FRRME), even after the American pull out of 2011, Canon White persists in supporting this initiative. Essential to peacebuilding endeavors of this nature is the importance of identifying and investing in local peacebuilders wherever they may be found. Ideally, such individuals would come from within the indigenous population of the Area of Operations (AO), where language, culture and, potentially, religion would be a common denominator. A rare occurrence here, Canon White, a Christian leader living in the midst of a predominantly Muslim culture, had earned the confidence and respect of religious leaders and their people alike (see ch. 4, Religious Communities: Promoting Local Ownership and Building Local Capacity). Hoyt's priority of aiding in the creation of structures committed to continuing the process of reconciliation comprised primarily of religious leadership indigenous to Iraqi culture has proven to be an effective means of sustaining the effort that began in 2006. It is not perfect and experiences the struggles of any organization faced with such complexities. However, as of the publication of this volume, the High Religious Council of Iraq meets regularly, a testament to the *mimetic modeling of the will to embrace* and the benefits of investing in faith-based organizations indigenous to the Area of Operations. Such is the *redemptive centering* of chaplains, ministering under command in collaboration with their Whole of Government partners, engaging the leadership of estranged religious communities with a view to seeding reconciliation—Religious Leader Engagement as conflict transformation.

NOTES

1. John Paul Lederach defines conflict transformation as a means to transform relationships and relational systems. RLE falls within this domain. "Conflict transformation . . . focuses on change, addressing two questions: "What do we need to stop?" and "What do we hope to build?" Since change always involves a movement from one thing to another, peacebuilders must look not only at the starting point, but also at the goal and the process of getting from one point to another. While conflict resolution focuses on de-escalation of conflict and diffusion of crises, transformation allows for an ebb and flow in conflict, and sees the presenting problem as a potential opportunity to transform the relationship and the systems in which relationships are embedded." See *Reflective Peacebuilding: A Planning, Monitoring and Learning Toolkit*, chapter 5, 17. http://www.google.ca/search?client=firefox-a&rls=org.mozilla%3Aen-US%3Aofficial&channel=s&hl=en-US&source=hp&biw=&bih=&

q=Reflective+Peacebuilding%3A+A+Planning%2C+Monitoring%2C+and+Learning+Tookit+
PDF&btnG=Google+Search&oq=&aq=&aqi=&aql=&gs_l=

2. The Iraq Study Group Report, December 2006, p.10. See http://media.usip.org/reports/
iraq_study_group_report.pdf.

3. The Iraq Study Group Report, p. 30.

4. See www.washingtonpost.com/wp-dyn/content/article/20.

5. Ellen Knickmeyer and K.I. Ibrahim, "Bombing Shatters Mosque in Iraq," *Washington
Post* Thursday, 23 February 2006.

6. For further discussion on the above Islamic terms see Hammudah 'Abd al 'Ati, *Islam in
Focus* (Beltsville, Maryland: Amana publications, 1998); Abdulkadar Tayob, *Islam, A Short
Introduction* (Oxford, England: One World Publications, 1999).

7. Drawn from public and private statements made by Sheikh Al Alani during the IIRC
initiative from October 2006 to May 2007. Sheikh Al Alani held the prestigious position of
Professor and PhD in Islamic and Shari'a science, University of Baghdad and Al Anbar province.

8. For Bin Laden's entire 1998 fatwa see http://www.pbs.org/newshour/terrorism/interna-
tional/fatwa_1998.html.

9. The Coalition Provisional Authority was the name given to the interim governing apparatus led by United States Ambassador Paul Bremmer to Iraq between June 03 and May 04.

10. Due to the security risks involved for those attending the June 07 meeting of the Iraqi
Inter-Religious Council (IIRC), media coverage was held to a minimum. Canon White and a
number of the Council members held a brief press conference following the historic meeting.
Robert McFarlane, former National Security Advisor to President Ronald Regan, attended the
IIRC meeting and penned a short column for the Washington Post, published in June 2007.
More commentary on the IIRC proceedings are offered by Canon White. See Canon Andrew
White, *Vicar of Baghdad: Fighting for Peace in the Middle East* (Oxford, UK: Monarch
Books, 2009), 91–103.

11. For more on this historic meeting see Canon Andrew White, *Vicar of Baghdad: Fighting
for Peace in the Middle East* (Oxford, UK: Monarch Books, 2009), 97, 103.

12. Canon Andrew White is actively involved with the High Religious Council of Iraq via
his Non-Governmental Organization, the Foundation for Relief and Reconciliation in the Middle East (FRRME). For more information see http://frrme.org/what-we-do/reconciliation/hcrli/

13. Theatre chaplain is a term used to describe the most senior chaplain of an operation. In
this instance, Chaplain Hoyt was responsible administratively for the supervision of not only
the scores of American chaplains in MNF-I, but those from partner nations as well. The
external ministry mentioned here refers to his functional role as a chaplain among the Iraqi
religious leadership and, consequently, the government bodies related to this unfolding initiative. Conversely, internal ministry is definitive of the sacramental and pastoral support provided for the troops under one's charge.

14. Albeit, this study pertains to the interface between Peacebuilding and Humanitarian
Operations in a post-conflict environment, *The Report on Integrated Missions* provides an
indication as to the present thinking around integrated approaches under consideration by the
United Nations. This was a study jointly organized and managed by the Office of the Coordination of Humanitarian Affairs' (OCHA) Policy Development and Studies Branch and Dept of
Peace Keeping Operations (DPKO) Peacekeeping Best Practices Unit, in full consultation with
the Dept of Political Affairs (DPA), the United Nations Development Group Office (UNDGO)
and the Executive Committee on Humanitarian Affairs (ECHA) Core Group. Their assessment
suggests an overall general acceptance throughout the UN system that *integrated* missions—in
some form—are the way of the future for the United Nations in post- conflict situations. This
acceptance must be acknowledged as a breakthrough; for whatever uncertainties surround the
theory and practice of *integrated* missions today, at least the need for practical manifestations
of system coherence has been accepted. Of particular interest were the inter-institutional relationships – it was assumed that one clear reflection of *integration* would be the ways that
institutions and their respective capacities related to one another. See *Report on Integrated
Missions: Practical Perspectives and Recommendations,* Independent Study for the Expanded

UN ECHA Core Group, p. 16, 47, 48, www.google.ca/search?q=United+Nations+Integrated+
Missions&ie=utf-8&oe=utf-8&aq=t&rls=org.mozilla:en-US:official&client=firefox-a.
   15. See http://frrme.org/.

Chapter Eight

New Zealand and Norway in Afghanistan

Additional Perspectives on Religious Leader Engagement: A Reconstruction Role (2009-2010) and Specialist Considerations (2007)

NEW ZEALAND IN BAMYAN PROVINCE

In Bamyan Province,[1] Afghanistan, RLE presents differently for New Zealand chaplains working out of their Provincial Reconstruction Team (PRT)[2]. Engagement in this case study is not with local/regional religious leaders but with the Provincial Director of Education. Although the orientation for the chaplain focuses on the reconstruction role (humanitarian/developmental), RLE remains the identifier due to the chaplain's involvement with local/regional civic leaders—external operational ministry. Pertinent to the thrust of this book is the integrative manner in which the chaplain conducts his *ministry* with his colleagues in the PRT. Significant, as well, is the "intentionality" associated with his developmental role—the *ad hoc* does not enter into the equation. His mandate, from the pre-deployment training phase, was to engage in a humanitarian role that would ameliorate life circumstances for the Afghan people in accordance with the PRT mission. This is somewhat of a departure from what has been presented thus far in previous case studies, the predominant focus of this overview. As per normal for a deploying chaplain, sacramental and pastoral support of the PRT contingent was part of his regular duties.

BACKGROUND: SHIA-SUNNI TENSIONS

Capt. Leon O'Flynn is a Protestant chaplain with the New Zealand Defence Forces (NZDF), who served in the Bamyan Province Provincial Reconstruction Team (PRT) from October 2009 to April 2010, based in Bamian City, Bamyan Province.[3] Using the PRT model as its primary vehicle, the New Zealand (NZ) Government has supported the reconstruction efforts in Afghanistan since 2002. Bamyan Province is divided into seven different districts, one of which is also confusingly called Bamyan. The NZPRT operates throughout the province, geographically located in the center of the country, an area perhaps most famously known for the Bamyan Buddhas[4] that the Taliban tragically destroyed in 2001. The total population of the province is approximately 600,000 of which one third live in the central district of Bamyan. Ethnically, the Shia Muslim Hazaras are the majority in this region, as compared with the Sunni Pashtun, by far the largest ethnic group in Afghanistan and farther to the south. A common sentiment in Bamyan is that the Kabul central government unfairly distributes resources due to the extant ethnoreligious differences. While the veracity of this common concern might be difficult to prove, its relevance to the reconstruction effort is significant, which exercises a quotidian interface with the local leadership and people. Any analysis of the dynamics of Bamyan Province with greater Afghanistan must consider the ethnic dimension. Earlier discussion cited reciprocal (*mimetic*) ethnic cleansing existing between Afghanistan's Pashtun Sunni majority and its Hazara Shia minority.[5] Such *historic enmity* in a tribal society is never far from memory. Related to such deep-seated sentiments, Dr. Habiba Sarabi,[6] Bamyan Province governor, and the only female governor in Afghanistan, speaks of the existing enmity between her native Hazara people and the predominantly Pashtun Taliban insurgents of neighboring Baghlan Province. Incursions in the northeast create instability in the area. Her aspiration is to establish a peace agreement between the insurgents and local tribal leaders, endeavoring to integrate those interested in peace and prosperity into Bamyan society. In her interview, Dr. Sarabi testifies to the scarred Hazara psyche due to the atrocities committed by the Taliban, some of whom originated within Bamyan Province, and are now desirous of laying down their arms and returning. She acknowledges that the people "will never forgive them," attesting to the intransigence often associated with *wounded memory* (see ch. 2, Wounded Memory).

Chaplain O'Flynn spoke of the common perception among the Hazara of unjust treatment at the hands of the central Kabul government (again, principally Pashtun Sunni) in terms of resource allocation. Unresolved feelings associated with the collective memory of past injustice—individual or group—eventually seep into the contemporary context. One must appreciate that memory functions in the temporal space; it knows no time, often keeping woundedness very much alive. Present circumstances may rupture memory's scar tissue, reviving sentiments previously thought long forgotten.

HUMAN IDENTITY NEEDS: A HAZARA PROFILE

As in all of the case studies, *human identity needs* come to the fore immediately. (see ch. 2, Human Identity Needs: Meaning; Connectedness; Security; Action; Recognition; and Being: An Integrated Sense of Self). A quick mention here will suffice. Promptly, *connectedness* for the Shia Hazaras with their Sunni "brothers," and any accompanying sense of belonging is strikingly absent, tenuous at best—a wanton interconnectedness. Apprehension exists over the welfare needs of *security* regarding the resources needed for the basic functions of life. The constant conflict with insurgents known to other parts of Afghanistan has been relegated, for the most part, to the northeastern part of the province bordering on Baghlan Province. Insurgent (Taliban) activity has been an irritant to tribal leadership, as the porous border lends itself to easy infiltration. In recent years, other regions have been relatively unmolested, rendering the work of the PRT much easier. Albeit, treachery at one another's hands is part of the Shia-Sunni shared history. Sadly, of late, the relative calm of other regions of Bamyan Province has begun to shift.[7] Due to its "secure" nature, the central government in Kabul selected Bamyan as the launching site to begin the gradual nation-wide handover from NATO troops to the newly trained Afghan National Army—the first phase of the NATO pullout. Not surprisingly, July and August of 2012 witnessed increased insurgent activity in the central region of the province, resulting in fatalities among New Zealand soldiers,[8] Afghan Nation Police and civilians. Such vulnerability to attack heightens the need for *security*, exacerbates Shia-Sunni tensions, negatively reinforces their historical enmity, and contributes to the hardening of "boundaries"—the *rigidification* of intractable conflict.

Action is manifest as the Hazaras project a sense of powerless to avoid being "acted upon" by the Sunni central government, accentuated by a perceived disadvantage with respect to the allocation of resources. This need for *recognition* goes to identity and the lack of respect for the Shia Hazara, leading to feelings associated with their complaint of persistent ill treatment at the hands of the Sunni Pashtun. Lastly, the need for *meaning* resonates with that of *recognition*—the Shia Hazara sense of fair and just treatment for what they believe to be a reasonable expectation in response to their well-intentioned actions is not forthcoming. All of this feeds *mimetic* rivalry (see ch. 2, Mimetic Rivalry) between these two ethnic groups. Aside from the Shia/Sunni animosity that percolates beneath the surface of most dealings with Kabul, and the simmering conflict in the northeast by insurgents, Bamyan Province was not experiencing the open conflict known to points farther south (Helmand and Kandahar provinces in particular) where insurgents were fighting government and ISAF forces. As such, the NZPRT was able to devote its energies to the reconstruction and development effort without the imposition of insurgent interference. The remainder of this overview will find its focus here.

RECONSTRUCTION: PROJECT SELECTION AND FUNDING PROCESS

Grasping something of how funding works in Bamyan Province is key to understanding how planning unfolds. The head of the various ministries in the province report to their respective ministers in Kabul, where the central government determines funding allocations and appointments at the provincial level. The central and provincial governments of Afghanistan have very little money to spend. The reality is that any building project, such as the construction of a new school or the building of a hospital, is paid for by a donor country or agency. Each country, including NZ, has preferred projects. NZ spends in the vicinity of $7 million dollars (NZD) per year, a great deal of it in the area of education. The United States provides the vast bulk of these funds in Bamyan (through USAID).[9] However, private organizations, NGO's and government agencies from other countries continue to be active in the region.

By way of example, Aga Khan[10] is an effective NGO operating in a number of countries around the world. As a well-funded private charity, this organization utilizes long-term planning, essential to major infrastructure projects such as the building and managing of a local hospital. Central to the NZPRT mandate is the support to local government in coordinating what can become numerous and diverse undertakings with little communication among the NGO community as to planning. At times, this has led to the duplication of effort. In one such case two private charities were concurrently building schools in the same village, only a few hundred meters apart.

The leadership of the mission operates in the normal army hierarchical manner. At times, in O'Flynn's experience, the commander would call upon various people to form *ad-hoc* groups for a specific project, task them and let them achieve the objective(s), a process punctuated with progress reports and briefings. The commander's team was made up of the following personnel: intelligence, operations, logistics, communications, planning, medical, chaplains, engineering and finance. A team was devoted to each area of responsibility. These were augmented by a contingent of infantry for security purposes.

Over the course of the tour, the command team created a three-year plan inclusive of roads, schools, irrigation and other key infrastructure projects. Strategically, this created congruence between PRT planning, the money it administered, and the governor's program for the province. More importantly, the next rotation enjoyed a head start in the development work; as a project neared completion, a new endeavor with further reaching timelines could be added to the list of scheduled tasks. The three-year plan afforded breathing space for planning, research and the awarding of contracts even if the building for such a project might be as much as two years away.

The PRT commander maintained a clear vision of what he wanted each member to achieve in the development area.[11] The expectation was to develop a series of projects that would assimilate into his larger strategic plan for the province—not simply a list of school buildings that had been approved for construction. Tasks were designed to support and, in fact, boost the local government. Paramount in the planning was the implication and involvement of local people, so as to engender local ownership.

MENTORING AFGHAN LEADERSHIP

As in other PRTs throughout Afghanistan, NZPRT personnel mentor local leadership. This necessitates the development of strong working relationships that allow team members to acquire sufficient information to identify the needs of the local community. Education, of course, was one sector among others that came under mission analysis. As the PRT chaplain, O'Flynn was tasked to engage the director of education (Mohamed Ada) as frequently as the director's schedule would permit—education, health and community engagement.

O'Flynn concentrated on nurturing an *open relational system* (see ch. 2, Open Relational Systems) with the director of education. His emphasis was to create and cultivate *interdependence* based on a respected and valued relation between them. Integrity and authenticity marked their collaboration. Continued *encounter* soon engendered a *working trust* that led to warming of relation and an open door invitation to his provincial office. While their discussions took place through an interpreter they came to know each other well, understood each other's tones, demeanor and expressions. The *collaborative activities* facilitated by O'Flynn between Director Ada and the various NGOs eventually resulted in a demonstrated *personal trust* between the two of them evidenced in their friendship (see ch. 4, Trust Development).

Islamic scholar Qamar-Ul Huda[12] underscores the salience of engaging Muslim educators in reconstruction efforts. He notes that such individuals often provide social, economic, and religious support to local communities. More highly educated than most, they often take on mediation roles in times of crisis, which may include interfaith dialogue programs or interfaith-reconciliation peacemaking projects. Mohamed Ada falls within this grouping. Albeit, Ada is not seen here acting in the capacity described by Huda, nonetheless, it is individuals of his ilk that possess such potential—influential leaders within communities and regions representing lasting change. *Networking* among educators is time well spent, an aspect of RLE by virtue of the chaplain's involvement.

THE ENORMITY OF THE TASK

The director had a number of incredibly difficult realities with which to deal. Bamyan Province had approximately 120,000 children of all ages in its schools, roughly a 50/50 split between boys and girls—the best ratio in the country. Approximately one third of his 140 schools were without classrooms; children were taught in fields under tents. Some schools, such as the Central Boys High School in Bamian Township, had over 4000 students, while others high in the mountains had as few as 30 pupils. Schools high in the Hindu-Kush Mountains were snow-bound seven months of the year. Only 5 percent of his teachers had graduated from teachers' training college. The rest of the teachers were often people who simply completed more schooling than the students, for example, year six students teaching year two.

The process began in the seven districts of Bamyan, each of which had its own deputy director of education. Local boards of village elders submitted plans to their respective deputies. District government leadership then discussed and prioritized projects according to importance for the district under review. Moving to the provincial planning level, the director of education made the final project selection based upon overall need and the availability of resources. PRT involvement ran in tandem with this entire process at all levels of government, offering guidance in accordance to the needs and requirements of each: local, district and provincial. At the grassroots, local Liaison Officers (LO) representing the PRT spent time explaining the process with councils in the villages. Survival is often day-to-day in a tribal society such as Afghanistan where resources are perpetually in short supply. As O'Flynn observed, due to such shortages it sometimes was taxing for communities to place the needs of other families, villages or tribes before their own. This grassroots engagement was critical to moving much needed infrastructure improvements to the next level—a "bottom up" endeavor. As Chaplain O'Flynn intimated, the PRT staff worked in concert with these efforts to assure safe passage of each initiative to both district and provincial stages of the process. Again, linking the director of education with the appropriate NGO for funding purposes became a 'top down' procedure as government structures already in place were accessed on behalf of grassroots requests. In this regard, the chaplain aided in the *circular causality* needed for grassroots initiatives to come to fruition—both 'bottom up' and 'top down' processes functioning together to bring about needed infrastructure changes in Bamyan Province (see ch. 4, Collaborative Activities: Towards Personal Trust and Integration). Advantageous too was the success of such reconstruction efforts, as it enhanced the central government's image among the people as they personally witnessed their provincial representatives making a difference—the *writing of new narratives*. By virtue of the chaplain facilitating such programming among government leadership and the NGO community it became a function of RLE, an added dimension of Whole of Government.

A pertinent example of the magnitude of the task was the aforementioned Central Boys High School. The need of additional classrooms was acute, as about half its students were meeting in tents on the school grounds. The PRT commander identified this project as key to his larger plan. One of the various NZPRT partners was approached to fund the construction. The Singapore team perceived the high school as an ideal project for national funding. As is frequently the case among government development agencies, imposed rules and guidelines as to project selection, group qualification and the disbursement of moneys can be a lengthy and arduous process. A reasonable approach to fieldwork, it remained a challenge for local populations to appreciate. Chaplain O'Flynn maintained a relationship based on co-operation and mutual respect with all concerned. During the technical engineering discussions his role consisted of keeping the provincial director informed of progress. Here the chaplain demonstrates his unique role as *facilitator*. Once the project was identified and the NGO selected, his function became one of *trusted friend* to be of assistance in any way deemed necessary (see ch. 4, Building Relation). The school extension was approved; construction began shortly after he redeployed for New Zealand. Essential to the completion of the high school project were the two following factors: (1) Both the local population and the NZPRT personnel were keen to see the project succeed—grassroots support due to thorough consultation; and (2) local leadership was implicated from its conception, an involvement that was maintained throughout the many meetings that led to getting this project to and across the starting line—local ownership.

Of note was a request that kept surfacing for the construction of a new headquarters for the Education Department in Bamian, a project that did not rate high on the NZPRT priority list. Its value to the mission was not appreciable. A quality admired by Chaplain O'Flynn in the PRT commander was his ability to adjust his plan based on presenting dynamics. He resisted leaving Afghan leadership with the impression that project selection was little more than randomly choosing locations on a map or that the PRT strategic mission was so entrenched that little tolerance existed for another viewpoint. The request for the new headquarters led to a great number of meetings with much time given to discussion and planning. It eventually found its way onto the construction docket. This is not to suggest that NZPRT planning was easily influenced, rather, as an organization, it maintained the capacity to be flexible when justifiable reasons to reconsider priorities were presented. Deliberations in the pre-deployment phase in NZ led to the development of a strategic plan for the entire tour. Once on the ground, a better understanding of the local situation had a way of informing and fine-tuning the original plan—a process not uncommon in missions. However the purpose behind the plan remained steadfast.

VALIDITY OF THE CHAPLAIN'S ROLE

A valid question at this point might be how did such 'ministry' fall to the chaplain? The NZ approach to deployments utilizes the Pre Deployment Training (PDT) to the fullest. This allows mission personnel a period of time before deploying to become acquainted and to receive additional skills training. Distinct to NZ is a season of pre-PDT training. In the case of the Bamyan PRT, all personnel designated to have contact with the local populace were directed to attend a two-week CIMIC[13] (Civil Military Cooperation) course. Included on the roster were patrol commanders, the mission doctor, nurse and chaplain. Emphasis lay on theory along with some practical exercises on how the military can cooperate with local originations. This was also a chance for various parts of the command team to meet each other for the first time.

The commander's perception of the chaplain's role led to greater inclusion in mission planning, an understanding facilitated by the Principal NZ Defence Forces Chaplain. From the inception of the mission, Chaplain Parker mandated NZ chaplains attached to the Bamyan PRT to demonstrate their utility as the mission dictated, provided that their role of the provision of sacramental and pastoral support to personnel was not compromised. Today's military leaders are experiencing a shift in how they perceive chaplains, a reality that will require many chaplains to broaden in their own self-understanding. Security operations of the twenty-first century will undoubtedly precipitate such reflection.

NETWORKING AND PARTNERING

Principal among Chaplain O'Flynn's contributions to the NZPRT reconstruction effort in Bamyan Province was his previously mentioned role as *facilitator* between Director Ada's office and the various NGOs called upon for funding assistance. O'Flynn's extensive *networking* precipitated *partnering* on a number of projects. Whole of Government emerges here as the chaplain moves within the Interagency environment of the Public space (JIMP) (see ch. 4, JIMP) of indigenous populations. RLE in this sense lay in his guiding these various processes through the labyrinth of potential miscommunication and misunderstanding. At times, this role extended to groups within the population where disappointment due to government project selection precipitated sentiments of favoritism among those communities not chosen for a reconstruction endeavor. In this light the chaplain worked to preclude *closed relational systems* from taking root. Breaches in relation—whatever the reason—create resentment, distance and isolation between principals. In a fashion, O'Flynn functioned as a "third party intervener," managing programs that necessitated keeping the channels of communication open between Afghan nationals in government, local communities, foreign NGOs and the NZPRT itself. In a very real sense, he *mimetically modelled* collaboration and *mutuality* for all concerned and a *will to embrace* the *other* despite cultural peculiarities, relational tensions or processes that sometimes left much to be desired. *Transcending* what for some would become impediments for the *greater good* aided others in maintaining their focus—a catalytic dimension of sorts (see ch. 2, Mimetic Modeling: Creating Openness to the Other).

UNDER COMMANDER'S AUTHORITY AND IN HIS EXPLICIT INTENT

A word must be also said in reference to the mandate Chaplain O'Flynn received from his chaplain chain of command prior to deployment and how the NZPRT functioned under the commander. Not all nations assign chaplains to PRTs with such intentionality. O'Flynn was course loaded for CIMIC training prior to deploying with the specific objective of assuming a humanitarian function for the duration of the operational tour. This was not to be *ad hoc* ministry, which, for the most part, is what humanitarian assistance has always been for chaplains. While not neglecting his traditional role, he was to be a full *partner* in the Whole of Government enterprise of the PRT. In this light, the *external operational ministry* of New Zealand chaplains is undeniably progressive. It offers a lens through which Whole of Government personnel can view the effectiveness of the chaplain's collaborative role in an integrated interagency environment. The commander of the NZPRT held the same expectation for Chaplain O'Flynn, directing him to concentrate his efforts within the Directorate of Education for the province. Initiating a three-year plan was strategically significant, creating the best opportunity for success for those who would follow. Ministering among the indigenous population under commander's authority and in his explicit intent was markedly easier for O'Flynn as both the Chaplaincy and the PRT chains of command acknowledged this was the desired outcome of his position. Evident also was the commanders concern for the people. He was not there simply to create sterling reports of his exploits as the PRT commander. He had the genuine interests of the people at heart, noticeable in his willingness to listen with openness to their concerns, acting upon them when deemed legitimate, even if it meant adjusting his own project strategies. Quality leadership of this nature holds promise for future Whole of Government endeavors.

Mention must be made with respect to chaplains as religious leaders ministering to indigenous populations. In their publication on *Trust Development*, Thompson et al. discuss trust *categories* in the sense of what additional qualities the *other* may possess. They illumine that where RLE is practiced as an aspect of the mission, chaplains project certain knowledge and expertise and a level of integrity and benevolence that is associated with their role, distinct from the attributes of any particular person. In establishing *trust* among indigenous leaders—religious or otherwise—within more faith-based societies, chaplains are more apt to be perceived as honorable and trustworthy individuals by leadership. As such, the inclination of indigenous leaders to trust chaplains more easily becomes a dynamic of such engagement. This is not to suggest that other personnel cannot achieve levels of trust—to the contrary. The point offered here is that Chaplain Leon O'Flynn found himself in the enviable position of engendering trust and enjoying acceptance far more effortlessly due to his identity as a religious leader. In Afghanistan, expectations and allowances are afforded religious leaders. One must exercise wisdom in not abusing such *trust*, for the integrity of engagement is crucial to continued respect and relation (see ch. 10, Instrumentalism). Notwithstanding, in a world where Western governments increasingly find themselves engaged in missions within more theocratic societies, personnel within the interagency environment of Whole of Government may come to benefit from such an association.

NORWAY IN FARYAB PROVINCE

Norway has been a world leader in peacekeeping[14] down through the decades, demonstrative of a national resolve to forge the way globally in other areas as well, e.g., paying other nations to refrain from destroying their rainforests.[15] It comes as no surprise that they also would be one of the frontrunners with respect to developing the capacity for Religious Leader Engagement (RLE). The Norwegians have led a Provincial Reconstruction Team (PRT)[16] in Meymaneh, Faryab Province[17] since September 2005 in collaboration with Latvia and Finland, later joined by Iceland. Chaplain Frode Lagset is a Norwegian Lutheran priest who served as the PRT field priest in 2007. His reflections on his role as chaplain to the PRT personnel as well as his *external operational ministry* among local religious and community leaders presents a Nordic perspective of the emerging dimension of Religious Leader Engagement (RLE). Significant to this series of case studies is Lagset's discussion published in *Pacem*, the Norwegian Chaplaincy Review.[18] Here he outlines some of the mechanics of such engagement but also candidly converses regarding how RLE may be maximized without diminishing the legitimacy of some of the more challenging questions associated with such ministry—a fitting way to conclude with this brief look at RLE in partnership with PRT personnel in the Whole of Government environment.

Lagset's Chaplaincy superiors are supportive of RLE, as a number of his predecessors at the Nordic PRT had been in contact with local religious leaders, as were those who followed him. He was encouraged to collaborate with the PRT staff in making inroads into the religious community. Notwithstanding, some Norwegian chaplains, as in other countries, remain cautious due to concerns of any additional duties that might distract from the primary role of ministering to the flock. Lagset was convinced that with a degree of planning and organization, both could be accomplished without one sacrificing the other.

THE RELIGIOUS COMMUNITY

In assessing the Meymaneh area, the center where the PRT resid, it was evident that the local mullahs are highly regarded community members. From Lagset's experience, lesser-developed parts of the country saw mullahs with relatively greater prestige and power than many of their urban counterparts. In villages and towns, where most could not read or write, the more educated mullahs were perceived by the people as community leaders— *middle range actors* (see ch. 4, The Tolerant Voice of Religion: Middle Range Actors). The majority of these clerics believed that traditional structures should be safeguarded, while others expressed need for new ways of thinking accompanied by structural change. Most often transforming tradition meant embracing an alternative understanding of the Koran espoused by proponents of Wahabbism[19] originating mainly from Saudi Arabia. Chaplain

Lagset's social *networking* also included the maulawis—plural of maulawi—a distinctive title of most educated mullahs, a number of whom received training abroad, normally in either Pakistan or Egypt. Lagset provides insight into the workings of the religious structures. In Faryab Province a hierarchy existed among the mullahs where those at the local level received payment from the people normally for reading Koranic verses in the home. He believed a portion of these funds went to the district and provincial levels where maulawis lived quite comfortably. One maulawi school existed for the entire province in Meymaneh with most of the madrassahhs located there. In addition to the provincial level gatherings, a national network of mullahs and maulawi existed with periodic meetings extending for several days. In this manner, communication from the more senior religious leaders worked its way down to local mosques and madrassahs quite effectively.

ENGAGING THE MULLAHS

Norwegian chaplains visit with local religious leaders both inside the PRT compound and in the community. Some arriving at the PRT do so cautiously, totally covered so as to avoid detection by "those who may be watching," while the majority come by taxi or are dropped off by a relative with no apparent concern. Planning for initial contact is intentionally minimal assuring an interpreter is available. It is recognized that the main points of the meeting will be passed on to the mullah's superiors. Courtesies are extended in the form of fruit, mineral water and tea, unless it is Ramadan. Good notes are taken, as the interpreter cannot be expected to remember everything. These are properly filed for the next chaplain. In such meetings, one must be careful not to make promises on behalf of the PRT unless prior approval for a given project has been given.

For the Nordic team, as it is for other PRTs, field trips are a serious matter and must exhibit a clear purpose if they are to be approved. Security is always a concern. A visit to a local mosque or madrassah includes a security squad with several vehicles—stressful for all implicated. The chaplain may be the first to visit from the local PRT, a gesture looked upon by the people as an honor. In calling on the maulawis of a local madrassah confidentiality during initial contact is not a concern. All attend the meeting: employees, colleagues and students, sitting cross-legged on the carpet, sipping on the traditional tea while conversing—a visit that can last for several hours. Chaplain Lagset recognized that these were early days in establishing rapport and, as such, it was important to lay a foundation for further dialogue where more meaningful discussion may take place (see ch. 4, Trust Development). He soon realized that any scholarly discussion about religious matters of any depth simply was not profitable, as much of the nuances of faith were lost in translation. It was beyond interpreters to convey the meaning of the extended responses that came with any questions relating to Islam or Koranic verses. Emphasis was placed on establishing relation with local religious leaders. A report of the meeting with the local maulawi is prepared for Command with comments and initial analysis: Who talked with whom? Where? What was said? (see ch. 4, Religious Area Analysis). In the Norwegian-led PRT, these reports are sent to Command, the civilian advisers and the Intelligence cell for assessment and archiving. Further discussion on this point will be offered under the upcoming section on *Intelligence.*

A SPECIALIST ROLE

Although Norwegian chaplains regularly engage the local religious leadership in Faryab Province, Lagset is the first to write about it. In his estimation, a distinction exists between *internal* pastoral ministries among the PRT personnel and the *external* role among the community religious leadership. The Norwegian chaplaincy is still exploring this new capacity within the Whole of Government environment of the PRT. Lagset sees benefit in developing a "specialist" role for a chaplain who would work in collaboration with PRT personnel in RLE activities. In such a scenario, a second priest would deploy to care for the sacramental and pastoral needs of the PRT personnel, precluding any undermining of the more traditional role due to a chaplain becoming too distracted by outside interests. The "specialist" would devote all of his/her energies to *networking, partnering* (see ch. 4, Building Relation) and eventual *peacebuilding* (see ch. 4, Collaboration Activities) among local religious communities, which would complement the diplomatic and development initiatives of his/her Whole of Government partners. Intimated here is the need for additional training beyond that which would prepare the chaplain for the priesthood, a notion worthy of consideration. Chaplain Lagset offered the intriguing observation that from the Afghan perspective, it was difficult to separate any *peacebuilding* initiatives from other PRT activities— a local Afghan did not make such a distinction. As the PRT chaplain, he was duly recognized as a religious leader within the community but never lost his attachment to the foreign European presence among them. How could he? Interestingly, Lagset did not see this as a detractor among the local populace. His impression was that in Afghan society for religious leaders to be involved in political and, sometimes, military endeavors, this was more the norm. In his estimation, affiliation with those in uniform was not as much of a problem for the local community as some would contend.

INTELLIGENCE (INT)

As with any new capability, taxing questions manifest in its application. The Norwegians fully recognize the difficulties the subject of Intelligence holds for chaplains conducting visits with local religious leaders. He cooperated with the INT Cell in the sense that he reported back on information from his visits with local mullahs related to current events and the basic structures of Afghan society. His function was not what some would label as "information gathering for intelligence purposes" (see the opening sections of chapter 8 for a discussion on the INT question). He viewed his *external* role as that of an intermediate. Lagset interpreted this as a cross between being a member of the Military Observation Teams (MOT) and, due to his engaging local religious leaders, that of a Political Advisor (PolAd). The MOT is comparable to what other nations might refer to as Key Leader Engagement (KLE)—traveling the district, talking with various individuals, and gathering general information. He was thoroughly convinced that confidentiality was not breached with the maulawis. It was his belief that these mullahs fully expected him as the local Christian priest to convey information given back to his authorities. They did not see him as their confessor. To withhold important points of their conversation would have been to deceive the maulawis. It is also true that as a priest and spiritual leader, Chaplain Lagset had greater experience and knowledge when it came to interpreting the religious leader's perspective— nuances that often escape leadership.

ESTABLISHING GOODWILL

In addition to conducting RLE activities throughout the district, Chaplain Lagset made mention of the *goodwill* that a number of his predecessors established among the local/district religious leadership by inviting a significant group of maulawis and mullahs to the PRT for lunch. The significance of *breaking bread together* has been cited in earlier case studies. Moreover, the *ritual* of the shared meal is a powerful conveyer of acceptance, interdependence and *mutuality* (see ch. 2, Formal and Informal Ritual). Such initiatives display a willingness to engage in what is held in high esteem in Afghan society and culture with respect to tradition and hospitality. In so doing, the Norwegian chaplains create a *safe space* for these local clerics where *kindness* is expressed and *trust* engendered—building relation (see ch. 2, The Place of Hospitality; ch. 4, Building Relation). *Cultural borrowing* may be seen in this invitation to dine together—respect for local custom is honored in offering them a traditional meal within the Nordic compound.

First meetings or sustaining relations beyond initial contact with local clerics can be perplexing for PRT staff. In bridging to the indigenous religious community, the Norwegian chaplains moved relation from a *closed relational system*, where communication was limited or non-existent, to that of an *open relational system* where *embracing* the *other* came in the form of *encounter* (see ch. 2, Relational Systems). Here they facilitated bringing the PRT staff together with the local religious leadership. It is in such exchanges, either visits outside the camp or inviting groups into the PRT compound, that chaplains *mimetically model* the desire for the wellbeing of the *other* (see ch. 2, Mimetic Modeling). This afforded the maulawis and mullahs an occasion to see the European staff in a different light. Many among their number heard for the first time just how much these Nordic advisors could help their communities. In such exchanges *double vision* has the opportunity to remove barriers and dispels suspicion, which so often accompanies stereotyping. These Islamic clerics not only saw these Europeans in a different perspective, they began to comprehend the perspective of the *other*. The power of *encounter* has such a lingering affect as something of the *other* remains in the *self*—seeds of change are sown (see ch. 4, Encounter). Due to the common ground between the priest and mullahs, PRT personnel, often secular in orientation, are able to present their objectives to an influential community body. Through such enterprise, these Norwegian chaplains aided in eroding local stereotypes that often encumber Whole of Government programming. It must be noted, as in earlier case studies, Chaplain Lagset and his Norwegian colleagues demonstrated the efficacy of the RLE role within the Public space known to the Comprehensive Approach in collaboration with their Whole of Government partners—the Interagency environment of operations (Joint, Interagency, Multinational, Public: JIMP—see ch. 4, JIMP). The spiraling effects of *mimetic structures of violence* in other parts of Afghanistan are far more menacing than in Faryab Province. Through the RLE of Norwegian chaplains a foundation for *mimetic structures of blessing* (ch. 2, Mimetic Structures of Blessing) continues to be laid in collaboration with their Whole of Government partners. Open and expanding options for communities are being explored through PRT programming that is life-oriented, creative and generous. The ease of movement and natural rapport of Chaplain Lagset and his colleagues within the social space of religious communities stands as yet another testament for the need to formally operationalize RLE as a capability within existing structures.

NOTES

1. The World Food Programme (United Nations) provides a thorough description and overview for Bamyan Province: Geography; Demography and Population; Current State of Development in the Province; Agriculture and Rural Development; Education; Health; Social Protection; and additional information. See http://www.foodsecurityatlas.org/afg/country/provincial-Profile/Bamyan, accessed 10 Aug 2012

2. See chapter 5, Canadian Case Study 2 (Afghanistan), Endnote 29 for a description of a PRT.

3. There are a number of spellings used; Bamiyan, Bamyan, and Bamian. The NZPRT used the Bamian spelling for the city, district and Bamyan for the province.

4. See "Afghan Buddha destruction revealed," http://news.bbc.co.uk/2/hi/south_asia/1222776.stm.

5. See chapter 5, Canadian Case Study 2 (Afghanistan), *Human Identity Needs*, particularly the section relating to *Security*, for further elaboration on the Hazara Shia and Pashtun Sunni animosity. Endnotes 9-11 offer additional references.

6. See http://www.youtube.com/watch?v=kutmNtCjeS0; see also http://www.khaama.com/bamyan-governor-warns-over-fragile-state-of-security/. For a map Afghanistan's provinces, see http://www.google.ca/imgres?imgurl=http://www.isaf.nato.int/templates/isaf3_project/images/mapAfghanistan.png&imgrefurl=http://www.isaf.nato.int/map-usfora/index.php&usg=__uKwvvjZtoGWLfbfSkltJGOo2-Ig=&h=877&w=900&sz=64&hl=en&start=11&sig2=zVzp3m_bv65iuY6-OYK_qQ&zoom=1&tbnid=iGjbaEPZtgan3M:&tbnh=142&tbnw=146&ei=UmgiUKL2LIP-8AS97oCQDg&prev=/search%3Fq%3Dafghan%2Bprovinces%2Bmap%26hl%3Den%26client%3Dsafari%26sa%3DX%26rls%3Den%26tbm%3Disch%26prmd%3Divns&itbs=1.

7. See "Afghanistan insurgency threatens previously peaceful Bamiyan province: Concerns growing over violence in central highland province after two bombs killed nine police officers earlier this month," http://www.guardian.co.uk/world/2012/jul/19/afghanistan-insurgency-threatens-bamiyan-province?INTCMP=SRCH, accessed 20 Aug 2012.

8. See "Three New Zealand soldiers killed by roadside bomb in Afghanistan," http://www.guardian.co.uk/world/2012/aug/20/new-zealand-soldiers-killed-afghanistan?INTCMP=SRCH, accessed 20 Aug 2012.

9. See http://www.usaid.gov/.

10. The Aga Khan Development Network (AKDN) is a group of development agencies with mandates that include the environment, health, education, architecture, culture, microfinance, rural development, disaster reduction, the promotion of private-sector enterprise and the revitalisation of historic cities. AKDN agencies conduct their programmes without regard to faith, origin or gender. See the Aga Khan Development Network, http://www.akdn.org/.

11. While Chaplain O'Flynn focused on education, other officers in the mission concentrated their efforts on such areas as roads, wells, health clinics, etc.

12. See chapter 5, Islamic Peacebuilding,

13. *Civil-Military Cooperation (CIMIC)*—coordination and cooperation in support of the mission between commanders and civil actors including the national population and local authorities as well as international, national and non-governmental organizations and agencies. CIMIC is a coordination and liaison function and leads to actions that support civilian authorities. Simply understood, this is a government funded cell within a deployed contingent that, among other things, targets the infrastructure needs of local populations . . . an additional element of capacity building.

14. See www.norway-un.org/NorwayandUN/Norwegian-UN-Politcies/Peace_Operations/, accessed 10 Aug 2012.

15. See "Norway to pay Guyana to save its rainforests," http://news.mongabay.com/2009/0204-guyana_norway.html, accessed 10 Aug 2012.

16. See "Norwegian Led PRT in Faryab," http://www.norway.org.af/News_and_events/prt/faryab1/; *Nordic Approaches to Whole of Government: Afghanistan and Beyond*, http://www.google.ca/search?q=Whole+of+Government+Finland&ie=utf-8&oe=utf-8&aq=t&rls=org.mozilla:en-US:official&client=firefox-a. See Chapter Five, Canadian Case Study 2 (Afghanistan), Endnote 2 for a description of a PRT.

17. The World Food Programme (United Nations) provides a thorough description and overview for Faryab Province: Geography; Demography and Population; Current State of Development in the Province; Agriculture and Rural Development; Education; Health; Social Protection; and additional information. See http://www.foodsecurityatlas.org/afg/country/provincial-Profile/Faryab, accessed 10 Aug 2012.

18. Pacem is published in Norwegian. Chaplain Lagset translated the article into English to assist the writing of this case study, continuing with email correspondence for further discussion and clarity. See DLCD for translation.

19. See Stephen Schwartz, *The Two Faces of Islam: Saudi Fundamentalism and its Role in Terrorism* (New York: Anchor Books, 2002), 96-97, 166-72, 175-79, 181-82; Ahmed Rashid, *Taliban* (New Haven and London: Yale University Press, 2000), 85, 132, 197, 199, 201-02, 211. See also "The Whabbi Threat to Islam" in *The Washington Post*, Mona Eltahawy, 6 June 2004, http://www.washingtonpost.com/wp-dyn/articles/A17037-2004Jun4.html; see "The Islamic Traditions of Wahabbism and Salafiyya" in *CRS Report for Congress*, Christopher M. Blanchard, 24 Jan 2008, http://www.fas.org/sgp/crs/misc/RS21695.pdf; "Islamic Radicalism: Its Whabbi Roots and Current Representation," *The Islamic Supreme Council of America*, http://www.islamicsupremecouncil.org/understanding-islam/anti-extremism/7-islamic-radicalism-its-wahhabi-roots-and-current-representation.html.

Chapter Nine

The Religious Directors of the Bosnia-Herzegovina Defense Forces

From Conflict to Collaboration — A Model of Reconciliation in Process

Given that the *impulse* for religious leader engagement (RLE) began for this author during the war in the Balkans in the early 1990s, it is only appropriate that these reflections conclude by returning there. Bosnia-Herzegovina has factored singularly in this research, as have the lives of the men of faith encountered on the outskirts of Sarajevo, shepherding their religious communities during a time of intense conflict among their respective identity groups. Since the Dayton Peace Accords[1] concluded the war in 1995, much has transpired. The journey toward reconciliation for the Bosniaks, Croats and Serbs residing in Bosnia-Herzegovina bear the marks and the scars of a post-war environment.

By way of context, one must consider their common history of five decades of communist rule following World War Two. Those years of communism were particularly arduous for those of religious faith. Religious belief and its institutions were relegated to the margins of Bosnian society. Authorities, espousing a more atheistic ideology, embarked upon an intense indoctrination of the people with the express purpose of negating any inherent sense of a human need for God. These years also brought much persecution for believers of all faiths—religious communities were confined to restricted areas while certain individuals were personally targeted, losing their property and freedom.[2]

The war in Bosnia resulting from the break-up of the former Yugoslavia brought still further degradation for those of genuine faith. Nationalist and, in some instances, religious exclusivity led to grave offenses against the humanity of the *other*. Indicative of such transgressions were the indiscriminate killing, the forced displacement of tens of thousands for the purposes of *ethnic cleansing*, the destruction of cultural and sacred sites, and the like. Compounding such egregious accounts was the reality that some committing these crimes did so in the name of their faith. Religious symbols were worn while attesting to a superficial faith conveniently *sacralized* for political agendas.[3] Imam Ismail Smajlovic, Military Mufti to the Bosnia-Herzegovina Defense Forces (BHDF) articulates that religious leaders are faced with the responsibility of cultivating self-control among their people when faced with war's ordeals through religious rituals and other means of fostering human virtues.[4] Sadly, some were implicated in the conflict while others offered little or no opposition. The many who chose to live according to the strength of their faith and the Divine principle of respect for human dignity[5] found such aggression and indifference toward the *other* by their religious brethren exceedingly difficult to comprehend.

THE RELIGIOUS DIRECTORATES OF THE BOSNIA-HERZEGOVINA DEFENSE FORCES

One cannot discuss post-war religious tolerance within Bosnia-Herzegovina without making reference to The statement of Shared Moral Commitment[6] struck in June, 1997, an agreement between the religious leadership of its four religious communities: Bosniak Muslim; Serbian Orthodox; Croatian Roman Catholic and Jewish. Together, they acknowledged the suffering of all during the war and recognized the need for a durable peace where truth, justice and common living were normative. The Statement recognized their differences, yet underscored their common values as a basis for mutual esteem, cooperation and coexistence, founded on the fundamental human rights of all. Abuses that occurred during the war were jointly condemned while each religious group committed to respect the rights of the *other*, pledging to be a support to one another in these pursuits.

In the years following the Bosnian war this author came to know Imam Smajlovic. The acquaintance of Fathers don Tomo Knezevic, Roman Catholic Religious Director, and Sladjan Vlajic, Orthodox Religious Director was made at the World Chiefs of Military Chaplains' Conference in Cape Town, South Africa, during the spring of 2009. That same fall presented the opportunity for a fact-finding mission to Sarajevo for the purpose of discerning more of how these three religious leaders ministered together in the military environment of post-war Bosnia: interviews were conducted, additional religious leaders and military officers were met, services of all three faith traditions were attended including a pilgrimage to a Roman Catholic holy site. Over the years, a warm comradery has developed.

Chronologically, Muslim religious services were the first to be integrated into the Bosnia-Herzegovina Ministry of Defense in 1999. The Roman Catholic Spiritual Care Office officially became a part of the forces in 2004, albeit the Vrhbosna Archdiocese had been offering sacramental and pastoral care for military personnel and prisoners some years prior. In 2008 the Serbian Orthodox religious directorate was formed to complete the spiritual support for all three ethno-religious groups represented in the BHDF. Further structuring of the BHDF Chaplaincy was in great part the work of American chaplains: SFOR[7] Theatre Chaplain, Colonel Robert R. Gilman, in collaboration with the USEUCOM[8] chaplain. Over a period of months in 2006 these chaplains aided in their adopting the laws and regulations on religious practices, now embedded in the BHDF doctrine. They were further assisted by a number of senior American Army officers who presented to their Bosnian counterparts on the significance of the faith dimension and religious leaders in the Armed Forces. Such formation of military personnel was deemed significant given that many in senior positions had undergone training during the former communist regime—an emphasis that was distinctly anti-religious. Ministry and activities for the Religious Directors of the BHDF are similar to those of other military chaplaincies: spiritual assistance and guidance for members in everyday life; religious services relating to the passages of life; religious ceremonies commemorating important historical moments; pastoral care for those in need; education and training of military personnel as required; interfacing with their civilian counterparts; and interacting with other military chaplaincies.

Paramount to the deliberations here is the collaborative nature of their ministry as religious directors and staffs on a number of fronts. What must be kept before the reader is that less than two decades have lapsed since these three religious communities were engulfed in the larger conflicts of their ethno-religious groups. This inter-religious endeavor has literally risen from the ashes of that conflict. There are few chaplaincies in the world today that can lay claim to such beginnings, the Chaplaincy of the South Africa Defense Forces being one exception. The Orthodox Religious Directorate is the most recently established of the three BHDF Directorates (2008). Father Vlajic testifies to receiving assistance from both the Muslim and Roman Catholic Directorates, support that continues to this day—solidarity bearing witness to fraternity. Each of the three directorates employs programming unique to their own constituency. Yet common questions and issues emerge requiring a united stance as a unique service with three equal components. Regular meetings are held to discuss such points as well as the exploration of how they may improve their common work in the field. One such ongoing collaborative project focuses more fully on exercising the religious rights and free-doms of military personnel. Visible signs of religious inclusivity among the three traditions are further buttressed for both military and civilian sectors by mutual visits during religious holidays and celebrations significant to a par-ticular group, something that does not escape detection by a populace still dealing with its past inflictions. These three Religious Directors are very much cognizant of the uniqueness of their role both within and without of the military. Of particular note is their interface with civilian society. Guided by the spiritual principle "to love one another," together they exemplify before local civilian communities how best to resolve disputes that may cross ethnic lines. As spiritual leaders representative of the predominant faith groups in Bosnia, they feel the burden of the past war and how, in the minds of many, the religious communities bear a degree of responsibility for enflaming the conflict. Their witness of love and solidarity for the *other* has become a means of disarming such sentiments, as their cooperation engenders trust and enhances reconciliation. Together they project a tangible image of peace and tolerance among the religious communities of the military and Bosnian soci-ety in general.

A PERMUTATION OF THE PARADIGM

In today's world, the religious directors of the BHDF represent not only a permutation of RLE paradigmatically but also an inspiring model of ministry for the religious leaders of other nations ravaged by the vagaries of war. These men of faith, and the religious leaders who covenanted with them, exemplify *transcendence*. Together, they have chosen to rise above the past—to put the repressive days of communism and a fractious war behind them in the desire to begin the *writing of a new narrative* of collegiality in ministry. Such *collaborative activity* exemplifies the *will to embrace* as the engendering of *trust* creates an ambience for *forgiveness* and the *healing of memory*. Reinforcing their profile with the Balkans was the response of Serbian scholars to their ministry.

In 2009, the Directors of the European Centre for Peace and Development (ECPD) in Belgrade, Serbia—a satellite of the University for Peace estab-lished by the United Nations—were undeniably astounded to learn of their collaboration within the BHDF. This author's proposal for a presentation at their "Fifth International Conference on National and Inter-Ethnic Reconcili-ation, Religious Tolerance and Human Security in the Balkans—Reconcilia-tion and Security" cited the religious directors of the BHDF as a cogent example for Bosnian society of renewed *interdependence* as a reconciling factor to sustained peace. The ECPD study[9] underway in preparation for the conference expressed palpable concern that ethno-religious tensions were resurfacing in certain regions of Bosnia. Upon learning of the BHDF Chaplaincy, UN representative to the ECPD Takehrio Togo and Executive Director, Negoslav Ostojic sent immediate invitations to all three religious directors to attend and present at the Croatian Conference. Imam Smajlovic brought greetings from all three Directorates in his address to the conferees, from North America, Western and Eastern Europe, inclusive of Russia. Poignant to this discussion is the significance this UN body attached to their collaboration, immediately recognizing its potential impact for Bosnian society still dealing with the effects of the war nearly fifteen years after its conclusion.

Where chaplains once modelled acceptance and tolerance of the *other* during a time of extreme conflict in Bosnian history, the religious directors of the BHDF now *mimetically model* the *will to embrace* for military and civilian society within Bosnia and the Balkans at large. These religious leaders of *tolerant voice, model* openness and acceptance of the *other*, a witness to all Bosnians regardless of faith or ethnicity of the path to reconciliation. The *open relational system* inclusive of Bosniak Muslim, Croatian Roman Catholic and Serbian Orthodox demonstrates a pluralism that relegates more exclusive practices to the margins. Demonstrative as well of the *embrace* of inter-religious acceptance is the *hermeneutic hospitality* that flourishes—the honoring of individual faith traditions for what each one brings to the collective understanding of God and truth. In such an *open relational system human identity needs* find greater fulfillment: renewed interdependence provides a greater sense of *connectedness; security* is far more certain due to such amiable relations; self worth is accentuated as each is *recognized* for the contribution they bring; *action* is experienced in a positive sense with no one being "acted upon" against their will; and the creation of a shared narrative gives *meaning* to all that they do in collaboration. These religious directors have moved from the *working trust* of the *fragile we*, known to *encounter* and coexistence, to the much deeper *personal trust* on the level of friendship that accompanies the cooperation of their *collaborative activity.* The common *superordinate* goal of building a multifaith chaplaincy has facilitated integration, as they strive together to ameliorate an organization that depends on their continued collaboration. More significant still is the *mimetic structure of blessing* these faith group leaders personify before Bosnian society. As an organization, the BHDF Chaplaincy is life oriented; past animosities that hampered religious groups were set aside for more congenial relations. Due to their generosity of spirit and penchant for creativity, options yet to be realized stretch out before these religious directors—a shared space that will continue to enlarge. Years prior, what began in the hearts of a few became a *bottom-up grassroots* initiative for the religious care of those in uniform. Over the course of time, this movement came to enjoy the *top down* support of government structures as the BHDF Chaplaincy began to take on form:

circular causality. Lastly, the journey of these religious directors demonstrates more than *instrumental reconciliation*, where the collaborative atmosphere of cooperation and *personal trust* move individuals toward reconciliation. These men of faith exemplify *socio-emotional reconciliation* where relation between individuals becomes such that past hardship may be *transcended* and the writing of *new narratives* of a shared journey may begin. It is in such collaboration that one sees oneself through the eyes of the *other*, providing *the healing of memory* an occasion to advance. Rather, the depth of their relation and integration of activities has created an atmosphere conducive to such reconciliation, a model for *others* who have yet to make that journey together.

NOTES

1. For a complete overview of the Dayton Peace Accords, see the Dept of State (U.S. government) website, http://www.state.gov/www/regions/eur/bosnia/bosagree.html, accessed 12 Aug 2012.

2. It was Reinhold Niebuhr that cited the fact that nations are held together largely by force and by emotion [Reinhold Nieburh, *The Nature and Destiny of Man*, vol. 1 (Louisville, KY; John Knox Press, 1996), 210 cited in *Balkan Idols: Religion and Nationalism in Yugoslav States*, Vjekoslav Perica, (New York, Oxford University Press, 2002), 95]. Perica builds on Neibuhr's notion by defining nationalism as a synthesis of nation building and human emotion that together join the individual with the collective whole (Perica, 2002, 95). President Tito, of the former Yugoslavia, endeavored to employ these two elements by introducing what can be described as *civil religion*, further amplified by Perica as, ". . . an alloy of myths, quasireligious symbols, cults, rituals, beliefs, and practice that secure the nation's legitimacy and convince the people that the system is good" (Perica, 2002, 95). In striving to develop a national consciousness, he attempted to create a Yugoslav national identity (Perica, 2002, 100). His communist doctrine emphasized ethnic diversity and distinctiveness in such a way that the people came to appreciate that unity meant freedom, pride and prosperity. They embraced the notion that to do otherwise was to return to strife, poverty and ultimate humiliation, reminiscent of the war years. The slogan of "brotherhood and unity" became Tito's communist party metatheme. While on the one hand the communists strove for unity among the ethno-religious groups as a means of control, they also concentrated on the subjugation of religious communities as a means of lessening their 'acknowledged' influence. In an effort to consolidate power they enacted a policy of an intentional undermining of religion as a Yugoslav *identity marker* in the hopes of rendering *civil religion* acceptable to all three groups. During the early post-war years faith groups and their leaders were under close surveillance and, at times, outright persecution [Paul Mojzes, "The Camouflaged Role of Religion in the War in B&H" in *Religion and the War in Bosnia*, Paul Mojzes, ed. (Atlanta, Georgia, Scholars Press, 1998), 80]. Related to the communist notion of *civil religion*, in *The Battle For God*, Karen Armstrong illumines how that during the 1970's the secular governments of both Egypt and Iran concurrently endeavored to institute *civil religion* while attempting to marginalize Islam and the influence of the traditional *Ulema*. During this "White Revolution," *modernity* was rigorously promoted to the masses where "literacy, build[ing] bridges and reservoirs, and vaccinat[ing] livestock' became nothing more than a 'transparent attempt to undermine the *ulema*" [Karen Armstrong, *The Battle For God* (Ballantine Publishing Group, New York, 2000), 219–58].

3. See Paul Mojzes, *Yugoslavian Inferno: Ethno religious Warfare in the Balkans* (New York: Continuum Publishing Company, 1995); Michael A. Sells, *The Bridge Betrayed: Religion and Genocide in Bosnia* (Berkley, Los Angeles, London: University of California Press, 1996); Paul Mojzes, *Religion and the War in Bosnia* (Atlanta, Georgia, Scholars Press, 1998);

R. Scot Appleby, "The Role of Religion in the Bosnian War" in *The Ambivalence of the Sacred: Religion, Violence, and Reconciliation* (Lanham, Maryland: Rowman and Littlefield Publishers, 2000), 64–71.

4. Ismail Smajlovic, Military Mufti, Bosnia and Herzegovina Defense Forces, "Believers in a Military Environment" in *National and Inter-Ethnic Reconciliation, Religious Tolerance and Human Security in the Balkans*, Proceedings of the Fifth ECPD International Conference, eds. Takehrio Togo and Negoslav P Ostojic (Belgrade, Serbia: European Center for Peace and Development, 2010), 76.

5. Smajlivoc, 2010, 76.

6. See http://www.bosnia.org.uk/bosrep/junaug97/moralcom.cfm, accessed 12 Aug 2012.

7. Security Forces.

8. United States European Command.

9. Todor Mirkovic, *Current Situation and the Ways Leading to Building Peace and Stability in the Balkans—An Assessment and Preliminary Study* (Belgrade, Serbia: ECPD, 2009).

Part III

Religious Leader Engagement in Application

Chapter Ten

Religious Leader Engagement in Implementation

Disclaimer: The opinions offered here are not those of the government of Canada or of the Canadian Forces. Policy has yet to be approved and doctrine has yet to be written regarding Religious Leader Engagement (RLE). The following musings are presented solely as a means of informing interested parties of advances in RLE thinking as an emerging domain and to promote discussion regarding its applicability to future operational environments.

The treatment of RLE presented in this book has attempted to put forward its benefits while touching on its limitations as well. Having conducted research in this domain well beyond the decade mark, this author is aware of the challenges that exist for this type of operational ministry for chaplains. A number of these questions have become more acute in recent years as a result of the move of the Canadian Forces (CF) Army and Chaplain Branch to see RLE—inclusive of Religious Area Analysis (RAA)—institutionalized as an operational capability for expeditionary, humanitarian and domestic operations. At the time of this writing, RLE had advanced through the Concept and Design phases of the capability development process under the auspices of the CF Army Land Warfare Centre (ALWC), formerly the Directorate of Land Concepts and Design (DLDC), best understood as an army *think tank* fostering a *futures* environment in which potential considerations of full spectrum operations of coming decades are explored and expanded—with a predominant focus on the Comprehensive Approach. RLE is seen to factor into this research due to the belief that religion, in one fashion or another, will present as an aspect of conflict well into the future, as does the potential for its peaceful applications.

Over the course of RLE development sobering questions with respect to its application have centered primarily on whether such activities would in any way jeopardize the protected (non-combatant) status of chaplains as articulated in the Geneva Conventions.[1] The first section of this chapter— *Caveats for Concern*—will deal specially with questions relating to these issues. The concern is if chaplains are engaging local religious leaders with the view to promoting a reconciling of differences are they in any way "influencing" them and, if so, could such engagement be interpreted as an Influence Activity[2] (IA)? If RLE was seen to fall within the domain of IA, encounters of this nature could be interpreted to be indirectly supporting hostilities. As such, this would place their protected status as chaplains at risk for they would be seen as contributing to the fight. Related to the IA question as well is the unease emanating from the Intelligence (INT) community surrounding RLE. "What does the chaplain do with sensitive information resulting from dialogue with local religious leaders? Who has access to this information? For what purposes might such information be used, e.g., Targeting Boards.[3] If the chaplain were to offer said information to Information Operations (IO), would RLE be tantamount to information gathering for intelligence purposes? Undeniably, these are taxing issues as chaplains consider functioning within this environment. In addition to the above, Instrumentalism finds its way into this discussion as well—the reductionist approach to RLE that perceives it simply as a tool to be used alongside of other techniques, undermining the integrity of *encounter*.

In addition to the above queries, the second section—*Areas for Advancement*—will offer a number of suggestions for consideration and future application. Identifying religious leaders of *tolerant voice* with whom to engage is critical to such processes, as is the potential contribution of select indigenous peacebuilders to the cultivation of local ownership and the sustaining of gains made. As an aspect of the Comprehensive Approach, the concept of embedding specialist chaplains and those of other faith traditions aside from Christian in PRT-like configurations will be probed due to its relevance for the future.

THE PROCESS

The Concepts Cell of ALWC is a seven-member team comprised of a defense analyst, a defense scientist, a chaplain and four additional military personnel, each with expertise in affiliated fields of research pertinent to conceptualizing future operational environments as far into the future as 2040. RLE development has benefited immensely from their knowledge of the full breadth of operations and insights as to how best to operationalize this unique capability, but more important has been their grasp of the capability development process within the Army. Culminating two years of in-depth research, RLE was presented to the CF Army Capabilities Development Board (ACDB),[4] the gatekeepers of equipment design and acquisition, in addition to new capabilities under consideration for development and implementation. In June 2011, RLE was endorsed by the ACDB as an operational capability under development, advancing it from the Concept Phase to that of Design—the second of a four-phase process, leaving the Build and Manage (Implementation) Phases to complete.[5]

Concomitant with the June 2011 presentation to the ACDB was an appreciable degree of discussion among the Board members as to the potential benefits and possible impediments to eventual RLE implementation as an operational capability. Most notable were the above-mentioned questions relating to Information Operations and Influence Activities. Of concern was the possible erosion of the chaplains' protected status under the Geneva Conventions. In endorsing the concept of RLE, the Board charged then DLCD with addressing these concerns and reporting back to the ACDB of their findings. A third year of research was devoted to this task. Eight senior chaplains (Maj/LCol) and three DLCD members (military and civilian) were selected to form a RLE Working Group (WG). Over a ten-month period the RLE WG convened three times to deliberate on the questions emanating from the ACDB. In addition to grappling with these concerns, these extended sessions served to prepare the ground for the culminating event of a Seminar War Game (SWG), an exercise whereby the principals invested in this discussion would come together with chaplains to deliberate—most notably, representatives from INT, IA and the Judge Advocate General (JAG).

In April 2012 a Seminar War Game (SWG) convened at the Canadian Army Staff College, Fort Frontenac, Kingston, Ontario with the task of further validating RLE as an operational capability. Representatives from related fields convened for four days of syndicate and plenary deliberation on two fictional scenarios featuring RLE in operations in the Horn of Africa region. The WG developed the scenarios with the express purpose of provoking discussion around possible RLE applications where religious communities factored into conflict situations. Among those in attendance were:

- Chaplain General of the Canadian Forces, BGen. Karl McLean
- Director of Chaplain Services, Col. Nigel Shaw
- Padre/Maj. S. K. Moore, Subject Matter Expert (SME)
- Senior Mentor, Col (ret.) Mike Hoyt, U.S. Army Chaplain Corps
- Dir/A DLCD, LCol. Ron Bell
- Concepts Team Leader, DLCD, LCol. Chris Rankin
- Conflict Studies, Saint Paul University — Dr. Vern Neufeld Redekop

- Judge Advocate General — Major Rory Fowler
- Military Intelligence — three senior members
- Influence Activities Task Force — three senior members
- Defence Analyst — Peter Gizewski
- Defence Research & Development Canada — four social psychologists
- Operational Researchers — two senior members
- DLCD — five senior analysts
- Chaplain Branch — an additional six senior chaplains

Much of what is to follow is a result of these discussions. Albeit, it must be stated that the findings presented here are not to be viewed as conclusive or binding. RLE is an evolving domain and, as such, further research is needed accompanied by continued dialogue among the principals in order to fully appreciate the nuances of this emerging operational capability. That said, one must not diminish the clarity brought and ground gained through the purposeful exercise of the RLE SWG. The reader must also keep in mind that references made to RLE throughout this chapter employ the full sense of the term, inclusive of RAA. The activities spanning RLE are *networking, partnering* and *peacebuilding* itself (see ch. 4). In this regard, the chaplain's role among religious communities within local indigenous populations may be viewed as one of *facilitation*—engagement that brings parties together, be they estranged religious leaders for dialogue / ritual events or linking identified community need with the appropriate mission partner(s) as a means of broadening participation in accomplishing mission objectives. Such co-operation is indicative of the contribution chaplains may make beyond their more traditional role of caring for the troops to that of collaborating within the Whole of Government environment of the Comprehensive Approach.

CAVEATS FOR CONCERN

International Humanitarian Law and the Protected Status of Chaplains

One of the more helpful contributions to clarifying the protected status of chaplains while conducting RLE came from JAG. Process dictated that the legal perspective come early in order to provide the scenarios prepared for syndicate discussion a frame of reference. The two terms, *religious personnel* and *ministry*, and their application in the context of conflict, were discussed at length. International Humanitarian Law (IHL) within the Geneva Conventions and Protocols was consulted: (1) for a definition of the term *religious personnel*, and (2) for the nuancing of the latitude of legitimate *ministry* of chaplains with religious communities of indigenous populations in Operations. In particular, that which would not jeopardize chaplains' protected status as non-combatants.[6] According to IHL, the term *religious personnel* refers to military or civilian persons *exclusively* engaged in the work of their *ministry* and attached to specific types of organizations.[7] In the instance of a military chaplain conducting RLE-type *ministry*, the organization would be the national forces chaplaincy of a signatory country to the Geneva Conventions. Notable here is the Convention's usage of the word *exclusively* in reference to the *ministry* of *religious personnel*. It must be understood, *where chaplains facilitate dialogue or collaborative activities between estranged religious leaders and their faith communities, the purpose is to seek consensus in the pursuance of peace, the resolution of conflict and reconciliation with their consent*—peacebuilding activities that may be viewed as exclusive and legitimate *ministry*. Commending peace and justice for all peoples is consistent with the *holy writ* of all major faith traditions. Chaplains bring this orientation with them to theaters of operation as an authentic aspect of their role as religious leaders—redemptive centering that is often overlooked. JAG posited that *exclusively* engaging in such *ministry* would not jeopardize the protected status of chaplains. It is the nuancing of this statement that becomes challenging, for if *ministry* of this nature is to maintain its legitimacy, how it is executed becomes paramount. It quickly becomes a question of not what RLE is "understood to be" but more importantly, what it is "intended to do" and what it "actually accomplishes." Employing RLE for purposes other than for what it is intended may undermine the protected status of chaplains and further alienate religious communities in the early stages of *trust development*. Safeguarding the integrity of RLE as *ministry* holds much promise for creating goodwill and improving relations between religious communities engulfed in the on-going conflict of their respective identity groups, or living with its residual effects—post-conflict environments.

Salutary to the understanding of RLE as *ministry* is the notion of *intent*, which alludes to the motivation behind such initiatives, the crux of the entire endeavor. The question that must be posed is, "What is its purpose?" Of necessity, the first order effect of RLE must preserve *benevolence* as its essential tenet—the incentive of seeking the *wellbeing*[8] of other persons. In so doing, the integrity of such *ministry* is assured. In order to guard against straying into activities that constitute contributing to or supporting hostilities, RLE must function within the bounds of *ministry* that proposes ameliorating the lives of *others*. This embraces *seeking consensus in the pursuance of peace and the resolution of conflict and reconciliation*. Initiatives of this nature are not designed to attack the opposing force's will to fight and, as such, would not be considered supporting the use of force. In this light, the chaplain's engagement in RLE does not put in jeopardy his/her protected status as a non-combatant. *RLE is best understood to be a unique chaplain capability conducted by credentialed religious personnel within boundaries of discrete religious interaction—a stand-alone line of operation along side other lines of operation.*

How RLE activities manifest may best be understood to be contextual. As a construct such *ministry* may be generalized from one context to another. Religious peacebuilding among indigenous populations may take the form of humanitarian aid in one situation, while another occasion may present to bring religious leaders together for dialogue or a ritual event. Still, where religious communities may be difficult to access for some, collaboration with other Whole of Government partners may serve as a means to advance initiatives more of a governance or developmental nature—*facilitation.* This is not to suggest that risks do not exist. Commanders and chaplains alike must be mindful that in the context of counterinsurgency operations non-state actors may not necessarily share the same commitment to the Conventions and Protocols, which are limited to "High Contracting Parties." Regardless of the protections afforded by both The Hague and Geneva Conventions, opposition forces may consider RLE as a hostile activity and respond in kinetic fashion. Consequently, chaplains themselves and indigenous religious leaders with whom they associate may become highly valued targets among opposition forces.

Influence Activities

In his Letter Report, "Ensuring Effective RLE: Some Initial Thoughts on its Place with the CF," Defense Analyst Peter Gizewski[9] notes that religious belief has become a key factor in contemporary conflict. Further to this observation, he suggests that the *ministry* of military chaplains among the religious communities of indigenous populations is of increasing value as a component of the Comprehensive Approach, "offering a key means of building the relationships of understanding, respect and trust essential to conflict mitigation and ultimately—resolution."[10] However, Gizewski also acknowledges that inherent in the challenge of moving RLE from concept to capability, one of the more significant hurdles may be that of perception. As a 'faith-based' capability, "rather than being regarded as a 'facilitator' of communication and dialogue, RLE may well raise suspicion that it is in reality simply another tool by which to propagandize, spy and deceive."[11] It is for this reason that the place RLE will eventually occupy within the conceptual / doctrinal landscape will be critical to "affecting not only the degree to which its true intent and purpose are accurately portrayed and perceived, but [also] the extent to which it can be effectively practiced."[12]

Gizewski's observations quite accurately reflect existing concerns surrounding RLE and its relationship with Influence Activities (IA) in particular and, by extension, the unsettling notion of information gathering for intelligence purposes. Information Operations[13] (IO) and most notably the domain of Influence Activities (IA) (one of IO's three core activity areas)[14] present the most obvious area of potential linkage to RLE. IA represents a continuum of capabilities on the psychological plane with the singular purpose of affecting the targets will, employed in gradations within operations to create desired effects with the express purpose of achieving military advantage.[15]

On the surface, similarities may appear to exist when comparing RLE with an Influence Activity (IA)—both are leader engagements, producing some degree of influence as an interactive, personal, and pragmatic method. RLE presents as a *unique capacity* (status) due to chaplains' ability to facilitate communication and dialogue between parties in environments in which religious communities are implicated. In this light, chaplains are seen to possess the potential of *influencing* indigenous religious leaders via their common ground as spiritual leaders of faith group communities—a facility that others lack. Similarly, RLE has as its goal to contribute to the easing of social tensions and resolving conflict by engaging those of *tolerant voice* (middle range actors) within religious communities. For some, such *ministry* may appear to be analogous with the act of *influencing.* Here, *intent* becomes the crucial indicator. That said, any inclusion of RLE as a capability within the IA domain remains problematic.

Nuanced above, what must be kept before the reader is the intended first order effect of each of these capabilities. As a first order effect, the *intent* of IA is in direct support of hostile activities simultaneous with and complementary to fires. This represents operational space that is incongruent with the purpose and *intent* of RLE and antithetical to the protected status of chaplains as non-combatants. The thin edge of the wedge emerges when considering the more "soft" IA capabilities such as Public Affairs (PA) or CIMIC activities (see endnote 15), which may be seen as somewhat complementary with RLE initiatives. In addition to IA and PA, Key Leader Engagement (KLE)[16] poses as a natural means of embedding chaplains for RLE *ministry.* By way of contrast, any association with Psychological Operations (PSYOPS) and Military Deception would taint RLE, thus undermining its effectiveness as a peacebuilding capability. The enticement to include RLE in a doctrinal category that incorporates capabilities that are clearly—and in some cases, directly—contrary to its purpose raises issues of concern. RLE is unique in content, expectations and the credentials of those engaged in its *ministry.* Its intended purpose is not to leverage relationships with religious leaders for military advantage. The aspiration of engagement is not simply to shape outcomes, but rather to appreciate the exceptional nature of religion as a catalyst to bridging divides—sometimes within faith communities, at other times across ethno-religious boundaries—with the first order effect of the *wellbeing* of the *other.* Future operational environments will undoubtedly benefit from such *ministry.* How one approaches RLE activities, and the motivation behind them, becomes the decisive factor. Where employed, commanders and Whole of Government personnel alike will need to appreciate its nuances. In so doing, access to religious communities, normally suspicious of more secular approaches, becomes a possibility for advancing additional altruistic activity.

Information Gathering for Intelligence Purposes

As an emerging capability, RLE has captured the attention of the Intelligence (INT) community and others. Commanders rely heavily on the information that comes to them via the various and sundry channels of Information Operations (IO) as an indispensable element of the decision-making process. The prospects of gleaning sensitive information from chaplains pertaining to—what constitutes at times as impenetrable—religious communities has been the theme of more than a few conversations among Intelligence officers and chaplains alike. This author has always maintained in bringing RLE forward, it could neither be developed nor employed in a vacuum. Dialogue with both the INT community and the IA Task Force has always been viewed as a necessary prerequisite to identifying space for RLE both in Operations and in the future writing of military doctrine. For this reason, the deliberations of the earlier-mentioned Seminar War Game (SWG) will be consulted, which hosted three seasoned Intelligence officers—two Canadian and one British. This event represents one of the few formal fora to date in any Western nation where INT officers came together with chaplains, IA and JAG personnel to examine the oft-contentious issue of information gathering for intelligence purposes and the chaplains role in *ministering* among the religious communities of indigenous populations.

Driving this interest is the recent emphasis on chaplain training in Religious Area Analysis (RAA), courseware now being integrated into curriculum at the U.S. Army Chaplain School and Center in Fort Jackson, South Carolina, and at the CF Chaplain School and Center at Canadian Forces Base (CFB) Borden, Ontario. Emphasized is the equipping of chaplains to accumulate and categorize information relating to the religious practices and traditions of indigenous populations within an Area of Operations (AO). Chaplains are credentialed religious leaders complete with advanced theological training, positioning them well to interpret the nuances of local religious belief that often escape detection. This process of analysis is on-going—a combination of pre-deployment open-source research and continued reflection during the common practice of *networking* among local religious leaders and their communities once in theater. Aside from knowledge about beliefs, religious festivals and sacred spaces, etc., chaplains are often able to discern how religious communities at the grassroots react to given mission initiatives, plans of action, and troop movements. Advising commanders of an inherent risk of a proposed course of action due to the religious sensibilities of a local community is viewed as a critical aspect of the role of chaplains.

Some within the INT community have likened RAA to the Intelligence Preparation of the Battlefield (IPB). There is a distinct difference between the two. The principal aim of the IPB process is to maximize information and translate it to military objectives. IPB directly contributes to hostilities as a targeting and information management platform designed to force a military response against a series of prescribed military outcomes. On the other hand, RAA is understood to be an academic process, analyzing the impact of religion on local culture, its people, and any detectable nuances of the practice of religion that may be helpful to know. Such information becomes part of the knowledge base. It serves no offensive purpose and is not linked to prescribed military objectives. As such, RAA may inform on the commander's spectrum of relative interest but its *intent* and purpose does not include targeting persons, or influencing any processes that would support such hostile activity.[17]

Returning to the SWG, syndicate discussions were aided by the use of scenarios created specifically for these discussions. The added presence of IA and Directorate of Land Concepts and Designs (DLCD) personnel, JAG, operational researchers, and social psychologists in each of the three syndicates aided deliberations markedly. Each day ended with plenary sessions at which time syndicates reported back on their findings followed by more open group deliberations. Intimated earlier, the opening session presented by JAG did much to provide the parameters for the subsequent syndicate work: further clarity on the protected status of chaplains and direct participation in hostilities assisted in developing the conclusions and framing the discussions.

> It was agreed by all that tasking the chaplain to provide a specific set of information requirements for programmed refinement into a larger intelligence collection platform was a violation of 'direct participation' in hostilities and jeopardized the chaplain non-combatant status. General inquiries dealing with local perceptions, attitudes, or issues were an expected part of any engagement but these would not be part of an intelligence debriefing or hostile act planning action.[18]

With the boundaries of the chaplain's involvement in IO more clearly defined, the exchange moved to the level of professional concern for the integrity and trustworthiness of chaplains as individuals and the Chaplaincy as an institution. All concurred that attempting to use chaplains as an intelligence source should be resisted. The INT personnel present also expressed concerns for the personal security of chaplains, possible hostile retaliation from "spoilers" and the issue of transparency—all viable considerations. Transparency drew the most attention in syndicate due to the sensitive nature of information that may be made known to the chaplain. An ideal solution to the handling of sensitive information by chaplains does not exist, should it fall into their hands. One must also take into consideration that in scenario deliberations, one is dealing in the hypothetical that pushes the envelope in terms of such engagement. Albeit, the potential for a chaplain to be caught in an ethical bind of this nature is real—maintaining the trust of a religious leader versus divulging information that may be vital to the mission or, more precarious still, the lives of others. With an increased intentionality associated with RAA, chaplains will make contact with religious leaders far more frequently. These encounters will no longer be left to the realm of the *ad hoc.* One must realize that the initial work of RLE is nested in the assessments provided by RAA. With a higher incidence of engagement, the greater the likelihood of sensitive information surfacing. It becomes a question of determining the most satisfactory approach among lesser desirables. In the event that a chaplain came to possess sensitive information that he/she deemed vital, the consensus was the most effective means of protecting the source (chaplain) and the integrity of the process (religious context and actors) was to exercise the chaplain's specialist officer status and report to the commander directly. Due to his/her grasp of the total mission, it was determined that the commander is best suited to decide in what manner to dispense with the information.

In this author's years of research of RLE-related *ministries* among a number of NATO and non-NATO military chaplaincies, an incident of this nature has not presented. This is not to suggest that it could not. Given the predilection toward training chaplains in RAA and RLE, it is in everyone's best interest to contemplate such potentialities. Of course, such an occurrence would more than likely carry serious ramifications for the continuance of such *ministry* among the implicated religious community. It would depend on how the chaplain elected to handle the transmission of such information. If the engendered trust between the religious leader and the chaplain was of sufficient strength, a meeting between the religious leader and the commander might be arranged. This would leave their relationship intact; yet, assure that the information was shared. Steps could be taken to protect the person's identity. Still, if information were of a serious enough nature that Command had to be informed, the relationship, and any promise it may have held, would have to be forfeited. At the end of the day, the safety of lives takes precedence—theirs and ours. In such circumstances, for U.S. Army chaplains, the spirit of Policy #3 relating to Religious Leader Liaison offers some guidance: "a member [of a Unit Ministry Team (UMT)] may report a personally-observed activity as long as he or she was not directed to do so in any prior intelligence-related tasking or as part of a HUMIT collection plan."[19]

Without question, RLE *ministry* and its "association" with Influence Activities and Information Operations are among the more perplexing questions surrounding such activity. There remains much work to be done in demarcating the lines of operation between RLE *ministry* and the domains of IA and IO. Where RLE should be situated in military doctrine continues to be debated. It seemed reasonable to the SWG participants to explore the Human Dimension (HD) as one possible doctrinal home for RLE. As a domain within doctrine, the HD focuses on such things as pursuing relationships, building trust and conflict resolution—capabilities that parallel RLE aspirations. The absence of an emphasis on hostile activities complements such *ministry*. However, a discussion of this nature does not by any means exhaust the challenges relating to RLE as an operational capability. The following discussion on *instrumentalism* stands among others as an area for education and growth, as RLE moves toward implementation.

Instrumentalism

Rabbi Marc Gopin defines *instrumentalism* as the undermining of genuine *relation*. Engagement is simply not an instrument that produces an outcome. In his research among Mennonite peacebuilders, he learned, ". . . it is the reduction of the human moment of relation to its instrumentality that is problematic."[20] Where chaplains have been the most effective in establishing working relationships with local/regional and, occasionally, national religious leaders, engendered *trust* and its associated *benevolence* in action have factored significantly into the equation. The leveraging of instrumentalism erodes such confidence. Chaplains will continue to voice their apprehension of such endeavors being co-opted by others. As this domain of operational ministry emerges, care must be taken to preserve the integrity of such engagement.

Gavin Buchan was introduced to the reader in the first Afghan Case Study, a Canadian Political Advisor (PolAd) who served with the Dept of Foreign Affairs and International Trade (DFAIT) at the Canadian Provincial Reconstruction Team[21] (PRT) in 2006. Returning to his panel presentation at the Generative Dialogue[22] in Ottawa in 2010, he astutely demonstrates the inherent nuances of this kind of ministry for chaplains and the binds that can occur. Although he did not use the term *instrumentalism* in his presentation, nonetheless, he spoke of its existence in other areas of operations and the need for chaplains to be wary of its presence.

> Another point is that we have to respect the independence of the people we engage. It's very tempting for a military commander to look at this and say, "Okay, right, we have a lever for influence, how can we get them to do what we want?" and that's a very dangerous route to go down. It's not that it's not done.

. . . We have to be wary, especially with an indigenous culture, in attempts at
having direct influence because we can destroy the credibility of the people
you're trying to reinforce, if you push too hard.[23]

Here Buchan cogently identifies a concern that is frequently voiced in chaplaincy circles. There are limitations to what chaplains can and cannot provide
as they engage local religious leaders and their faith group communities. This
operational space for chaplains must be clearly defined so as not to impose
undue expectations on lines of communication that depend upon mutual
trust, transparency and respect. Anything less will surly scuttle the long-term
benefit of contributing to eventual *inter*communal integration. Commanders
must view RLE through the lens of its benefits and resist seeing it simply as
another tool to be used, which tends toward reductionism. Engagement of
this nature is far more than a technique. The building of relation and its
concomitant seeding of reconciliation rests on the *benevolence* of the actor
and the *trust* engendered. Reducing such encounter, to leverage for advantage, rings hollow, undermines the integrity of engagement, and more dis-
concertingly, is soon perceived as such by indigenous religious leaders, who
are genuinely interested in transcending the conflict that has consumed their
communities. In the end, *instrumentalism* represents missed opportunities,
for collaboration built on *trust* is that which sustains such endeavors.

AREAS FOR ADVANCEMENT

Identifying the Tolerant Religious Voice

Information referencing the identity of local religious leaders more inclined
to engage in constructive dialogue may be available once the chaplain has
deployed into theatre. Resources exist within the military that can be drawn
upon as well as trusted interpreters who frequently become indispensable
aids in navigating local communities. That said, additional sources may be
accessible that are seldom employed in operations, which could prove indispensable to engaging local religious communities in the future. Such international religious organizations as *Religions for Peace* and the *World Council
of Churches* possess global capabilities and, as such, may be of assistance.

The largest international coalition of representatives from the world's
great religions dedicated to promoting peace is the faith-based NGO *Religions for Peace*. A tour of their website lists regional, sub-regional and national councils active globally and in some of the most troubled areas of the
world, creating multi-religious partnerships to confront civilization's most
dire issues: stopping war, ending poverty, and protecting the earth. Among
their varied initiatives globally are conflict transformation efforts. The following quote from their website provides an indication of how they are

advancing conflict transformation, with whom, and where their energies are being focused.

> Inter-religious councils and groups formed and supported by Religions for Peace have played key roles transforming conflict and rebuilding peaceful societies in the Balkans, West Africa and the Middle East. In the past decade, Religions for Peace has engaged its leadership of prominent international religious figures to bring together diverse Bosnian religious leaders in the aftermath of civil war and to support multi-religious peacebuilding efforts in West Africa. Currently, Religions for Peace is also facilitating emerging efforts for peacebuilding collaboration among religious leaders in Sri Lanka, Iraq, Sudan, and the Korean Peninsula.
>
> To date much of Religions for Peace's conflict transformation and peacebuilding programming has centered on sub-Saharan Africa, where its network of inter-religious councils and groups is the most developed. In West Africa and the Great Lakes region of Africa Religions for Peace has facilitated multi-religious collaborations working to prevent conflicts from developing, to mediate peace negotiations among warring parties, and to rebuild peaceful societies in the aftermath of violence. [24]

This author's experience with *Religions for Peace* offers encouragement in terms of potential collaboration. While researching the model of ministry (2009) with the religious directors of the Bosnia-Herzegovina Defense Forces (BHDF) Chaplaincy—an example to other nations endeavoring to put conflict behind them—Father Sladjan Vlajic (Orthodox Religious Director) made arrangements to meet certain leaders of the Inter-Religious Council in Bosnia-Herzegovina,[25] an NGO established by *Religions for Peace* following the war. Comprised of Bosniak [Muslim], Croat Roman Catholic, Serbian Orthodox and Jewish religious leaders and scholars, their commitment to peace and religious freedom has resulted in their shepherding a law on religious freedom[26] through Parliament, now enshrined within the Constitution of Bosnia-Herzegovina—given their recent history, a monumental accomplishment. Olivera Jovanovic is an Orthodox theologian and senior advisor on the council; a woman clearly committed to the cause of peace among the ethno religious groups of Bosnia-Herzegovina. Her many years of experience with inter-confessional dialogue convinced her that impacting concrete steps are the most practical approach to lasting and improved relations in post-conflict Bosnia-Herzegovina. In her mind, reconciliation remained an admirable goal but was a process requiring many years of patient labor measured in concrete and tangible efforts that promote mutuality.[27] Jovanovic was well aware of the challenges that remained in integrating the three ethnoreligious communities. The intensity of her desire and the strength of her commitment to further amenable relations conveyed an openness to external actors who may have something to bring.

As an organization, *Religions for Peace* works closely with religious leaders and their communities in many of the more conflicted areas of the world, some of which may involve the deployment of international forces due to the intractability of hostilities. In such cases chaplains would deploy to these areas as well. It would seem reasonable that during the pre-deployment phase of a given operation, inquiries into the activities of *Religions for Peace* in the AO in question could be made. It may be they are already active in the area or it could be they have yet to establish dialogue among the religious communities engulfed in the conflict. Either way, assistance in contacting religious leaders within the geographical boundaries of the Operation would be of immeasurable help to a chaplain interested in offering support to existing endeavors or initiating dialogue among religious communities where it is non-existent. Technology will only continue to advance, making ease of contact with key individuals, even in remote areas of the globe, more accessible. Dialogue may begin prior to deploying. Of course, venturing into this domain is never initiated without thorough investigation and approval of Command. This will necessitate a well-prepared briefing denoting a clear rationale as to the benefits of such civic engagement to the mission, complete with background information of implicated religious leaders, resources needed and proposed progress reports.

Granted, reticence may exist on the part of locals to align themselves with the military regardless of origin. Disdain among the people for any military may be a residual effect from having suffered violence at the hands of local forces or para-military groups during the height of conflict. *Trust* engendered by the authentic engagement of a chaplain among religious leaders desirous of change has a proven track record. Initiated dialogue is inclusive of hearing the needs raised in conversation and addressing them. Such genuine engagement may bridge the distance that suspicions and misgivings often create. Where conflict is ongoing, progressive indigenous leaders often live in precarious circumstances. At times the mere appearance of aligning with international forces can quickly escalate into a confrontation with insurgents. Care must be taken not to provoke a threatening situation due to well-intentioned, yet hastily planned encounters. Assistance may be available from other operators as to the safest way to proceed, which may be to make the initial overtures on behalf of chaplains, deciding how best to facilitate a meeting and where. Post-conflict environments may not be as openly hostile. However, tension may be such that intergroup relations remain delicate. Discretion is called for in planning so as not to exacerbate any residual tension.

The World Council of Churches (WCC) is a Christian ecumenical organization, spanning the globe and comprised of 349 different Christian denominations. Their core tenets are visible unity, common witness and Christian service. WWC initiatives are many in number, impacting a broad section of societal challenges: Justice and accountability (nuclear arms control), racism, people with disabilities, human rights, HIV/AIDS in Africa, poverty, and ecology are but a few examples. As an ecumenical Christian organization the WWC is interested in *inter*-religious dialogue, especially in countries where Christian churches are in situations of conflict.

> [The *World Council of Churches*] accompanies churches faced with religious intolerance, discrimination and conflict, and advocates for inter-religious cooperation, human dignity, sustainable values and just relationships. It emphasizes those aspects in all religions that promote harmony among communities, which help people to live their individual faith with integrity while living together in mutual respect and mutual acceptance of each other's faiths.[28]

Again, the World Council of Churches may be an organization predisposed to assisting chaplains interested in promoting dialogue and reconciliation in conflict zones. As the largest ecumenical Christian organization globally, the WWC would be cognizant of religious leaders in countries predominantly Christian. That said, the Roman Catholic Church is not a member of the WWC. In cases where religious demographics cite Roman Catholicism as the principal Christian expression—Burundi being a likely example—the *Community of Sant'Egidio* would be strategically placed to be of assistance. Noted earlier, this is a lay organization within the Roman Catholic Church with considerable peacebuilding experience in conflict areas around the world. Roman Catholic chaplains are well positioned to investigate such possibilities. Of singular importance to this discussion, there are organizations that may be of assistance to deploying chaplains in identifying local religious leaders interested in dialogue across ethno-religious lines where conflict has created tense relations.

Where future RLE *ministry* implicates religious leaders affiliated with such organizations, a reasonable approach would be for national chaplaincy representatives to establish dialogue with the leadership of their respective organizations. It cannot be assumed that reservations would not exist with respect to any alliances with chaplains as members of military forces. A proactive strategy of engagement and exchange of information regarding the operational *ministry* of chaplains would aid in preparing an NGO for a request for collaboration in a given AO. This would be one approach, among others, where a chaplain could facilitate religious peacebuilding in a WoG setting by communicating with faith-based NGOs active in the AO.

THE COLLABORATIVE ROLE OF CHAPLAINS WITHIN THE WHOLE OF GOVERNMENT AS AN ASPECT OF THE COMPREHENSIVE APPROACH

Few people are as knowledgeable about the Comprehensive Approach as LCol. (ret.) Mike Rostek, PhD, the main thrust of his research for a number of years. In his recent publication, *Security Operations in the Twenty-First Century: The Canadian Perspective on the Comprehensive Approach* (McGill and Queen's University Press, 2011), he and Peter Gizewski (co-editor) bring together a confluence of contributors spanning the full spectrum of Whole of Government entities: military, government departments and agencies and the NGO community. RLE is one of the featured chapters. Dr. Rostek's role in the development of RLE has been as supervisor of the conceptual process relating to capability development, one of consistent academic rigor and scrutiny. In the following excerpt from an unpublished article, he articulates how RLE—with its interoperable facility in the multi-disciplinary environment of operations—functions as a *new norm* within the Whole of Government (Interagency) domain of the Comprehensive Approach.

First articulated as "3D" or "whole-of-government" (WoG), the Comprehensive Approach (CA) seeks to move beyond the interagency environment where ". . . diverse situationally-aware actors resolve complex issues through the purposeful coordination and de-confliction of their information, actions and effects."[1] Interest in the CA and the capacity to practice it reflects a growing belief in the importance of achieving greater interoperability, collaboration or awareness among key players in the operational arena as well as in the development of the requisite networking capabilities and skills essential to achieving one's objectives.[2] Properly conceived and implemented, this would offer an effective, efficient means of applying diverse and often disparate assets to a problem and could potentially lead to the creation of synergies in capability that would not otherwise exist.

Even more fundamentally, support for adoption of a comprehensive approach stems from a growing consensus that outward-focused, integrated and multidisciplinary approaches to security threats and challenges must become the new norm given the complex problems and challenges posed by a multidimensional security environment. As noted in the [earlier Case Studies], RLE has an instrumental role to play as part a comprehensive approach; indeed, military chaplains have already established a track record in working constructively with religious leaders in theatres of violent conflict thereby contributing to the peace process. However, the question remains, how do you operationalize RLE as a new norm as part of a comprehensive approach.

The successful creation of new norms begins with the emergence of norm entrepreneurs and the art of persuasion. Entrepreneurs are critical to the emergence of new norms as they call attention to, or even create, issues focused on appropriate behaviour within their community.[3] Motivated by altruism, empathy or ideational commitment, their advocacy must be underpinned by strong communication skills if they are to convince other actors to adopt the new norm. The work of Canadian Forces Chaplain Imam Suleyman Demiray and diplomat Gavin Buchan provide evidence of entrepreneurial roles while in Afghanistan [ch. 5, Case Study 2]. From an operational perspective, a political advisor collaborating with a chaplain in engaging spiritual leaders as a means of accessing the religious sector of society—frequently leery of Western overtures—is a new development. . . . The use of military Chaplains in RLE through WoG and subsequently CA attaches meaning to its action and builds on structures and processes already in place. Indeed, the Comprehensive Approach and one of its component parts—RLE—represent a collective expectation about how to deal with complex security situations, in essence a new norm.

The successful creation of new norms begins with the emergence of norm entrepreneurs and the art of persuasion. Entrepreneurs are critical to the emergence of new norms as they call attention to, or even create, issues focused on appropriate behaviour within their community.[3] Motivated by altruism, empathy or ideational commitment, their advocacy must be underpinned by strong communication skills if they are to convince other actors to adopt the new norm. The work of Canadian Forces Chaplain Imam Suleyman Demiray and diplomat Gavin Buchan provide evidence of entrepreneurial roles while in Afghanistan [ch. 5, Case Study 2]. From an operational perspective, a political advisor collaborating with a chaplain in engaging spiritual leaders as a means of accessing the religious sector of society—frequently leery of Western overtures—is a new development. . . . The use of military Chaplains in RLE through WoG and subsequently CA attaches meaning to its action and builds on structures and processes already in place. Indeed, the Comprehensive Approach and one of its component parts—RLE—represent a collective expectation about how to deal with complex security situations, in essence a new norm.

1. Chief of Force Development, "The Comprehensive Approach Concept" (Ottawa: National Defence, 2010), 1.

2. Interoperability will occur in three broad domains: information interoperability (the way we share information including technological and procedural aspects); cognitive interoperability (the way we perceive and think reflected in doctrine and decision processes); and behavioural interoperability (the way we carry out the selected course of action). See Canadian Forces Experimentation Center Glossary of Terms Website at: http://www.ops.forces.gc.ca/cfec/viewHTML_e.asp?islandid=452.

3. Martha Finnemore and Kathryn Sikkink, "International Norm Dynamics and Political Change" in *International Organization*, Vol. 52, No.4, International Organization at Fifty: Exploration and Contestation in the Study of World Politics, 1998, 897 (887–917).

In addition to Rostek's perception of the potential role of chaplains within PRT-like formulations, further benefit to Whole of Government would be the interface chaplains would bring with local indigenous peace endeavors. The *external operational ministry* of chaplains will not always require creating new initiatives. Local peacebuilding structures already in place may simply require assistance. Here, again, the rapport and trust that a chaplain engenders as a religious leader within indigenous cultures cannot be understated. Their *networking* in an Area of Operations may reveal the presence of Community Peace Councils[29] (CPCs). These are community forums mainly comprised of local citizens drawn from the ethnic mix representative of the community at large. Courageous and caring individuals, theirs' is a commitment to dialogue and harmonious living often in the midst of situations where co-opted religious belief, in an already tension-charged environment, exacerbates conflict and violence. CPCs exemplify dialogical peacebuilding, which cultivates an environment of *working trust* and co-operation across ethnic boundaries—community-based conflict transformation (Endnote #29 cites several examples from among the numerous CPCs active globally: India, Kenya, Nepal and Afghanistan). Where CPCs exist, chaplains may be of assistance by listening to the presenting needs of the leadership. Resources at the chaplain's disposal are significant in comparison to those of local communities. It is not inconceivable that trainers could hold community-wide workshops for the leadership where conflict resolution skills, sensitive to community custom and tradition, could be taught. Implicating indigenous trainers would be advantageous to such processes.

Where communities are in conflict and/or living with its residual alienation, chaplains trained in peacebuilding may discover interest across ethnic lines for dialogue. As a collaborative activity, establishing a Community Peace Council may prove to be an effective means of developing a forum where common interests can be discussed, solutions proposed and conflicts resolved. Over the long-term, a new generation of leaders may be nurtured, committed to preventing/transforming conflict and empowered to act. Where such initiatives hold promise, Whole of Government personnel could do much to further such development:

1. Where local / regional religious leaders from the affected identity groups of a conflict are desirous of dialogue, provide trained facilitators to aid with the process, indigenous to the culture where possible;
2. Integrate such initiatives into national reconciliation endeavors, benefiting from their example in other regions;
3. Aid chaplains in identifying collaborative development projects that incorporate *superordinate* goals designed to enhance greater integration between ethno-religious communities;
4. Provide assistance to bona fide faith-based organizations, identified by chaplains as having legitimate developmental goals / projects, including such groups in overall strategic planning.

For the chaplain it is often more about being cognizant of the resources available and bringing them to bear on the presenting need—*facilitation*.

THE POTENTIAL ROLE OF INDIGENOUS RELIGIOUS PEACEBUILDERS WITHIN THE WHOLE OF GOVERNMENT ENVIRONMENT

The intent here is not to replicate what has already been presented in chapter 3 with respect to religious peacebuilding. The case was sufficiently made for the legitimacy and prevalence of such initiatives from a number of faith traditions globally. Moreover, several distinguished secular organizations were identified as embracing religious approaches to conflict resolution in recognition of the need to expand the range of actors to be more representative of the realities of contemporary conflict. The Washington-based Center for Strategic and International Studies (CSIS) received a cursory mention as one of these organizations. Their contribution to this discussion will be revisited here.

"In July 2007, CSIS released a Report entitled *Mixed Blessings: US Government Engagement with Religion in Conflict-Prone Settings.* At the heart of this document is the dual-pronged acknowledgement that: (1) successful resolution to conflict abroad will necessitate the engaging of the religious *other* and, (2) at present, government departments and agencies are inadequately prepared to do such. Continuing further, the authors explicate,

> In a world heavily influenced by religion, U.S. government intelligence, military, diplomatic, and development tools must be properly prepared to engage these religious elements. . . . Religious leaders, organizations, institutions and communities can mobilize religion to sanction violence, draw on religion to resolve conflicts, or invoke religion to provide humanitarian and development aid. To engage successfully, government analyses, policy, training, and pro-

gramming must fully incorporate an understanding of the varied roles for religion in conflict-prone settings.

The Recommendations issuing from the Report called for a sweeping increase to the knowledge base of the religious dynamics of today's world. Among these were: additional government expertise in all departments with respect to religion; expanding outside partnerships with academics in related fields; and linking this community of experts as a force multiplier. Poignant to the discussion to follow, and under the heading "Sensitize Programming to Religious Realities," CSIS forcefully advocates the engaging of a broader range of leaders in conflict-prone parts of the world, specifically identifying religious leaders and faith-based groups as potential partners integral to resolving contemporary conflict where the manipulative processes of religious extremists have become a component of the conflict. The suggestion is that working with religious peacebuilders indigenous to the Area of Operations (AO) would hold dividends for inter- and intra-faith dialogue."[30]

In 2009 the United States Agency for International Development (USAID) published, *Religion, Conflict & Peacebuilding: An Introductory Program Guide*, a Toolkit specifically designed "to help lower the discomfort of USAID staff in making the analytical and programmatic connections between conflict, religion and peacebuilding."[31] In this document, an internal department within USAID, the Office of Conflict Management and Mitigation, attests to the increased role of religion as a driver of conflict and acknowledges its capacity as a resource for mitigating its impact. Again, crucial here is the realization that USAID is a secular organization within government. The study cites religion as a common source of core identity in cultures around the world that may exist interdependent with ethnicity, yet has the ability to transcend ethnic differences. A number of attributes pertaining to religious actors (leaders) are listed: (1) religious leaders and institutions are often considered trustworthy and credible before the eyes of the people; (2) these same leaders often share a respected set of values across ethnic divides, e.g., forgiveness, reconciliation and sacred texts that may inspire change; (3) religious leaders often are able to bring abut such change among the people in ways that cannot be replicated by secular approaches; (4) they possess a deep understanding of the local context, offering a greater occasion for successful programming at the local level; and (5) religious leaders have access to levels of power—community, regional, and at times, international—providing opportunity to address conflicts on multiple levels.[32] Both CSIS and USAID are implicated in initiatives globally. A few moments browsing their websites soon gives one an indication of the breadth of their work. Their endorsement of training for government and agency personnel specific to greater religious understanding and garnering the support of local religious leaders in conflict mitigation and development projects is a significant departure from past practices. Given the complexities associated with the resurgence of religiously inspired conflict in today's context, recognition of these realities and openness to new approaches from within secular and government organizations are a welcome development.

This author has consistently advocated for the involvement of religious actors within PRT-like configurations in operational environments. The case for chaplains to fulfill this role has been forcefully made here. In the future, those with specialist training could work alongside their Whole of Government partners, aiding them in advancing principles of governance, development projects and, where identified, furthering reconciliation within the religious sector of the indigenous populace—admittedly, where more conservative strains of religion prevail, often a closed community to secular approaches. Extending the logic further—given the increasing recognition within government of the potential place of religion in resolving conflict—it is not inconceivable to imagine a day when religious peacebuilders indigenous to the local population, may become of strategic import to reconstruction and stabilization processes.

Along these lines, the promise of implicating religious actors of the same faith tradition as the indigenous population was made abundantly clear to this author while conducting doctoral research in Kandahar, Afghanistan. Featured in an earlier case study, Imam Capt. Suleyman Demiray was the chaplain attached to the Canadian PRT in Kandahar during the summer of 2006. Although not Afghan, being Turkish in origin, rapport was established immediately with the Islamic leadership and local populace. It was during a televised CIMIC[33] event at the Kandahar PRT that the magnitude of the impact of the Imam's presence was truly appreciated. Twelve Toyota trucks (extended-cab) were presented to the Afghan National Police as an aspect of the broader program of capacity building.

> Approaching the podium in CF arid pattern (desert) uniform, wearing the traditional Islamic *takke* (headdress), he began his prayers with an Arabic recitation, concluding with prayer both in Arabic and English. The effect was immediate and electrifying for the Muslim audience as astonishment gave birth to sheer delight. Individuals among this predominantly Sunni Pashtun assembly began tugging on their own clothing, excitedly exclaiming in hushed tones to their neighbours that the Imam praying to Allah before them was in a CF uniform. With eyes flashing back and forth between Capt Demiray and their friends, they continually gestured to each other their obvious enchantment. Bringing his prayer to a close, Imam Demiray used the traditional Islamic hands gesture to the face (ears, eyes and mouth) with the *Amen*. Like a startled school of shimmering fish uniformly turning in clear water, a multitude of hands flashed out of nowhere instinctively accompanying the Imam in the Islamic Amen, vanishing as quickly as they had appeared. At the conclusion of the ceremony, Afghan dignitaries and people alike queued to hug and shake hands with this Imam in Canadian uniform. The majority of the Pashtun

presents poke little Arabic and no English. Imam Demiray spoke not Pashtun, only English, Arabic, Turkish, his native tongue. It was truly of no consequence. The spontaneous *connectedness* was evident for all to see. . . . Although not Afghan, nonetheless he was *kin* . . . belonging to the *umma*, the international community of believers in which national boundaries are of no consequence.[34]

This operational anecdote is offered as a lens through which to view the astounding effectiveness among the people of one who is accepted as one of their own. It would stand to reason that a religious peacebuilder indigenous to the population would experience a similar, if not greater, reception among those interested in putting conflict behind them. Where language, religion and culture are held in common, fewer barriers exist to be overcome in gaining confidence and establishing trust. In bringing RLE forward, the intention has never been to make conflict resolution experts out of chaplains. Aiding in resolving conflict, as a *facilitator*, is a more accurate depiction of the role of chaplains—staying in their own lane. Where RLE *ministry* brings religious leaders from estranged identity-groups together, the long view maintains placing such initiatives in the hands of those with expertise in peacebuilding—indigenous to the local population if at all possible. Ideally, such individuals would be identified prior to deployment, a resource for consultation in a *reach back* capacity, brought into theatre if warranted. In such instances, the chaplain would remain engaged in a *facilitative* role as the *trusted friend* who initiated the process. Beneficial to the strategy of involving indigenous peacebuilders is the key feature of placing the initiative in the hands of local leadership. Sustaining any reconciling effort requires local ownership. Still in other cases, there may be pre-existing peace initiatives already in place and active. Careful not to undermine such endeavors due to "foreign involvement," support may be offered in whatever form is deemed appropriate to the situation.

A word must also be stated for collaborating with a faith-based NGO operating in the AO. CH Hoyt's involvement with Canon Andrew White (ch. 7, Case Study 4) is demonstrative of the efficacy of linking with a religious peacebuilder well connected with the principal religious leaders across ethnic lines. The chaplain is well suited to make overtures to such organizations: establishing their credibility; evaluating their programs; and determining if any form of partnership is in the best interests of the mission.

CHRISTIAN CHAPLAINS AND THE RUDIMENTS OF ISLAMIC PEACEBUILDING

Operations extending to or beyond the decade mark in Iraq and Afghanistan hold lessons for future missions. In the years to come, the likelihood of

Western governments to call upon their military leaders to mount operations somewhere in the world is hardly remote. One can also surmise, with a certain degree of certainty, that wherever such missions may take troops, chances are the religious factor, as an aspect of conflict, will play a role. Recent experience would indicate that groups purporting extreme expressions of Islam have, and may for the foreseeable future, seek predominantly Islamic societies in which to propagate their views and activities, a phenomenon that transpires where Islam shares the cultural space with other faith traditions as well. It is also true, where the *tolerant voice* of religion exists in such venues, the desire for peace initiatives normally ensues.

With military leadership recognizing the *strategic* contribution of chaplains among indigenous religious communities, a major challenge for RLE is the reality that the vast majority of chaplains in Western nations are Christian in orientation. As such, the lens used in RLE activities is predominately one of Christian belief and practice. Where opportunities present, chaplain formation must include greater familiarity with Islamic faith and cultural *peacebuilding* and conflict transformation principles. Future research must tap more deeply into the *ethos* of chaplaincy, further honing the inherent *peacebuilding* capabilities of chaplains' prevalent in fulfilling their unique role as *agents* of peace.

This knowledge gap necessitates chaplains be better equipped to recognize Islamic *peacebuilding* models indigenous to local culture and tradition, linking Christian and Islamic principles that resonate inter-religiously. Western approaches to resolving conflict often seem foreign—at times suspect—to indigenous populations where different values and norms exist. A growing number of Islamic scholars suggest that a rudimentary understanding of *peacebuilding* inherent to Islam will enable Christian peacebuilders to discern and reinforce local rituals, customs and methods more conducive to creating greater co-operation and interdependence where tensions exist across communal lines.[35] Such *inter*communal cooperation also underscores maintaining commendable human relationships, which the piety and religiosity of Islam strongly advocates. Outcomes in Islamic processes to resolving conflict are often less tangible, posing a challenge for the more Western style of individualism and negotiation. As spiritual leaders, chaplains are attuned to 'measuring results' in more qualitative terms. Implicating the *tolerant religious voice* in peacebuilding activities integral to culture and community life holds promise in creating community ownership of the process. Whole of Government personnel are well positioned to integrate such grassroots, or 'bottom up' initiatives, into 'top down' structures at the regional and national levels of reconciliation and nation building endeavors.

Designing skills development in peacebuilding and conflict transformation need not come in the form of courseware alone. For most, operational tours do not come regularly. Yet, given the operational environments over the last two decades, the probability of a chaplain deploying for six months or longer to a region where Christianity is but one faith tradition among others, or not at all, is not unrealistic. Scores of Christian chaplains deploy with little awareness of the religious *other*; yet find themselves navigating in an AO where coming face to face with religious leaders of other faith traditions is a regular occurrence. Much benefit may be derived from cultivating a degree of inter-religious sensitivity prior to an overseas tour. Most major centers in the West are multi-ethnic. Where geographically accessible, an aspect of chaplains' formation could include regular attendance at a Christian/Jewish/Muslim dialogue group for an extended period—a minimum of one season during the calendar year. This would aid in achieving the much-needed synthesis between training and praxis as chaplains apply their knowledge of other faith traditions in real time situations of interfaith dialogue—culture, values and norms. Dialogue groups of this nature are normally known for their acceptance and tolerance of diversity—something that would necessitate verification. National-level religious organizations could be of assistance in effecting such a strategy, e.g., identifying and interfacing with bona fide dialogue groups demonstrating the capacity to accommodate chaplains. In a time of much stereotyping and polarization around faith as identity, such exposure would be particularly conducive to the requisite formation necessary for inter-religious engagement in operational environments. It need not be an expeditionary mission. Both humanitarian and domestic operations could potentially have a religious dimension. Participating in interfaith dialogue groups might also involve citizens from the country to which the chaplain is deploying. Hearing their perspective on the cultural/religious practices and its nuances would do much to prepare the chaplain for a tour of duty in another culture, as well as inform the Religious Area Analysis underway. Encounters of this nature offer distinct advantage to understanding the religious *other*—a necessity for RLE in operations.

The above treatment of RLE has provided a summary of a number of the major challenges inherent in its implementation. Military chaplains are strategically situated to make a timely and valuable contribution to peace related initiatives in support of mission mandates and potentially in collaboration with their Whole of Government partners. As religious leaders in their own right, they bring a unique yet complementary capability to the operational environment. The closing chapter will consider the role of RLE from a theological perspective, delving into what goes to the core identity of chaplains as religious leaders—a calling to be a *reconciling* influence as *agents of peace.* Exclusion of the *other* is at the seat of conflict with its dehumanizing practices and ensuing violence, often balanced by the *will to embrace,* as *self* reaches out to the *other* in an act of mutuality that transcends barriers.

NOTES

1. *Geneva Convention for the Amelioration of the Condition of the Wounded and Sick in Armed Forces in the Field of August 12, 1949*, 75 U.N.T.S. 970, Entry into Force 21 October 1950. The remaining Geneva Conventions (II, III and IV) are 971, 972 and 973.

2. "Influence Activities are meant to influence and affect understandings, perceptions and will, cannot be considered separately from other operations, for they themselves are operations, that is, they are tactical activities undertaken to create desired effects. The deception of an enemy commander, the use of flyers to convince conscripts to flee, the building of civilian infrastructure to take support away from an insurgency and win the support of a populace, and other such activities seeking psychological effects are all tactical activities that must be conceived, planned, and targeted as part of an overall plan, simultaneous with and complementary to fires. Like physical activities, they may be classified in the functional and effects frameworks and described by their effects of shaping decisive, or sustaining." Definition provided by the Canadian Forces Influence Activities Task Force, CFB Kingston, Ontario. For further expansion see Influence Activity in *Land Operations*, Chapter Five, Section 9, 5, 51–54, https://info.publicintelligence.net/CanadaLandOps.pdf; see also Information Operations—Influence Activities in *Land Force: Counter-Insurgency Operations*, Chapter 8, http://info.publicintelligence.net/CanadaCOIN.pdf; Chapter 3: How the Army Fights, 3–5. Supporting Ideas, f (2) *Influence* in *The United States Army Operating Concept*, http://www.tradoc.army.mil/tpubs/pams/tp525-3-1.pdf; Chapter 6, Influence Activity, Section 2 Influence Activities in the *British Army Field Manual*, Volume 1 Part 10, Countering Insurgency, http://news.bbc.co.uk/2/shared/bsp/hi/pdfs/16_11_09_army_manual.pdf.

3. The targeting of people is an activity in all Operations, not simply Counterinsurgency Operations (COIN) where both insurgents and noncombatants are identified. The targeting process may be in support of Information Operations (IO), civil-military operations (CMO), and even meetings between commanders and host nation (HN) leaders, based on the commander's desires. In a COIN environment, which has been the case in Iraq and Afghanistan, potential targets have been insurgents and the support to their activities that is both internal and external to the Area of Operations (AO). Targeting may be both lethal and non-lethal: (1) lethal targets focus on capturing or killing; (2) nonlethal targets normally involve CMO, IO, negotiation, political, economic or social programs and other non-combatant methods. In a theatre of operations, an actual Targeting Board is essentially the responsibility of the Intelligence Cell comprised of representatives from the implicated domains relating to target selection and plan implementation. See "Targeting" in *Counterinsurgency*, FM 3-24, Chapter 5, 29–31, http://usacac.army.mil/cac2/Repository/Materials/COIN-FM3-24.pdf; also, "The Target Process" in *Land Operations*, Chapter 7, Section 4, 9–17, https://info.publicintelligence.net/CanadaLandOps.pdf; see also the *British Army Field Manual*, Volume 1 Part 10, Countering Insurgency, Chapters 5 (Intelligence) and 6 (Influence Activity) which contains elements of targeting, http://news.bbc.co.uk/2/shared/bsp/hi/pdfs/16_11_09_army_manual.pdf.

4. The Army Capability Development Board consists of Chief of Staff Land Strategy Directors, the Directors of Army Doctrine and Training, Arms and Branch Advisors, and representatives from the Science and Technology community, and with direct support and collaboration from other Land Staff and Chief of Force Development Directorates. The Board deals with proposed doctrinal changes / additions, inclusive of an operating concept for achieving desired outcomes, its potential impact on the force employment structure, a relevant equipment project, and the master implementation plan needed to fully develop, integrate and generate the pertinent capability. See http://www.army.forces.gc.ca/DLCD-DCSFT/pubs/armyoftomorrow/DesigningCanadasArmyofTomorrow_full_e.pdf, accessed 19 Aug 2012.

5. For an overview of the Capability Development Process used by the CF Army, see "The Capability Development Environment" in *Designing Canada's Army of Tomorrow: A Land Operations 2021 Publication*, 25-28. See http://www.army.forces.gc.ca/DLCD-DCSFT/specialPubs-eng.asp.

6. Non-combatants are defined as follows, "Non-combatants comprise all persons who are not combatants. Provided they do not take a direct part in hostilities, non-combatants are not legitimate targets. Civilians are generally the largest category of non- combatants. Religious

and medical personnel are non-combatants, even if they are in uniform and members of the armed forces of a party to the conflict." See *Law of Armed Conflict at the Operational and Tactical Levels,* Joint Doctrine Manual, B-GJ-005-104/FP-021, 2001, Office of the Judge Advocate General, National Defence, Canada, GL-13, http://www.forces.gc.ca/jag/publications/oplaw-loiop/loac-ddca-2004-eng.pdf. For citations from the Geneva Conventions stipulating the protected status of chaplains, see *Convention for the Amelioration of the Condition of the Wounded and Sick in Armies in the Field. Geneva,* 6 July 1906, Article III, Chapter III, paragraph 9, chaplains have protected status as non-combatants, "The personnel charged exclusively with the removal, transportation, and treatment of the sick and wounded, as well as with the administration of sanitary formations and establishments, and the chaplains attached to armies, shall be respected and protected under all circumstances. If they fall into the hands of the enemy they shall not be considered as prisoners of war." See http://www.icrc.org/ihl.nsf/WebART/180-170010?OpenDocument. Refer also to the *Convention for the Amelioration of the Condition of the Wounded and Sick in Armies in the Field.* Geneva, 27 July 1929. Ch III: Personnel, Art. 9, "The personnel engaged exclusively in the collection, transport and treatment of the wounded and sick, and in the administration of medical formations and establishments, and chaplains attached to armies, shall be respected and protected under all circumstances. If they fall into the hands of the enemy they shall not be treated as prisoners of war. See http://www.icrc.org/ihl.nsf/WebART/300-420015?OpenDocument.

7. See *Law of Armed Conflict at the Operational and Tactical Levels,* Joint Doctrine Manual, B-GJ-005-104/FP-021, 2001, Office of the Judge Advocate General, National Defence, Canada, GL-16, http://www.forces.gc.ca/jag/publications/oplaw-loiop/loac-ddca-2004-eng.pdf.

8. Without launching into a philosophical treatise, something should be offered with respect to the meaning of the term *well being of the other.* A term first used in the 16th century, much has been written on this topic. Today, science is also offering its viewpoint. One must consider that a Western view of *well being* may appear to be presumptuous or even convey the notion of Western imperialism (i.e. we know what is good for them…etc). In some sense, this may be a culturally bound construct. This would be consistent with Shin and Johnson who define *well being* as "a global assessment of a person's quality of life according to his/her own chosen criteria." (D. Shin & D. Johnson. "Avowed happiness as an overall assessment of the quality of life" in *Social Indicators Research,* 1978, *5*(1), 475–492). See http://nwia.idwellness.org/2011/02/28/definitions-of-wellbeing-quality-of-life-and-wellness/, accessed 23 July 2012. The NEF organization is an independent think-and-do tank in the UK committed to enhancing individual and collective well-being in ways that are environmentally sustainable and socially just. Their National Accounts of Well Being stresses "…that people feel a sense of relatedness to other people, so that in addition to the personal, internally focused elements, people's social experience—the degree to which they have supportive relationships and a sense of connection with others—form a vital aspect of well being. In addition they state, "Because of this dynamic nature, high levels of well-being mean that we are more able to respond to difficult circumstances, to innovate and constructively engage with other people and the world around us. As well as representing a highly effective way of bringing about good outcomes in many different areas our lives, there is also a strong case for regarding well-being as an ultimate goal of human endeavour." See http://www.nationalaccountsofwellbeing.org/learn/what-is-well-being.html, accessed 24 July 2012. In Chapter Three of this volume the Buddhist movement in Sri Lanka known as *Sarvodaya Shramadana* may best exemplify what caring for the well-being of the *other* might encompass. For more than 50 years and in more than 15,000 villages they have been addressing basic human needs as a central tenet to creating harmony among people: a clean environment inclusive of access to potable water, clothing, good, housing, health care, energy requirements, education, communication facilities, and a focus on cultural and spiritual needs. See http://www.savodaya.org/about, accessed 11 April, 2011. Suffice it to say that the employment of the term *well being* here is in no way meant to impose Western notions of what that might mean on *others.* Rather, a more universal understanding of peaceful and just relationships with *others* is implied, combined with an addressing of welfare needs, all the while keeping the cultural context in mind.

9. A member of the Concept Cell of the CF Army Land Warfare Centre, Peter Gizewski has contributed to the development of RLE. Acknowledged here, his thinking has informed this section on the relationship between Influence Activities and RLE.

10. Peter Gizewski. "Religious Leader Engagement: thoughts on its place in CF thinking," Defence Research and Development Canada — Centre for Operational Research and Analysis, March 2012, 1.

11. Gizewski, 2012, 2.

12. Gizewski, 2012, 2.

13. Information Operations are defined as ". . . coordinated actions to create desired effects on the will understanding and capability of adversaries, potential adversaries and other approved parties in support of overall objectives by affecting their information, information based processes and systems while exploiting and protecting one's own." As reported in Neil Chuka, "Note to File—A Comparison of the Information Operations Doctrine of Canada, the United States, the United Kingdom and NATO," *Canadian Army Journal*, Vol. 12.2 (Summer, 2009), p. 93.

14. These are: 1) Influence Activity, 2) Counter-Command Activity, and 3) Information Protection Activity. Reported in Ibid.

15. To these ends, IA can involve action drawing from a repertoire of five core capabilities:

- *Psychological Operations (PSYOPS)* - planned psychological activities designed to influence attitudes and behaviour affecting the achievement of political and military objectives.
- *Public Affairs (PA)* - a staff function within DND/CF that helps establish and maintain mutual lines of communications, understanding, acceptance and cooperation between an organization and its audiences.
- *Presence, Posture and Profile (PPP)* — the explicit use of the appearance, presence, attitude and profile of forces to impact on perceptions and attitudes — particularly of neutral and potentially adversarial audiences.
- *Civil-Military Cooperation (CIMIC)* — coordination and cooperation in support of the mission between commanders and civil actors including the national population and local authorities as well as international, national and non-governmental organizations and agencies. CIMIC is a coordination and liaison function and leads to actions that support civilian authorities.
- *Military Deception* — those measures designed to mislead the enemy by manipulation, distortion or falsification of information to induce him to react in a manner prejudicial to his interests.

For more detailed information, see Canadian Department of National Defence, B-GL-323-004/ FP-003 *Counterinsurgency Operations* (Kingston: Army Publishing Office, 2009), http://info.publicintelligence.net/CanadaCOIN.pdf. See especially chapter 8.

16. Key Leader Engagement is an Influence Activity used at commander's discretion. It may be defined as "the conduct of a deliberate and focused meeting with a person of significant importance in order to achieve a desired effect." Land Force Doctrine Note 2-09 Key Leader Engagement (KLE) — Approval Draft, Oct 2009, p.1.

17. Chaplain (Colonel) Mike Hoyt, U.S. Army-Retired, Senior Mentor, DLCD RLE SWG formal report, April 2012, 8.

18. Chaplain (Colonel) Mike Hoyt, U.S. Army-Retired, Senior Mentor, DLCD RLE SWG formal report, April 2012, 5.

19. The U.S. Army Chief of Chaplain's policy states, "When conducting Religious Leader Liaison (RLL), a chaplain and/or chaplain assistant will not collect or provide information as a human intelligence (HUMINT) source (FM 2–22.3, Para 1–4 through 1–7). A Unit Ministry Team (UMT) member may report a personally-observed activity as long as he or she was not directed to do so in any prior intelligence-related tasking or as part of a HUMIT collection plan." U.S. Army Chief of Chaplain's Policy #3—Religious Leader Liaison, 4–2a, 30 September 2008

20. Marc Gopin, *Between Eden and Armageddon: The Future of World Religions, Violence, and Peacemaking* (New York: Oxford University Press, 2000), pp. 154–158.

21. "Provincial Reconstruction Teams (PRTs) were designed to spread a peacekeeping effect without creating a large peacekeeping force. They are the grease, not the wheel. . . . The policy is to establish PRTs in locations [helping to] stabilize the region by extending the reach of the central government and facilitating increased reconstruction efforts. As a location becomes more secure, the PRT should shift from brick and mortar reconstruction efforts to governmental capacity building and focus on such tasks as security planning for elections, DDR (disarmament, demobilization, and reintegration), police mentoring, and so forth. In this case, the number of civilian representatives should increase, and their areas of expertise should be tailored to the evolving tasks at hand." Michael J. Dziedzic and Colonel Michael K. Seidl, "Provincial Reconstruction Teams and Military Relations with International and Nongovernmental Organizations in Afghanistan" in *Special Report*, United States Institute of Peace, No 147, September 2005, 8.

22. A three-day Generative Dialogue (GD)—*Vision and Strategy for Reconciliation as an Aspect Of the Whole of Government Approach to Nation Building*—was held at Saint Paul University (SPU), Ottawa, Canada, June 6-8, 2010. The GD was a collaborative effort implicating the Dept of Conflict Studies of the Faculty of Human Sciences at SPU and the Canadian Forces (CF) Directorate of Land Concepts and Designs. The conference was a first attempt within the Canadian context to bring stakeholders together to deliberate on the emerging theme of Religious Leader Engagement. The process combined brief presentations with plenary and small group discussions led by trained facilitators. Of interest were: first, a recognition that the interagency collaboration of Whole of Government (WoG)—a pillar of the Comprehensive Approach (CA)—is essential to nation building endeavours as a means of intervening in conflict and post-conflict situations; second, the increasing recognition that for many regions globally, religion is an integral dimension of life—mostly manifested peacefully and yet, at times, an element of conflict. Engaging the *tolerant voice* of religion may hold dividends in situations of protracted conflict. Already military chaplains have established a track record in working constructively with religious leaders in theatres of violent conflict. Over thirty people took part in the GD including personnel from the CF, Dept of National Defence, Dept of Foreign Affairs and International Trade, the Canadian International Development Agency (retired Director), NGOs, Pearson Peacekeeping Centre, and a number of academics from the United States and Canada. Of particular note was panelist General (ret'd) John de Chastelain, former Chief of the Defence Staff for the CF and Ambassador to the United States. Most recently, de Chastelain completed 13-year Northern Ireland involvement in aiding in the decommissioning of arms for the IRA, as an aspect of the Good Friday Accord. His co-panelist was General (ret'd) Maurice Baril, also a former Chief of the Defence Staff. General Baril served as military advisor to Koffi Annon at the UN Peacekeeping Operations during the Rwanda genocide. For a PDF of the Concept Paper for the Generative Dialogue—"Vision and Strategy for Reconciliation as an Aspect Of the Whole of Government Approach to Nation Building: A Generative Dialogue," see
http://www.amiando.com/eventResources/t/U/lLGwe2dwAa4xrq/Concept%20Paper.Generative%20Dialogue..pdf.

23. Gavin Buchan, Panel Discussion, Vision and Strategy for Reconciliation as an Aspect of the Whole of Government Approach to Nation Building: A Generative Dialogue, Saint Paul University, Ottawa, Canada, 7 June 2010.

24. *Religions for Peace*, http://religionsforpeace.org/initiatives/violent-conflict/conflict-transformation/, accessed 17 Aug 2010.

25. The Inter-Religious Council in Bosnia-Herzegovina is an NGO that comes under the umbrella of The World Conference of Religions for Peace, headquarted in New York and has been operating since 1996. I conversed with Olivera Jovanovic 25 and 26 Oct 2009, while visiting the Bosnian Defence Forces Chaplaincy—an inter-confessional body comprised of Muslim (Bosniak), Roman Catholic (Croatian) and Orthodox (Serbian) chaplains.

26. The Inter-Religious Council in Bosnia-Herzegovina, Law on Freedom of Religion and Legal Positions of Churches and Religious Communities in Bosnia-Herzegovina, the Parliamentary Assembly of Bosnia and Herzegovina, at the 28th session of the House of Representatives held on January 22, 2004 and passed on the 17th session of the House of Peoples held on January 28, 2004. See http://www.mrv.ba/, accessed 25 March 2011.

27. S. K. Moore, "Interdependence and the Role of Religious Leaders: Embracing the Other—Bridging Alienation" in National and Inter-ethnic Reconciliation, Religious Tolerance and Human Security in the Balkans: Proceedings of the Fifth ECPD International Conference, Takehiro Togo and Negoslav P. Ostojic eds. (Brijuni Islands, Croatia European Centre for Peace and Development International Conference, Conference Proceedings, 2009), 97-98.

28. *The World Council of Churches*, http://www.oikoumene.org/en/programmes/interreligiousdialogue/churches-in-situations-of-conflict.html, accessed 17 August 2010.

29. Reference has already been made to the **Peace Councils of India—the Mohalla** neighborhood commmittees. See Ashutosh Varshney, *Ethic Conflict and Civic Life: Hindus and Muslims in India* (New Haven, CN: Yale University Press, 2002; Varshney, *Social Policy, Conflict and Horizontal integration*, http://siteresources.worldbank.org/INTRANETSOCIAL-DEVELOPMENT/Resources/Varshney%5B1%5D%5B1%5D.rev.1.pdf, accessed 13 Aug 2012; Varshney, Ethnic Conflict and Civil Society: India and Beyond," http://chenry.webhost.utexas.edu/core/Course%20Materials/Varshney/53.3varshney.pdf, accessed 13 Aug 2012; Julia Eckert, "Reconciling the Mohalla: Politics of Violence and the Strength and Limits of Mediation in Bombay" in *Religion Between Violence and Reconciliation*, Introduction, ed. Thomas Scheffler (Beirut: Orient-Institute, 2002), 365-389. Committees. See **Kenyan Peace Committees**: Practical Action, "The Concept Peace Committee" http://practicalaction.org/concept-peace-committee-1, accessed 4 May 2011. See the same website for Mohamud Adan and Ruto Pkalya, "The Concept Peace Committee: A Snapshot Analysis of the Concept Peace Committee in Relation to Peacebuilding Initiatives in Kenya" (Nairobi, Kenya: Practical Action, 2006). See **Nepalese Peace Committees**: Andries Odendaal and Retief Oliver, *Local Peace Committees: some Reflections and Lessons Learned. A study report commissioned by The Academy for Educational Development, Dilli Bazar, Kathmandu, Nepal* and the United States Agency for International Development, 2009. http://www.google.ca/search?client=firefox-a&rls=org.mozilla%3Aen-US%3Aofficial&channel=s&hl=en&source=hp&biw=1280&bih=582&q=Peace+Committees& btnG=Google+Search, accessed 5 May 2011. See **Afghan Peace Councils**, http://humansecuritygateway.com/documents/CPAU_TrendsInLocalAfghanConflicts.pdf, accessed 11 June 2011.

30. Liora Danan and Alice Hunt, *Mixed Blessings: U.S. Government Engagement with Religion in Conflict-Prone Settings*, A Report of the Post-Conflict Reconstruction Project, Introduction (Washington, D.C.: Center for Strategic and International Studies Press, 2007), 1. See http://csis.org/files/media/csis/pubs/070820_religion.pdf. Informed by Major S.K. Moore, "Operational Chaplains: Establishing Trust with the Religious Other through the Building of Relation" in *In Harms Way* (Kingston, Ontario: Canadian Defence Academy, 2008), 73–74.

31. *Religion, Conflict & Peacebuilding: An Introductory Program Guide*, United States Agency for International Development, 2009, 3. See http://transition.usaid.gov/our_work/cross-cutting_programs/conflict/publications/docs/Religion_Conflict_and_Peacebuilding_Toolkit.pdf.

32. *Religion, Conflict & Peacebuilding*, 2009, 5–6. See http://transition.usaid.gov/our_work/cross-cutting_programs/conflict/publications/docs/Religion_Conflict_and_Peacebuilding_Toolkit.pdf.

33. CIMIC is an acronym meaning Civilian and Military Co-operations. Simply understood, this is a government funded CF cell within a deployed contingent that, among other things, targets the infrastructure needs of local populations . . . an additional element of capacity building.

34. Major S.K. Moore, CD, PhD C and Capt Imam Suleyman Demiray. "The Canadian Forces Chaplain Branch: Modeling Interfaith Cooperation and Pluralism in Afghanistan" in *Ecumenism*, No. 165, March 2007, 6–7. [*Pashtun* is the largest ethnic group in Afghanistan comprising 44 per cent of the population, predominantly in the south. The majority of the Taliban are Pashtun, a shared ethnicity with the neighboring population of southeastern Pakistan. See http://www.dfait-maeci.gc.ca/asia/main/country/afghanistan-_facgtsheet-en-asp, accessed 24 July 2006; *Umma* definition: Peter Marsden, *The Taliban: War, Religion and the New Order in Afghanistan* (New York: Oxford University Press, 1998), 69].

35. Mohammed Abu-Nimer. "Peacebuilding and Nonviolence in Islamic Religion and Culture: A theoretical Framework" in *Nonviolence and Peacebuilding in Islam: Theory and Practice* (Gainesville, Florida: University Press of Florida, 2003), 5–84; Mohammed Abu-Nimer. *Reconciliation, Justice and Coexistence: Theory and Practice* (Lanham, Maryland: Lexington Books, 2001); Qamar-Ul Huda. "Enhancing Skills and Capacity Building in Islamic Peacebuilding" in *Crescent and Dove: Peace and Conflict Resolution in Islam*, ed. Qamar-Ul Huda (Washington, D.C.: United Institute of Peace Press, 2010), 205–25; Abdulaziz Sachedina. *The Islamic Roots of Democratic Pluralism* (New York: Oxford University Press, 2001).

Chapter Eleven

A Practical Theology of Reconciliation in Theatres of War

In considering Religious Leader Engagement, one might be tempted to question why such operational initiatives would fall to the purview of chaplains. Are there not others deemed qualified to aid local religious leaders and their communities with resolving conflict and its effects? Ostensibly, the answer is yes. There is no question to the skills and expertise of others that could be brought to bear in such circumstances. However, one could also ask if there are particular reasons why chaplains ought to be involved. What is the value-added dimension that comes with chaplaincy? The answer is not only a matter of pragmatic consideration, though that comes into the equation as well. Rather, a theological reflection around the identity, calling and mission of chaplains reveals that RLE gives expression to what is at the core of chaplaincy.

Previous chapters highlighted the efficacy of religious peacebuilding: (1) among conflicting communities where religiously motivated violence factors into conflict; (2) within cultures that experience identity as inherently religious; and, (3) as religious leaders chaplains are uniquely qualified and positioned for peacebuilding endeavors among religious leaders and their communities. From a theological perspective, the chaplain's predisposition to peacebuilding and reconciliation emanates from the spiritual imperative to be *reconciled* one*self* with God and, concomitantly, to be a *reconciling* influence with the *other* (2 Corinthians 5: 18–19). Underpinning the chaplain's quest for peace and justice for all, regardless of faith or ethnicity, is the compelling truth that *self's* identity is inextricably tied to that of the *other*.

For the chaplain as religious leader, restoring proper balance to this interdependence among conflicting communities—a *reconciling* of the *self* with the *other*—is much more than techniques and strategies, it goes to the core of identity as *agents of peace.*

As a military chaplain and practical theologian, this author recognizes that ministry contexts do not remain static, as has been the case in operations around the world in recent decades. Documented evidence suggests an emerging *impulse* and sense of calling among deployed chaplains to be *reconciling agents* among estranged religious communities either engulfed in the larger conflicts of their identity groups or facilitating dialogue among faith groups living in alienation in post-conflict environments. In the language of Robert Doran, chaplains engaging in such operational ministry would be viewed as "catalytic agent[s] for an alternative situation in the world [whereby one] cooperates with God in working out God's solution to the problem of evil."[1]

As a multi-faith community, military chaplaincy represents numerous religious traditions, each with its own understanding and interpretation of belief based upon the sacred texts and teachings of their particular tradition. At the heart of this interfaith collaboration resides a *hermeneutics of peace* that recognizes peace and justice as a sacred priority in bridging alienation among those enduring conflict or its residual effects.[2] Religious leaders in uniform, these men and women of faith frequently witness the horrific acts of violence and their consequences apparent in theatres of war, manifest in the tragic loss of life and livelihood, often accompanied by the staggering movements of refugees in search of safety. It is circumstances in time and space such as these that challenge one's belief and time-honored traditions, precipitating new self-understandings of ministry and, by extension, chaplaincy. Demonstrative of this expanding *hermeneutic* is the *impulse* among chaplains to draw on the understanding, imagination and requisite values of their collective faith traditions to aid conflicting groups in *re-humanizing* the *other*, often the first step in the journey toward reconciliation. *Hermeneutically*, this *impulse* to engage indigenous populations is visible in its many forms among those struggling to rebuild their lives either in the midst of conflict or in its wake. From the humanitarian assistance of earlier times—something that continues today—to building relation with the religious *other(s)* through dialogue, thus spanning the divide of estranged communities (*encounter*), to the subsequent *collaborative activities* that engender trust and cooperation between/among estranged groups: hence, *agents of peace.*

Resulting from this expanding *hermeneutic* has been the development of a practical theology pertaining to the peacebuilding and reconciliation efforts of chaplains in conflict or post-conflict environments. Either through interfaith celebrations, intergroup sharing of humanitarian assistance or reinstated cooperation through the facilitation of dialogue where none existed, chaplains have patiently—yet intentionally—brought alienated religious leaders together in situations where such communication would otherwise not have occurred. The aim here will be twofold: (1) to grasp theologically something of the *reconciling* role of the chaplain as a bridge between alienated groups, and (2) to reflect theologically on the evils that stalk such environments as well as the shafts of light that repel such darkness. Embryonic in nature, these are the beginnings of the process of reconciliation to which chaplains prayerfully aspire often in the midst of conflict and overt violence. What is to follow is by no means exhaustive. However, it does represent where this struggle has brought this chaplain in his quest to understand and make a difference.

MIROSLAV VOLF: A THEOLOGIAN FOR OUR TIMES

Reflecting on the early 1990's implosion of the former Yugoslavia, Croatian-born Miroslav Volf[3] recognized early what lay before humanity as its core crisis. Two decades later, the world has endured tragedies still more horrific than those experienced in the Balkans. At the height of this crisis for his former homeland, Volf's proclamation comes to us as being no less pertinent, "the practice of ethnic and the other kinds of 'cleansing' in the Balkans forces us *to place the otherness at the center of theological reflection.*"[4] His challenge for Christians to "reflect on their identity as a people of God among the struggling peoples of the world" stands before us as a call to people of all faith traditions everywhere. He opines that religious wars were not the threat of earlier times, yet his caution not to underplay the existence of a religious component in much of the conflict of that time was prescient to where we find ourselves today. In so doing, Volf confronted Christians with the need to "rethink their mission as agents of peace" in light of "the resurgence of ethnic strife." He enjoined believers everywhere to engage in introspection: "What vision of the relations between cultures do we have to offer to communities at war? What paths to suggest?"[5]

To those of other faith traditions, the intent of these reflections is not to impose an exclusive Christian theology for conflicted peoples, rather as contemplations relating to this author's faith stance and experience of war. Recognized is the realization that other faith expressions hold within them like truths. The hope is that these musings may in some way inspire discussion and enhance understanding. Transforming conflict will ultimately require people of faith to mine the truths of their traditions in leading their people to peace and justice, cultivating the truths that are universal to all faiths.

In developing a practical theology for conflict zones and post-conflict environments, Volf will be the primary source. Intimately acquainted with the intercommunal conflict of a nation at war within, he offers a perspective that few theologians are able to bring today. His themes of exclusion and embrace are particularly poignant as a means of grappling with the notions of identity, *otherness* and reconciliation. Albeit, the emphasis will draw from the corpus of Volf's work, additional sources will be consulted as his themes are developed, keeping ethno-religious conflict as the focus. The reader will note that Volf has been drawn upon in earlier chapters. For the sake of continuity and clarity, some passages may bear a certain familiarity to what has come before. By way of clarification, the term "relation" is defined as the "act of relating," hence the emphasis on *agency*. The usage of "relationship" is interpreted as the "state of being related." Greater emphasis will be placed on relation, although relationship will appear when appropriate. The *agency* of relation illuminated in Volf adapts well to the *agency* of the operational ministry of chaplains.

By way of overview, exploration will begin with the relation of the *self* and the *other*, as inscribed within the patterns of relation of the order of *creation*—interdependence. Building on the creation theme of interdependence, Volf reveals how creating space in the *self* for the *other* is depicted in the cross—an opening of a fissure to humanity as Christ calls all people to reciprocally *create* space for the *other* within in mutuality. In the *new covenant* relation translates to journeying with the *other*—making space for the changing *other* within one*self* by a willingness to re-negotiate one's identity in relation to the fluidity of theirs. From here exclusion and embrace will be considered respectively.

Theologically speaking, it is the sin of exclusion that diminishes the bonds of relation, precipitating *self's* abandonment of the *other*. Numerous convulsing societies around the globe give testimony to what transpires once the *other* is dehumanized and objectified. Countering such egregious acts of violence is *the will to embrace*, or grace in action, as barriers become bridges. It is a grace-enabled *self* that reaches across the divide, creating space in the *self* for the *other*, initiating the beginnings of reconciliation. The *self/other* relation will remain a principal element of the sin of *exclusion* with its distortion of relation leading to conflict and its ensuing violence. *Embrace*, an expression of grace, bridges the chasm of alienation in its initial gesture of the *will to embrace*, as *self* reaches out to the *other* in the desire to transcend conflict and violence. These themes will build on each other as this practical theology for operational contexts is advanced, a construct that may be generalized to conflict and post-conflict environments.

RELATION IN CREATION

Relation is the lens through which Volf is viewed, the axis that cuts through the corpus of his work—a perspective relevant to chaplains, as the building of relation is the fulcrum upon which all endeavors balance. Revisiting the creation story, he introduces the dialectic of interdependence and independence in describing the nature of God's relation with humanity and, in turn, the relation between *self* and the *other*. Citing God's activity in creation, he expands on Cornelius Plantinga's notion of "separating and binding."

He contends that in the creation story God separated the "light from darkness, day from night, water from land, the sea creatures from the land cruisers" each "separate" yet "bound" in their binary relation. Concurrently, continues Plantinga, God "bound humanity to the rest of creation as stewards and caretakers of it, to [Godself] as bearers of [God's] image, and to each other as perfect complements—a matched pair of male and female persons who fit together and whose fitting harmony itself images God."[6] Inscribed within patterns of relation in the order of creation is a binding of the *self* and the *other* together in interdependence, understood to be an "intricate pattern of separate-and-bound-together entities."[7] Volf refers to this creative activity as *differentiation* where *self* and *other* "negotiate their identities in interaction with one another."[8] *Interdependence* in relation is of pivotal importance to humanity as created beings. He sums up the fulfillment found in the interdependence of relation in the following quote. "We are who we are not because we are separate from the others who are next to us, but because we are both separate and connected, both distinct and related; the boundaries that mark our identities are both barriers and bridges."[9] In their absence, identities would seep into "the dense pond of indistinguishables."[10] However, it is in relation that both define identity, that which distinguishes us from others and by what we have in common with others. Including the *other* is offered as "an alternative way to construe identity,"[11] which more than alludes to mutuality and interdependence. Charles Taylor reinforces this assertion in *Sources of the Self* by theorizing that one cannot be a self on one's own. Becoming a fulfilled *self* is coupled to one's relation to other interlocutors: "those conversation partners who are essential to [our] achieving self-definition [and] those who are now crucial to [our] continuing [to] grasp [the] languages of self-understanding."[12] Cited earlier, interdependence in the thinking of Paul Ricoeur employs *otherness* in relation to *selfhood* to such an intimate degree that one cannot be thought of without the other.[13]

Few individuals in today's world can speak as authoritatively to interdependence and identity as South Africa's archbishop Desmond Tutu. His emphasis on the theology of *ubuntu* is particularly relevant to *relation*, explaining it to mean, "each individual's humanity is ideally expressed in relationship with others."[14] Echoing Volf's depiction of *differentiation*, he articulates, "a person is a person through other persons,"[15] and, as Michael Battle affirms, Tutu demonstrates that "We are made for togetherness; we are made for family, for fellowship, to exist in a tender network of interdependence . . .

the fundamental law of our being is interdependence, and if this network is interrupted, the whole network breaks."[16]

Increasingly in Volf, relation of the *self* with the *other* becomes vital to wholeness, identifying a sense of relational reciprocity with respect to 'making room' for the *other* within the *self*. As such, the binary language of "separate yet bound," and 'taking in' balanced with 'keeping out' serves as a precursor to the emergence of Volf's recurring relational theme of *creating space in self for the other* also described as the *fissure in the self for the other*. No greater depiction is there of God's self-giving love than in the *cross* where a *fissure* of created space is manifest for humanity. Relational ties are strained to the point of rupture in conflict situations. Concretely or tacitly, in engaging the *other(s)* the chaplain *mimetically models* such openness of the *self* to the *other*, offering a vision of renewed relation—mutuality.

RELATION IN THE CROSS

For Volf, *solidarity* stands as paramount in the cross. Relation is profoundly epitomized in Christ's suffering on the cross, as are also "the sufferings of the poor and weak, which Jesus shares in his own body and in his own soul, in solidarity with them."[17] In the cross, the *self*-giving and *other*--receiving love of God reaches out in desired relation with victim and perpetrator alike: solidarity with the victim and atonement for the perpetrator. He states, "at the heart of the cross is Christ's stance of not letting the *other* remain an enemy and of creating space in himself for the offender to come in." In the cross, "God's self-giving love overcomes human enmity [through] the creation of space in [God-self] to receive estranged humanity."[18]

It is in the cross that relation, that *self*-giving and *other*-receiving love, is so convincingly and movingly exhibited. The message is that grace-enabled mutuality is manifest in inclusivity in relation, victim and perpetrator alike. Volf illuminates further, "Just as the oppressed must be liberated from the suffering caused by oppression, so the oppressors must be liberated from the injustice committed through oppression."[19] His depiction of a *fissure* that appears and opens to humanity during the agony of the passion, profoundly beckons humanity to reciprocally *create space* for the *other* in the *mutuality* of relation—*embrace*.

Recognizing that the thrust of this exercise is to develop a contextual theology grounded in Volf's thinking, it is imperative that one heed his admonishment with respect to *covenant*. Again, he calls for any serious theological reflection on social issues to consider the relation between the *cross* and the *new covenant*.

RELATION IN THE NEW COVENANT

With respect to *covenant*, Volf illumines that "the indisputable human capacity to make covenants is matched by their incontestable capacity to break them."[20] In much of today's fratricidal conflict, the erosion of trust in relation of the *self* with the *other* has led to the breach of covenant. Alternatively, relation between God and humanity is such that we are "*always already in the covenant* as those who have *always already broken the covenant.*"[21] This understanding of covenant unquestionably reflects the *self*-giving of God's love in *other*-receiving—God's unchanging faithfulness to relation with humanity regardless of humanity's failings. Relation in the new covenant is in "response to a persistent pattern of breaking of the covenant [and God's desire] to transcribe the covenantal promises written on the 'tablets of stone' onto 'hearts of flesh' (Jeremiah 31:31ff)."[22]

Consistent with Volf's understanding of *covenant* is Paul Ricoeur's own observation that *covenant* is primarily about *relation*. He illumines how humankind is "implicated in an initiative taken by someone who on [humanity's] side, is essentially turned toward [humankind] . . . a god concerned about [humanity]."[23] Ricoeur notes that in the bond of the *covenant*, relation precedes the notion of law. It is at this point of transition, from the dialogal relation—that is to say, God's calling and initiating relation—to that of the giving of the law, which marks a difference in God's revelation to humanity. It is at this juncture that 'Thou shalt' is heard for the first time which bespeaks the existence of a prior Legislator.[24] Of significance is that relation is viewed primordially, coming before sin is articulated in the law and the prophets, thus, endowing the role of relation as paramount. Most notably is God's *initiating* the dialogal relation, a notion that will be revisited in *embrace.*

Underscoring further the notion of *covenant*, Dale Aukerman articulates, "Yahweh had *drawn* Israel to [Godself] as covenant partner," again inferring the initiative of God and God's desire to be in relation with humanity. He states that the intention was for "wholeness of that relationship to [God] and of the relationships among the people."[25] Aukerman expounds that the Hebrew term *mishpat* describes the "harmony of interrelationships lived under the gracious ordering sway of [the] covenant Lord [who was] continuously active in human affairs to maintain or, more often, to restore right relationships and as constantly moving against whatever (and whoever) broke away from the coherence and fractured relationships."[26]

In Volf, the covenant is renewed in the cross by "making space for humanity in God's self,"[27] a recurring theme in his work. Citing Michael Welker, he depicts *creating space* for the *other* in the renewal of covenant to mean "attend[ing] to the shifts in the identity of the *other*, to make space for the changing other in ourselves, and to be willing to re-negotiate our own identity in interaction with the fluid identity of the other."[28] The resolution of conflict requires mutuality in relation evident in a reciprocal *creating of space* in the self for the *other* that "re-arrange[s] the self in light of the other's presence."[29]

Again, in renewing covenant the theme of God's *self-giving* on the cross offers meaning for conflictual relation. As in God's *self-giving*, Volf articulates further how in a broken covenant it is often the suffering innocent who take the first steps in repairing the breach.

> The one party has broken the covenant, and the other suffers the breach because it will not let the covenant be undone. If such suffering of the innocent party strikes us as unjust, in an important sense it *is* unjust. Yet the "injustice" is precisely what it takes to renew the covenant. . . . In a world of clashing perspectives and strenuous self-justifications, of crumbly commitments and strong animosities, covenants are kept and renewed because those who, from their perspective, have not broken the covenant are willing to do the hard work of repairing it.[30]

In the likeness of God who, in spite of the enmity of broken covenant, continues to seek the *other*, the renewed mutuality of relation often requires sacrifice.

Somehow such a depiction of reconciliation disturbs one's contemporary sense of justice. It resonates within, yet one struggles with such seeming out-of-kilter balancing of accounts. In *Reconciliation: Restoring Justice*, South African theologian John W. de Gruchy consults the scholarship of S.E. Porter as a means of informing this seeming paradoxical aspect of reconciliation. Porter states, "Paul is the first attested Greek author to speak of the offended party (God) initiating reconciliation . . . in which God is not only the agent or instigator of reconciliation, but is the goal toward whom reconciliation is directed."[31] Distinguishing Apostle Paul's rendering of reconciliation is that in other languages and cultures it is normally the party responsible for the alienation and acrimony who initiates dialogue, "hence the acknowledgement of guilt becomes a precondition for reconciliation."[32] Sadly, assuming responsibility by those guilty of crimes against the *other* is not often witnessed. Consistent with this thesis is de Gruchy's insistence that God's *initiating* reconciliation between Godself and humankind reflects the *relational* character of God and *covenant*. God *initiates* the end of hostility by *seeking* those who are *out* of fellowship with Godself, which "turns enemies into friends thereby creating peace."[33]

Lastly, William B. Oglesby underscores God's continually *initiating relation* as being pivotal to the concept of *covenant* and the impetus to affect the building of community between persons. He writes,

Indeed, in the biblical sense, covenant can be understood only in terms of the relationship between God and [humankind] as continually God moves toward the effecting of the community between person with person, and persons with God. . . . Throughout the entire scope of covenant, the basic factor is God's initiative; it is [God] who moves towards [humankind] to re-establish the broken relationships, it is [God] who again and again renews the Covenant which [humankind] ignores or breaks.[34]

From *creation* to the *cross* and on into *covenant*, the theme of *interdependence* in relation is one of fulfillment by *creating space* in the *self* for the *other*. As well, it is one of *initiating* reconciliation with the *other* just as God seeks out those who are out of fellowship with Godself when the responsibility of the breach of *covenant* rests with humankind. It is this sense of the *self/ other* relation that Volf uses as a lens to further articulate his major themes of exclusion and embrace.

Noted mediator Herbert W. Kelman earlier stated that the negation of the *other* was at the crux of conflict.[35] Volf intuits such negation of the *other* as exclusion, diminished relation manifest in entrenched estrangement, discernible in overt conflict or in the subsequent alienation of formerly accepting and neighborly groups. Chaplains witness firsthand the forceful destructiveness of such exclusion impacting individuals and communities alike—the evil of exclusion.

EXCLUSION

This segment will examine exclusion's distortion of relation, illuminating its linkage to conflict and, if left to its own devices, its ensuing violence, be that individual or group—its ultimate expression in the horrors of war. Scrutinized for their complicity in the undermining of *interdependence* will be Volf's themes of Wilful Independence, the Logic of Purity—with its related False Purity: Renewing and Remaking in Relation—and, finally, Societal Defilement. In Volf, the antithesis of interdependence is manifested in a *wilful independence* where *self* intentionally alienates the *other*. That said, one must recognize that a degree of independence is necessary for maintaining one's own identity. The difficulty emerges where wilful independence becomes *totalizing*, where the *other* is no longer needed. As an aspect of exclusion, the Logic of Purity sees the *other* as an intrusion into *their* space—often a defiling ethnic presence that must be "cleansed." In False Purity, re-naming that which is falsely labelled as impure and re-making the ostracized as members of community unmasks such false perceptions of legitimacy. Finally, the exclusion of Societal Defilement speaks of the structures that insidiously ensnare both the dominant and subjugated in perpetual estrangement that breed reciprocal violence.

EXCLUSION: WILFUL INDEPENDENCE

Wilful independence exerts relentless pressure on the *self* to push the *other* away, resisting any synergy of relation. Volf affirms, "Our very *selves* have been shaped by the climate of evil in which we live. Evil has insinuated itself into our very souls and rules over us from the very citadel erected to guard us against it."[36] One cannot improve on Apostle Paul's depiction of the inner struggle of the *self* with evil in Romans 7:14-20: "*self*, split into a weaker *self* that knows and wants the good, and the stronger *self* dominated by sin, which does the evil a person is then capable of willing but not of doing what is right."[37] In *The Symbolism of Evil*, Ricoeur speaks of this inner struggle as "the duality of two tendencies—a good inclination and an evil inclination . . . a permanent temptation that gives opportunity for the exercise of freedom of choice, an obstacle transformed into a springboard."[38] Impacting the *self's* relation with the *other* is the externality of evil that exists outside of human-kind, an external objective evil. Consulting Ricoeur once more, he articu-lates, "Externality is so essential to human evil that [humanity's] wickedness is always secondary."[39] Such externality works in tandem with the infection of evil—that evil inclination—within the *self* to bring about its seduction. Evil is at once outside and within, something that is brought about and yet is already there. Volf connotes, "This partly explains the power of sin, which is located neither simply inside nor simply outside of the person but both in a person and in social relations."[40] Violently manifested in today's genocidal ethnic strife are the exclusionary practices of evil. Some that come to mind are the killing fields of Cambodia,[41] the Muslim men and boys of Srebreni-ca,[42] the Tutsi's of Rwanda,[43] the Hutu refugees in the Democratic Republic of the Congo,[44] or the non-Arabs of the Darfur.[45] At the epicenter of such convulsing violence is seductive *evil* and *sin*, undermining and destroying the *mutuality* and *interdependence* of relation.

Ultimately, it is the deceptiveness of exclusion that causes *self* to "pretend that the *other* is not included within [*self's*] own identity."[46] Although a well-formed identity is desirable, the tendency for *self* is to "become the infinite basis and reference point for all objects, thus usurping the place of God."[47] Sin's reconfiguration of God's intended relational *interdependence* for hu-manity is most notably observed in how *wilful independence* begins the formation of boundaries as an expression of *exclusion*. The decline into the sinfulness of *exclusion* begins with the *self* "putting boundaries around the soul" with a view to becoming the *totality* of all that is needed. The *self* soon begins to use its surroundings in an effort to assert itself.[48] The *will* to an *exclusionary independent identity* demonizes the *other* not because the *self* doesn't know any better, rather because the *self* refuses to recognize what is manifest and instead chooses to know what serves the *self's* interest. *Self's* sinful independence of the *other* can reach such wretched depths of hatred that the means of destruction of the *other* knows no bounds. Volf writes, "Some of the most brutal acts of exclusion depend on hatred, and if the common history of persons and communities does not contain enough reasons to hate, masters of exclusion will rewrite the histories and fabricate injuries in order to manufacture hatreds."[49]

Returning to Plantinga, Volf describes sin as exclusion—not so much the will to undo God's creation, but rather to violently *reconfigure* its patterns of *interdependence*.[50] It is the violent reconfiguration of *interdependence* that alienates the *self* from the *other* in relation. Such reconfiguring is consistent with Ricoeur's description of sin's distortion of that which is good. He views "wickedness [as] not something that replaces the goodness of [humanity]; it is the staining, the darkening, the disfiguring of an innocence, a light, and a beauty that remain."[51] Here relation degenerates as one takes "oneself out of the pattern of *interdependence* and place[s] oneself in a position of sovereign [or wilful] independence."[52] Relation as *wilful independence* deteriorates as *other*,

> . . . emerges either as an enemy that must be pushed away from the *self* and driven out of its space or as a nonentity—a superfluous being—that can be disregarded and abandoned . . . exclusion can entail erasure of separation, not recognizing the *other* as someone who in his or her *otherness* belongs to the pattern of *interdependence* . . . an inferior being who must either be assimilated by being made like the *self* or be subjugated to the *self*.[53]

In her rendering of Christ's encounter with the Samaritan woman at the well (John 4:1–38), Judith Gundry-Volf aptly describes the face of exclusion. One who had fallen in disfavor with her own people, she had come to draw water at the sixth hour. Calculating from 6 a.m., this registers as the hottest time of the day. Most would come to the well during the cooler evening hours for the next day's replenishments. Gundry-Volf discerns the Samaritan woman's alienation from her own people, exemplified in her avoidance of social contact; as such, "Jacob's well stands for the bitter water of her marginalization."[54] Suffering, seemingly alone, she demonstrates the relational impoverishment of one who, for whatever reason, had been pushed or driven out from among her own people. Not in the literal sense, as she still lived in the same town, but, somehow worse, in that the bonds of relation were severed. *Interdependence* was denied as the rigidity and coldness of wilful independence condemned her to live in alienation and isolation in their midst. Denied her was the *mutuality* of relation that nurtures community and, as such, she lived relationally isolated and spiritually impoverished. Such is the evil of exclusion.

In wilful independence we have seen how sin's reconfiguration of the patterns of interdependence has resisted the synergy of relation, leaving the *self* relationally isolated and the *other* relationally impoverished. Volf's logic of purity delves more deeply into the subtleties of exclusion. Here the synergy of relation is opposed for fear of melding a "low-grade alloy" with the *other*, thus surrendering all prospects of forging the 'pure metal' to which 'destiny' has called the *self*.

EXCLUSION AS THE LOGIC OF PURITY

The Samaritan woman serves as a cogent example of Volf's insight into what he terms the *logic of purity*. It is his contention that those most culpable of sin are "not the outcast[s] but [those] one who cast other[s] out."[55] He poignantly identifies the root issue that, "sin is not so much a defilement but a certain kind of purity. Emerging is the desire "to purge the *other* from one's world, by ostracism or oppression, deportation or liquidation"[56] as *self* seeks to cleanse the world of the *other* rather than the heart of evil.[57]

The exclusive language of purity becomes a moral rationale and motivation for violence against the *other*. The violence of *self*-preservation, indeed *self*-purification, is taken by the pure and deemed legitimate as *other* is construed to be a defiling influence, and therefore, must be removed or eradicated. In this sense, *ethnic cleansing* is a related metaphor emerging from the logic of purity whereby *self* and, by extension community, cleanses it-*self* from the defiling *other*. The logic of purity renders such an exclusive notion of identity that careful attention is given to assure "that no external elements enter [*self's*] proper space so as to disturb the purity of identity."[58] Expounding further, Volf identifies the obsession with purity as demonstrated in wanting "our world to ourselves, and so we create a monochrome world without *others*, we want to be identical with ourselves, so we exclude *others*."[59] To be in relation with the ethnic *other* soils the *self*, as the *other* is unjustly indicted to be void of goodness, rendering the *other* 'unworthy' of relation with a *self*-proclaimed superior *self*. Relegating the *other* to the margins of the *self's* existence, the logic of purity attempts to remove any occasion for relation. Relation is resisted to the degree that "we strive to get rid of that which blurs accepted boundaries, disturbs our social identity and disarranges our symbolic cultural maps."[60]

Volf draws on Christ's parable of the Good Samaritan (Luke 10: 25-37) as a means of lifting his logic of purity to another level of abstraction. He uses this Gospel account to accomplish two objectives: (1) to introduce in more depth the exclusive nature of *false purity* depicted in the behavior of the religious leaders, and (2) to underscore the inclusiveness of Christ's "renewing" and "remaking" of the marginalized in community. Significant to our purposes is the centrality of relation to Christ's ministry with the estranged *other*.

False Purity Rebuked: Relation—Remaking as Renewal

Volf's hermeneutic of the parable of the Good Samaritan (St. Luke 10: 25–37) quite naturally introduces Christ's condemnation of *false purity* as it relates to the "renewing" and "remaking" of relation. The obvious evil is the brutal assault and robbery, leaving the victim for dead. Warranting further reflection is the more subtle sin committed against the *other* by the busy dignitaries, that of "pass[ing] by on the other side (vv. 31–32)." Says Volf, "these heartless acts of seeing but refusing to be bothered, of treating the others as a 'surplus people' who are of no use and therefore of no consequence, are exclusion by abandonment."[61] The false purity of the religious elite of Christ's day withheld relation from those they pronounced as "unclean," abandoning them to the extremities of "community." As such, a relational gulf lay between the *self* and the *other*. It is this withered spirit of exclusion's false purity that exudes from the religious leaders in the parable of the Good Samaritan.

Their wilful relational abandonment of the victim is striking by contrast with Jesus' intentional detour from Judea to Galilee through Samaria in his encounter with the Samaritan woman. Volf observes the circuitous route seldom traveled by Jews for the express reason of relational avoidance of the "unclean" Samaritan *other*.[62] Christ's encounter with the Samaritan woman radiates relational inclusivity, thus redeeming her as "clean." The evil of self-perceived (false) purity resists relation with the *other*, condemning the "clean" as "unclean" and shrinking from the responsibility of making "clean" those who are "unclean."[63]

False Purity Rebuked: Relation—Remaking as Renaming

Continuing with this theme, Volf enunciates the revolutionary relation-oriented ministry of Christ: (1) the re-naming of that which the "religious elite" of his day had falsely labelled as "sinful," and; (2) his re-making of individuals who had become entangled in sin and left to suffer, ostracized from community.[64] Denounced and re-named as exclusionary was the division of clean and unclean foods (Mark 7: 14–23), the flow of blood from a woman's body as not clean (Mark 5: 25–34) and laws of purity for women that promoted false boundaries of marginalization. Volf rightly states that such labelling served only to reinforce the binary logic of "us" and "them," a "superior in-group" and an "inferior out-group," unnecessarily separating people.[65] The *self*, claiming purity as its state, deems the *other* as being defiled and, by extension, pushes the "defiled" to the margins of society for fear of contamination. In Christ's extending welcoming relation to all, it should be underscored that "an indiscriminate welcome of everyone by no means entails an indiscriminate affirmation of everything."[66]

Christ's remaking of those with unclean spirits was liberating. They were cut off from community and forced to live among the dead. Once healed, these people were delivered from oppression and reintegrated into community (St. Mark 5:1–20). Tax collectors and prostitutes, ensnared in lives of sin, were the bane of their society. Forgiven and transformed by Christ, they were re-made, welcomed at his table and brought back into community where the mutuality of relation with God and the *other* was restored. L.E. Klosinski, an anthropological authority, amplifies Volf's attributing the welcoming at table as tantamount to being included in community. Exemplifying *hospitality*, he explains how "eating at table" symbolized for the discerning Jew feelings and relations, reflecting social status and the boundaries of group identity. [67] Quoting Volf,

> The double strategy of re-naming and re-making, rooted in the commitment to both the outcast *and* the sinner, to the victim *and* the perpetrator, is the proper background against which an adequate notion of sin as exclusion can emerge. . . . By the double strategy of re-naming and re-making Jesus condemned the world of exclusion—a world in which the innocent are labelled evil and driven out and a world in which the guilty are not sought out and brought into the communion. [68]

Originating in the heart, the *self's* will to purity finds expression in culture and politics. The desire for the all-encompassing 'oneness' of a group, to protect and maintain the group purity and identity, necessitates a severing of relation evidenced in the elimination of the *other* from the *self's* world. The subtler version of elimination is assimilation, where a minority group is "granted residency" in the land as long as they submit to the dominance of the majority group. Exclusion by assimilation therefore rests on the compromise of a relation oppressively defined and enacted: the dominant group will refrain from vomiting the minority group out, if they allow themselves to be swallowed up. [69] Structurally such exclusion by domination is hegemonic, relegating relation with the *other* to the status of the inferior with its enforced limitations: designated neighborhoods, certain kinds of jobs, less pay or honor. "These people must stay in their proper place," goes the logic. The *other* is dealt with in finality through the exclusion of relational abandonment, which keeps the *other* at a safe distance. Having no need of the *other's* goods or services, it is easier for the *self* to close them off; where the *self* is not reminded of any claim the *other* might have on them. Volf remarks,

> What differentiates us from the others, we claim, is something that we have as properly our own. We define ourselves by difference, and we want our difference to be pure. Blood ought to be pure, soil ought to be pure, language ought to be pure. This logic of purity often attends our understanding of identity. [70]

Over time exclusion of this nature evolves structurally within societies. Entrenched in law and practice, governments create and maintain such alienating structures, quickly ossifying into the status quo. Sadly, instances do occur where the subjugated *other* comes to believe the rhetoric of the dominant group and embraces their circumstances in life as the "designed" end state—a theme which will now be discussed—*Exclusion as Societal Defilement.*

EXCLUSION AS SOCIETAL DEFILEMENT

The life and theology of Dr. Martin Luther King, Jr. offers us a porthole through which to grasp something of Volf's notion of *societal defilement* and how our recognition of its insidious nature may serve to engender our willingness to embrace the *other.* Andrew Young, an intimate friend and associate of King's, offers a cogent vignette of the soul of this incredible gift to humanity.

In 1955 Dr. Martin Luther King, Jr. rallied black America to confront the blatant *exclusion* and injustice of Alabama's hegemonic policy of segregation where whites maintained societal privilege and dominance over blacks. As the civil rights movement evolved in the southern United States, Dr. King coined the phrase "no-fault justice"[71] as a descriptor of transcending the injustice and violence of whites toward blacks. He purported that responsibility for the injustice of segregation rested with neither white nor black, rather with the injustice of the situation itself. In so doing, he moved the struggle to the sphere of *societal defilement*, where existing and pernicious social structures insidiously contaminated the white community. King was oft to quote, states Young, the famed black thinker Frederick Douglass by exclaiming to black Americans that their struggle for freedom was "a struggle to save black men's bodies and white men's souls."[72] In seeking justice in the midst of an unjust situation, King epitomized the *will to embrace* by refusing to abandon the "perceived" evildoer.

King's refusal to make reference to the *other* in a manner debasing to their humanity enabled him to resist placing the perpetrator beyond redemption. Eruditely, he fathomed what most could not: *societal defilement* had become a systemic *stain* of entanglement menacingly permeating white southern culture. The entrenched structures were such that society in the south had become *normalized* for its white population: a pre-existing distortion into which one was born—a defilement of sorts that had been perpetuated from one generation to the next.

In his *Engaging the Powers: Discernment and Resistance in a World of Domination*, Walter Wink defines such systemic stain as "natal alienation," where people are "born into a world in which one is condemned in advance, by virtue of one's skin color, or gender, or disability, or malnutrition, or a mother's addiction, or AIDS, to a future more or less blocked off."[73] As such, an image of *self* as a creation of one's own culture emerges, where predetermined and confining structures condemn and sentence countless lives to injustice and misery. *Normalized* to such systemic defilement, the *self* practices exclusivity towards the *other* while believing itself to be tolerant and accepting.

Where conflict has become overt violence, tracing the roots of violence back to such systemic exclusion of the *other* is not uncommon. *Societal defilement* of this nature may be deemed as a "good" by the dominant, while the oppressed, having previously believed their state to be the "accepted order," now "enlightened," have risen up to resist their oppressors. Girardean scholar, Vern Neufeld Redekop, explains how such *mimetic* structures of violence[74] have, over extended periods of time, created an imbalance of pervasive domination and intolerable oppression. Once conflict erupts it frequently takes on an especially vicious tenor, as the thirst for vengeance and reprisal seems to know no bounds. Such structures give rise to an ever-increasing escalation of conflict—a phenomenon earlier depicted as *mimetic.*

Returning to King, his choosing to transcend conflict with his no-fault-justice platform personified the *will to embrace* as he held out hope for the remaking of the *other.* Grace transcending affirmed justice by exceeding its limits—*embrace* eclipsing *exclusion.* King elected to see the humanity of the *other,* which, in turn enabled him to unconditionally initiate relation with those who opposed him, believing that through dialogue and relation, justice would emerge.

Epitomized by King, the *will to embrace* is 'unconditional and indiscriminate' but yet not *full embrace* itself "that neither play-acts acceptance nor crushes the other [something which] cannot take place until justice is attended to."[75] The first step toward reconciliation, intrinsic to the notion of *will* as it relates to *embrace,* is one's resolve to see the eventual rectifying of wrongs and relationships reshaped to correspond to justice. Volf rightly illumines the impossibility of redeeming *community* and its social relations aside from the grace of *embrace* as depicted below.

> Indeed, the pursuit of embrace is precisely an alternative to constructing social relations around strict justice. It is a way of creating a genuine and deeply human community of harmonious peace in an imperfect world of inescapable injustice. Without the grace of embrace, humane life in our world—in which evil is inescapably committed but our deeds are irreversible—would be impossible.[76]

THE WILL TO EMBRACE — A BALANCE TO STRICT JUSTICE

Volf employs the theme of the *will to embrace* as a means of bridging the chasm separating exclusion from embrace. He deems this theological construct to be an expression of grace. It is in the *will to embrace* that the initiation of relation moves the conflicted *self* and the *other* toward reconciliation, a journey in process and goal. Here justice is transcended in the sense that willingness within the *self* emerges for initial engagement with the *other*, recognition of the humanity of the *other*. In the *will to embrace* justice is affirmed. Inherent in its promise is an eventual attending to injustice as former enemies move from entrenched positions to taking small steps toward renewed relation. He speaks of the willingness of usually the wounded party to see the good in a gesture of the *other*, often over against a backdrop of the tremendous hurt and suffering known to conflict. Movement toward the *other* often precipitates a reciprocal reaction. The *will to embrace* involves not only seeing the *other* from a different perspective, but also seeing the *self* from the perspective of the *other*, something Volf calls *double vision*.

The *will to embrace* is *mimetically modeled* by chaplains in their willingness to engage the *other*, most often leaders of religious communities whose respective identity groups are at odds. Exemplifying the opening of a space within one*self* to receive the *other* in a very real sense precipitates *encounter* between alienated leaders. Such incremental steps toward openness resembles accommodating the *other* within the *self's* identity boundaries, results in something of the *other* remaining within the *self* upon the conclusion of the initial *encounter*—a reflection of Volf's double vision. Cumulative small steps toward renewed relation become evident in *collaborative activities* at the community level. In Redekop's language, such mutuality would be defined as *mimetic* structures of blessing, as *inter*communal engagement engenders relational dynamics more open and expanding, life-oriented, creative and generous.

The term, *will to embrace*—what some would define as restorative justice—is introduced as a means of balancing strict or retributive justice. As will be seen, Volf resists the thinking that insists on the satisfaction of strict justice as a precursor to reconciliation, i.e., the 'balancing of accounts' of past injustice. He is persuaded that such rigidity precludes any movement between victim and perpetrator. The *will to embrace* presents the added dimension of grace, whereby the initiation of movement toward relation is offered by one of the two parties . . . usually the victim. Amplified below, Volf contests that such grace-enabled movement does not equate with the "assuaging" of offenses, something he refers to as 'cheap reconciliation'. Rather the *will to embrace* is the hesitant yet hopeful opening of the *self* to the *other* in the arduous task of bridging the chasm of alienation and separation. Perceiving an insidious injustice in holding to strict justice, Volf states "given the nature of human beings and their interaction, there is too much injustice in an uncompromising struggle for justice."[77] The *will to embrace* is the recognition of the 'injustice' of such intransigence. The overarching grace of the *will to embrace* affirms justice in its inherent promise of an eventual attending to injustice as grace brings *self* to recognition of the humanity of the *other* in the initiation of relation. In some sense, justice is deferred in the interest of establishing relation with the other. Holding out for the settling of accounts prior to the beginnings of constructive dialogue tends to perpetuate intercommunal estrangement.

PAUL'S CONVERSION

Volf's hermeneutic of Paul's Damascus road experience (Acts 9:1-19) re-enforces the prominent role of relation as it pertains to justice and reconciliation. The Acts account depicts the post-resurrection Jesus confronting Paul for the wickedness of his persecution of the church, which was indeed a justice issue. Succinctly put, "grace is unthinkable without justice, justice is subordinate to grace." Amplifying this notion is Volf's interpretation, "[T]hough clearly opposed to Paul's intentions, God did not let the demands of justice govern God's actions toward him but instead showed love by offering reconciliation to Paul, the enemy."[78] A strategic hinge to Volf's hermeneutic of strict justice is the notion that attending to justice did not supersede Christ's initiating relation with Paul as a means of reaching out to him in reconciliation.

He contends that "first justice, then reconciliation" is not a realistic approach to resolving conflict between injured parties as justice has a tendency to be relative. Opposing views exist with respect to responsibility for atrocities and ongoing conflict. Comparatively speaking, the measure of 'merited justice' varies from group to group, individual to individual, testifying to its seeming elusiveness. Strict justice or, "as much justice as possible," prior to the initiation of relation exacerbates the process of reconciliation by never enough justice being realized. More justice is always possible than what in reality is achieved.[79] As such, strict justice potentially creates a situation where the healing of relation is in fact undermined. Volf adds, "But it should be clear that if we pursue 'street justice' in such ways, the result will be a maimed and finally humanly unsustainable world."[80] Where retributive justice is sought to the degree that 'an eye for an eye, a tooth for a tooth' serves as the standard, vengeance would appear to be the motivation rather than justice. Such sentiments, though understandably issuing from the intense pain of loss, serve to fuel *mimetic* violence. Hence, Gandhi's sage remark, "an eye for an eye will soon leave us all blind" succinctly captures the wisdom of this concept.

Volf does not suggest that justice is not deemed vital to reconciliation. To the contrary, it is a question of priority and process. The *will to embrace* is a "grace-enabled" movement toward reconciliation and the *full embrace* of restored relation. In an eschatological sense, full "embrace is the horizon for the struggle for justice . . . oriented toward the larger goal of healing relationships."[81] An enforced justice would rectify past wrongs but fall far short of creating communion between victims and perpetrators. That said, "Some form of communion—some form of relation—needs to be established if the victim and perpetrator are to be fully healed."[82]

THE REFRAMING OF RELATION

Volf appreciates the magnitude and delicacy of reconciliation's task as he insightfully remarks how 'the inscriptions of hatred must be carefully erased and the threads of violence gently removed."[83] However, embedded in this acknowledgment is his hermeneutic of Christ's radical call to repentance. Understandably and without compunction, he condemns the perpetrators of sin and the structures that label innocence as being sinful and the unrelenting oppression of society's vulnerable. Revolutionary was Christ's calling of the oppressed to repentance. Although the Jewish population of Palestine clearly suffered under the weight of the oppressive Roman regime, Christ did not neatly divide society between the oppressors and the victims, naming one guilty and the other innocent. Without question, those guilty of sins against the innocent felt the sting of Christ's rebuke. The hope that he offers the oppressed is undeniably connected to the radical change he requires of them . . . that of repentance.

Volf illuminates further that if social change is to reflect the "vision of God's reign, [it cannot happen] without a change of the heart and behavior."[84] It is the grace-enabling light of the *will to embrace* that filters the heart with the reversing perspectives of *double vision* enabling the *self* to view the *other* through one's own eyes and, more importantly, to see one*self* from the perspective of the *other*. Amplifying further *double vision's* role in the reframing of relation, Volf states,

> I can't simply see myself the way I see myself. I have to expose myself to hearing how I am perceived. Then, as we are seen, we can exchange perspectives. It is only though exchanging perspectives that we can gain an adequate perception both of ourselves and of the other.[85]

Charles Villa-Vicencio, of the University of Cape Town, South Africa, contends that such "partisan memories" must be integrated into the greater story that unites.[86] Fashioning a less fractious future,

[I]nvolves telling our stories to one another and listening intently to the stories
we are told . . . reaching beyond the words and the 'facts' to what lies behind
the words . . . of gaining an understanding from the perspective of another's
experience. It is a process that involves more than empathy. It involves hermeneutical relocation whereby we see, hear, and understand in a different way. [87]

Recognizing one's tendency to nurture and feed feelings of bitterness and
hatred for the oppressor is an aspect of the *self*-revelation of double vision.
The *will to embrace* must eventually lead to the uprooting of the bitterness
that often takes root in the soil of the tortured heart of victims. Perhaps a long
road, and too difficult to contemplate early on, but such is the healing nature
of forgiveness.

Having deployed to various conflict zones, troops are well acquainted
with the ebb and flow of conflict. Eventually oppressive regimes are toppled,
providing occasion for former victims to visit their brand of "justice" on
those who so brutally oppressed them. Needing to be broken is the hold of
such dominant values and practices on the hearts and minds of victims. [88]
Volf illumines,

For a victim to repent means not to allow the oppressors to determine the terms
under which social conflict is carried out, the values around which the conflict
is raging, and the means by which it is fought. Repentance thus empowers
victims and disempowers the oppressors. It "humanizes" the victims precisely
by protecting them from either mimicking or dehumanizing the oppressors.
Far from being a sign of acquiescence to the dominant order, repentance
creates a haven of God's new world in the midst of the old and so makes the
transformation of the old possible. [89]

Far too often such reactive behavior is justified and rationalized either by
asserting that "they are not responsible for it or that such reactions are a
necessary condition of liberation." [90]

For many interventionists, the brutality that victims have suffered at the
hands of their perpetrators is beyond their comprehension. Volf's interpretation of repentance is not meant to belittle the horrific experiences that undoubtedly leave indelible scars at all levels. However, he contends that even
in the midst of,

[E]xtreme brutality, an inner realm of freedom to shape one's self must be
defended as a sanctuary of a person's humanity. Though victims may not be
able to prevent hate from springing to life, for their own sake they can and
must refuse to give it nourishment and strive to weed it out. If victims do not
repent today they will become perpetrators tomorrow who, in their self-deceit,
will seek to exculpate their misdeeds on account of their own victimization. [91]

MAKING SPACE IN SELF FOR THE OTHER: THE DRAMA OF EMBRACE

An appropriate manner by which to complete this journey through Volf is to reflect on his "phenomenology of embrace" depicted as the drama of embrace, as restored relation gives birth to reconciliation. A vision of two individuals standing face to face is used in this depiction. Four acts in this drama symbolically enact 'the dynamic relationship between the *self* and the *other*' as a means to "thinking about identity—personal as well as communal—in relation to the other under the conditions of enmity."[92]

ACT ONE—*OPENING THE ARMS*

This is a gesture of the body reaching for the *other*. In so doing the *self* emits the sign of discontent with one's own self-enclosed identity while gesturing a code of desire for the *other*. Such movement simultaneously signifies the *self* has created space within for the *other* to come in, while indicating motion to enter the space created by the *other*. "*Self* makes room for the *other* and sets on a journey toward the *other* in one and the same act." Implied as well is a fissure in the *self*, "an aperture on the boundary of the *self* through which the *other* can come in." Denoted is the gesture of invitation, which in a state of mutual enmity remains conditional "in the sense that certain conditions need to be fulfilled not before the invitation can be issued but before 'entering in' can take place."[93] More than an invitation; Volf suggests that it is a soft knock on the *other's* door.

ACT TWO—*WAITING*

At this juncture the *self's* open arms stretch out toward the *other* but stop at the boundary of the *other* before touching. The desire for relation must arise in the *other* signified by open arms if movement is to proceed.

ACT THREE—*CLOSING THE ARMS*

The *telos* of embrace is that of reciprocity evidenced in both holding and being held. Citing Nobel Laureate, Elie Wiesel, Volf offers the following portrayal:

> In an embrace I also close my arms around the other—not tightly, so as to crush her and assimilate her forcefully into myself—for that would not be an embrace but a concealed power-act of exclusion—but gently, so as to tell her that I do not want to be without her in her otherness. I want her to remain

independent and true to her genuine self, to maintain her identity and, as such, to become part of me so that she can enrich me with what she has and I do not.[94]

ACT FOUR—*OPENING THE ARMS AGAIN*

Self must preserve the *self's* own identity by releasing the *other*, but is forever enriched by the traces of the presence of the *other* that have been left. Volf speaks of identity boundaries that are permeable and shifting,[95] allowing for "incursions of the *other* into the *self* and of the *self* into the *other*."[96] He clarifies,

> In personal encounters, that which the other person is flows consciously or unconsciously into that which I am. The reverse is also true. In this mutual giving and receiving, we give to the others not only something, but also a piece of ourselves, something of that which we have made of ourselves in communion with the others; and from the others we take not only something, but also a piece of them. Each person gives of himself or herself to the others, and each person in a unique way takes up the others into himself or herself.[97]

The image here is one of mutuality, where the identity of the *self* is enriched and enlarged by that of the *other*. "The *otherness* is reciprocal," says Volf, "a mutual *relation*."[98]

The above drama of embrace has much to do with identity as it reflects the mutuality of interdependence: the integrity of the *self* yet impacted by the *other*. With such mutuality comes the need for a degree of boundary maintenance, "a certain kind of assertion of the *self* in the presence of the *other* and a certain kind of deference of the *other* before the *self*:"[99] a sense of the earlier discussed notion of "separate but bound." Volf speaks of identity boundaries that are permeable and shifting,[100] a porosity that allows "incursions of the *other* into the *self* and of the *self* into the *other*."[101] He contends, "identity is not self-enclosed" as "the *other* is already in the *self*" meaning that the *self* cannot simply be defined "oppositionally."[102] The *self's* identity is not defined solely on the basis of the *self's* independence of the *other*, rather it is created in relation with the *other*.

Echoing Volf, Fumitaka Matsuoka[103] describes how in a gesture of openness, *self* pulls back from the edges of *self's* identity boundary to make room for the *other*. Such encounters are likened to an "antechamber" where the participants come to what is defined as the liminal experience of mutual participation. Liminal space may be understood as the approaching of a "threshold" of something new; an experience of the *other* that is "barely perceptible." The *self's* granting of access to the *other* within the *self's* boundaries leaves an altered and lingering impression of the estranged *other* once the encounter is finished. It is in such encounters that the humanity of the *other* emerges.

AN APPLICATION IN BRIEF

External operational ministry in conflict zones is frequently met with ethno-religious groups still embroiled in hostilities of one nature or another. In many instances these people are either fighting overtly or are in entrenched positions of estrangement where the renewal of communication has yet to begin. *Exclusion* is manifest in deep-rooted conflict, as the heightened *human identity needs* of *security* and *connectedness* have driven once integrated neighborhoods to becoming completely separated behind not only geographical boundaries but those of identity as well. Here suspicion and hatred grow as leaders bent on creating followings of their own, misconstrue truth and fabricate lies in an effort to keep conflict alive for their own purposes. Soon the *logic of purity* emerges in their rhetoric, engendering an environment where the "defiling" *other* is castigated for their sullied influence and the historical enmity that "they perpetuate" with their "aggression." Religious belief is often co-opted—along with some of its leaders—as an additional lever to apply sway over desperate and vulnerable minority groups. Reciprocal violence escalates (*mimetic*) as one group strikes back at another in retaliation for aggression toward them—hostilities that find their origin in their own offering of violence to the *other*. *Exclusion* known to deep-rooted conflict feeds the spiralling effect of the reversing roles of perpetrator and victim.

In the midst of such turmoil there often exist religious leaders not desirous of conflict for their peoples. Individuals of influence within communities (middle-range actors), these are they who often exhibit a *willingness* to reach across ethnic lines to their religious counterparts in the hopes that together they may model transcending the conflict that has consumed their respective communities. Chaplains may serve as catalysts for such displays of the *will to embrace*. Where opportunity presents and security permits, chaplains identify and bring together like-minded religious leaders—such is *encounter.* It is in peacebuilding endeavors of this nature that the *will to embrace* comes into view. Literally, these leaders come together for dialogue against a backdrop of alienation and intercommunal division. New narratives of *mutuality* and *interdependence* begin to take shape as renewed cooperation creates a different vision of the *other*. As trust develops between religious leaders and their communities, damaging effects of intercommunal violence may be lessened among the people due to the channels of communication established across ethnic lines via the religious community leadership. Building on such beginnings, collaborative activities with superordinate goals among faith groups may be one approach to sustaining further cooperation. As opportunity arises, bringing estranged religious leaders together in encounter witnesses an approaching of the *will to embrace*. Here the opening of the *fissure* within the *self* to the *other* begins the journey of re-humanizing the *other*. These are the seeds of reconciliation.

The above has considered the theological underpinnings of the chaplain's orientation toward reconciling ministries among those entangled in conflict or living with its resulting alienation—a *hermeneutics of peace*. As *interdependence*, the *self/other* relation became the lens through which to view the origins of the *exclusion* of the *other*. Together, the subtleties of *willful independence*, the *logic of purity*, and *societal defilement* were shown to manifest in conflict, offering some understanding of the dynamics at play where violence was a factor. The *will to embrace* with its *double vision* was seen to transcend conflict, as restored relation became a bridge rather than a barrier to the reconciling of differences. Perceiving one*self* through the eyes of the *other* held great value in better understanding one*self* as well as comprehending afresh the conflict at hand.

NOTES

1. Robert Doran, "Psychic Conversion" in *Theology and the Dialectics of History* (Toronto, Buffalo, London: University of Toronto Press, 1990), 44.

2. Informed by David Little, *Peacemakers in Action: Profiles of Religion in Conflict Resolution* (New York: Cambridge University Press, 2007), 438.

3. Miroslav Volf is the Henry B. Wright Professor of Systematic Theology and Director of the Yale Center for Faith and Culture, Yale University. See http://www.yale.edu/divinity/faculty/Fac.MVolf.shtml

4. Miroslav Volf, "Exclusion and Embrace: Theological Reflections in the Wake of 'Ethnic Cleansing'" in *Journal of Ecumenical Studies*, Vol. 29, No. 2, Spring, 1992, 234.

5. Miroslav Volf, "A Vision of Embrace: Theological Perspectives on Cultural Identity and Conflict" in *Ecumenical Review*, Vol. 47, No. 2, 2001, 196.

6. Cornelius Plantinga, *Not The Way It's Supposed To Be: A Breviary of Sin*, (Grand Rapids, Michigan: William B Eerdmans Publishing, 1995), 29 cited in Miroslav Volf, *Exclusion and Embrace: A Theological Exploration of Identity, Otherness, and Reconciliation* (Nashville, TN: Abingdon Press, 1996), 65–66. (More inclusive language is used)

7. Volf, 1996, 65.

8. Volf, 1996, 66.

9. Volf, 1996, 66.

10. Miroslav Volf, "Conversations with Miroslav Volf: Part 1" in *The Conrad Grebel Review*, Vol. 18, No. 3, Fall 2000, 73.

11. Miroslav Volf, "The Role of the Other," *Institute for Global Engagement*, http://www.globalengagement.org/issues/2001/09/mvolf-bwf-the other-p.htm, accessed 11 Nov 2005.

12. Charles Taylor, *Sources of the Self: The Making of the Modern Identity* (Cambridge, Mass, Harvard University Press, 1989), 36.

13. Paul Ricoeur, *Oneself as Another* (Chicago: The University of Chicago Press, 1992), 3.

14. Michael Battle, *Reconciliation: The Ubuntu Theology of Desmond Tutu* (Cleveland, Ohio: Pilgrim Press, 1997), 40.

15. Desmond Tutu, *No Future Without Forgiveness* (New York: Doubleday, 1999), 31.

16. Michael Battle, *Reconciliation: The Ubuntu Theology of Desmond Tutu* (Cleveland, Ohio: Pilgrim Press, 1997), 65–66, 73.

17. Jürgen Moltmann, *The Spirit of Life: A Universal Affirmation*, translated by Margaret Kohl (San Francisco: HarperCollins, 1992), 130 cited in Volf, 1996, 22. The theme of *solidarity* in Volf derives from theologian Jürgen Moltmann, under whom Volf received his theological formation. He credits the most recent significant contributions on the theology of the cross for life in the world to Moltmann.

18. Volf, 1996, 126–27. (Italics mine; insertion of God-self mine in an effort to keep with inclusive language).

19. Volf, 1996, 23.

20. Volf, 1996, 153.

21. Volf, 1996, 153.

22. Volf, 1996, 153.

23. Paul Ricoeur, *The Symbolism of Evil* (Boston: Beacon Press, 1967), 50–52.

24. Ricoeur, 1967, 50–52.

25. Dale Aukerman, *Reckoning With Apocalypse: Terminal Politics and Christian Hope* (New York: Crossroad Publishing, 1993), 37. Jürgen Moltmann also cites that the initiative of *relationship* with humanity originates with God, establishing and committing Godself to the covenant, which is aligned towards the reciprocity of *relationship*. See Jürgen Moltmann, 2000. *Experiences in Theology: Ways and Forms of Christian Theology*, translated by Margaret Kohl (Minneapolis: Fortress Press), p. 96

26. Aukerman, 1993, 37.

27. Volf, 1996, 154.

28. Michael Welker, *Kirch im Pluralismus* (Kaiser Taschenbuch 136. Gütersloh: Christian Kaiser, 1995a), 54ff cited in Volf, 1996, 154.

29. Volf, 1996, 154.

30. Volf, 1996, 155.

31. S.E. Porter, "Peace, Reconciliation" in Hawthorne and Martin, *Dictionary of Paul and His Letters* (Downers Grove, Illinois: Intervarsity Press, 1993), 695-696 cited in John W. De Gruchy, *Reconciliation: Restoring Justice* (Minneapolis: Fortress Press, 2002), 52.

32. John W. De Gruchy, *Reconciliation: Restoring Justice* (Minneapolis: Fortress Press, 2002), 52.

33. De Gruchy, 2002, 52.

34. W. B. Oglesby Jr., *Biblical Themes For Pastoral Care* (Nashville: Abingdon Press, 1980), 46-47. Inclusive language is used.

35. See Ch 2, Intractable Conflict, Introduction, xx.

36. Volf, 1996, 89.

37. Volf, 1996, 89.

38. Ricoeur, 1967, 131.

39. Ricoeur, 1967, 155. For Ricoeur's full discussion on the Servile Will see *Symbolism of Evil*, 151-157. The bracketed words are in keeping with the inclusive language of this thesis. Later references to [humanity] will substitute [a man].

40. Miroslav Volf, "The Final Reconciliation: Reflections on a Social Dimension of the Eschatological Transition" in *Modern Theology* Vol. 16, No.1, 2000, 100.

41. See http://news.bbc.co.uk/2/hi/asia-pacific/7814000.stm

42. See http://www.martinfrost.ws/htmlfiles/srebrenica_massacre.html

43. See the International Criminal Tribunal for Rwanda http://www.unictr.org/Home/tabid/36/Default.aspx

44. "GENEVA (1 October 2010)—The UN High Commissioner for Human Rights released Friday a 550-page report listing 617 of the most serious violations of human rights and international humanitarian law over a ten-year period by both state and non-state actors in the Democratic Republic of the Congo (DRC). Tens of thousands of people were killed, and numerous others were raped, mutilated or otherwise victimized during the decade. The report also examines in detail various options for truth and reconciliation, as well as for bringing those responsible for serious crimes to justice, thereby ending a climate of near-total impunity and setting the foundation for sustainable peace and development in the DRC." http://www.ohchr.org/en/

NewsEvents/Pages/DisplayNews.aspx?NewsID=10404&LangID=E, accessed 6 Oct 2010. For the full Report see http://www.ohchr.org/EN/Countries/AfricaRegion/Pages/RDCProjetMapping.aspx

45. A distinction is made between the "Arabs" and "non-Arabs" in the Darfur, both African and both Muslim. "The Save Darfur Coalition has adopted the terms 'non-Arab black African Muslims' and 'Arab black African Muslims,' suggesting that both groups share a black African Muslim identity that is differentiated by distinctions between 'Arabs' and 'non-Arabs', not 'Arabs' and 'Africans'." The Fur, the Masalit, and the Zaghawa are principal among "non-Arab black African Muslim" ethnicities that have suffered at the hands of the "Arab black African Muslim" Janjaweed militia sponsored by the Sudanese Government. See Amanda F. Grzyb ed., 2009. *The World and Darfur: International Response to Crimes Against Humanity in Western Sudan,* Introduction (Montreal & Kingston: McGill-Queen's University Press), 8.

46. Volf, 2000, 73.

47. Wolfhart Pannenberg, *Anthropology in Theological Perspective*, translated by Michael J. O'Connell (Philadelphia: Westminster, 1985), 261 cited in Volf, 1996, 90.

48. Pannenberg, 1985, 85.

49. Volf, 1996, 77.

50. Volf, 1996, 66. Volf concurs with Cornelius Plantinga's portrayal of sin as the violent reconfiguration of the inscribed patterns of relation (interdependence) in the order of creation. In Volf, *exclusion* is meant to convey reconfiguration in the sense that sin does not destroy what God has created; rather its subversive nature brings distortion, deformity and disharmony to God's purposes.

51. Ricoeur, 1967, 156.

52. Volf, 1996, 67.

53. Volf, 1996, 67 (Italics mine).

54. Judith Gundry-Volf, "Spirit, Mercy and the Other" in *Theology Today*, Vol. 51, No. 4, Jan 1995, 511.

55. Volf, 2002, 241.

56. Judith M. Gundry-Volf and Miroslav Volf, "Exclusion and Embrace: Theological Reflections in the Wake of Ethnic Cleansing" in *A Spacious Heart: Essays on Identity and Belonging* (Harrisburg, Pennsylvania: Trinity Press International, 1997), 49.

57. Volf, 1996, 74.

58. Miroslav Volf, "The Healthy Church: Embodying Diversity," in *Catalyst On Line: Contemporary Evangelical Perspectives for United Methodist Seminarians*, http://catalystresources.org/issues/293volf.html, accessed 26 Nov 2005, 4.

59. Miroslav Volf, "A Vision of Embrace: Theological Perspectives on Cultural Identity and Conflict" in *Ecumenical Review*, Vol. 47, No. 2, 2001, 201. (Italics mine).

60. Mary Douglas, *Purity and Danger* (London: Routledge, 1966); Julia Kristiva, *Powers of Horror: An Essay in Abjection* (New York: Columbia University Press, 1982), 4 cited in Volf, 2001, 201.

61. Volf, 2001, 202.

62. Gundry-Volf, 1995, 509.

63. Volf, 1996, 74.

64. Miroslav Volf, "'The Trinity Is Our Social Program': The Doctrine of the Trinity and the Shape of Social Engagement" in *Modern Theology*, Vol 14, No 3, July 1998, 416.

65. Judith Romney Wegner, *Chattel or Person? The Status of Women in the Mishnah* (New York: Oxford University Press, 1988), 162-167 cited in Volf, 1996, 73.

66. Volf, 1998, 416.

67. L.E. Klosinski, *The Meals in Mark* (Ann Arbor, Mich.: University Microfilms International, 1988), 58 as quoted by John D. Crossan, *The Historical Jesus* (San Francisco: Harper & Row, 1991), 341,cited in D.W. Shriver, in *An Ethic For Enemies* (Oxford University Press, NY, NY. 1995), 40.

68. Volf, 1996, 73–74.

69. Claude Lévi-Strauss, *Triste Tropiques* (Paris: Librarie Plon, 1955), 417 cited in Volf, 1996, 75.

70. Volf, http://www.globalengagement.org/issues/2001/09/mvolf-bwf-the other-p.htm.

71. Andrew Young, 'Martin Luther King as Political Theologian' in *Theology, Politics, and Peace*, ed. Theodore Runyon (Maryknoll, NY: Orbis Books, 1989), 81.

72. Young, 1989, 81.

73. Walter Wink, *Engaging the Powers: Discernment and Resistance in a World of Domination* (Minneapolis: Fortress Press, 1992), 82.

74. *Mimetic structures of violence* may be described as follows. "When the attitudes and orientation of both parties are turned against one another as they attempt to control, hurt, diminish or otherwise do violence to one another, we have a mimetic structure of violence. Here we see the mutual hate between groups taking on a life of its own. It is *mimetic* because groups are imitating one another in hurting each other; it is a structure because it is an ongoing pattern that creates and sustains harm. Mimetic structures of violence constrict the movement of people, limit life's options, and are directed toward death. Groups develop competing interpretive frameworks and public relation strategies to disclaim any culpability of their own all the while maximizing the responsibility for the violence on the other side—the "perpetrator." So it's not just that groups strike back in retaliation, reversing the roles of victim and perpetrator, but a relationship builds up in such a way that the parties in the relationship continually say and do things to harm one another. In that sense it becomes a structure that can be prolonged over extended periods of time, even decades or longer." See Vern Neufeld Redekop, (2002). *From Violence to Blessing: How an understanding of deep-rooted conflict can open paths to reconciliation* (Toronto: Novalis), 161-172.

75. Miroslav Volf, "Forgiveness, Reconciliation, and Justice: A Christian Contribution to a More Peaceful Social Environment" in *Forgiveness and Reconciliation*, eds., Raymond G. Hemlick, S.J. and Rodney L. Peterson (Philadelphia/London: Templeton Foundation Press, 2001), 43.

76. Volf, 2001, 43.

77. Volf, 2000, 43–44.

78. Miroslav Volf, 'The Social Meaning of Reconciliation', *Interpretation*, Vol 54, No.2, 2001, pp. 165-166.

79. Volf, 2000, 39.

80. Miroslav Volf, *From Exclusion to Embrace: Reflections on Reconciliation*, http://www.christianembassyun.com/speech_by_dr_volf.htm, accessed 30 Dec 2005.

81. Volf, http://www.christianembassyun.com/speech_by_dr_volf.htm.

82. Volf, 2000, 40.

83. Volf, 1996, 111.

84. Volf, 1996, 111.

85. Volf, http://www.globalengagement.org/issues/2001/09/mvolf-bwf-the other-p.htm.

86. Charles Villa-Vicencio, "Telling One Another Stories: Toward A Theology of Reconciliation" in *The Reconciliation of Peoples: Challenge to the Churches*, eds., Gregory Baum and Harold Wells (Maryknoll, New York; Geneva, Switzerland: Orbis Books, World Council of Churches Publications, 1997), 34.

87. Villa-Vicencio, 1997, 34.

88. Volf, 1996, 116.

89. Volf, 1996, 116.

90. Volf, 1996, 117.

91. Volf, 1996, 117.

92. Volf, 1996, 140–141.

93. Volf, 1996,141–142.

94. Elie Wiesel, *From the Kingdom of Memory: Reminiscences* (New York: Summit Books, 1990), 61 in Miroslav Volf, "Theological Reflections in the Wake of 'Ethnic Cleansing,'" 247.

95. Miroslav Volf, *A Voice of One's Own: Public Faith in a Pluralistic World*, presented at the American Academy of Religion, Philadelphia, 19 Nov 2005, 14.

96. Volf, "The Trinity Is Our Social Program," 1998, 410.

97. Miroslav Volf, *After Our Likeness: The Church as the Image of the Trinity*, (Grand Rapids: Eerdmans, 1998), 211.

98. Volf, http://www.globalengagement.org/issues/2001/09/mvolf-bwf-the other-p.htm.

Relation is substituted for "relationship" to accent its agency. Paul Ricoeur reinforces Volf's inclusion of mutuality in his depiction of the otherness. Mutuality in Ricoeur is seen in such statements as, "selfhood of oneself implies the otherness to such an intimate degree that one cannot be thought of without the other." See Paul Ricoeur, *Oneself as Another* (Chicago: The University of Chicago Press, 1992), p. 3.

99. Volf, 1998, "The Trinity Is Our Social Program," 410.

100. Miroslav Volf, *A Voice of One's Own: Public Faith in a Pluralistic World*, presented at the American Academy of Religion, Philadelphia, 19 Nov 2005, p. 14.

101. Volf, "The Trinity Is Our Social Program," 1998, 410.

102. Volf, 1998, "The Trinity Is Our Social Program,"1998, 410.

103. Fumitaka Matsuoka, "A Reflection on 'Teaching Theology from an Intercultural Perspective,'" *Theological Education* 36, no 1 (1989), 35-42 cited in Robert Schreiter, *The New Catholicity: Theology Between the Global and the Local* (Maryknoll, N.Y.: Orbis Books, 2000), 40–41.

Conclusion

The inspiration for this book originates with the people of war. For this author, the impact of engaging local and regional religious leaders on the outskirts of Sarajevo during the Bosnian war was transformative. Journeying with Christian and Muslim clerics alike at the height of the conflict provided a rare occasion to connect with faith group leaders wrestling with how to live out their faith before their communities in such times. Building relation with these men of faith led to the development of a *trusting* environment where true *encounter* with the *other* transpired. These initial brushes with Religious Leader Engagement (RLE) have led to years of research into the external operational ministry of chaplains among the religious communities of indigenous populations. With its sundry manifestations, an identifiable *impulse* to engage the religious *other* has emerged among chaplains in theatres of operation around the world. Spanning as much as two decades, these *ad hoc* liaisons have grown in number and gained significance in terms of their strategic value to mission mandates. Commanders have come to recognize RLE as an effective means of interfacing with local populations, at times enhancing security through inter-communal dialogue. With this book, the hope is to broaden the discourse among government, military and academic circles as to the inherent benefits of institutionalizing RLE as a construct in conflict and post-conflict operational environments.

In much of contemporary conflict, unabated religious extremism serves as an added layer of complexity enflaming sentiments and fuelling conflict. Extremism's overpowering rhetoric often renders the *religious tolerant voice* inaudible. Developing RLE as a capability—inclusive of Religious Area Analysis (RAA)—within present operational structures promises to aid religious leaders beginning the arduous task of countering such rhetoric and its effects. The conceptual framework presented here clearly delineates the religious peacebuilding attributes of RLE and its dividends for operations. *Networking* among indigenous religious communities, chaplains bring to the table what others cannot—grasping something of the nuances of faith community issues that often escape detection, sometimes carrying heavy consequences. In future, with greater clarity to their role, chaplains may more consistently contribute to Key Leader Engagement teams, establishing contact with the religious element in their Area of Operations. Emphasized has been their natural rapport as religious leaders, creating the common ground necessary to listen and discern the needs of religious leaders and their communities, *partnering* with organizations committed to development and reconstruction. As a new paradigm, RLE advances further to include actual *peacebuilding* endeavors, manifesting differently depending on the type of operation: expeditionary, humanitarian or domestic. Underscored also is the adaptability of the construct, as principles may be generalized from one context to another—recognizing the reality that one size does not fit all. Whether RLE takes the form of humanitarian assistance (HA), dialogue (*encounter*), inter/intra-faith initiatives (*ritual*), or collaborative activities (*superordinate goals*), such initiatives advance conflict transformation. The injunction for chaplains is to stay in their own lane, yet offer more in terms of advising commanders on the religious terrain (RAA) and facilitating greater coexistence/integration among faith communities caught in conflict or experiencing its residual effects.

Where *mimetic* structures of violence plague communities with reciprocal and escalating hostilities, protracted conflict often becomes entrenched. For this reason the social psychology of inter-group reconciliation was consulted. Such grassroots initiatives hold within them the prospects for inter-communal dialogue and collaborative activities where greater levels of engendered trust and cooperation lead to the sure steps of instrumental reconciliation. Where conflict carries with it a religious dimension, those functioning within conflict resolution circles may want to consider the contributions chaplains potentially bring. The religious domain represents a pervasive and influential sector within indigenous cultures, often presenting to those espousing more western and secular approaches the added challenge of gaining access to key community leadership. As such, RLE presents as an emerging operational construct, seminal to the domain of religious *peacebuilding* and *conflict transformation*. Reaching across ethnic and religious divides in conflict zones to the estranged *other* RLE demonstrates an embryonic seeding of reconciliation. This catalytic (*mimetic modeling*) ministry of chaplains' draws alienated people together, thus commencing the process of conflict transformation as individuals and groups transcend conflict and begin the writing of new narratives. As was seen, such processes are integral to a reframed *interdependence*—renewed relation invoked by the *will to embrace*.

The case studies more than validate the versatility of this construct. Not only were chaplains featured in different operational environments and at different levels of Command, principles of RLE applied in one milieu were adaptable to another. Such malleability substantiates the assertion that rudiments of RLE may be generalized from one context to another. This is of increasing importance as one considers where the operational emphasis may lay in the years and decades to come. The necessity of military strength will assuredly remain a component of operations where conflicts persist. Denying extremist militants strategic advantage, while extracting failed and failing states from the quagmire of conflict internal to their borders, stands to extend evolving formulations of reconstruction and stabilization efforts well into the future. The complexity of contemporary conflict will continue to drive the requirement for further advancement in multidisciplinary approaches to resolving discord. Integrated *peacemaking* and *peacebuilding* initiatives will emanate from within the civil-military structures as well as from the interagency environment of International Organizations and NGOs. Whether future configurations of civil-military collaboration will be in the form of PRTs, one can only surmise. What is for certain is that the present trend toward greater civilian involvement will continue. Increased numbers of academics and practitioners possessing pertinent knowledge and honed skills applicable to resolving conflict and sustaining peace efforts is likely. It is hoped that a portion of these will be indigenous to the ethnic groups present. Military presence will always remain substantial due to security concerns vastly outnumbering any civilian contingent. Where there are concentrations of troops, chaplains will be among them. Given the adaptability of RLE as a conceptual model and operational construct, whatever the civil-military configuration, it is conceivable that a demand for chaplains with more specialist training in *peacebuilding* and *conflict transformation* could develop.

As RLE becomes more institutionalized, the probability of specialist chaplains embedded in PRT-like organizations holding to a civil-military configuration is on the horizon. Chaplains at the strategic level will be compelled to develop such formation. Training all chaplains is the ideal. Creating the expertise will require time, energy and resources. At a minimum, where chaplains network among local/regional religious leaders as members of Key Leader Engagement teams, tactical chaplain team leaders will require a greater understanding of how *peacebuilding* and *conflict transformation* principles permeate operational ministry: relation building, dialogue, intercommunal ritual events and *collaborative activities*, etc. More senior chaplains at the higher levels of Command will need similar training. Maintaining its chaplain focus is of singular importance to such instruction. It is due to the uniqueness of what the chaplain brings that RLE is finding its place as a structural construct within operational mandates. Much can be done by way of training to enhance the chaplains' role.

Be it conflict or post-conflict environments, much of the challenge of today's religious extremism finds its roots in Islam. It presents as a perversion of the hallowed truth found in Koranic scripture, yet persists as a powerful motivator among the uninformed and impressionable. The emphasis here is not intended to lessen the importance of acquiring knowledge of faith traditions outside of the Abrahamic fold. Rather, it is to underscore the reality that attention must be directed toward grasping something of the causes of Islamic militancy and the *peacebuilding* principles found within Islam that will counter its influence within communities struggling under its effects.

Salutary to future formation will be a familiarity with *peacebuilding* principles of faith traditions other than Christian, Islam in particular. Identifying models and methodologies indigenous to local culture and tradition will be helpful in giving balance to what is often seen by indigenous religious leaders as approaches too secular in nature. Conflict resolution based on Western values and norms cannot automatically be applied to Muslim cultural contexts. Islamic scholars and practitioners in the West explicate that different values and norms come into play in Islam. Compounding this, outcomes in Islamic approaches to resolving conflict are often less tangible—posing a challenge for the more Western style of individualism and negotiation. The suggestion here is not that chaplains become conflict resolution experts. There are many highly qualified and effective conflict resolution practitioners who will continue to perform an integral role in resolving conflicts among indigenous peoples. That said, as religious leaders in theatres of operation, the natural rapport and common ground that chaplains share with their religious counterparts will increasingly be of value to such efforts; chaplains are more able to span the secular-religious divide. Desirable also will be the capacity to make the links between what chaplains naturally bring and what resonates within the presenting faith tradition and culture. Absorbing the rudiments of *peacebuilding* inherent to Islamic tradition and culture will enable chaplains to discern and reinforce indigenous rituals and customs conducive to creating greater co-operation and *interdependence* among estranged communities. Indigenous religious leaders of *tolerant voice* are key to shaping ritual events. Peacebuilding activities integral to culture and community life hold far more promise than Western approaches that may be sound in principle and well-intentioned, yet appear foreign to indigenous faith group leaders and their communities. Local ownership of *peacebuilding* processes may be cultivated in such ways. *Collaborative activities* can function in a similar fashion. Community Peace Councils are one such instrument.

The international response to today's protracted conflicts has given rise to the advent of the Comprehensive Approach with its JIMP emphasis focusing here primarily on the Interagency and the Public Space aspects of operations. Interagency—Whole of Government for others—proposes intensified collaboration of military and civilian entities as a means of enhancing stability and reconstruction efforts. Concomitant with greater civil-military integration is the incorporation of a Phase 0 into campaign planning, with its aspiring emphasis on prevention by attending to strategies designed to preclude and resolve conflict before it has a chance to ossify—operational objectives for the future. These are consequential shifts in focus indicative of a move to greater inclusivity. Converging with such openness, RLE at tactical and operational levels represents an added dimension of mission effectiveness now recognized by leadership at strategic levels. The concept of chaplains with specialized training, conducting RLE-type activities within religious communities, collaborating with their Whole of Government partners has come of age. As government departments and agencies move toward incorporating a religious element within their approach to *peacebuilding* and *reconciliation* efforts, serious reflection must be given to the unique contribution chaplains bring as an operational resource.

To conclude these thoughts without mentioning some of the tensions surrounding RLE would be dismissive. There will always be those who will endeavor to co-opt chaplains' ability to easily *network* among religious communities for purposes other than what are intended. The non-combatant status of chaplains cannot be compromised, something that the mere perception of information gathering for intelligence purposes would jeopardize. Aligning RLE with Influence Activities presents similar challenges. *Ministry* first-order effects must focus on the *well-being* of the *other*, the pursuance of peace and the resolution of conflict. Delineating clear lines as to the employment of RLE and to whom the chaplain reports will reduce the likelihood of such occurrences. Understandable as well is the tendency for Command to see RLE as simply another tool to be utilized in the accomplishment of the mission. Religious leaders often measure continued dialogue and co-operation with chaplains by the degree of trust and authenticity they detect. In contributing to overall mission effectiveness, chaplains will need to guard against *instrumentalism* that undermines the integrity that genuine *encounter* with the *other* fosters.

These are some of the more pronounced tensions that exist for RLE in operational environments. For some chaplains *external operational ministry* of this nature may simply be a bridge too far. As RLE emerges as an operational construct each will have to determine what their role will be in this regard. Granted, tensions do exist. This need not become an impediment. Chaplains will become more adept at managing such concerns and educating leadership as to the benefits and limitations of RLE. The complexities of current and future operational environments will undoubtedly implicate the religious dimension. The Religious Leader Engagement of chaplains with those of the *tolerant voice of religion* among indigenous populations stands as an untapped resource for Command and the Whole of Government community in the collaborative efforts of mitigating and resolving conflict.

Bibliography

Abd al Ati, Hammudah. *Islam in Focus.* Beltsville, Maryland: Amana Publications, 1998.

Abu-Nimer, Mohammed. "Peacebuilding and Nonviolence in Islamic Religion and Culture: A theoretical Framework." Pp. 5–84 in *Nonviolence and Peacebuilding in Islam: Theory and Practice.* Gainesville: University Press of Florida, 2003.

———. *Reconciliation, Justice and Coexistence: Theory and Practice.* Lanham, Maryland: Lexington Books, 2001.

Adams, George. "Chaplains as Liaisons with Religious Leaders: Lessons from Iraq and Afghanistan." *Peaceworks*, No. 56. Washington D.C.: The United States Institute of Peace, 2006. http://www.usip.org/publications/chaplains-liaisons-religious-leaders-lessons-iraq-and-afghanistan.

Agnew, John. "Beyond Reason: Spatial and Temporal Sources of Ethnic Conflicts." Pp. 41–52 in *Intractable Conflicts and Their Transformation*, eds. Louis Kriesberg, Terrell A. Northrup & Stuart Thorson. Syracuse, New York: Syracuse University Press, 1989.

Annan, Kofi A. *Prevention of Armed Conflict: Report of the Secretary* General, A/55/985–S/2001/574, United Nations General Assembly, Fifty-fifth Session, 2001. http://www.reliefweb.int/library/documents/2001/un-conflprev-07jun.htm

Anwar, Raja. *The Tragedy of Afghanistan: A First-hand Account*, translated from the Urdu by Khalid Hasan. London and New York: Verso, 1988.

Apostolov, Mario. *Religious Minorities, Nation States and Security: Five Cases from the Balkans and Eastern Mediterranean.* Aldershot, Hampshire, England: Ashgate, 2001.

Appleby, R. Scott. *The Ambivalence of the Sacred: Religion, Violence, and Reconciliation.* Lanham, Maryland: Rowman and Littlefield, 2000.

———. "Retrieving the Missing Dimension of Statecraft." Pp. 231–58 in *Faith-based Diplomacy: Trumping Realpolitik*, ed. Douglas Johnston. Oxford: Oxford University Press, 2003.

——— and Richard Cizik. *Engaging Religious Communities Abroad: A New Imperative for U.S. Foreign Policy*, Report of the Task Force on Religion and the Making of Foreign Policy. Council on the Global Affairs: Chicago, 2010.

Armstrong, Karen. *The Battle For God*, New York: Ballantine Publishing Group, 2000.

Aukerman, Dale. *Reckoning With Apocalypse: Terminal Politics and Christian Hope.* New York: Crossroad Publishing, 1993.

Avruch, Kevin. *Culture and Conflict Resolution.* Washington, D.C.: United States Institute of Peace Press, 1998.

Baron, Ruben M. "Reconciliation, Trust, and Cooperation: Using Bottom-Up and Top-Down Strategies to Achieve Peace in Israeli-Palestinian Conflict." Pp. 275–98 in *The Social Psychology of Intergroup Reconciliation*, eds. Arie Nadler, Thomas E. Malloy and Jeffery D. Fisher. New York: Oxford University Press, 2008.

Bar-Tal, Daniel and Gemma H. Bennink. "The Nature of Reconciliation as an Outcome and as a Process." Pp. 11–38 in *From Conflict Resolution to Reconciliation*, ed. Yaacov Bar-Siman-tov. New York: Oxford University Press, 2004.

Bartoli, Andrea. "Christianity and Peace." Pp. 147–56 in *Religion and Peacebuilding*, eds. Harold Coward and Gordon S. Smith. Albany: State University of New York Press.

Battle, Michael. *Reconciliation: The Ubuntu Theology of Desmond Tutu.* Cleveland, Ohio: Pilgrim Press, 1997.

Blanchard, Christopher M. "The Islamic Traditions of Wahabbism and Salafiyya." *CRS Report for Congress.* 24 Jan 2008. http://www.fas.org/sgp/crs/misc/RS21695.pdf.

Bloomer, Fiona and Peter Weinreich. "Cross-community Relations Projects and Interdependent Identities." Pp. 141–62 in *Researching the Troubles: Social Science Perspectives on the Northern Ireland Conflict*, eds. Owen Hargie and David Dickson. Edinburgh and London: Mainstream Publishing, 2003.

British Army Field Manual, Volume 1, Part 10, Countering Insurgency, Army Code 71876, October 2009. http://news.bbc.co.uk/2/shared/bsp/hi/pdfs/16_11_09_army_manual.pdf.

Building on Success: The Afghanistan Compact. London Conference on Afghanistan. London, England, 31 Jan–1 Feb 2006. http://www.ssrnetwork.net/document_library/detail/5034/building-on-success-the-afghanistan-compact

Burton, John. *Conflict: Human Needs Theory.* New York: St. Martin's Press, 1990.

Carter, Judy and Gordon S. Smith. "Religious Peacebuilding: From Potential to Action." Pp. 279–301 in *Religion and Peacebuilding*, eds. Harold Coward and Gordon S. Smith. Albany: State University of New York Press, 2004.

Civil-Military Agenda, Danish Institute for International Studies (DIIS), http://www.diis.dk/sw69236.asp

Cohen, Raymond. *Negotiating Across Cultures: International Communication in an Interdependent World*, revised ed. Washington, D.C.: United States Institute of Peace Press, 1991.

Comprehensive Approach: Trends, Challenges and Possibilities for Cooperation in Crisis Prevention and Management. Based on Comprehensive Approach Seminar 17 June 2008 Helsinki, Articles from International Actors and from National Delegations, Work of the CAS Research Team and Expertise of the Crisis Management Initiative. Ministry of Defence: Helsinki, Finland, 2008.

The Comprehensive Approach Concept. Ottawa, Canada: Chief of Force Development, National Defence, 2010.

Convention for the Amelioration of the Condition of the Wounded and Sick in Armies in the Field. Geneva, 6 July 1906. http://www.icrc.org/ihl.nsf/WebART/180-170010?OpenDocument.

Convention for the Amelioration of the Condition of the Wounded and Sick in Armies in the Field. Geneva, 27 July 1929. http://www.icrc.org/ihl.nsf/WebART/300-420015?OpenDocument.

Counterinsurgency, FM 3-24, MCWP 3-33.5 Headquarters, Dept. of the Army, 2006. http://usacac.army.mil/cac2/Repository/Materials/COIN-FM3-24.pdf.

Crossan, John D. *The Historical Jesus.* San Francisco: Harper & Row, 1991.

Currall, S. and T. Judge. "Measuring trust between organizational boundary persons." Pp. 151–70 in *Organizational Behavior and Human Decision Processes* 64 (2), 1995.

Cusimano Love, Maryann. "Partnering for Peace in the Philippines: Military and Religious Engagement." Paper presented at the Chaplains Workshop on Religion, Conflict and Peace at the Pentagon, hosted by Georgetown University's Berkley Center for Religion, Peace & World Affairs and National Defense University's Institute for National Security, Ethics and Leadership, Washington, D.C., 24–25 March 2010.

Danan, Liora and Alice Hunt. *Mixed Blessings: U.S. Government and Engagement with Religion in Conflict Prone Settings.* Centre for Strategic and International Studies: Washington, D.C., 2007. http://csis.org/files/media/csis/pubs/070820_religion.pdf.

Darby, John. "Northern Ireland: The Persistence and Limitations of Violence." Pp. 151–59 in *Conflict and Peacemaking in Multiethnic Societies*, ed. Joseph Montville (Lexington/Toronto: Lexington Books, 1990.

Davie, G. *Religion in Modern Europe: A Memory Mutates.* Oxford: Oxford University Press, 2000.

――――. *Religion in Britain since 1945: Believe without Belonging.* Oxford: Blackwell, 1994.

Deady, Timothy K. "Lessons from a Successful Counterinsurgency: The Philippines, 1899–1902." Pp. 53–68 in *Parameters*, Spring 2005. http://www.carlisle.army.mil/ USAWC/parameters/Articles/05spring/deady.pdf.

De Gruchy, John. W. *Reconciliation: Restoring Justice.* Minneapolis: Fortress Press, 2002.

Designing Canada's Army of Tomorrow: A Land Operations 2021 Publication. IDDN-NDID B-GL-300-000/AG-002. Kingston, Ontario: Dept. of National Defence, 2011.http://www. army.forces.gc.ca/DLCD-DCSFT/specialPubs-eng.asp.

De Vos, George A. "Ethnic Pluralism: Conflict and Accommodation: The Role of Ethnicity in Social History." Pp. 15–47 in *Ethnic Identity: Creation, Conflict, and Accommodation*, eds. Lola Lomanucci-Ross and George A. De Vos. Walnut Creek, California: Altamira Press, 1995.

Diamond, Louise and John MacDonald, *Multi-track Diplomacy: A Systems Approach to Peace-building.* West Hartford, Connecticut: Kumarian Press, 1996.

Doran, Robert. "Psychic Conversion." Introduction, pp. 8–9 in *Theology and the Dialectics of History.* Toronto, Buffalo, London: University of Toronto Press, 1990.

Douglas, Mary. *Purity and Danger.* London: Routledge, 1966.

Duffy Toft, Monica, 2007. "Getting Religion: The Puzzling Case of Islam and Civil War." Pp. 97–131 in *International Security Vol. 31, Issue 4*, Spring 2007. http://www.mitpressjournals. org/doi/pdfplus/10.1162/isec.2007.31.4.97 .

Dupree, Louis. *Afghanistan.* Karachi, Pakistan: Oxford University Press,1973.

Dziedzic, Michael J. and Colonel Michael K. Seidl. "Provincial Reconstruction Teams and Military Relations with International and Nongovernmental Organizations in Afghanistan - *Special Report.* United States Institute of Peace, No 147, September 2005. http:// www.usip.org/files/resources/sr147.pdf.

Eckert, Julia. "Reconciling the Mohalla: Politics of Violence and the Strength and Limits of Mediation in Bombay." Pp. 365–89 in *Religion Between Violence and Reconciliation*, ed. Thomas Scheffler. Beirut: Orient-Institute, 2002.

Eide, Espen Barth, Anja Therese Kaspersen, Randolph Kent and Karen von Hippel. *Report on Integrated Missions: Practical Perspectives and Recommendations,* Independent Study for the Expanded UN ECHA Core Group, May 2005. http://www.google.ca/ search?q=Report+on+Integrated+Missions&ie=utf-8&oe=utf-8&aq=t&rls=org.mozilla:en-US:official&client=firefox-a.

Emadi, Hafzullah. *Culture and Customs of Afghanistan.* Westport, Connecticut: Greenwood Press, 2005.

English, Allen, Daniel Gosselin, Howard Coombs, and Laurence M. Hickey. *The Operational Art, Canadian Perspectives – Context and Concepts.* Kingston, Ontario: Canadian Defence Academy Press, 2005.

――――. "The Operational Art: Theory, Practice, and Implications for the Future." Pp. 1–74 in *The Operational Art, Canadian Perspectives – Context and Concepts*, eds. Allen English, Daniel Gosselin, Howard Coombs, and Laurence M. Hickey. Kingston, Ontario: Canadian Defence Academy Press, 2005.

Ewans, Martin. *Afghanistan: A Short History of Its People and Politics* (New York: HarperCollins, 2002.

――――. *Conflict in Afghanistan: Studies in Asymmetric Warfare.* Oxon and New York: Routledge, 2005.

Farmer, Paul. *Pathologies of Power: Health, Human Rights and the New War on the Poor.* Berkley and Los Angeles: University of California Press, 2003.

Finnemore, Martha and Kathryn Sikkink. "International Norm Dynamics and Political Change." Pp. 887–917 in *International Organization*, International Organization at Fifty: Exploration and Contestation in the Study of World Politics, Vol. 52, No.4, 1998.

Fukuyama, Francis. *Nation Building: Beyond Afghanistan and Iraq.* Baltimore, MD: Johns Hopkins University Press, 2006.

Geneva Convention for the Amelioration of the Condition of the Wounded and Sick in Armed Forces in the Field of August 12, 1949, 75 U.N.T.S. 970, Entry into Force 21 October 1950. http://www1.umn.edu/humanrts/instree/y1gcacws.htm.

Girard, René. *Deceit, Desire and the Novel: Self and the Other in Literary Structure* , trans. by Yvonne Freccero, Original Publication, 1961: Trans. 1965, Paperback edition. Baltimore and London: Johns Hopkins University Press, 1976.

———. *Violence and the Sacred*, trans. by Patrick Gregory. Baltimore, MD: John Hopkins University Press, English Translation, 1977.

———. *The Girard Reader*, ed. James G. Williams 2nd edition. New York: Crossroad Publishing Company, 1996.

Gizewski, Peter. "Religious Leader Engagement: thoughts on its place in CF thinking," Toronto: DRDC CORA 2012, p. 212, 19 September, 2012.

Global Peace and Security Program (GPSP), Foreign Affairs and International Trade Canada, 10 August 2010. http://www.international.gc.ca/START-GTSR/gpsp-ppsm.aspx.

Gohari, M. J. *The Taliban Ascent to Power*. Oxford, England: Oxford University Press, 2000.

Gopin, Marc. *Between Eden and Armageddon: The Future of World Religions, Violence, and Peacemaking.* New York: Oxford University Press, 2000.

———. "The Religious Component of Mennonite Peacemaking and Its Global Implications." Pp. 233–55 in *From the Ground Up: Mennonite Contributions to International Peacebuilding*, eds. Cynthia Sampson and John Paul Lederach. New York: Oxford University Press, 2000.

———. *Holy War, Holy Peace: How Religion Can Bring Peace to the Middle East*. New York: Oxford University Press, 2002.

———. *To Make the Earth Whole: The Art of Citizen Diplomacy in an Age of Religious Militancy*. Lanham, Maryland: Rowan and Littlefield, 2009.

Gross Stein, Janice and Eugene Lang. *The Unexpected War.* Toronto: Viking Canada, 2007.

Grzyb, Amanda F. *The World and Darfur: International Response to Crimes Against Humanity in Western Sudan*. Montreal & Kingston: McGill-Queen's University Press, 2009.

Guiding Principles for Stabilization and Reconstruction. Washington, D.C.: the United States Institute of Peace Press & The United States Peacekeeping and Stability Operations Institute, 2009. http://www.usip.org/files/resources/guiding_principles_full.pdf.

Gundry-Volf, Judith. "Spirit, Mercy and the Other." Pp. 508–23 in *Theology Today*, Vol. 51, No. 4, January 1995.

———. and Miroslav Volf. "Exclusion and Embrace: Theological Reflections in the Wake of Ethnic Cleansing." Pp. in *A Spacious Heart: Essays on Identity and Belonging.* Harrisburg, Pennsylvania: Trinity Press International, 1997.

Gurr, Tedd Robert. *Minorities at Risk: A Global View of Enthnopolitical Conflicts*. Washington, D.C.: United States Institute of Peace, 1993.

Herbst, Ambassador John E. *2009 Year in Review: Smart Power in Action*. United States Department of State, Coordinator for Reconstruction and Stabilization, http://www.state.gov/j/cso/scrsarchive/releases/183741.htm.

Hertog, Katrien. *The Complex Reality of Religious Peacebuilding: Conceptual Contributions and Critical Analysis*. Lanham, Maryland: Lexington Books, 2010.

Hewstone, Miles, Jared B. Kenworthy, Ed Cairns, Nocole Tausch, Joanne Hughes, Tania Tam, Alberto Voci, Ulrich Von Hecker, and Catherine Pinder. "Stepping Stones to Reconciliation in Northern Ireland: Intergroup Contact, Forgiveness, and Trust." Pp. 199–226 in *The Social Psychology of Intergroup Reconciliation*, eds. Arie Nadler, Thomas E. Malloy and Jeffery D. Fisher. New York: Oxford University Press, 2008.

Hoffman, Bruce. *Inside Terrorism: Revised and Expanded Edition.* New York: Columbia University Press, 2006.

Horowitz, Donald A. *Ethnic Groups in Conflict*. Berkeley: University of California Press, 1985.

Huda, Qamar-ul. "Enhancing Skills and Capacity Building in Islamic Peacemaking." Pp. 205–25 in *Crescent and Dove: Peace and Conflict Resolution in Islam*, ed. Qamar-ul Huda. Washington D. C.: United States Institute of Peace, 2010.

Hull, Jeanne F. *Iraq: Strategic Reconciliation, Targeting and Key Leader Engagement*—Summary. Carlisle, PA: Strategic Studies Institute, U.S. Army War College, 2009. http://www.strategicstudiesinstitute.army.mil/pubs/display.cfm?pubID=938

Ignatieff, Michael, *The Warrior's Honour*. Toronto: Penguin Books, 1998.

Janoff-Bulman, Ronnie. *Shattered Assumptions: Towards a New Psychology of Trauma*. New York: Free Press, 1992.

JIIM Lessons Learned Report (Joint, Interagency, Intergovernmental, Multinational). Center for Army Lessons Learned, Fort Leavenworth, Kansas: OIF and OEF Joint Context and Knowledge Training Gaps, No. 07-24, May 2007. http://www.google.ca/search?q=JIIM&ie=utf-8&oe=utf-8&aq=t&rls=org.mozilla:en-US:official&client=firefox-a#q=US+Army+and+JIIM&hl=en&client=firefox-a&rls=org.mozilla:en-US:official&prmd=ivns&ei=d_AkTYeOKs6Qswax1rHdAg&start=10&sa=N&fp=825210affd154cf0.

Johnston, Douglas. "Introduction: Beyond Power Politics." Pp. 3–7 in *Religion, the Missing Dimension of Statecraft*, eds. Douglas Johnston and Cynthia Sampson. New York: Oxford University Press, 1994.

———. *Faith-Based Diplomacy: Trumping Realpolitik*. New York: Oxford University Press, 2003.

Joint Doctrine and Concepts Centre. Joint Discussion Note 4/05, *The Comprehensive Approach*. 2006. http://www.google.ca/search?client=safari&rls=en&q=Joint+Doctrine+and+Concept+Centre,+The+comprehensive+Approach&ie=UTF-8&oe=UTF-8&redir_esc=&ei=ukPQS_C1KIT68Abvh62oDw.

Juergensmeyer, Mark. *Terror in the Mind of God*. Berkeley, Los Angeles, London: University of California Press, 2000.

Kaldor, Mary. *New & Old Wars: Organized Violence in a Global Era, 2nd Edition*. Stanford, California: Stanford University Press, 2006.

Kaplan, R.D. *Balkan Ghosts: A Journey Through History*. New York: Vintage Books, 1993.

Kelman, Herbert C. "Reconciliation From a Social-Psychological Perspective." Pp. 15–32 in *The Social Psychology of Intergroup Reconciliation*, eds. Arie Nadler, Thomas E. Malloy and Jeffery D. Fisher. New York: Oxford University Press, 2008.

Kennedy, John F. *Profiles in Courage*. New York: Harper & Row, 1956.

Kim, Sebastian C. H., Pauline Kollontai and Greg Hoyland. *Peace and Reconciliation: In Search of Shared Identity*. Hampshire, England and Burlington, Vermont: Ashgate, 2008.

King, Craig. "Effects Based Operations: Buzzword or Blueprint." Pp. 313–30 in *The Operational Art, Canadian Perspectives – Context and Concepts*, eds. Allan English, Daniel Gosselin, Howard Coombs, and Laurence M. Hickey. Kingston, Ontario: Canadian Defence Academy Press, 2005.

Klosinski, L.E. *The Meals in Mark*. Ann Arbor, Michigan.: University Microfilms International, 1988.

Kramer, R.M. and P.J. Carnevale. "Trust and intergroup negotiation." Pp. 432–50 in *Intergroup Processes*, eds. R. Brown and S. Gaertner. Malden, MA: Blackwell, 2003.

Kraybill, Ron. "Reflections on Twenty Years of Peacebuilding." Pp. 30–44 in *From the Ground Up: Mennonite Contributions to International Peacebuilding*, eds. Cynthia Sampson and John Paul Lederach. New York: Oxford University Press, 2000.

Kriesberg, Louis. "Comparing Reconciliation Actions within and between Countries." Pp. 81–110 in *From Conflict Resolution to Reconciliation*, ed. Yaacov Bar-Siman-Tov. New York: Oxford University Press, 2004.

Kristiva, Julia. *Powers of Horror: An Essay in Abjection*. New York: Columbia University Press, 1982.

Land Force: Counter-Insurgency Operations B-GL-323-004/FP-003. Kingston, Ontario: Army Publishing Office, 2008. http://info.publicintelligence.net/CanadaCOIN.pdf.

Land Operations, B-GL-300-001/FP-001 (209-01-01). Ottawa: DND, 2008. https://info.publicintelligence.net/CanadaLandOps.pdf.

Landau, Yehezkel, 2003. Healing the Holy Land, *Peaceworks,* No. 51. Washington, D.C.: United States Institute of Peace. http://www.usip.org/publications/healing-holy-land-interreligious-peacebuilding-israelpalestine.

————. "Peacebuilding in Israel/Palestine: A 25-Year Retrospective" in Waging Peace: A Two-Part Discussion of Religion-Based Peacemaking, Washington National Cathedral, November 2003.

Law of Armed Conflict at the Operational and Tactical Levels, Joint Doctrine Manual, B-GJ-005-104/FP-021, 2001, Office of the Judge Advocate General, National Defence, Canada, GL-13. http://www.forces.gc.ca/jag/publications/oplaw-loiop/loac-ddca-2004-eng.pdf.

Lebaron, Michelle and Venashri Pillay. *Conflict Across Cultures: A Unique Experience of Bridging Differences.* Boston and London: Intercultural Press, 2006.

Lederach, John Paul. *Building Peace: Sustainable Reconciliation in Divided Societies.* Washington, D. C.: United States Institute of Peace, 1997.

————. "Journey From Resolution to Transformative Peacebuilding." Pp. 45–55 in *From the Ground Up: Mennonite Contributions to International Peacebuilding*, eds. Cynthia Sampson and John Paul Lederach. New York: Oxford University Press, 2000.

————. *The Moral Imagination: The Art and Soul of Building Peace.* New York: Oxford University Press, 2005.

————, Reina Neufeldt and Hal Culbertson. *Reflective Peacebuilding: A Planning, Monitoring, and Learning Toolkit.* Notre Dame, Indiana and Bangkok, Thailand: Kroc Institute for Peace Studies and Catholic Relief Services, East Asia Regional Office, 2007.

————, and R. Scott Appleby. "Strategic Peacebuilding: An Overview." Pp. 19–44 in *Strategies of Peace: Transforming Conflict in a Violent World*, eds. Daniel Philpot and Gerard Powers. New York: Oxford University Press, 2010.

Lee, William Sean, Chaplain (Col.) army, LtCol. Christopher J. Burke, USAF and LtCol. Zonna M. J. Crayne. "Military Chaplains as Peacebuilders: Embracing Indigenous Religious in Stability Operations," in *The Cadre Papers*, No. 20, February, 2005.

Leslie, Lieutenant-General Andrew, Mr. Peter Gizewski, and Lieutenant-Colonel Michael Rostek. "Developing a Comprehensive Approach to Canadian Forces Operations." Pp. 11–20 in *Canadian Military Journal*, Vol. 9. No. 1, 2008. http://www.journal.forces.gc.ca/vo9/no1/04-leslie-eng.asp.

Levinas, Emmanuel. *Totality and Infinity: An Essay on Exteriority*, trans. Alphonso Lingis. Pittsburgh: Duquesne University Press, 1969.

Lévi-Strauss, Claude. *Triste Tropiques.* Paris: Librarie Plon, 1955.

Levy, Jack S. "International Sources of Interstate and Intrastate War." Pp. 17–38 in *Leashing the Dogs of War: Conflict Management in a Divided World*, eds. Chester A. Crocker, Fen Osler Hampson and Pamela Aall. Washington, D.C.: United States Institute of Peace, 2007.

Lewicki, R.J. & C. Wiethoff. "Trust, Trust Development, and Trust Repair." Pp. 86–107 in *The Handbook of Conflict Resolution*, eds. M. Deutsch & P.T. Coleman. San Francisco: Josey-Bas Publishers, 2000.

———— and Edward C. Tomlinson, "Trust and Trust Building" in *Beyond Intractability*, eds. Guy Burgess and Heidi Burgess (Boulder, Colorado: Conflict Resolution Consortium, 2003), <http://www.beyondintractability.org/essay/trust_building/.

Little, David. *Peacemakers in Action: Profiles of Religion in Conflict Resolution.* New York: Cambridge University Press, 2007.

MacAskill, Ewen. "Invisible man at the United Nations: A leaked memo has questioned Ban Ki-moon's skill at global diplomacy." pp. 30-31 in *Guardian Weekly.* 6–12 August 2010.

Marsden, Peter. *The Taliban: War, Religion and the New Order in Afghanistan.* New York: Oxford University Press, 1998.

Matsuoka, Fumitaka. "A Reflection on 'Teaching Theology from an Intercultural Perspective.'" Pp. 35–42 in *Theological Education* 36, no 1, 1989.

McConnell, John A. *Mindful Meditation: A Handbook for Buddhist Peacemakers.* Thailand: Buddhist Research Institute & Mahachula Buddhist University, 1995.

McFate, Sean. "U.S. Africa Command: A New Strategic Paradigm?" Pp. 10–21 in *Military Review* 17. January–February, 2008: 10–21.

McLeod. C. *Trust, The Stanford Encyclopedia of Philosophy.* Spring 2011 Edition, ed. Edward N. Zalta, http://plato.stanford.edu/archives/spring2011/entries/trust

Mirkovic, Todor. *Current Situation and the Ways Leading to Building Peace and Stability in the Balkans—An Assessment and Preliminary Study.* Belgrade, Serbia: European Centre for Peace and Development, 2009.

Mitchell, Christopher. "Mennonite Approaches to Peace and Conflict Resolution." pp. 218–32 in *From the Ground Up: Mennonite Contributions to International Peacebuilding*, eds. Cynthia Sampson and John Paul Lederach. New York: Oxford University Press, 2000.

Mitchell, Claire. *Religion, Identity and Politics in Northern Ireland.* Aldershot, England & Burlington, Vermont: Ashgate, 2006.

Mojzes, Paul. *Yugoslavian Inferno: Ethnoreligious Warfare in the Balkans.* New York: Continuum Publishing Company, 1995.

———. *Religion and the War in Bosnia.* Atlanta, Georgia: Scholars Press, 1998.

———. "The Camouflaged Role of Religion in the War in B&H." Pp. 74–98 in *Religion and the War in Bosnia*, ed. Paul Mojzes. Atlanta, Georgia: Scholars Press, 1998.

Moltmann, Jürgen. *The Spirit of Life: A Universal Affirmation*, translated by Margaret Kohl. San Francisco: HarperCollins, 1992.

Moore, S.K. and Capt. Imam Suleyman Demiray. "The Canadian Forces Chaplain Branch: Modeling Interfaith Cooperation and Pluralism in Afghanistan." Pp. 5–8 in *Ecumenism*, No. 165, March 2007.

———. *Military Chaplains as Agents of Peace: The Theology and Praxis of Reconciliation in Stability Operations* (Dissertation). Ottawa, Canada: University of Ottawa / Saint Paul University, 2008.

———. "Operational Chaplains: Establishing Trust with the Religious Other through the Building of Relation." Pp. 73–86 in *In Harms Way: Leveraging Trust—A Force Multiplier for Today.* Kingston, Ontario: Canadian Defence Academy, 2008.

———. "Interdependence and the Role of Religious Peacebuilders: Embracing the Other—Building Bridges." Pp. 83–99 in *National and Inter-Ethnic Reconciliation, Religious Tolerance and Human Security in the Balkans*, Proceedings of the Fifth ECPD International Conference, eds. Takehrio Togo and Negoslav P Ostojic. Belgrade, Serbia: European Center for Peace and Development, 2010.

———, and Vern Redekop. *Vision and Strategy for Reconciliation as an Aspect Of the Whole of Government Approach to Nation Building: A Generative Dialogue.* Saint Paul University, Ottawa, Canada, 6–8 June 2010. http://www.amiando.com/eventResources/t/U/lLGwe2dwAa4xrq/Concept%20Paper.Generative%20Dialogue.pdf.

———. "Religious Leader Engagement and the Comprehensive Approach: An Enhanced Capability for Operational Chaplains as Whole of Government Partners." Pp. 179–92 in *Security Operations in the 21st Century: Canadian Perspectives on the Comprehensive Approach*, eds. Michael Rostek and Peter Gizewski. Montreal and Kingston: McGill-Queen's University Press, 2011.

Moses, Rafael, M.D. "Self, Self-View, and Identity." Pp. 47–55 in *The Psychodynamics of International Relationships*, Vol. 1, eds. Vamik D. Volkan, Demetrios A. Julias & Joseph V. Montville. Lexington, Toronto: Lexington Books, 1990.

Nadler, Arie and Nurit Shnabel. "Instrumental and Socioemotional Paths to Intergroup Reconciliation and the Needs-Based Model of Socioemotional Reconciliation." Pp. 37–56 in *The Social Psychology of Intergroup Reconciliation*, eds. Arie Nadler, Thomas E. Malloy and Jeffery D. Fisher. New York: Oxford University Press, 2008.

Nieburh, Reinhold. *The Nature and Destiny of Man*, vol. 1. Louisville, Kentucky: John Knox Press, 1996.

Northrup, Terrell A. "The Dynamic of Identity in Personal and Social Conflict." Pp. 55–82 in *Intractable Conflicts and Their Transformation*, eds. Louis Kriesberg, Terrell A. Northrup and Stuart Thorson. Syracuse, New York: Syracuse University Press, 1989.

Oglesby, W.B. Jr. *Biblical Themes For Pastoral Care.* Nashville: Abingdon Press, 1980.

Otis, Pauletta. "Religion and War in the Twenty-first Century." Pp. 11–24 in *Religion and Security: The New Nexus in International Relations*, eds. R. A. Seiple & D. R. Hoover. Lanham. Maryland: Rowan and Littlefield, 2004.

Pannenberg, Wolfhart. *Anthropology in Theological Perspective*, translated by Michael J. O'Connell. Philadelphia: Westminster, 1985.

Party, Bernard, and M. P. Chair. *Exploring Canada's Relations with the Countries of the Muslim World.* Report of the Standing Committee on Foreign Affairs and International Trade: Ottawa, Canada, 2004.

Perica, Vjekoslav. *Balkan Idols: Religion and Nationalism in Yugoslav States.* New York: Oxford University Press, 2002.

Petito Fabio and Pavlos Hatzopoulos. *Religion in International Relations: The Return from Exile.* New York: Palgrave Macmillan, 2003.

Plantinga, Cornelius. *Not The Way It's Supposed To Be: A Breviary of Sin.* Grand Rapids, Michigan: Eerdmans, 1995.

Porter, S.E. "Peace, Reconciliation." Pp. 695–96 in Hawthorne and Martin, *Dictionary of Paul and His Letters.* Downers Grove, Illinois: Intervarsity Press, 1993.

Powers, Gerard F. "Religion and Peacebuilding." Pp. 317-52 in *Strategies of Peace: Transforming Conflict in a Violent World*, eds. Daniel Philpott and Gerard F. Powers. New York: Oxford University Press, 2010.

Principles for Good International Engagement in Fragile States, Organization for Economic Cooperation and Development (OECD). http://www.oecd.org/document/40/ 0,3343,en_21571361_42277499_42283112_1_1_1_1,00.html.

Rashid, Ahmed. *Taliban.* New Haven: Yale Nota Bene, 2001.

Redekop, V.N. "Deep-Rooted Conflict Theory and Pastoral Counselling: Dealing With What One Sees." Pp. 9–24 in *Pastoral Sciences*, Vol 20, No. 1, 2001. http:// www.counsellingandspirituality.com/english/journal.php?annee=2001#resume.

———. *From Violence to Blessing: How An Understanding of Deep-Rooted Conflict Can Open Paths to Reconciliation.* Toronto: Novalis, 2002.

———, and O. Gasana. "Implication of Religious Leaders in Mimetic Structures of Violence: The Case of Rwanda." Pp. 117–37 in *Journal of Religion & Society, Supplement Series 2*, 2007. http://moses.creighton.edu/jrs/toc/2007SS.html

——— and Shirley Paré. *Beyond Control: A Mutual Respect Approach to Protest Crowd-Police Reactions.* New York: Bloomsbury Academic, 2010.

Religion, Conflict & Peacebuilding: An Introductory Program Guide, United States Agency for International Development, 2009. http://transition.usaid.gov/our_work/crosscutting_programs/conflict/publications/docs/Religion_Conflict_and_Peacebuilding_Toolkit.pdf.

The Responsibility to Protect: Report of the International Commission on Intervention and State Sovereignty. Ottawa, Canada: International Development Research Centre, 2001.

Ricoeur, Paul. *Oneself as Another.* Chicago: The University of Chicago Press, 1992.

———. *The Symbolism of Evil.* Boston: Beacon Press, 1967.

Rogers, Rita, M.D. "Intergenerational Transmission of Historical Enmity." Pp. 91–96 in *The Psychodynamics of International Relationships, Vol 1*, eds. Vamik D. Volkan, Demetrios A. Julias and Joseph V. Montville. Lexington, Toronto: Lexington Books, 1990.

Romney Wegner, Judith. *Chattel or Person? The Status of Women in the Mishnah.* New York: Oxford University Press, 1988.

Rosen, Frederik. "Third-generation Civil-Military Relations." Pp. 27–42 in *Prism 2*, No. 1, 2010.

Rostek, Michael and Peter Gizewski. *Security Operations in the 21st Century: Canadian Perspective on the Comprehensive Approach.* Montreal and Kingston: McGill-Queens University Press, 2011.

Rubin, Barry. "Religion and Internal Affairs." Pp. 20–34 in *Religion, the Missing Dimension of Statecraft*, eds. Douglas Johnston and Cynthia Sampson. New York: Oxford University Press, 1994.

Runyon, Theodore. *Theology, Politics, and Peace.* Maryknoll, New York: Orbis Books, 1989.

Ryan, Stephan. *Ethnic Conflict and international Relations.* Aldershot, England and Burlington, Vermont: Ashgate, 1995.

Sachedina, Abdulaziz. *The Islamic Roots of Democratic Pluralism.* New York: Oxford University Press, 2001.

Sampson, Cynthia. "Religion and Peacebuilding." Pp. 273–318 in *Peacemaking in International Conflict*, eds. I. William Zartman and J. Lewis Rasmussen. Washington, D.C.: United States Institute of Peace, 1997.

Samuel, R. and P. Thompson. *The Myths We Live By.* London: Routledge, 1990.

Schirch, Lisa. *Ritual and Symbol in Peacebuilding.* Bloomfield, Connecticut: Kumarian Press, 2005.

———. "The Civil Society-Military Relationship in Afghanistan" in *Peacebrief.* Washington, D.C.: United States Institute of Peace, No. 56, September 24, 2010.

Schreiter, Robert J. *Reconciliation: Mission & Ministry in a Changing Social Order.* Maryknoll, New York and Newton, Massachusetts: Orbis Books and Boston Theological Institute, 1992.

———. *The New Catholicity: Theology Between the Global and the Local.* Maryknoll, New York: Orbis Books, 2000.

———. *The Ministry of Reconciliation: Spirituality and Strategies.* Maryknoll, New York: Orbis Books, 2002.

Schwartz, Stephen. *The Two Faces of Islam: Saudi Fundamentalism and its Role in Terrorism.* New York: Anchor Books, 2002.

Sells, Michael A. *The Bridge Betrayed: Religion and Genocide in Bosnia.* Berkeley: University of California Press, 1996.

———. "Religion, History, and Genocide in Bosnia-Herzegovina." Pp. 23–43 in *Religion and Justice in the War over Bosnia*, ed. G. Scott Davis: Routledge, New York 1997. http://coursesa.matrix.msu.edu/~fisher/bosnia/readings/sells1.html.

Selvanayagam, Israel. "Truth and Reconciliation: An Interfaith Perspective from India." Pp. 35–49 in *Peace and Reconciliation: In Search of Shared Identity*, eds. Sebastian C. H. Kim, Pauline Kollontai and Greg Hoyland. Hampshire, England and Burlington, Vermont: 2008.

Shore, Megan. *Religion and Conflict Resolution: Christianity and South Africa's Truth and Reconciliation Commission.* Surrey, England and Burlington, Vermont: Ashgate, 2009.

Shriver, D.W. *An Ethic For Enemies.* Oxford University Press: New York, 1995.

Smajlovic, Ismail. "Believers in a Military Environment." Pp. 71–82 in *National and Inter-Ethnic Reconciliation, Religious Tolerance and Human Security in the Balkans.* Proceedings of the Fifth ECPD International Conference, eds. Takehrio Togo and Negoslav P Ostojic. Belgrade, Serbia: European Center for Peace and Development, 2010.

Smith, Rupert. *The Utility of Force: The Art of War in the Modern World.* London: Penguin Books, 2006.

Smock, David. *Religion in World Affairs: Its Role in Conflict and Peace*, Special Report 101. Washington, D.C.: United States Institute of Peace, 2008. http://www.usip.org/publications/religion-world-affairs-its-role-conflict-and-peace.

——— and Qamar-ul Huda. *Islamic Peacebuilding Since 9/11*, Special Report 218. Washington, D.C.: United States Institute of Peace, 2009.

Stability Operations, Field Manual, Dept. of the Army, Washington, D.C., http://downloads.army.mil/docs/fm_3-07.pdf.

Svensson, Isak. "Fighting with Faith: Religion and Conflict Resolution in Civil Wars." Pp. 930–49 in *Journal of Conflict Resolution*, Vol. 51, No. 6, December 2007. http://jcr.sagepub.com/content/51/6/930.full.pdf+html.

Tanner, Stephan. *Afghanistan: A Military History from Alexander the Great to the Fall of the Taliban.* New York: Da Capo Press, 2002.

Taylor, Charles. *Sources of the Self: The Making of the Modern Identity.* Cambridge, Mass, Harvard University Press, 1989.

Tayob, Abdulkadar. *Islam, A Short Introduction.* Oxford: One World Publications, 1999.

Thompson, M. M. & R. Gill. "The Role of Trust in Whole of Government Missions." Pp. 225–44 in *Mission Critical: Smaller Democracies Role in Global Stability Operations*, eds. C. Leuprecht, T. Jodok, & D. Last. Montreal & Kingston: McGill-Queen's University Press, 2010.

———, and Ritu Gill, Angela Febbraro & Kelly Piasentin. "The Role of Trust in Religious Leader Engagement." Defence Research and Development Canada, 3772-12og04, 30 April 2012.

Tibi, Bassam. *The Challenge of Fundamentalism: Political Islam and the New World Disorder.* Berkeley: University of California Press, 1998.

———. *Islam Between Culture and Politics.* Basingstoke: Palgrave, 2001.

Tutu, Desmond. *No Future Without Forgiveness.* New York: Doubleday, 1999.

Tyler T.R. & R.M. Kramer. "Whither Trust" in *Trust in Organizations: Frontiers of Theory and Research.* Thousand Oaks, CA: Sage Publications, 1996.

United Nations Peacekeeping Operations: Principles and Guidelines: Capstone Document. United Nations Dept. of Peacekeeping Operations, Dept. of Field Support, 2008. http://pbpu.unlb.org/pbps/Library/Capstone_Doctrine_ENG.pdf

United States Army Operating Concept, TRADOC Pam 525-3-1, 2016-2028. Dept of the United States Army: 19 August 2010. http://www.tradoc.army.mil/tpubs/pams/tp525-3-1.pdf.

USAID, *Religion, Conflict & Peacebuilding: An Introductory Programming Guide,* http://www.usaid.gov/our_work/cross-cutting_programs/conflict/publications/docs/Religion_Conflict_and_Peacebuilding_Toolkit.pdf.

Varshney, Ashutosh. *Ethic Conflict and Civic Life: Hindus and Muslims in India.* New Haven, Connecticut: Yale University Press, 2002.

———. *Social Policy, Conflict and Horizontal integration.* Boston: Arusha Conference-New Frontiers of Social Policy, 12–15 December 2005. http://siteresources.worldbank.org/INTRANETSOCIALDEVELOPMENT/Resources/Varshney%5B1%5D%5B1%5D.rev.1.pdf.

———. "Ethnic Conflict and Civil Society: India and Beyond." Pp. 362–98 in *World Politics 53,* April 2001. http://chenry.webhost.utexas.edu/core/Course%20Materials/Varshney/53.3varshney.pdf

Villa-Vicencio, Charles. "Telling One Another Stories: Toward a Theology of Reconciliation." Pp. 30-42 in *The Reconciliation of Peoples: Challenge to the Churches,* eds. Gregory Baum and Harold Wells. Maryknoll, New York; Geneva, Switzerland: Orbis Books, World Council of Churches Publications, 1997.

Volf, Miroslav. "Exclusion and Embrace: Theological Reflections in the Wake of 'Ethnic Cleansing'" in *Journal of Ecumenical Studies,* Vol. 29, No. 2, Spring 1992. http://journal.jesdialogue.org/back_issues/volume_29_1992/.

———. *Exclusion and Embrace: A Theological Exploration of Identity, Otherness, and Reconciliation.* Nashville, Tennessee: Abingdon Press, 1996.

———. "'The Trinity Is Our Social Program': The Doctrine of the Trinity and the Shape of Social Engagement." Pp. 403–23 in *Modern Theology,* Vol. 14, No. 3, July 1998. http://onlinelibrary.wiley.com/doi/10.1111/moth.1998.14.issue-3/issuetoc.

———. *After Our Likeness: The Church as the Image of the Trinity.* Grand Rapids, Michigan: Eerdmans, 1998.

———. "The Social Meaning of Reconciliation." Pp. 158–72 in *Interpretation,* Vol 54, No.2, 2000. http://int.sagepub.com/content/54/2/158.full.pdf+html.

———. "Conversations with Miroslav Volf: Part 1" in *Conrad Grebel Review,* Vol. 18, No. 3, Fall 2000. https://uwaterloo.ca/grebel/publications/conrad-grebel-review/list-past-issues.

———. "The Healthy Church: Embodying Diversity," in *Catalyst On Line: Contemporary Evangelical Perspectives for United Methodist Seminarians,* http://catalystresources.org/issues/293volf.html.

———. *From Exclusion to Embrace: Reflections on Reconciliation.* http://www.christianembassyun.com/speech_by_dr_volf.htm.

———. "The Final Reconciliation: Reflections on a Social Dimension of the Eschatological Transition." Pp. 91–113 in *Modern Theology* Vol. 16, No.1, 2000. http://onlinelibrary.wiley.com/doi/10.1111/moth.2000.16.issue-1/issuetoc

———. "Forgiveness, Reconciliation, and Justice: A Christian Contribution to a More Peaceful Social Environment." Pp. 27–49 in *Forgiveness and Reconciliation,* eds. Raymond G. Hemlick, S.J. and Rodney L. Peterson. Philadelphia/London: Templeton Foundation Press, 2001.

———. *A Voice of One's Own: Public Faith in a Pluralistic World,* presented at the American Academy of Religion, Philadelphia, 19 November 2005, 14.

Volkan, Vamik. *Blood Lines: From Ethnic Pride to Ethnic Terrorism.* Boulder, Colorado: Westview Press, 1997.

Vrcan, Srdjan. "Religious Factors in the War in Bosnia-Herzegovina." Pp. 108–131 in *Religion and the War in Bosnia*, ed. Paul Mojzes. Atlanta, Georgia: Scholars Press, 1998.

White, Canan Andrew. *Vicar of Baghdad: Fighting for Peace in the Middle East.* Oxfords: Monarch Books, 2009.

Wiesel, Elie. *From the Kingdom of Memory: Reminiscences.* New York: Summit Books, 1990.

Wilson, G. I., John P. Sullivan and Hal Kempfer. "4GW Tactics of the Weak Confound the Strong." Military.com (8 September 2003).

Witter Turner, Victor. *Dramas, Fields, and Metaphors: Symbolic Action in Human Society.* Ithaca, New York.: Cornell University Press, 1974.

Whole of Government Approaches to Fragile States: Governance, Peace and Security, DAC Guidelines and Reference Series, Organization for Economic Cooperation and Development (OECD), 2006. http://www.oecd.org/dataoecd/15/24/37826256.pdf.

Williams, P. "The competent boundary spanner." Pp. 103–24 in *Public Administration* 80, 2002.

Wink, Walter. *Engaging the Powers: Discernment and Resistance in a World of Domination.* Minneapolis: Fortress Press, 1992.

Yakovleva, M., R.R. Reilly & R. Werko. "Why do we trust? Moving beyond individual to dyadic perceptions." Pp. 79–91 in *Journal of Applied Psychology* 95 (1), 2010.

Zartman, William I. "Toward the Resolution of International Conflicts." Pp. 3–19 in *Peacemaking in International Conflict: Methods & Techniques*, eds. I. William Zartman and J. Lewis Rasmussen. Washington, D.C.: United States Institute of Peace Press, 1997.

Zuckerman, M. J. "Can 'Unofficial' Talks Avert Disaster? Defining Track II: Meet Joseph Montville" in *Carnegie Reporter*, Vol. 3. No. 3, 2005. http://carnegie.org/publications/carnegie-reporter/single/view/article/item/136/.

Index

Abrahamic faith traditions / partners, 84, 85, 110, 143, 296
Abu-Nimer, Mohammed, 257, 264n35
Ada, Mohamed, 211–212
Adams, George, 112
Aga Khan Development Network, 87
Akasaka, Kiyo, 50
Al Qaeda, 194
Al Rubaie, Mowaffaq, 191, 203
Annan, Kofi, 50, 79
apology, 121, 130n75, 178, 181
Appleby, R. Scott: hermeneutics, 101; religion as barriers, 72; religion as identity marker, 71; religion's public-private dictum, 66; religion transcending conflict, 79; role of external actors, 80; sacredness of land, 20; space of ambivalence, 65, 76; strong and weak religion, 75
Armstrong, Karen, 75, 230n2
Army Capabilities Development Board (CF), 236, 259n4
Asian Muslim Action Network, 87
Askariya Shrine, 188
Avruch, Kevin, 45. *See* cultural cliché, causal, psychogenic and sociogenic.

Baron, Reuben M., 115–116, 119–122
Bartoli, Andrea, 82
Battle, Michael, 269–270
Battle of the Boyne, 37

benevolence, 116–119, 177, 200, 216, 239, 245, 246
Bishop: Archbishop of Canterbury, England, 81, 189; Archbishop Desmond Tutu, South Africa, 269–270; Bishop's-Ulama Forum, Mindanao, Philippines, 87, 89; Roman Catholic Bishop's of Mindanao, Philippines, 89; Serbian Orthodox Bishop Teodosije. Kosovo, 172, 174–175, 177–179; Roman Catholic Bishop Maco Sopi of Prizren, Kosovo, 176
Bosnia-Herzegovina Defense Forces, 125, 226
boundary spanners, 98, 118, 119. *See also* religion–tolerant voice; middle-range actors
Burton, John, 29

Canadian International Development Agency (CIDA), 262n22
Carter, Judy, 78, 110
Center for Religious Dialogue, 87
Center for Strategic and International Studies (CSIS), 100
Chicago Council on Global Affairs Task Force, 99, 107, 124–125
chosen glories, 59n37
chosen trauma, 38, 59n37, 69, 156, 199
circular causality, 119, 213, 230

About the Author

Steve Moore is an ordained elder with the United Church of Canada. He is married to Deborah, who is a successful watercolor artist in Ottawa, and they have three sons: Ryan (30), Josh (26) and Andrew (21). Moore served as a chaplain in the Canadian Forces (CF) for twenty-two years, with operational tours including Bosnia during the war (1993), Haiti (1997) and the Kandahar Provincial Reconstruction Team, Afghanistan for research purposes (2006). The experience of engaging the religious leaders of greater Sarajevo left an indelible mark on his life. These were men of faith and leaders of religious communities, endeavoring to lead their people during a time of intense turmoil.

Dr. Moore's doctoral dissertation focused on the development of a practical theology emphasizing the role of chaplains engaging local religious leaders in an environment of deep-rooted conflict—Conflict Studies. Upon the completion of his PhD from the University of Ottawa / Saint Paul University, he joined the Directorate of Land Concepts and Designs—now Canadian Army Land Warfare Centre—a *futures* environment (*think tank*) within the CF emphasizing the Army of Tomorrow. Here he further developed his concepts for an additional three years. Concurrently with this assignment, he served as a Visiting Research Fellow with the Faculty of Human Sciences (Conflict Studies) at Saint Paul University, Ottawa, Canada. In June 2011, the Army Capabilities Development Board (ACDB) of the CF endorsed Religious Leader Engagement (RLE) as a capability under development. Dr. Moore is currently developing a one-year, five-module, online program at Saint Paul University in Integrative Peacebuilding.

About the Cover

At first glance, this drawing, done in watercolor and charcoal, depicts the desert environment of Afghanistan. The tone is evocative of the emerging idea of chaplains engaging religious leaders in dialogue in conflict situations. As the leader appears amidst the desert heat and the blowing sand, the drawing becomes a metaphor for this nascent concept in a time when more peaceful and sustainable approaches to resolving conflict are sought.

—Deborah Moore, *artist*